Ethics and
Corporate Social
Responsibility

Also by Ronald R. Sims

An Experiential Learning Approach to Employee Systems (1990)

Training Enhancement in Government Organizations (1993)

Diversity and Differences in Organizations: An Agenda for Answers and Questions (1993) *(edited, with Robert F. Dennehy)*

Ethics and Organizational Decision Making: A Call for Renewal (1994)

Changes and Challenges for the Human Resource Professional (1994) *(with Serbrenia J. Sims)*

Human Resource Management and the Americans with Disabilities Act (1995) *(edited, with John G. Veres III)*

Corporate Misconduct: The Legal, Societal, and Management Issues (1995) *(edited, with Margaret P. Spencer)*

Accountability and Radical Change in Public Organizations (1998) *(edited)*

Reinventing Training and Development (1998)

Keys to Employee Success in Coming Decades (1999) *(edited, with John G. Veres III)*

The Challenge of Front-Line Management: Flattened Organizations in the New Economy (2000) *(with John G. Veres III, Katherine Jackson, and Carolyn L. Facteau)*

Organizational Success through Effective Human Resources Management (2002)

Teaching Business Ethics for Effective Learning (2002)

Managing Organizational Behavior (2002)

Changing the Way We Manage Change (2002)

Ethics and Corporate Social Responsibility

Why Giants Fall

Ronald R. Sims

Westport, Connecticut
London

Library of Congress Cataloging-in-Publication Data

Sims, Ronald R.
  Ethics and corporate social responsibility : why giants fall / Ronald R. Sims.
    p. cm.
  Includes bibliographical references and index.
  ISBN 0-275-98039-1 (alk. paper)
    1. Business ethics. 2. Social responsibility of business. I. Title.
  HF5387.S569 2003
  174'.4—dc21   2003045767

British Library Cataloguing in Publication Data is available.

Library of Congress Catalog Card Number: 2003045767
ISBN: 0-275-98039-1

First published in 2003

Praeger Publishers, 88 Post Road West, Westport, CT 06881
An imprint of Greenwood Publishing Group, Inc.
www.praeger.com

Printed in the United States of America

The paper used in this book complies with the
Permanent Paper Standard issued by the National
Information Standards Organization (Z39.48-1984).

10 9 8 7 6 5 4 3 2

Contents

Contents

Acknowledgments

Once again a very, very special thanks goes to Herrington Bryce, who continues to serve as a colleague, a mentor, and a valued friend. The administrative support of Larry Pulley, Dean of the School of Business Administration at the College of William and Mary, is also acknowledged. I am also indebted to Eric Valentine, former publisher of Quorum Books, a former imprint of Greenwood Publishing Group, who provided an outlet for my ideas.

My thanks and appreciation as usual also goes out to my wife and the rest of the gang, Nandi, Dangaia, Sieya, and Kani, who have supported me during those times when it seemed as if all I ever did was read and sit in front of the computer. A special thanks goes out to Ronald, Jr., Marchet, Vellice, Shelley, and Sharisse.

Ethical Business Missteps: The Former and Current State of Affairs

INTRODUCTION

No matter which way we turn, it appears that the entire population is whirling within a vortex of mistrust, distrust, misinformation, disinformation, and disclosures. Corporate managements, meanwhile, are scrambling to mend miles of fences between themselves and their boards of directors, banks, investment bankers, stockbrokers, auditors, the media, Senate and House committees, the Justice Department, and the Securities and Exchange Commission (SEC). An array of scandals afflicting corporations and Wall Street over the last few years have created what has been referred to as "a triple-tier Who's Who" for officials under investigation—those who are jail bound, those who might be sentenced and those who have the good luck merely to be greatly embarrassed (Hahn 2002).[1] For example, Timothy Ganley, former VP of software maker Critical Path Inc., was sentenced to six months in federal prison plus two months of supervised release for insider trading. The former president, David Thatcher, has pleaded guilty to one count of conspiring to commit securities fraud and awaits sentencing, as do two vice presidents (Jonathan Beck and Kevin Clark) who have admitted guilt on insider-trading charges; a third veep got six-months jail sentence. Ganley also paid $107,908 in a civil case brought by the SEC.

Tyco International CEO Dennis Kozlowski, former CFO Mark Swartz, and former general counsel Mark Belnick were all indicted on charges that Kozlowski and Swartz, among others, stole $170 million from the company and pocketing $430 million from the fraudulent sale of Tyco stock. Belnick was charged with hiding $14 million in loans to himself. Tyco's management fired back as well. It filed a lawsuit against Kozlowski looking to recoup $244 million in pay and benefits.

Finally, some officials found themselves simply having to deal with bad publicity. Former General Electric CEO Jack Welch was revealed to have received such lifetime perks as front-row seats to New York Knicks games and the use of a company jet, according to his wife's divorce filings. Adelphia Corp. chief executive John Rigas, whose $4.2 million cash severance package was revoked by Adelphia's new board (his severance agreement can be revoked in the case of a felony conviction), has been another official on the ropes. Although Martha Stewart skirted legal problems for a while, the House Energy and Commerce Committee turned over its investigation of Stewart to the Justice Department after her attorneys said she would refuse to testify about the sales of ImClone Systems stock hours before the stock value plummeted. In June 2003 Stewart was indicted by a federal grand jury on five criminal counts of securities fraud, conspiracy and making false statements to federal agents.

Salomon Smith Barney chairman and CEO Michael Carpenter was left more than embarrassed from his firm's recent troubles: he was ousted and replaced with former general counsel and current chief operating officer (and Citigroup chairman Sanford Weill's right arm) Charles Prince. Salomon is currently embroiled in a congressional probe into the firm's IPO practices during the telecom bubble. Carpenter took over Citigroup's global investment group, while speculation mounted that Prince was on a path that could lead him ultimately to succeed Weill as Citigroup head. One would think that Salomon would have learned not to raise suspicion that it might be outside ethical bounds, given its problems with the bond-trading scandal in the 1990s that helped lead to its eventual fall as a giant in the bond-trading industry.

Citigroup was also nearing a possible $200 million settlement with the Federal Trade Commission (FTC) over a lawsuit alleging predatory lending to consumers by Associates First Capital Corp., the Dallas-based sub-prime lender the firm bought for $27 billion in 2000. The $200 million could be the largest ever consumer-protection settlement with the FTC.

Such news stories as the fall of the once giant Enron continue to bring to the attention of the public social and ethical issues that help to frame the relationship between society and business organizations. The reporting of these stories is highlighted by criticisms of various actions, decisions, and practices on the part of business leaders. Criticisms have included exposé of Beech-Nut Nutrition Company's practices of selling adulterated apple juice and passing it off to the public as "100% fruit juices," accusations against H. B. Fuller Co. that it was selling glue in Honduras that was being recklessly used for "sniffing" by Honduran street children, allegations that Sears Roebuck & Co. engaged in sales abuses at its auto centers by pressuring customers to purchase un-needed or unwanted services, lawsuits against Dow Corning for its sale of defective silicone breast implants, and lawsuits against the tobacco industry for manufacturing and marketing what an increasing number of people consider to be an inherently dangerous product. Though the litany of concerns raised about the safety of cell phones, SUVs, and other issues could go on and on, these examples illustrate the continu-ing tensions between society and business organizations, which can be traced to specific incidents or events. However, despite the media coverage, organizations and their respective leaders still find ways to further decrease stakeholder confidence in their ability to "do the right things."

This book is concerned with "doing the right thing" and more specif-ically with increaseing our understanding of why organizations stray from "doing the right thing." Such behavior often leads to an ethical and financial fall, a fall that they find themselves unable to recover from. As for Humpty Dumpty, all the kings horse's and all the king's men are unable to help many organizations to get up from their ethical fall. Today's organizations increasingly confront many issues that carry social or ethical implications that result from a more visible relationship between business and the broader society. Issues such as toxic waste disposal, sexual harassment in the workplace, AIDS in the workplace, drug testing, insider trading, political action committees supported by business to influence the outcome of legislation, whistle-blowing, and the use of lie detectors typify the stories about society and business that the media focus on in television, newspapers, and magazines.

Some situations that seem to capture the headlines almost daily are situations in which the public or some segment of the public (e.g., various stakeholders) believes that an organization has done wrong or has treated some individual or group unfairly. Ethical questions are typically raised in such situations. In some cases, major laws have been broken. In most, questions have arisen of whether or not the organiza-tions have been socially responsible or ethical. Organizations find themselves frequently on the defensive in today's socially aware envi-ronment, being criticized for some action they have taken or failed to take. Whether these organizations are right or wrong sometimes does not matter. Powerful stakeholder groups, aided by a cooperative media with a flair for the dramatic, are often able to exert enormous pressure

on these organizations and wield significant influence on public opinion, causing organizations to take or not to take particular courses of
action.

In other instances, organizations are attempting to deal with broad
societal concerns (such as AIDS in the workplace, discrimination in the
workplace, and the employee "rights" movement). Today's organizations must increasingly weigh the pros and cons of these issues and
adopt the best postures, given the conflicting points of view expressed
by key stakeholders. Organizations must respond and be willing to live
with the consequences, even though correct responses are not always
easy to identify.

At a broad level, we are discussing the role of business in society. In
our effort to understand why giants fall, we will address such issues as
what an organization must do to be considered socially responsible and
what organizational leaders must do to be considered ethical. The
ethical missteps, the societal responses, and our need to be proactive in
preventing the ethical fall of organizations require immediate attention
and definite courses of actions, which may become the next subject of
debate in years to come.

As we move further into the twenty-first century, there is every
indication that times will continue to be turbulent; the future will be
characterized by significant changes in the economy, in society, in
technology, and in the global marketplace. Against this continuing
turbulence it is important to set forth briefly some ideas that will be
discussed in more detail later in this book; they are fundamental to
increasing our understanding of why giants fall.

THE CHALLENGE OF BUSINESS ETHICS AND CORPORATE SOCIAL RESPONSIBILITY

As evidenced by the number of ethical missteps in the news, today
we pay the piper as we tally the sorry record of organizational wrongdoings, infractions, and white-collar crimes, all of which can be traced
to a diminishing interest in standards, controls, integrity, and that
nineteenth-century commodity known as good reputation. Yet as a
society, we define ourselves by the values we choose to emphasize.
Beginning in the 1980s, a frenzied quest for efficiency led to the endorse-
ment of individualism over community. The resulting emphasis on
short-term returns encouraged a speculative frenzy in the stock markets
and merger mania on Wall Street, variously described as "the casino
society"[2] and a "circus of ambition,"[3] attacked in the Oliver Stone film
Wall Street, and satirized in Tom Wolfe's popular book *The Bonfire of the
Vanities.*[4] The reputation of the business community as a whole fell to

an all-time low. On into the 1990s and today, companies like E. F. Hutton, Drexel Burnham Lambert, and Salomon Brothers committed very public ethical wrongdoings, while others saw their reputations become severely tarnished. Once-giant organizations took a fall, never to recover to their previous grandeur. As suggested by Fombrun,[5] the corporate world has squandered much of its reputational capital and its ability to survive and thrive in the years to come.[6]

Business Ethics Missteps

While several business ethics scandals piqued the public's attention, two notable examples are worth brief mention here. The Salomon Brothers bond-trading scandal helped to usher in the 1990s. Salomon Brothers, the world's fourth-largest underwriter of securities, admitted in 1991 to repeatedly violating Treasury rules against buying more than 35 percent of a Treasury issue of securities at auction. The scandal led to the resignation of three top officials, among other consequences.[7] It should not have come as a surprise that the U.S. Sentencing Commission in 1991 created new federal sentencing guidelines designed to deter corporate crime by creating incentives for corporations to report and accept responsibility for unlawful behavior.

In the second half of the 1990s, many of the ethical scandals found in business involved massive charges of sexual harassment and racial discrimination. Among the well-known companies that experienced such allegations were Mitsubishi, Coca-Cola, Home Depot, and Texaco. The Texaco case involved a $196 million settlement in a class-action race discrimination lawsuit brought by employees fighting for equal pay and a chance for promotions. Bari-Ellen Roberts, lead plaintiff in the case against the oil company, revealed a dark side of corporate America in her 1998 book, *Roberts vs. Texaco: A True Story of Race and Corporate America*.[8]

During the first years of the new century, business ethics scandals continued in the headlines. Archer Daniels Midland pleaded guilty to a price-fixing conspiracy that cost consumers millions in higher prices for soft drinks and detergents. ADM agreed to pay a $100 million fine. Royal Dutch Shell scrapped its plans for sinking a North Sea oilrig that environmentalists said was contaminated. They were later accused of colluding with the Nigerian government in the oppression of the Ogoni people and of failing to speak out against the execution of one of its leaders. In 2001, Bridgestone/Firestone and the Ford Motor Company apologized to consumers for a pattern of deadly tire failures, while blaming each other for the debacle.[9] Once again, major corporations are enveloped in ethics scandals that are generating new tremors of public distrust of large corporations.

Corporate Social Responsibility

About public interest in business ethics and corporate social responsibility (CSR) during the past three or four decades, two conclusions can be drawn. First, interest in business ethics and social responsibility has heightened during each of the past forty years. Second, interest in business ethics and CSR seems to have been spurred by major headline-grabbing scandals. Certainly, society has taken an on-again, off-again interest, but lately this interest has grown to a preoccupation or obsession.

Because of ethical missteps like those just alluded to, business has been undergoing the most intense scrutiny it has ever received from the public. As a result of the many allegations—charges that it has little concern for the consumer, cares nothing about the deteriorating social order, has no concept of acceptable behavior, and is indifferent to the problems of minorities and the environment—concern continues to be expressed as to what responsibilities business has to the society in which it resides. These concerns have generated an unprecedented number of pleas for CSR, more recently included in the broad term of corporate citizenship.

The basic CSR issue can be framed in terms of two key questions: Does business have a social responsibility? If so, how much and what kind? This book explores several facets of CSR and provides some insights into these questions. Chapter 3 is dedicated to the CSR issue and concepts that have emerged from it because that core idea underlies a great deal of the discussion in this book.

No one would argue that life in most business organizations was much simpler in the past, in a less complex period, with minimal and clearly understood expectations among the various parties. Investors put up money to start or finance the business, owners and employees kept the business running, suppliers made raw materials available for production, and customers purchased the product or services. In today's society, organizations face a more complex state of affairs. The public recognizes that today's business organization has evolved to a point where it is no longer the sole property or interest of the founder, the founder's family, or even a group of owner-investors. That development has been a principal driving force behind this societal transformation.

Today's Organization and Stakeholders

Today's modern organization in many instances is the institutional centerpiece of a complex society made up of many people with a multitude of interests and with many expectations as to what organizations ought to provide. As highlighted in this book, the social contract between organizations and various stakeholders (e.g., employers and employees) has continually changed, producing new demands that all parties rethink their relationships. Those organizations likely to survive in the future will pay particular attention to how to successfully respond to ever-changing expectations. These organizations will need to meet many legal, ethical, and social or philanthropic expectations while still being able to change proactively in response to economic incentives.

Ethical and socially responsible employee behavior is important to the viability of all organizations as they attempt to change and respond to stakeholder expectations. "Doing what's right" matters to organizations, related stakeholders, and the public-at-large. To organizations and employees, acting ethically and legally means saving billions of dollars each year in theft, lawsuits, and settlements. Research has shown that corporations also have paid significant financial penalties for acting unethically. Carnival Cruise Lines realized that illegally dumping wastes from its ships into the world's waterways wasn't worth the $18 million fine it recently paid. The tobacco industry discovered that lying about nicotine could be costly to business. Dow Corning paid heavy penalties for manufacturing and selling unsafe products, and Arthur Andersen has not recovered from its shredding of documents involved with the Enron debacle.

It has been estimated that workplace theft costs U.S. businesses $40 billion each year. In particular, some have found that employees accounted for a higher percentage of retail thefts than did customers; it has been estimated that one in every fifteen employees steals from his or her employer. Costs to businesses also include ineffective information flow throughout the organization; deterioration of relationships; declining productivity, creativity, and loyalty; and absenteeism. Organizations that have a reputation for unethical and uncaring behavior toward employees also have a difficult time recruiting and retaining valued professionals.

Today's organizations must be responsive to an increasingly diverse audience, made up of individuals and groups that they may have been able to ignore in the past. The growing importance of the role of stakeholders in the organizational equation over the past few decades has made it apparent that organizations must address the legitimate needs and expectations of stakeholders if they want to be successful in the long run. "Stakeholder inclusion" is the key to company success in the twenty-first century. Today's businesses must continuously address stakeholders; it is the ethical course of action to take, and stakeholders clearly have claims, rights, and expectations that should be honored. A stakeholder approach to understanding organizational situations like the Enron debacle can help us to understand better why such ethical organizational demises occur.

Organizational management that truly cares about business and corporate social responsibility is proactive rather than reactive in linking strategic action and ethics. It steers away from ethically and morally questionable business opportunities and business practices. It goes to considerable lengths to ensure that its actions reflect integrity and high ethical standards such as Warren Buffett attempted to introduce in Salomon Brothers following its ethical fall. If an organization's stakeholders conclude that management is not measuring up to ethical standards, they have recourse. For example, concerned investors can protest at the annual shareholders' meeting, appeal to the board of directors, or sell their stock. Concerned employees can unionize and bargain collectively, or they can seek employment elsewhere. Customers can switch to competitors. Suppliers can find other buyers. The community and society can do anything from staging protest marches and urging boycotts to stimulating political and governmental action.

THE FOCUS OF THIS BOOK

Being socially responsible, ethical, and a good corporate citizen is important to meeting and exceeding the expectations of any organization's stakeholders. Unless today's organizations recognize the importance of developing and sustaining a reputation that is built on "doing the right things" and "doing things right" as viewed by their key stakeholders, they will not survive or thrive, as has been the case with several organizations over the last few decades. This book is intended to help readers better understand some of the organizational sins of the past, with the goal of preventing more "Enrons" in the future. The book assumes that individuals, groups, and organizations of all sizes will at some point find themselves confronted with challenges to do the right ethical things; and if they fail, they may not recover from their ethical fall. The book also offers some insights into how organizations can get up from such falls by restoring their ethical reputation, being proactive by institutionalizing ethics and building and maintaining ethical employer-employee relationships.

The issues surrounding business ethics, corporate social responsibility, and stakeholder management are treated at various points in this book. Special treatment is also given to Salomon Brothers and related organizational missteps at Enron to gain insight into why such social irresponsible and unethical behavior occurs. The role of various stakeholders (internal and external) and the impact of such missteps on these stakeholders make up the focus of several chapters. Workplace issues like employee rights are considered important topics in our efforts to make sense of organizational missteps and attempts to resurrect organizational reputation. Readers will gain an appreciation of how important it is that organizational decision makers integrate socially responsible and ethical wisdom with management wisdom in all they do.

For those interested in understanding what contributed to organizational debacles and ethical falls like the Enron's and Archer Daniels Midland's of today and the Salomon Brothers and E. F. Hutton a decade or so ago, this book provides some answers. This book employs a stakeholder framework for emphasizing business's social and ethical responsibilities to both external and internal stakeholder groups. An analytical perspective is embedded within the book's themes of business ethics, corporate social responsibility, and stakeholder management. The book stresses that these perspectives are essential because they require organizations and their leaders to recognize the importance of socially responsible and ethical decision making and behavior that continually incorporates the stakeholders (e.g., customers, employees, government, suppliers, and the public-at-large) into the organizations' strategic initiatives and plans.

Clearly, there is every indication that the American society of today is clamoring for a renewed emphasis on values, morals, and ethics and that the business ethics and social responsibility debates of this period are but a subset of this larger societal concern. Whether organizations and their leaders will be able to respond and ratchet their reputation to a new plateau remains to be seen. One thing is sure: The renewed interest in business ethics and corporate social responsibility is accompanied by increased calls for ethical accountability. We hope that, this time, that accountability will be institutionalized in the fabric of our society and each organization in hopes that no more giants will fall.

Given the notoriety of the Enron demise, discussions will continue on the why and how of the situation. Pundits will also undoubtedly focus on Enron specifically and offer various views on why the company fell so far so fast. This book suggests that organizations like Enron take ethical falls because of failed leadership, an unethically oriented culture, socially irresponsible behavior and operational activities that lead to unethical employee practices.

Against the backdrop of the Enron disaster, this book discusses business ethics, specifically, in Chapter 2. In Chapters 3 and 4 the discussion turns to corporate social responsibility and stakeholder management. Chapter 5 focuses on why unethical behavior occurs in organizations. Chapters 6–8 address specific examples of unethical behavior in action, in an effort to answer to questions like, "What brings a giant like Enron to its knees?" Chapters 9–11 attempt to answer questions like, "How can organizations recover from unethical and socially irresponsible missteps?" "How can organizations be proactive in avoiding such missteps in the first place?" Finally, in Chapter 12 attention turns to concluding comments based upon major points discussed throughout the book.

NOTES

1. Avital L. Hahn, "The Jailed, The Probed, The Embarrassed: A New Who's Who of the Afflicted in the Business and Street Worlds," *The Investment Dealers' Digest* (Sept. 16, 2002), 4.

2. Susan Strange, *Casino Capitalism* (London: Oxford, Blackwell, 1986).

3. John Taylor, *Circus of Ambition* (New York: Warner Books, 1989).

4. Tom Wolfe, *The Bonfire of the Vanities* (New York: Farrar, Strauss, 1987).

5. Charles J. Fombrum, *Reputation: Realizing Value from the Corporate Image* (Boston: Harvard Business School Press, 1996).

6. Ronald R. Sims, "Enron: How a Failure of Leadership, Culture and Unethical Behavior Brought a Giant to Its Knees" (*William and Mary Business* (Fall/Winter, 2002), 18–19.

7. David R. Francis, "How Wall Street Ethics Slipped," *The Christian Science Monitor* (August 21, 1991).

8. Bari-Ellen Roberts, with Jack E. White, *Roberts vs. Texaco: A True Story of Race and Corporate America* (New York: Avon Books, 1998).

9. Amy Zipkin, "Management: Getting Religion on Corporate Ethics: A Scourge of Scandals Leaves Its Mark," *New York Times* (October 18, 2000).

2

The Nature of Business and Managerial Ethics

INTRODUCTION

For the past few decades, many executives, administrators, social scientists, and the public at large have seen unethical behavior as a cancer working on the tissue of society. Many are concerned that a crisis of ethics in the West is undermining our competitive strength. This crisis involves businesspeople, government officials, customers, and employees. Especially worrisome is unethical behavior among employees at all levels of the business organization. For example, consider the notion that employees account for a higher percentage of retail thefts than do customers or the suggestion that one in every fifteen employees steals from his or her employer.

In addition, we are all too familiar with illegal and unethical behavior on Wall Street, pension scandals in which executives gamble on risky business ventures with employees' retirement funds, companies that expose their workers to hazardous working conditions, and blatant favoritism in hiring and promotion practices. Although such practices occur throughout the world, their presence serves to remind us of the challenge facing organizations in the twenty-first century.

This challenge is especially difficult because standards for what constitutes ethical behavior lie in a gray zone where clear-cut right-or-wrong answers may not exist. As a result, sometimes a case can be made that unethical behavior is forced on organizations by the environment and by laws such as the Foreign Corrupt Practices Act. For example, if you were a sales representative for an American company abroad and your foreign competitors used bribes to get business, what would you do? In the United States such behavior is illegal, yet it is perfectly acceptable in other countries. What is ethical here? Similarly, in many countries women are systematically discriminated against in the workplace; it is felt that their place is in the home. In the United States, this practice is illegal. If you ran an American company in one of these countries, would you hire women in important positions? If you did, your company might be isolated in the larger business community, and you might lose business. If you did not, you might be violating what most Americans believe to be fair business practices.

Effective leadership and management of ethical issues require that organizations ensure that their managers and employees do not commit unethical acts and are familiar with how to deal with ethical issues in their everyday work lives. These charges are especially important today as it appears that American society in the first decade of the 2000s is clamoring for a renewed emphasis on values, morals, and ethics and that the business debate of this period is but a subset of this larger societal concern. Whether the business community will be able to respond and raise its reputation to a new plateau remains to be seen. One thing is sure: This renewed interest in business ethics is not likely to dissipate in the near term. Organizational members can effectively respond to the public's new expectations by first understanding what it means for their organizations to be socially responsible, as discussed in Chapter 3; why a commitment to high ethical standards is good business, which is the focus of this chapter; and some of the factors contributing to why individuals commit unethical acts, as discussed in Chapter 4.

WHAT IS BUSINESS ETHICS?

Almost every year, it seems, some major corporation is enveloped in an ethics scandal that generates a new tremor of public distrust of large corporations.[1] As a result of these never-ending scandals, the word "ethics" is often a major part of the news. *Ethics* is a philosophical term derived from the Greek word "ethos," meaning character or custom. This definition is germane to effective leadership in organizations in that it connotes an organization code conveying moral integrity and consistent values in service to the public. History shows us that certain organizations will commit themselves to a philosophy in a formal pronouncement of a Code of Ethics or Standards of Conduct. Once written, the recorded idealism is distributed or shelved, and all too often that is that. Other organizations, however, are increasingly concerned with aspects of ethics of greater specificity, usefulness, and consistency.

Ethical behavior is that which isaccepted as morally "good" and "right" as opposed to "bad" or "wrong" in a particular setting. For the individual that means acting in ways consistent with one's personal values and the commonly held values of the organization and society. Is it ethical, for example, to pay a bribe to obtain a business contract in a foreign country? Is it ethical to allow your company to withhold information that might discourage a job candidate from joining your organization? Is it ethical to ask someone to take a job you know will not be good for their career progress? Is it ethical to do personal business on company time?

The point of asking is to remind organizations that the public-at-large is demanding that government officials, business leaders and managers, workers in general, and the organizations they represent all act according to high ethical and moral standards. There is every indication that the future will bring a renewed concern with maintaining high standards of ethical behavior in organizational transactions and in the workplace.

To understand business ethics, it is useful to comment on the relationship between ethics and morality. *Ethics* is the discipline that deals with what is good and bad and with moral duty and obligation. Ethics can also be regarded as a set of moral principles or values. *Morality* is a system or doctrine of moral conduct. Moral conduct refers to that which relates to principles of right and wrong in behavior. We can think of ethics and morality as being so similar that we may use the terms interchangeably to refer to the study of fairness, justice, and right and wrong behavior in business.

Business ethics, therefore, is concerned with good and bad or right and wrong behavior and practices within a business context. Concepts of right and wrong are increasingly being interpreted to include the more difficult and subtle questions of fairness, justice, and equity.

Normative and descriptive ethics are two key branches of moral philosophy or ethics. Each takes a different perspective. *Normative* ethics is concerned with supplying and justifying a coherent moral system of thinking and judging. Normative ethics seeks to uncover, develop, and justify basic moral principles that are intended to guide behavior, actions, and decisions.[2] Normative business ethics, therefore, seeks to propose some principle or principles for distinguishing ethical from unethical in the business context. It deals more with "what ought to be" or "what ought not to be" in terms of business practices. Normative ethics is concerned with establishing norms or standards by which business might be guided or judged.

Descriptive ethics, by contrast, is concerned with describing, charac-
terizing, and studying the morality of a people, a culture, or a society.
It also compares and contrasts different moral codes, systems, practices,
beliefs, and values.[3] In descriptive business ethics, therefore, the focus
is on learning what is occurring in the real of behavior, actions, decisions, policies, and practices of business organizations, managers, or
specific industries. Public opinion polls like the 2000 Gallup Poll on
Honesty/Ethics in the Professions give us glimpses of descriptive ethics—what people believe to be going on based on their perceptions and
understandings. Descriptive ethics focuses on "what is"—the prevailing set of ethical standards in the business community or specific
organizations or on the part of specific managers. A real danger in
limiting our attention to descriptive ethics is that some people may
adopt the view that "if everyone is doing it," it must be acceptable. For
example, if a survey reveals that 77 percent of employees in retail are
stealing from work, this describes what is taking place but it does not
describe what should be taking place. Just because many are participating in this questionable activity doesn't make it an appropriate practice.
This is why normative ethics is important.

In our study of and efforts to increasingly understand business ethics,
we need to be ever mindful of this distinction between normative and
descriptive perspectives. It is tempting to observe the prevalence of a
particular practice in business (for example, deceptive advertising or
discrimination) and conclude that because so many are doing it (descriptive ethics), it must be acceptable behavior. Normative ethics
would insist that a practice be justified on the basis of some ethical
principle, argument, or rationale before being considered acceptable.
Normative ethics demands a more meaningful moral anchor.

Operational Levels of Business Ethics

As ethical problems are not only an individual or personal matter, it
is useful to see the different levels at which issues originate and how
they often move to other levels. Since today's business leaders must
manage a wide range of stakeholders inside and outside their organizations, understanding the levels of issues that stakeholders face facilitates our understanding of the complex relationships within and
among those addressing ethical problems.

Ethical and moral issues in business can be examined from several
levels: individual or personal, organizational, industry, societal, and
international.[4]

Individual Level

We all experience ethical challenges at the individual or personal
level. These include situations we face in our personal lives that are

generally outside the work context. Questions or dilemmas that we might face at the personal level include:

- Should I tell the cashier that he gave me change for a $20 bill when I gave him a $10 bill?
- Should I notify my bank that it credited someone else's $100 to my checking account?
- Should I cheat on my income tax return by inflating my charitable contributions?
- Should I return the extra merchandise that a store accidentally sent me?

If an ethical issue involves or is limited to an individual's responsibilities, that person may examine her or his own ethical motives and standards before choosing a course of action.

Organizational Level

People also confront ethical issues at the organizational level in their roles as managers or employees. Certainly, many of these issues are similar to those we face personally. However, these issues may carry consequences for the company's reputation and success in the community and also for the kind of ethical climate or culture that will prevail on a day-to-day basis at the office. Issues posed at the organizational level might include:

- Should I overlook the wrongdoings of my peers and direct reports in the interest of company harmony?
- Should I perform an unethical or illegal act to earn a division or work-unit profit?
- Should I offer a kickback to ensure I get the client's business to meet my sales quota?
- Should I make this product safer than required by law, because I know the legal standard is grossly inadequate?
- Should I accept this gift or bribe that is being given to me to close a big deal for the company?

If an ethical issue arises at the organizational level, the organizational members should examine the company's policies and procedures and code of ethics, if one, exists before making a decision or taking action.

Industry Level

An organization or manager also might influence business ethics at the industry level. The industry might be insurance, stock brokerage, manufactured homes, real estate, automobiles, or a host of others.

Related to the industry might be the profession of which an individual is a member—law, medicine, accounting, pharmacy, or engineering. Some examples of questions that might pose ethical problems or dilemmas at this level include the following:

- Is this standard contract we condominium sellers have adopted really in keeping with the recently strengthened financial disclosure laws?
- Is this practice that we stockbrokers have been using for years with prospective clients really fair and in their best interests?
- Is this safety standard we mechanical engineers have passed really adequate for protecting the consumer in this age of do-it-yourselfers?
- Is this standard we physicians have adopted violating the Hippocratic oath and the value it places on human life?

Conflicts of interest and conscience can arise in such situations. At this level, professionals can refer to their professional association's charter code of ethics for guidelines on conducting business or the set of ethical practices of a particular industry. For example, in the summer of 2001, an industry-level group of fourteen Wall Street firms endorsed a set of ethical practices for the industry covering broad areas such as analysts' compensation, personal ownership of stocks by analysts, and the objectivity of reports.[5]

Societal and International Levels

At the societal and international levels, laws, norms, customs, and traditions govern the legal and moral acceptability of behaviors. Business activities acceptable in Turkey or Russia may be immoral or illegal in the United States, and vice versa. At these levels it becomes very difficult for the individual manager to have any direct effect on business ethics. However, managers acting in concert through their companies and trade and professional associations can definitely bring about high standards and constructive changes. Because the industry, societal, and international levels are quite removed from the practicing manager, we will focus our attention in this chapter primarily on the personal and organizational levels. The greatest impact of managers can be felt through what they do personally or as members of the management team.

It is also important to recognize that managers have an important role to play as ethical role models for society. To the extent that they successfully convey to the public that they believe in the importance of integrity in business and throughout society, managers may have a significant impact on society's general level of ethics and on the future course of the free enterprise system.[6]

WHY ETHICS MATTERS IN BUSINESS

Ethical behavior by employees is important to the viability of all organizations. "Doing what's right" matters to organizations, their employees, stakeholders, and the public-at-large. To organizations and employees, acting ethically and legally means saving billions of dollars each year in theft, lawsuits, and settlements. As noted in Chapter 1, a number of organizations have paid significant financial penalties for acting unethically.[7] And many of them will undoubtedly never fully recover from their ethical misdeeds. Studies have estimated that workplace theft costs U.S. businesses $40 billion each year and that employees accounted for a higher percentage of retail thefts than did customers.[8] Costs to businesses also include ineffective information flow throughout the organization; deterioration of relationships; declining productivity, creativity, and loyalty; and absenteeism.[9] Organizations that have a strong reputation of unethical and uncaring behavior toward employees also have a difficult time recruiting and retaining valued professionals.[10]

For today's business leaders, and managers, leading and managing ethically also means managing with integrity.[11] Integrity cascades throughout an organization. It shapes, influences and maintains the values, tone, climate, or culture of the organization; communications among all its members; and the commitment, imagination, and realism of everyone in the organization. Ethics matters in business because all the internal and external stakeholders stand to gain when organizations, groups, and individuals seek to do what is right, as well as to do things the right way.

Employees care about ethics because they are attracted to ethically and socially responsible companies.[12] A list of the 100 best companies to work for is regularly published in *Fortune* magazine.[13] While the list continues to change, it is instructive to observe some of the characteristics of good employers that surveyed employees repeatedly cite. The most frequently mentioned characteristics include profit sharing, bonuses, and monetary awards. However, the list also contains policies and benefits that balance work and personal life and those that encourage social responsibility, all of which are part of the new social contract discussed in Chapter 11. Consider these policies described by employees:

- "When it comes to flextime requests, managers are encouraged to 'do what is right and human.'"

- "An employee hotline to report violations of company values."
- "Will fire clients who don't respect its security officers."
- "Employees donated more than 28,000 hours of volunteer labor last year."

There are moral benefits to business ethics as well as other types of benefits. The following paragraphs describe various types of benefits from managing ethics in the workplace.

Attention to business ethics has substantially improved society. For example, some decades ago, when workers' limbs could be torn off on the job, and disabled workers were condemned to poverty and often to starvation. Children in our country worked sixteen-hour days. Trusts controlled some markets to the extent that prices were fixed and small businesses choked out. Price fixing crippled normal market forces. Employees were terminated based on personalities. Influence was applied through intimidation and harassment. Then society reacted and demanded that businesses place high value on fairness and equal rights. Anti-trust laws were instituted. Government agencies were established. Unions were organized. Laws and regulations were established.

Ethics programs help maintain a moral course in turbulent times. Attention to business ethics is critical during times of fundamental change—times much like those faced now by businesses, both nonprofit or for-profit. During times of change, there is often no clear moral compass exists to guide leaders through complex conflicts about what is right or wrong. Continuing attention to ethics in the workplace sensitizes leaders and staff to how they want to act—consistently.

A commitment to ethics cultivates strong teamwork and productivity, two very important characteristics for today's successful organizations. Ethics programs align employee behaviors with the most important ethical values preferred by leaders of the organization. Ongoing attention and dialogue regarding values in the workplace build openness, integrity, and community—critical ingredients of strong teams in the workplace. Employees feel strong alignment between their values and those of the organization. They react with strong motivation and performance.

Ethics programs support employee growth and meaning. Attention to ethics in the workplace helps employees face reality, both good and bad, in the organization and themselves. Employees feel full confidence they can admit and deal with whatever comes their way.

Ethical climates and institutionalized organizational ethics are an insurance policy; they help ensure that policies are legal. There are an increasing number of lawsuits over human resources management (HRM) matters and over the effects of an organization's services or products on stakeholders. Ethical principles are often state-of-the-art legal matters. These principles are often applied to current major ethical issues to become legislation. Attention to ethics ensures highly ethical policies and procedures in the workplace. It's far better to incur the cost of mechanisms to ensure ethical practices now than to incur costs of litigation later. A major intent of well-designed HRM policies is to ensure ethical treatment of employees, e.g., in matters of hiring, evaluating, disciplining, and firing. Some have noted that "an employer can be subject to suit for breach of contract for failure to comply with any promise it made, so the gap between stated corporate culture and actual practice has significant legal, as well as ethical implications."[14]

Organizational ethics emphases help avoid criminal acts "of omission" and can lower fines. Ethics programs tend to detect ethical issues and violations early so that they can be reported or addressed. In some cases, when an organization is aware of an actual or potential violation and does not report it to the appropriate authorities, this failure can be considered a criminal act, as in business dealings with certain government agencies such as the Defense Department. The Federal Sentencing Guidelines specify major penalties for various types of major ethics violations. However, the guidelines allow for lower fines if an organization has clearly made an effort to operate ethically.

Ethics programs identify preferred values and ensure that organizational behaviors are aligned with those values. This effort includes recording the values, developing policies and procedures to align behaviors with preferred values, and then training all personnel about the policies and procedures. This overall effort is very useful for several other programs in the workplace that require behaviors to be aligned with values, including quality management, strategic planning, and diversity management. For example, successful team performance in a "Six Sigma" quality organization includes high priority on certain operating values such as trust among stakeholders, performance, reliability, measurement, and feedback. Many of these organizations use ethics tools in their quality programs to ensure integrity in their relationships with stakeholders. Ethics management techniques are also highly useful for managing strategic values, such as expand marketshare or reduce costs. Ethics management programs are also useful in managing diversity. Diversity programs require recognizing and applying diverse values and perspectives; these activities are the basis of an organization committed to sound ethics.

As noted earlier, a commitment to ethics promotes a strong public image. Attention to ethics is strong public relations. Admittedly, managing ethics should not be done primarily for reasons of public relations. But, frankly, the fact that an organization regularly gives attention to its ethics can portray a strong positive to the public. People see those organizations as valuing people more than profit, as striving to operate with the utmost of integrity and honor. Aligning behavior with values is critical to effective marketing and public relations programs. Consider how Johnson & Johnson handled the Tylenol crisis versus how Exxon handled the oil spill in Alaska. In companies like Johnson & Johnson ethical values, consistently applied, are the cornerstones in building a competitive, successful and socially responsible busines

A commitment to ethical values in the workplace legitimizes managerial actions, strengthens the coherence and balance of the organization's culture, improves trust in relationships between individuals and groups, supports greater consistency in standards and qualities of products, and cultivates greater sensitivity to the impact of the enterprise's values and messages.

Last—and most important—an unwavering commitment to ethics in the workplace is the right thing to do.

There is evidence that paying attention to ethical issues pays off for companies. In the early 1990s, James Burke, then the CEO of Johnson & Johnson, put together a list of companies that devoted a great deal of attention to ethics. The group included Johnson & Johnson, Coca-Cola, Gerber, Kodak, 3M, and Pitney Bowes. Over a forty-year period the market value of these organizations grew at an annual rate of 11.3 percent, as compared to 6.2 percent for the Dow Jones industrials as a whole.[15] Other evidence has also demonstrated that ethics and financial performance are linked. In a recent study of the 500 largest U.S. public corporations, those that claim a commitment to ethical behavior toward their stakeholders have a better financial performance than those firms that do not.[16] While these results do not demonstrate a causal relationship between ethics and performance, the findings hint at the presence of a relationship between the two. Doing the right thing can have a positive effect on an organization's performance.

MYTHS ABOUT BUSINESS ETHICS

Not everyone agrees that ethics is a relevant or necessary subject for business dealings or education.[17] Some have argued that business ethics is an oxymoron, or a contradiction in terms. While we do not advocate or promote a particular ethical position or belief system in this book, we do see that ethics is relevant to business transactions.

Over the years, lack of involvement by organizational leaders and managers in the field of business ethics has spawned a great deal of confusion and misunderstanding among them about business ethics. Often when someone brings up the topic of business ethics "it tends to bring up cynicism, righteousness, paranoia, and laughter."[18] Many leaders and managers believe business ethics is religion because it seems to contain a great deal of preaching.

Certain myths persist about business ethics. Some of these myths arise from general confusion about the notion of ethics. Other myths arise from narrow or simplistic views of ethical dilemmas. A myth "is a belief given uncritical acceptance by members of a group, especially in support of existing or traditional practices and institutions."[19]

1. Ethics is personal. This myth holds that individual ethics is based on personal or religious beliefs and that one decides what is right and wrong in the privacy of one's own conscience.
2. Business ethics and ethics do not mix. This popular myth holds that business practices are basically amoral (not necessarily immoral), since businesses operate in a free market.[20] This myth also asserts that management is based on scientific, rather than religious or ethical, principles.
3. Business ethics is more a matter of religion than management. A cornerstone of this myth is the belief that "altering people's values or souls isn't the aim of an organizational ethics program—managing values and conflict among them is."[21]
4. Business ethics is relative. This myth holds that no right or wrong way of believing or acting exists. Right and wrong are in the eye of the beholder.
5. Good business means good ethics. The reasoning here is that executives and organizations that maintain a good corporate image, practice fair and equitable dealing with customers and employees, and earn profits by legitimate means are de facto ethical.[22] Such organizations, therefore, would not have to be concerned explicitly with ethics in the workplace. Just do a hard, fair day's work, which has its own moral goodness and rewards.
6. Information is neutral and amoral. This myth holds that information and computing are neither moral nor immoral, but amoral, that is, they are in a "gray zone," a questionable area regarding ethics.
7. Business ethics is still a fad or a discipline touted by philosophers, academics, and theologians. Many believe that business ethics is a fad or movement, having little to do with the day-to-day realities of running an organization. They believe business ethics is primarily a complex philosophical debate or a religion.
8. Business ethics is superfluous—it only asserts the obvious: "Do good!" Those who support this myth react that codes of ethics or lists of ethical values to which the organization aspires are rather superfluous because they represent values to which everyone should naturally aspire.

9. Business ethics is a matter of the good guys preaching to the bad guys. Some claim a moral high ground while lamenting the poor condition of business and its leaders. However, those people well versed in managing organizations realize that good people can take bad actions, particularly when stressed or confused.
10. Ethics can't be managed. Some are still skeptical about business ethics, believing you can't manage values in an organization.

Logical problems occur in all of these myths. In many instances, the myths hold simplistic and even unrealistic notions about ethics in business dealings. While these myths can be refuted, they persist in the minds of many who will never believe that ethics is relevant or necessary to business dealings or education.

ETHICS AND THE LAW

Ethical behavior is typically thought to reside above behavior required by the law. This is the generally accepted view of ethics. It should be clear, however, that in many respects the law and ethics overlap. To really appreciate this, one needs to recognize that the law embodies notions of ethics. That is, the law may be seen as a reflection of what society thinks are minimal standards of conduct and behavior. Both law and ethics have to do with what is deemed appropriate or acceptable, but law reflects society's *codified* ethics. Therefore, if a person breaks a law or violates a regulation, he or she is also behaving unethically. In spite of this overlap, our view is that desirable ethical behavior is behavior that extends beyond what is required by law. Viewed from the standpoint of minimums, we would definitely say that obedience to the law is generally regarded to be a minimum standard of behavior.

The law does not address all realms in which ethical questions might be raised. Thus, there are clear roles for both law and ethics to play. It should be noted that research on illegal corporate behavior has been conducted for some time. Illegal corporate behavior, of course, comprises business practices that are in direct defiance of law of public policy.

ETHICAL AND UNETHICAL BEHAVIOR

We're [Pepsico] committed to being environmentally responsible and to minimizing the impact of our business on the Earth. We encourage conservation, recycling and energy use programs that promote clean air and water and reduce landfill.[23]

The company's [DuPont] business ethics policy is the cornerstone of our internal control system. This policy sets forth management's commitment to conduct business worldwide with the highest ethical standards and in conformity with applicable laws.[24]

It has always been the policy and practice of the Company [Johnson & Johnson] to conduct its affairs ethically and in a socially responsible manner. This responsibility is characterized and reflected in the company's Credo and Policy on Business Conduct which are distributed throughout the Company. Management maintains a systematic program to ensure compliance with these policies.[25]

These excerpts from corporate annual reports illustrate that some organizations attempt to make ethics an integral part of the organization's culture and control systems. It is also quite easy to confirm that ethical behavior does not characterize the actions of all managers and their organizations.

Ethical behavior is acting in ways consistent with one's personal values and the commonly held values of the organization and society. Ethical issues are a major concern in organizations, and failure to handle situations in an ethical manner can cost companies.

Unethical behavior by employees can affect individuals, work teams, and even the organization. Organizations thus depend on individuals to act ethically. Observations of widespread illegality, unethical behavior, and cynicism have led to researchers of managerial values to conclude that it is important to keep a "continued vigilance . . . focusing attention on values and ethical behavior."[26] Concerns of this nature have led to the emergence of organizations like London's Institute of Social and Ethical AccountAbility and their efforts to establish standards for ethical and social behavior and the public accounting of behavior along both of these lines.

Influences on Unethical Behavior

Before continuing with our discussion of business ethics, it is important to take a brief look at why employees choose to behave unethically (A topic explored in more detail in Chapter 5). Sometimes employees behave unethically simply because they don't take the time to think about the implications of their behavior. For example, today's managers are commonly overworked and highly stressed. Under these conditions, people sometimes do things they later regret. Employees sometimes behave unethically for other reasons. The behavior of one's supervisors is one of the strongest influences on employees and the ethical or unethical decisions they make.

Personality characteristics can also influence unethical behavior. Persons most likely to behave unethically are those who believe that the ends justify the means; that what happens is due to luck or change, not to their actions; and that economic and political values are of great importance. Several traits appear to make some people less ethical than others. For example, people who rate low on conscientiousness are more likely to steal from their employers than people who rate high on this personality dimension. It has also been shown that people placed in competitive situations are more likely to behave unethically.

Rewards and punishments are among the most powerful determinants of ethical and unethical behavior. People who are rewarded for unethical behavior (such as receiving a pay increase for providing a kickback to a customer) are much more likely to behave unethically than those who are punished for unethical behavior—people, after all, generally do that for which they are rewarded. Punishing unethical behavior frequently leads to higher levels of ethical behavior. Rewards and punishment probably influence the ethics of behavior both because rewards increase the likelihood that behavior will be repeated and punishment decreases the likelihood of repetition, and because rewards call attention to the potentially unethical behavior.

Ethical Standards and the Employee's Dilemma

An independent set of standards does not exist for ethical behavior in organizations. Ethics for organizations derive from the ethics of the society within which they exist. Thus, societal standards are the ultimate guide for employees. When employees confront an ethically difficult decision, they should consider how societal standards apply to their situation and should try to incorporate the most relevant ones within their moral reasoning.

Employees can look at several theories to guide their decision making. Utilitarian theory concentrates on the social consequences that an action is likely to produce. An action is considered morally right if its consequences for everyone affected by the action are greater than those which would be realized by a different action. Labor unions often negotiate across-the-board pay raises for the employees that they represent. Everyone gets the same pay increase in such situations, even though some employees perform at higher levels than others, and perhaps deserve a larger pay increase. Unions resist this notion, because they believe they can maximize the total return to all members by focusing on the size of the increase for everyone, not just for a few. In rights theory, decision makers are concerned with respecting the rights to which people are entitled—these may be legal rights or moral rights.

In the United States, these rights include the right of free consent, the right to privacy, the right to freedom of conscience, the right to free speech, and the right to due process. Organizational leaders operating under a rights theory would not prohibit its employees from speaking in favor of a gay rights bill, endorsing gay partner benefits, or participating in a same-sex marriage.

Organizations that subscribe to the theory of justice emphasize engaging in acts that are fair and impartial. They would not consider a managerial action as just if it benefited some, while resulting in an injustice to others. Managers operating under a theory of justice try to prevent their direct reports from feeling cheated. For example, they make their expectations for performance clear to everyone, and then reward most of those employees who have met or exceeded those expectations. Everyone may not get a large pay increase, but they understand how the pay increases were determined. This is often referred to as procedural justice.

The suggestion that employees should consider the social consequences, the rights of others, and other ethical standards when making decisions sounds reasonable; however, doing so will not prevent individuals from encountering ethical dilemmas from time to time. Consider, for example, the dilemma posed by new scientific developments. In one recent case, the Environmental Protection Agency (EPA) caused public controversy by announcing that it would allow BioTechnica International, Inc., to test genetically altered organisms on a Wisconsin farm.[27]

THE LINK BETWEEN ETHICS, SOCIAL RESPONSIBILITY, AND STRATEGY

Organizational manager's choices about what strategic courses to steer are typically influenced by their ambitions, values, business philosophies, attitudes toward risk, and ethical beliefs. Sometimes the influence of a manager's personal values, experiences, and emotions is conscious and deliberate; at other times it may be unconscious. As one expert noted in explaining the relevance of personal factors to strategy, "People have to have their hearts in it."[28]

Managerial values shape the ethical quality of an organization's strategy. Managers with strong ethical convictions take pains to see that their companies observe strict codes of ethics in all aspects of the business. They expressly forbid such practices as accepting or giving kickbacks, badmouthing rivals' products, and buying political influence with political contributions. Instances where a company's strategic actions run afoul of high ethical standards include charging excessive interest rates on credit card balances, employing bait-and-switch sales tactics, continuing to market products suspected of having safety problems, and using ingredients that are known health hazards.

Every strategic action an organization takes should be ethical. It should involve rightful actions, not wrongful ones; otherwise it won't past the test of moral scrutiny. This means more than conforming to what is legal. Ethical and moral standards go beyond the law and the language of "thou shall not." They address the issues of duty and the language of "should do and should not do." Ethics concern human duty and the principles on which this duty rests.[29]

Every business has an ethical duty to its stakeholders. Stakeholders affect the organization and are affected by it, with certain expectations as to what the organization should do and how it should do it. A company has a duty to shareholders, for instance, who rightly expect a return on their investment. Even though investors may individually differ in their preferences for profits now versus profits later, their tolerance for greater risk, and their enthusiasm for exercising social responsibility, business executives have a moral duty to pursue profitable management of the owners' investment.

A company's duty to employees arises out of respect for the worth and dignity of individuals who devote their energies to the business and who depend on the business for their economic well-being. Principled strategy making requires that employee-related decisions be made equitably and compassionately, with concern for due process and for the impact that strategic change has on employees' lives. At best, the chosen strategy should promote employee interests as concerns compensation, career opportunities, job security, and overall working conditions. At least, the chosen strategy should not disadvantage employees. Even in crisis situations, businesses have an ethical duty to minimize whatever hardships have to be imposed in the form of workforce reductions, plant closings, job transfers, relocations, and loss of income.

The duty to the customer arises out of expectations that attend the purchase of a good or service. Inadequate appreciation of this duty led to the product liability laws and a host of regulatory agencies to protect consumers (see Chapter 4). All kinds of strategy-related ethical issues still abound, however. Should a seller voluntarily inform consumers that its product contains ingredients that, though officially approved for use, are suspected of having potentially harmful effects? Is it ethical for the makers of alcoholic beverages to sponsor college events, given that many college students are under the age of twenty-one? Is it ethical for manufacturers to stonewall efforts to recall products they suspect have faulty parts or defective designs? Is it ethical for the makers of athletic apparel and equipment to make substantial payments to college coaches in return for having the school's athletic teams wear their apparel or use their equipment?

An organization's ethical duty to suppliers arises out of the market relationship that exists between them. They are both partners and adversaries. They are partners in the sense that the quality of suppliers' parts affects the quality of a company's product and in the sense that their businesses are connected. They are adversaries in the sense that the supplier wants the highest price and profit it can get while the buyer wants a cheaper price, better quality, and speedier service. An organization confronts several ethical issues in its supplier relationships. Is it ethical to purchase goods from foreign suppliers who employ child labor, pay substandard wages, or have sweatshop working conditions in their facilities? Is it ethical to threaten to cease doing business with a supplier unless the supplier agrees not to do business with key competitors? Is it ethical not to give suppliers advance warning of an intent to discontinue using their materials?

An organization's ethical duty to the community at large stems from its status as a member of the community and as an institution of society. Communities and society are reasonable in expecting businesses to be good citizens—to pay their fair share of taxes for fire and police protection, streets and highways, waste removal, and so on, and to exercise care in the impact their activities have on the environment, society, and the communities in which they operate. Is it ethical for firearms makers to make just enough changes in the designs of their automatic weapons to escape the bans and prohibitions on automatic firearms instituted by Congress? Is it ethical for a brewer of beer to advertise its products on TV at times when these ads are likely to be seen by underage viewers?

Ultimately, an organization's community citizenship is demonstrated by whether it refrains from acting in a manner contrary to the well-being of society and by the degree to which it supports community activities, encourages employees to participate in community activities, handles health and safety aspects of its operations, accepts responsibility for overcoming environmental pollution, relates to regulatory bodies and employee unions, and exhibits high ethical standards.

Organizational management that truly cares about business and corporate social responsibility is proactive rather than reactive in linking strategic action and ethics. It steers away from ethically and morally questionable business opportunities and business practices. And it goes to considerable lengths to ensure that its actions reflect integrity and high ethical standards. If any of an organization's stakeholders conclude that management is not measuring up to ethical standards, they have recourse (see Chapter 3). Concerned investors can protest at the annual shareholders' meeting, appeal to the board of directors, or sell their stock. Concerned employees can unionize and bargain collectively, or they can seek employment elsewhere. Customers can switch to competitors. Suppliers can find other buyers. The community and society can do anything from staging protest marches and urging boycotts to stimulating political and governmental action.

The Kroger Company provides an excellent example of how an organization intends to live up to or satisfy its ethical responsibilities to various stakeholders. More specifically, company documents state:

> Our mission is to be a leader in the distribution and merchandising of food, health, personal care, and related consumable products and services. In achieving this objective, we will satisfy our responsibilities to shareowners, employees, customers, suppliers, and the communities we serve.
>
> We will conduct our business to produce financial returns that reward investment by shareowners and allow the Company to grow. Investments in retailing, distribution and food processing will be continually evaluated for their contribution to our corporate return objectives.
>
> We will constantly strive to satisfy consumer needs better than the best of our competitors. Operating procedures will reflect our belief that the organizational levels closest to the consumer are best positioned to respond to changing consumer needs.
>
> We will treat our employees fairly and with respect, openness, and honesty. We will solicit and respond to their ideas and reward meaningful contributions to our success.
>
> We value America's diversity and will strive to reflect that diversity in our workforce, the companies with whom we do business, and customers we serve. As a company, we will convey respect and dignity to each individual.
>
> We will encourage our employees to be active, responsible citizens and will allocate resources for activities that enhance the quality of life for our customers, our employees, and the communities we serve.[30]

As evidenced in the Kroger Company's efforts, organizations must commit themselves to pursuing their missions in a manner that satisfies their responsibilities to its stakeholders. One of the best ways organizations can achieve such objectives is by continually improving the organization-employee relationship, as discussed in the next section.

ETHICS AND THE ORGANIZATION-EMPLOYEE RELATIONSHIP

The organization-employee relationship has changed in today's high-involvement organizations (HIO). High involvement refers to "a participative process [that uses] the entire capacity of workers, designed to encourage employee commitment to organizational success."[31] High involvement management argues that the individual as an organizational member is a valuable organizational resource, in fact more valu-able than the organization's buildings, equipment, and inventory. High-involvement management sees the organization's human re-sources as one of the few resources that grows, develops, and increases in value with the "right use." For example, as people become better informed about the affairs of the organization, they increase in their value to the company as future decision makers. Thus, effective organ-izational management calls for the careful, strategic, efficient, and ef-fective utilization of all the organization's resources. Organizational managers need to be sensitive to the ethical nature of their actions, which undoubtedly influence employee behavior that contributes to the organization's functioning.

Classical economics and classical management theory tell us that employees are economically motivated. Knowing that employees have economic needs, should a manager offer economic incentives to encour-age employees to come to work and to come to work on time? The Hawthorne studies and the human relations model sensitized us to the ideal that social needs motivate behavior in the workplace. Knowing that employees have social needs, should a manager engage in pater-nalistic management practices to shape employee attitudes and pro-mote job satisfaction so that they will be less likely to seek employment elsewhere? From Abraham Maslow we learned that individuals have the need to know and the need to understand. Knowing that employees have these growth needs, should a manager provide employees with opportunities to grow and develop with the belief that this will moti-vate the employee to higher levels of performance? Knowing that salespeople with a strong need for achievement generally have more job satisfaction and are higher performers, should managers profile job applicants on the strengths of their need for achievement to improve the selection process?

In each of these instances, managers consciously use knowledge about personality, employee attitudes, and motivation to influence behavior that serves the organization's needs. Is this ethical? Is it ethical in some instances and not in others? What ethical standards guide the management of the individual-organization relationship? If managers intend no harm to the employee, if their actions produce positive effects for the employee and positive effects for the organization, is their behavior ethical?

These are important questions. And answering them requires a delicate balancing act—for example, on management practices and how they influence employee job satisfaction, organizational commit-ment, and psychological ownership. In each instance, managers must confront the inevitable question: What is the "right" thing to do? Is it ethical for a manager to consciously engage in management practices, design social systems (organizations), and structure the work that people do with an eye toward impacting employee motivation, job satisfaction, organizational commitment and identification, work as a central life interest, psychological ownership, work attendance, and performance?

While each manager must answer this question for themselves, it is our belief that each manager must develop the habit and the ability to create organizational systems that ask the question, What is the socially responsible and ethical thing to do? every time a decision is made.

With regard to employee job satisfaction, many different arguments are given as to why job satisfaction is important. Some argue from (1) a utilitarian perspective—job satisfaction is important because it impacts the organization's bottom line through tardiness, absenteeism, turnover, union activity, and performance; (2) a social welfare perspective—job satisfaction is important because prolonged job dissatisfaction contributes to poor mental health, which carries with it costs to society; (3) an altruistic perspective—job satisfaction is a valued outcome in the lives of people as an end in and of itself; or (4) a rights perspective—employees have a right to job satisfaction. Building on the "rights" argument, it is our position managers have no right to make the work lives of those who work for them miserable—thus, job dissatisfying. While we are not arguing that it is management's responsibility to create job satisfaction for everyone, we do believe that organizational decision making should, in part, be guided by a concern for the welfare of all organizational members. The managerial compass points "true north" (a metaphor for that which is socially responsible and the right thing to do) when management effectively strives to prevent the onset of job dissatisfaction.

The idea that management should consciously engage in strategies that strengthen employee commitment and loyalty also has ethical implications. We are of the opinion that commitment has a beneficial symmetry relationship. Therefore, ethical management actively commits to employees in the hope that employees will actively commit to the organization. We question the ethicality of consciously attempting to build employee commitment to management and the organization that is greater than the strength of the commitment that the organization is willing to extend to the organizational member.

We have addressed only the issues pertaining to job satisfaction/dissatisfaction and commitment. There are many more employee attitudes, motives, and behaviors that managers affect for which a question of ethics arises. What prescriptions can management employ to encourage ethical and socially responsible behavior? In general managers should use a quality-of-work-life barometer, which measures whether a managerial/organizational act creates an upward or a downward pressure on the organizational member's current quality-of-work-life. If an act is anticipated and intended to be neutral or to have a positive impact on the quality-of-work-life, it can usually be judged as socially responsible and ethical. If, however, the act is intended or anticipated to lower the quality-of-work-life, the act can be judged to be socially irresponsible and unethical.

It is important to recognize that every managerial act affects the attitudes, motivation, and behavior of the members of the organization. It is better (that is, more ethical and socially responsible) to consciously direct managerial actions toward enhancing the quality of the organizational member's work life than not to do so. It is our contention that as long as the manager's intention is not to harm the employee and to try to increase the quality-of-work life, the conscious management of employee work-related attitudes, motivation, and behavior is not an unethical act per se.

Ethics are rarely clear cut. Although many behaviors are clearly ethical or unethical, the vast majority of decisions employees make concern "gray" areas. When people cannot agree on whether a particular behavior is ethical, employees' personal values and the cultural values of an organization come into play. Employees must let their behavior reflect their values.

DIVERSITY: A CONTEMPORARY ISSUE WITH ETHICAL AND SOCIALLY RESPONSIBLE UNDERPINNINGS

Countless contemporary ethical and socially responsibility issues confront organizations and their members today. Among them are ethics and use of the Internet and e-commerce, stewardship of financial resources, environmental stewardship, sweatshops, the exploitation of labor and child labor, the emergence of mega-organizations and the potential reduction of competition in a variety of industries, genetic engineering, the commercialization of health care and education, and issues of diversity in the workplace.

The changing demographics of the workforce, with the increase in organizational diversity, is an extremely important philosophical issue intimately linked to ethics and socially responsive behavior. The changing nature of the workforce (for example, increased gender and ethnicity in the workforce) challenges businesses throughout America.

Compounding this workforce challenge is the fact that many companies are having a difficult time finding, hiring, and keeping skilled workers. In their efforts to remain competitive many organizations are keeping employees whom they might have ignored or discarded just ten years ago. These workers include not only people who have historically been victims of discrimination in the United States, such as women, African Americans, and Native Americans, but also older workers, people with a wider variety of educational and socioeconomic backgrounds, people with disabilities, and people who are gay or lesbian. In short, the workforce will be ever more diverse. Henceforth we will all be expected to work effectively with people who are different from ourselves.

Over the past three decades, American businesses have been aware that they may not intentionally or unintentionally discriminate in employment on the basis of race, color, creed (religion), sex, national origin, or age. Various federal acts have guaranteed all eligible workers in the United States those rights. Even though few laws require business to diversify their workforce, many organizations are actively pursuing diversification. Why? One major reason is that they don't have much choice. In most large cities in the United States, where most large companies conduct their business, the influx of immigrants combined with the decreasing workforce participation rate of whites means that the new applicant pools are increasingly diverse. In addition, most large companies have come to understand that they have an ethical and social responsibility to create and value diversity among employees, as suggested in the following excerpts:[32]

Texas Instruments: "Our effectiveness at using the talents of people of different backgrounds, experiences and perspectives is key to our competitive edge. . . . Diversity is a core TI value; valuing diversity in our workforce is at the core of the TI values statement." (see http://www.ti.com/corp/docs/diversity/world.htm for the complete TI definition of diversity.)[33]

Computer Sciences Corporation: "We value the diversity of our employees and the unique perspectives they bring to CSC. Diversity at CSC includes functional roles within the company, the markets and industries we serve, our length of service, geographic, location, educational background, age, race, gender, ethnicity, and whether we joined CSC independently or though an acquisition. By valuing differences, we demonstrate our commitment to treating everyone with fairness and respect." (see http://www.csc.com)

Microsoft Corporation: "At Microsoft, we believe that diversity enriches our performance and products, the communities in which we live and work, and the lives of our employees. As our workforce evolves to reflect the growing diversity of our communities and global marketplace, our efforts to understand, value, and incorporate difference become increasingly important. At Microsoft, we have established a number of initiatives to promote diversity within our own organization, and to demonstrate this commitment nationwide."[34]

Importance of Valuing Diversity

Valuing diversity is ethical—doing what is right and just in human actions. Our commonsense definitions of justice and fairness are usually in line with the principle that individuals should not encounter discrimination because of some unchangeable characteristic they possess, like their age. Organizations that truly value diversity agree that discriminating against people who have brown eyes, are short, or were born in Steubenville, Ohio is not ethical, because it is not fair. Similarly, it isn't ethical to treat West Indians, the older, and the obese with less dignity or respect than people who are Muslim, young, or slim.

Valuing diversity is socially responsible. When organizations promote diversity and train and require all employees to treat each other with respect, irrespective of their backgrounds, they advance the organizational community. Every person's unique talents and perspectives can be better used to the benefit of all.

Why Valuing Diversity Is Good Business

Some individuals are not convinced that they or their organizations have a responsibility to respond to societal needs. They focus only on maximizing shareholder wealth. However, a recent survey suggests that such individuals are in the minority. Of executives at Fortune 500 companies, 84 percent think diversity management is important, as do 67 percent of human resource management professionals in companies outside the Fortune 500.[35] Sempra Energy, Toyota Motor Sales, SBE Communications, Advantica, Fannie Mae, Darden Restaurants, Public Service Company of New Mexico, Lucent Technologies, Wal-Mart, and Union Bank of California were listed in the top 10 of Fortune's "50 Best Companies for Asians, Blacks, and Hispanics" at the close of the twentieth century. Fortunately, it turns out that valuing diversity is compatible with maximizing profits. Organizations (like Avon, Inland Steel, and Ortho Pharmaceuticals) often improve their bottom line when they put diversity management strategies in place. Fortune observes that many of the "best companies for minorities" matched Standard and Poor's 500 over the past year, and their performance surpassed them over the past three and five years.[36] Lucent Technology's CEO stated, "The company adopted its diversity stance because it made good business sense, . . . in addition, it was the right thing to do." The CEO goes on to say that "Diversity is a competitive advantage. Different people approach similar problems in different ways."[37] There are several reasons that diversity program can add to a company's bottom line:[38]

- Diversity improves the workforce. When employees treat one another with respect, less time is wasted on interpersonal conflicts and politicking. More time is devoted to working together to maximize organization effectiveness.
- Diversity facilitates hiring the best and brightest employees. Many companies are finding it difficult to find qualified workers, especially well-educated professionals. When organizations develop a reputation for supporting people of all backgrounds with respect, people from diverse backgrounds are more likely to seek employment there. The employer gets to choose from the "cream of the crop."
- Diversity helps to prevent discrimination lawsuits. If employees value and treat one another with respect, they will be less likely to sue for employment discrimination. Discrimination lawsuits can be costly, as Texaco found out when it lost a $176 million judgment in 1996.
- Diversity improves marketplace understanding. Just as diversity promotes creativity in decision-making, so too do diverse perspectives bring a broader understanding of the marketplace. The spending power of ethnic minorities in the United States will be $650 billion in the early twenty-first century.[39] Tapping into this lucrative market requires understanding their needs and values.
- Diversity capitalizes on new markets. Consumers eventually know which companies value people from all backgrounds. Diverse consumers are more likely to make purchases from companies who value employees like themselves. Conversely, they are less likely to make purchases from companies they perceive as discriminatory.
- Diversity facilitates the building of global relationships. Organizations who are comfortable with diversity do better in the global marketplace. Becoming truly at ease with diversity is not longer an option; it is a necessity.

It is critical that today's organizational managers and leaders develop a mindset that values diversity and sees diversity as an organizational resource, while also seeing the integration of diversity into the organization's culture as the right and socially responsible thing to do. Organizations that view valuing and managing diversity as the ethical and socially responsible thing to do can reap the rewards of increased productivity and improved organizational health.

CONCLUSION

Ethical behavior is that which is morally accepted as "good" and "right" as opposed to "bad" or "wrong" in a particular setting. For the individual that means acting in ways consistent with one's personal values and the commonly held values of the organization and society. Is it ethical, for example, to pay a bribe to obtain a business contract in a foreign country? Is it ethical to allow your company to withhold information that might discourage a job candidate from joining your organization? Is it ethical to do personal business on company time?

The public-at-large is demanding that government officials, business leaders and managers, workers in general, and the organizations they represent all act according to high ethical and moral standards. There is every indication that the future will bring a renewed concern with maintaining high standards of ethical behavior in organizational transactions and in the workplace.

One writer on the ethical organization provides the following four principles for highly ethical organizations:

- They are at ease interacting with diverse internal and external stakeholder groups. The ground rules of these firms make the good of these stakeholder groups part of the organizations' own good.
- They are obsessed with fairness. Their ground rules emphasize that the other persons' interests count as much as their own.
- Responsibility is individual rather than collective, with individuals assuming personal responsibility for actions of the organization. These organizations' ground rules mandate that individuals are responsible to themselves.
- They see their activities in terms of purpose. This purpose is a way of operating that members of the organization highly value. And purpose ties the organization to its environment.[40]

Additionally, we offer the following characteristics of a high-integrity organization:

- There exists a clear vision and picture of integrity throughout the organization.
- The vision is owned and embodied by top management, over time.
- The reward system is aligned with the vision of integrity.
- Policies and practices of the organization are aligned with the vision; no mixed messages.
- It is understood that every significant management decision has ethical value dimensions.
- Everyone is expected to work through conflicting stakeholder value perspectives.

NOTES

1. A. Zipkin, "Management: Getting Religion on Corporate Ethics: A Scourge of Scandals Leaves Its Mark," *New York Times* (October 18, 2000), 1, 3.

2. R. DeGeorge, *Business Ethics*, 5th ed. (Upper Saddle River, N.J.: Prentice-Hall, 2002).

3. Ibid; R. A. Buchholtz and S. B. Rosenthal, *Business Ethics* (Upper Saddle River, N.J.: Prentice Hall, 1998).

4. Archie B. Carroll, *Business and Society: Ethics and Stakeholder Management*, 3rd ed. (Cincinnati, Ohio: South-Western, 1993), 110–12; J. W. Weiss, *Business Ethics: A Stakeholder and Issues Management Approach*, 3rd ed. (Mason, O.: South-Western, 2003), 8; A. B. Carroll and A. K. Buchholtz, *Business and Society: Ethics and Stakeholder Management*, 5th ed. (Mason, O.: South-Western, 2003).

5. G. Morgenson, "Wall Street Firms Endorse Ethics Standards for Analysts," *New York Times* (June 13, 2001). See: NewYorkTimes.com.

6. Carroll and Buchholtz, *Business and Society*.

7. J. Frooman, "Socially Irresponsible and Illegal Behavior and Shareholder Wealth," *Business & Society* 36, no. 3 (1997), 221–29.

8. R. Zemke, "Employee Theft: How to Cut Your Losses," *Training* (May 1986), 74–78; S. Silverstein, "One in 15 Employees in Study Caught Stealing," *Los Angeles Times* (December 2, 1989), D-1.

9. KPMG Report, "Managing Ethics Costs and Benefits," *Ethics and Integrity*. See also *www.kpmg.ca/ethics/vl/ethben.htm* (Nov. 27, 1999).

10. Weiss, *Business Ethics*.

11. KPMG, "Managing Ethics Costs and Benefits."

12. R. Levering and M. Milton, "The 100 Best Companies to Work For," *Fortune* (January 10, 2000), 82-114.

13. See: *www.fortune.com*.

14. B. H. Drake and E. Drake, "Ethical and Legal Aspects of Managing Corporate Cultures," *California Management Review* 16 (1988), 107–23.

15. Debra L. Nelson and James C. Quick, *Organizational Behavior: Foundations, Realities, and Challenges*, 4th ed. (Mason, O.: South-Western, 2003).

16. C. C. Verchoor, "A Study of the Link Between Corporation's Financial Performance and Its Commitment to Ethics, *Journal of Business Ethics* 17 (1998), 1509–16.

17. Johannes Brinkmann and Ronald R. Sims, "Stakeholder-Sensitive Business Ethics Teaching," *Teaching Business Ethics* 5, no. 2 (2001), 171–93.

18. G. McDonald and R. Zepp, "What Should Be Done? A Practical Approach to Business Ethics," *Management Decision* 28, no. 1 (1990), 9–13.

19. Weiss, *Business Ethics*, 15.

20. DeGeorge, *Business Ethics*.

21. D. E. Kirrane, "Managing Values: A Systematic Approach to Business Ethics," *Training and Development Journal* (November 1990), 53–60.

22. C. D. Stone, *Where the Law Ends* (New York: Harper, 1975).

23. "We're Building a Premier Company," *Annual Report*, PepsiCo, Inc., 1999, 10.

24. E. I. DuPont de Nemours and Company, *Annual Report*, 1996, 28.

25. Johnson & Johnson, *Annual Report*, 1996, 40.

26. Barry Z. Posner and William H. Schmidt, "Values and the American Manager: An Update," *California Management Review* 26, no. 3 (1984), 202–16.

27. J. Wilke, "BioTechnica to Get OK to Test Genetically Altered Bacteria," *Boston Globe* (May 7, 1987), 61.

28. Kenneth R. Andrews, *The Concept of Corporate Strategy*, 3rd ed. (Homewood, Ill.: Richard D. Irwin, 1987).

29. H. Downs, "Business Ethics: The Stewardship of Power," cited in A. A. Thompson Jr., and A. J. Strickland III, *Strategic Management: Concepts and Cases*, 13th ed. (New York: McGraw-Hill, 2003), 64.

30. "The Kroger Company's Commitments to Its Shareholders," from: Company Web site (*www.kroger.com*), as cited in A. A. Thompson Jr., and A. J. Strickland III, *Strategic Management*, 69.

31. J. L. Cotton, *Employee Involvement: Methods for Improving Performance and Work Attitudes* (Newbury, Calif.: Sage, 1993).

32. Society for Human Resource Management, *Workplace Diversity: A Product of the SHRM Diversity Initiative* (Alexandria, Va.: The Society for Human Resource Management, 1999).

33. See *http://www.ti.com/corp/docs/diversity/world.htm*.

34. Society for Human Resource Management, *Workplace Diversity.*

35. See *http://www.ti.com/corp/docs/diversity/world.htm*.

36. G. Colvin, "The 50 Best Companies for Asians, Blacks, and Hispanics," *Fortune* (July 19, 1999), 53–88.

37. Ibid.

38. Society for Human Resource Management, *Workplace Diversity*; Robinson and K. Dechant, "Building a Business Case for Diversity," *Academy of Management Executive* 11, no. 3 (1997), 21–31.

39. C. Eichenwald, "Texaco to Let U.S. Check Bias-Law Compliance," *New York Times* (January 4, 1997), 36.

40. M. Pastin, *The Hard Problems of Management: Gaining the Ethics Edge* (San Francisco: Jossey-Bass, 1986).

3

Understanding Corporate Citizenship: Social Responsibility, Responsiveness, and Performance

INTRODUCTION

The history of U.S. business is riddled with sordid tales of magnates who went to any length in their quest for success, in the process destroying not only the country's natural resources and the public's trust but also the hopes and dreams of millions of people. For example, John D. Rockefeller, founder of Standard Oil, regularly bribed politicians and stepped over others in his quest to monopolize the oil industry.

Of course, unsavory business practices are not merely a relic of the past. For example, recent reports of bribes and kickbacks have tarnished the reputation of the International Olympic Organizing Committee, accusations of fraudulent practice in its auto-repair business raised ethical questions about the venerable retail giant Sears, and the bond-trading scandal at Salomon Brothers led to the company's demise. Clearly, human greed has not faded from the business scene. Something, however, has changed—the public's acceptance of unethical or socially irresponsible behavior by organizations. Consider this statement by a leading expert on business ethics: "Ethical standards, whether formal or informal, changed tremendously in the twentieth century and there is every indication that they will continue to do so throughout this century."[1] Standards are considerably higher as many organizations, as well as the public, expect more sensitive behavior in the conduct of business. The issue is not having the standards, however. It is living by them on a daily basis.

To the extent that people are increasingly intolerant of unethical or socially irresponsible business activity, it makes sense for organizational members to increase their understanding of corporate social responsibility (CSR), which is the focus of this chapter, and the nature of managerial ethics as discussed in the next chapter.

A STAKEHOLDER APPROACH TO CORPORATE SOCIAL RESPONSIBILITY

Organizations must recognize the rights or interests of various stakeholders—not only stockholders and employees but also outsiders affected by the company's actions. As we have said, such outsiders include customers, suppliers, governments, unions, competitors, local communities, and the general public. Stakeholder groups justifiably expect (and often demand) that the firm satisfy their claims in a responsible manner. In general, stockholders claim appropriate returns on their investment; employees seek broadly defined job satisfactions; customers want what they pay for; suppliers seek dependable buyers; governments want adherence to legislation; unions seek benefit for their members; competitors want fair competition; local communities want the company to be a responsible citizen; and the general public expects the company's existence to improve the quality of life.

To be successful in today's complex and dynamic environment, organizations must attempt to incorporate the interests of these groups when defining their strategy or making business decisions. These steps should be taken:

1. Identification of the stakeholders
2. Understanding the stakeholders' specific claims vis-á-vis the company
3. Reconciliation of these claims and assignments of priorities to them
4. Coordination of the claims with other elements of the company

The left-hand column of Table 3.1 lists the commonly encountered stakeholder groups, to which the company's senior officer group is often added. Obviously, though, every business faces a slightly different set of stakeholder groups, which vary in number, size, influence, and importance. Organizational leaders and managers must take the time to identify all the stakeholder groups and to weigh their relative rights and their relative abilities to affect the company's success.

The concerns of the principal stakeholder groups tend to center on general claims, as listed in the right-hand column of Table 3.1. However,

TABLE 3.1   Stakeholder View of Corporate Responsibility

Stakeholder	Nature of the Stakeholder Claim
Shareholders	Participation in distribution of profits, additional stock offerings, assets on liquidation; vote of stock; inspection of company books; transfer of stock; election of board of directors; and such additional rights as have been established in the contract with the corporation.
Employees	Economic, social, and psychological satisfaction in the place of employment. Freedom from arbitrary and capricious behavior on the part of company officials. Share in fringe benefits, freedom to join union and participate in collective bargaining, individual freedom in offering up their services through an employment contract. Adequate working conditions.
Customers	Service provided with the product; technical data to use the product; suitable warranties; spare parts to support the product during use; R&D leading to product improvement; facilitation of credit.
Creditors	Legal proportion of interest payments due and return of principal from the investment. Security of pledged assets; relative priority in event of liquidation. Management and owner prerogatives if certain conditions exist with the company (such as default of interest payments).
Suppliers	Continuing source of business; timely consummation of trade credit obligations; professional relationship in contracting for, purchasing, and receiving goods and services.
Unions	Recognition as the negotiating agent for employees. Opportunity to perpetuate the union as a participant in the business organization.
Competitors	Observation of the norms of competitive conduct established by society and the industry. Business statesmanship on the part of peers.
Governments	Taxes (income, property, and so on); adherence to the letter and intent of public policy dealing with the requirements of fair and free competition; discharge of legal obligations of businesspeople (and business organizations); adherence to antitrust laws.
Local communities	Place of productive and healthful environment in the community. Participation of company officials in community affairs, provision of regular employment, fair play, reasonable portion of purchases made in the local community, interest in and support of local government, support of cultural and charitable projects.
The general public	Participation in and contribution to society as a whole; creative communications between governmental and business units designed for reciprocal understanding; assumption of fair proportion of the burden of government and society. Fair price for products and advancement of the state-of-the-art technology that the product line involves.

the organization's leaders and managers should understand the specific demands of each group. They then will be better able to initiate actions that satisfy these demands.

Unfortunately, the claims of various stakeholder groups often conflict. For example, the claims of governments and the general public tend to limit profitability, which is the central claim of most creditors and stockholders. Claims must be reconciled in a way that resolves the conflicting, claims of stakeholders. For organizational objectives and strategies to be internally consistent and precisely focused, leaders must display a single-minded, though multidimensional, approach to the company's aims.

Claims on an organization may include high wages, pure air, job security, product quality, equal employment opportunity regulations, product variety, wide markets, company growth, investment security, high return on investment (ROI), and more. Although most of these claims may be desirable ends, they cannot be pursued with equal emphasis. They must be assigned priorities in accordance with the emphasis that the organization will give them. That emphasis is reflected in the criteria that the company uses in its strategic decision making; in the company's allocation of its human, financial, and physical resources; and in the company's long-term objectives and strategies.

The demands of stakeholder groups constitute only one principal set of inputs to decisions on such things as mission and strategic direction. The other principal sets are the managerial operating philosophy and the determinants of the product- or service-market offerings. Those determinants constitute a reality test that the accepted claims must pass. The key question is: How can the company satisfy its claimants and at the same time optimize its economic success in the marketplace?

Today's organizations must increasingly learn how to respond to this question if they are going to survive and thrive. They must be financially successful while responding claims that the organization be more socially responsible. The issues that surround the call for more socially responsible organizations are numerous, complex, and contingent on specific situations. Rigid rules of business conduct cannot deal with them. Today's organizational managers must be concerned about the social responsibility of their organizations. Failure to do so may result in their inability to sustain a competitive advantage.

THE CONCEPT OF CORPORATE SOCIAL RESPONSIBILITY

To understand better why some organizations fall ethically, we can explore organizational attitudes toward stakeholders in the form of corporate social responsibility (CSR). For many organizations, commitment to CSR is shown in references to stakeholders and "triple bottom line" thinking (i.e., financial, environmental, and social responsibility bottom lines). One useful definition of CSR is that it requires "the continuing commitment by business to behaving ethically and contributing to economic development while improving the quality of life of the workforce and their families as well as of the community and society at large."[2]

Criticism of business over the years has led to an increased concern for the social environment and a changed social contract. Out of suuvh criticism has grown the notion of corporate social responsibility, or CSR. Let us take a closer look at the nature of social responsibility.

Many argue strongly that organizations and their leaders must consider the impact of their decisions and actions on society as a whole and that they must assume responsibility for their activities. It is argued further that organizations should take steps to protect and improve the welfare of society. Some have suggested that organizations exist to serve the needs of society. Therefore, being a steward of the needs of society is a socially responsible, appropriate, and natural act."[3] In short, leaders and managers must evaluate their decisions and actions not merely from the perspective of organizational effectiveness, but also from the perspective of the greater good.

An early view of CSR is as follows: "Corporate social responsibility is seriously considering the impact of the company's actions on society."[4] Another definition that may be helpful is, "The idea of social responsibility . . . requires the individual to consider his [or her] acts in terms of a whole system, and holds him [or her] responsible for the effects of his [or her] acts anywhere in that system."[5] A third definition places social responsibilities in context vis-à-vis economic and legal objectives. That is, "the idea of social responsibility supposes that the corporation has not only economic and legal obligations, but also certain responsibilities to society which extend beyond these obligations."[6]

A fourth definition relates CSR to business management's growing concern with stakeholders and ethics. According to this definition, "Corporate social responsibility relates primarily to achieving outcomes from organizational decisions concerning specific issues or problems which (by some normative standard) have beneficial rather than adverse effects upon pertinent corporate stakeholders. The normative correctness of the products of corporate action have been the main focus of corporate social responsibility."[7] This definition concentrates on the outcomes, products, or results of corporate actions for stakeholders. Over the decades, a number of different views on CSR have evolved.

Finally, a four-part definition of CSR focuses on the types of social responsibilities that it might be argued belong to business. That is, as Archie Carroll says, "The social responsibility of business encompasses the economic, legal, ethical and discretionary (philanthropic) expectations that society has of organizations at a given point in time."[8] Carroll's definition attempts to place the economic and legal expectations of business in context by relating them to more socially oriented concerns. These social concerns include ethical responsibilities and philanthropic (voluntary/discretionary) responsibilities. This definition, which includes four kinds of responsibilities, elaborates and builds upon the definition proposed by McGuire. Carroll suggests portraying the four parts of his definition of CSR in pyramid form, beginning with the building block of economic performance at the base. At the same time, business is expected to obey the law, because the law is society's codification of acceptable and unacceptable behavior. Next is business's responsibility to be ethical, which at its most basic level is the obligation to do what is right, just, and fair and to avoid or minimize harm to stakeholders (employees, consumers, the environment, and others). Finally, business is expected to be a good corporate citizen—to fulfill voluntary/discretionary or philanthropic responsibility to contribute financial and human resources to the community and to improve the quality of life.[9]

All these definitions provide some insight into the ideal of CSR. Social responsibility goes beyond the letter of the law. For our purposes, social responsibility is an organization's obligation to engage in activities that protect and contribute to the welfare of society. CSR refers to an organization's moral obligation toward others who are affected by the organization's actions. An organization's social responsibilities are always shaped by the culture and the historical period in which the organization operates. Just as a society's values, norms, and mores change over time, so does the definition of what is socially responsible behavior. Differences in societal values and the shift of public attitude can be seen in the tobacco industry and in the public's response to the genetic alteration of seeds and dairy products. In the tobacco industry, the old thinking was that "if you smoke cigarettes, whatever happens to your heart and lungs is your own fault. Cigarettes are legal and are voluntarily purchased and consumed. Don't come whining to the courts when you see a shadow on the X-ray. Caveat fumor." During the latter part of the twentieth century, the old thinking shifted to the new thinking that "Big Tobacco knowingly sells a defective product that when used exactly as intended (that is, you smoke the thing), addicts the consumer to nicotine and eventually sickens and kills him. Big Tobacco should pay billions."[10] What was once considered socially acceptable and legal is now considered socially irresponsible, and it has been punished to the tune of billions of dollars! Passions in many Western European countries ran extremely high during the 1990s with regard to importing U.S. dairy products, which use growth hormones to stimulate milk production. Similar feelings do not exist throughout much of the United States.

Just exactly what is an organization's social responsibility? At one extreme, there are those who strongly believe that organizations are in business solely to produce goods and services that societies want—be they life-saving devices, legal advice, or atomic weapons—and that they are entitled to make a profit in return. For these people, social responsibility is simply not an issue. At the other extreme, there are those who believe that organizations should be allowed to do business only if they do no harm, help solve social problems, and put some of the profits they earn back to work for society. This disagreement does not lend itself to quick and easy resolution.

The concept of CSR grew out of business criticism and increased concern for the social environment and the changed social contract. Many organizations have responded to these new ideas with a commitment to social responsibility that has led to increased corporate responsiveness to stakeholders and improved social (stakeholder) performance.

Some individuals today prefer the language of "corporate citizenship" to collectively embrace the host of concepts related to CSR. In their view corporate citizenship concepts include CSR, which emphasizes obligation and accountability; corporate social responsiveness, which emphasizes action and activity; and corporate social performance (CSP),which emphasizes outcomes and results. The growth of these ideas has brought about a society more satisfied with business. However, although this satisfaction has countered some criticisms of business, it has also led to increased expectations that will inevitably result in more criticism. It has been suggested "that the net result of this double effect is that the overall levels of business performance and societal satisfaction should increase with time in spite of this interplay of positive and negative factors. Should business not be responsive to societal expectations, it could conceivably enter a downward spiral, resulting in significant changes in the business/society relationship."[11]

FACTORS SHAPING ORGANIZATIONS AND THEIR DECISIONS

All organizations operate within the broader community of society. What an organization can and cannot do is always constrained by what is legal, by what complies with government policies and regulatory requirements, by what is considered ethical, and by what is in accord with societal expectations and the standards of good community citizenship. Outside pressures also come from other sources—special-interest groups, the glare of investigative reporting, a fear of unwanted political action, and the stigma of negative opinions. Societal concerns over gun control, health and nutrition, alcohol and drug abuse, smoking, environmental pollution, sexual harassment, and the impact of plant closings on local communities have caused many companies to temper or review aspects of their organizational decisions. American concerns over jobs lost to foreign manufacturers and political debate over how to cure the chronic U.S. trade deficit are driving forces in the decisions of foreign companies to locate plants in the United States. Heightened consumer awareness about the hazards of saturated fat and cholesterol have driven most food products companies to phase out high-fat ingredients and substitute low-fat ingredients.

Factoring in societal values and priorities, business ethics, community concerns, and the potential for onerous legislation and regulatory requirements is a regular part of external situation analysis at more and more companies. Intense public pressure and adverse media coverage make such a practice prudent. For our purposes, the task of making an organization socially responsible means (1) conducting organizational activities within the bounds of what is considered ethical and in the general public interest, (2) responding positively to emerging societal pressures and expectations, (3) demonstrating a willingness to take action ahead of regulatory confrontation, (4) balancing stockholder interests against the larger interests of society as a whole, and (5) being a good citizen in the community.

CORPORATE SOCIAL RESPONSIBILITY AND THE LAW

The two concepts "social responsibility" and "legality" are not one and the same. CSR is often seen as acts that go beyond what is prescribed by the law. In fact, many individuals believe that certain existing laws do not encourage socially responsible behavior.[12] For example, oceangoing ships are currently (and legally) allowed to dump their ballast water into the Great Lakes. This water brings many nonnative species to the Great Lakes, such as lamprey, which nearly destroyed the trout population in Lake Superior, and zebra mussels, which have damaged the water intake systems of communities and businesses located along the lakes. The dumping of ballast water may be legal but it is not socially responsible.

Thinking about legality and responsibility identifies four distinct organizational approaches to social responsibility: illegal and irresponsible, illegal and responsible, irresponsible and legal, and legal and responsible.

Some organizations behave illegally and irresponsibly. For example, an investigation was launched to examine claims that some companies took advantage of the catastrophic Pennsylvania Ashland Petroleum tank collapse by dumping their own toxic wastes into the already polluted Monongahela River. Dumping this type of material into the river is prohibited by law, and it was clearly irresponsible to further contaminate the water. In recent years there have been numerous reports of contractors illegally dumping asbestos removed from schools as a way of avoiding the costs associated with proper disposal. Today, an illegal and irresponsible strategy is a high-risk strategy that may be fatal to an organization, because a broad spectrum of society will no longer tolerate such behavior.

Some organizations follow strategies that are socially conscious and responsible, but that violate the letter of the law. Greenpeace has on many occasions engaged in illegal acts in an effort to protect the environment. For example, during the mid-1990s, they attempted to block French nuclear tests in the South Pacific by illegally occupying French territory and harassing French military operations.

Some organizations operate without violating a single law, but still do not act in a socially responsible manner. For example, beer companies produce commercials that appeal to underage drinkers, and casinos sometimes make special offers that encourage people to trade their Social Security checks for gambling chips. These organizations are acting within the letter of the law but not the spirit of the law.

Finally, some organizations obey the law and at the same time engage in socially responsible behavior. For example, since 1984 Patagonia has given 10 percent of its pretax profits to such groups as the Wolf Fund, the Audubon Society, and the Nature Conservancy. Ben & Jerry's gives 7.5 percent of its pretax profits to charity, while the Hallmark Corporation for the past 80 years has donated more than 5 percent of its corporate pre-tax profits to charitable causes. These charitable acts on the part of Patagonia, Ben & Jerry's, and Hallmark are both legal and highly socially responsible.

A HISTORICAL PERSPECTIVE ON CSR

There were few corporate acts of charity at the start of the twentieth century. Instead, wealthy business people engaged in philanthropy as they gave as individuals from their personal wealth to charitable and other worthy causes. How, then, did corporate commitment to social responsibility evolve? Two principles provided the foundation for contemporary views on social responsibility.[13] The first of these, the principle of charity, is rooted in religious tradition and suggests that those who have plenty should give to those who do not. Under the influence of this principle, individuals in the business community increasingly decided to use some of their corporate power and wealth for the social good. These voluntary community obligations to improve, beautify, and uplift were quite evident by many business leaders. One early example was the cooperative effort between the railroads and the YMCA immediately after the Civil War to provide community services in areas served by the railroads. Although these services economically benefited the railroads, they were at the same time philanthropic. In another example, steel magnate Andrew Carnegie put much of his great wealth to work for education. Henry Ford adopted a paternalistic style of management and made recreational and health programs available to Ford employees. The company town was one of the most visible examples of paternalism. Although business's motives for creating company towns (for example, the Pullman/Illinois experiment) were mixed, business had to do a considerable amount of work in governing them. Thus, the company accepted a form of paternalistic social responsibility. Over time, an increasing number of business leaders adopted and spread the idea that business has a responsibility to society beyond simply providing necessary goods and services.

A second principle that shaped CSR is the principle of stewardship, which asserts that organizations have an obligation to see that the public's interests are served by corporate actions and the way in which profits are spent. Because corporations control vast resources, because they are powerful, and because this power and wealth come from their operations within society, they have an obligation to serve society's needs. In this way, corporations and their leaders and managers become stewards, or trustees for society. Under the influence of this principle, Congress, the popular press, and other factions started to attack many large and powerful organizations whose attitudes they perceived to be both anticompetitive and antisocial. Antitrust laws and other legislation began to place constraints on the actions of organizations.[14] In general, there was a shift in the public perception of a corporation's place within and obligation to society.

Attitudes about what is and is not considered socially responsible behavior also have changed substantially over time. This change is reflected by the following three phases.

Phase One: Profit-Maximizing Management

During the period of economic scarcity in the nineteenth century and the early part of the twentieth century, most American business managers felt they had one primary responsibility to society. They were to underwrite the country's economic growth and oversee the accumulation of wealth. Business leaders could pursue, almost single-mindedly, the objective of maximizing profits. Leaders essentially felt that what was good for business was good for the country. The strong business ethos was shattered, however by the Great Depression of the 1930s.

Phase Two: Trusteeship Management

After the Great Depression, the number of privately held American corporations began to decline. Organizations found themselves having to respond to the demands of both internal and external groups, such as stockholders, customers, suppliers, and creditors. This phase signaled a transition from a predominantly laissez-faire economy to a mixed economy in which business found itself one of the constituencies monitored by a more active government. As a consequence, organizations had to shift their orientation to social responsibility, and the result was the emergence of trusteeship management. Corporate leaders needed to maintain an equitable balance among the competing interests of all groups with a stake in the organization. Pressure from these groups led to the use of some corporate wealth to meet social needs. From this time well into the 1950s, business's social responsibilities grew to include employee welfare (pension and insurance plans), safety, medical care, retirement programs, and so on. It has been suggested that these new developments were spurred by governmental compulsion and by an enlarged concept of business responsibility.[15]

Phase Three: Quality-of-Life Movement

This phase may be considered part of the modern era in which the concept of corporate social responsibility gained considerable acceptance and broadened in meaning. During this time, a new set of national priorities began to develop and the pressure on corporations and their business leaders to behave in socially responsible ways intensified as the emphasis moved from little more than a general awareness of social and moral concerns to a period in which specific issues such as product safety, honesty in advertising, employee rights, affirmative action, poverty, environmental pollution, deteriorating inner cities, and ethical behavior raised widespread concern about the quality of life in the United States. The consensus was that corporations and their managers had to do more than achieve narrow economic goals. They are to enhance our quality of life by helping solve society's ills.[16] The issues of charity and stewardship were firmly in place (see Table 3.2).

The community involvement of the Control Data Corporation (CDC) provides an illustration of this approach to CSR. CDC built plants in Minneapolis, St. Paul, and Washington, D.C., to provide jobs and de-

TABLE 3.2 Comparison of Managerial Values

Profit Maximization Management	Trusteeship Management	Quality-of-Life Management
Economic Values		
1. Raw self-interest	1. Self-interest 2. Contributors' interest	1. Enlightened self-interest 2. Contributors' interest 3. Society's interest
What's good for me is good for my country.	What's good for GM is good for the country.	What is good for society is good for our company.
Profit maximizer	Profit satisfier*	Profit is necessary, but. . . .
Money and wealth are most important.	Money is important, but so are people.	People are more important than money.
Let the buyer beware (*caveat emptor*).	Let us not cheat the customer.	Let the seller beware (*caveat venditor*).
Labor is a commodity to be bought and sold.	Labor has certain rights, which must be recognized.	Employee dignity has to be satisfied.
Accountability of management is to the owners.	Accountability of management is to the owners, customers, employees, suppliers, and other contributors.	Accountability of management is to the owners, contributors, and society.
Technology Values		
Technology is very important.	Technology is important but so are people.	People are more important than technology.
Social Values		
Employee personal problems must be left at home.	We recognize that employees have needs beyond their economic needs.	We hire the whole person.
I am a rugged individualist, and I will manage my business as I please.	I am an individualist, but I recognize the value of group participation.	Group participation is fundamental to our success.
Political Values		
The government is best that governs least.	Government is a necessary evil.	Business and government must cooperate to solve society's problems.
Environmental Values		
The natural environment controls the destiny of humankind.	Human beings can control and manipulate the environment.	We must preserve the environment in order to lead a quality life.
Esthetic Values		
Esthetic values? What are they?	Esthetic values are okay, but not for us.	We must preserve our esthetic values, and we will do our part.

Profit satisfier means generating a satisfactory return.

velop an economic base for inner-city residents of poor urban areas. They have also undertaken numerous other projects to assist the disabled with vocational training programs and have created Rural Ventures and City Venture Corporation to encourage rural and urban revitalization projects.

CORPORATE SOCIAL RESPONSIVENESS: LEVELS AND TYPES OF SOCIAL COMMITMENT

We have discussed the evolution of corporate social responsibility and the arguments for and against it. It is now important to address a concept that has arisen over the use of the terms *responsibility* and *responsiveness*. We will briefly consider the views of several writers before taking a more in-depth look at Sethi's view on getting from social responsibility to social responsiveness.

A number of writers have provided conceptual schemes that describe the responsiveness facet. A general argument that has generated much discussion over the past several decades holds that the term *responsibility* is too suggestive of efforts to pinpoint accountability or obligation. Therefore, it is not dynamic enough to fully describe business's willingness and activity—apart from obligation—to respond to social demands. Some have criticized the CSR term by stating, "The connotation of 'responsibility' is that of the process of assuming an obligation. It places an emphasis on motivation rather than on performance." They go on to say, "Responding to social demands is much more than deciding what to do. There remains the management task of doing what one has decided to do, and this task is far from trivial."[17] They argue that "social responsiveness" is a more apt description of what is essential in the social arena.

Corporate social responsiveness has been discussed within the context of a broader concept that he calls the corporate social policy process. In this context, the *process* aspect of social responsiveness is emphasized. He asserts that corporate social responsiveness focuses on the individual and organizational processes "for determining, implementing, and evaluating the firm's capacity to anticipate, respond to, and manage the issues and problems arising from the diverse claims and expectations of internal and external stakeholders."[18]

One author asserts that there are four possible business strategies: reaction, defense, accommodation, and proaction.[19] Another writer has likewise described four social responsibility philosophies that mesh well with Wilson's and describe the managerial approach that would characterize the range of the responsiveness dimension: "Fight all the way," "Do only what is required," "Be progressive," and "Lead the industry."[20] Alternative responses to societal pressures have been described as follows:[21] withdrawal, public relations approach, legal approach, bargaining, and problem solving. Finally, three major social responsiveness categories have been articulated: adaptive, proactive, and interactive.[22]

SETHI'S THREE-STAGE SCHEMA: TYPES AND LEVELS OF SOCIAL COMMITMENT

What makes managers in some organizations respond so vigorously to social issues, while others seem to do only what the law forces them to do? The intensity with which managers involve their organizations in social issues varies according to the principles that motivate them.[23] Table 3.3 depicts the levels of social commitment.

At the lowest level of social commitment are the organizations whose managers adhere to the principle of social obligation. Social obligation is corporate behavior in response to market forces or legal constraints.[24] These managers confine their responses to social issues to those mandated by prevailing laws and the operation of the economic system. They engage in philanthropic acts only when they believe their organization will benefit directly. Social contributions are viewed as the responsibility of individuals and not of an organization. Such organizations might adhere to the letter of federal and local environmental protection laws, yet willingly allow pollution when no legal punishment is likely.

At an intermediate level of commitment are organizations who are socially responsible; their managers go beyond merely fulfilling their social obligation. Social responsibility "implies bringing corporate be-

TABLE 3. 3   Levels of Social Commitment

Social Obligation Low	Social Responsibility	Responsiveness High
Reactive	Prescriptive	Proactive
Proscriptive*	Does more than required by law	Anticipates and prevents problems
Adheres to legal requirements	Does more than required by economic considerations	Searches for socially responsible acts
Adheres to economic considerations	Avoids public stands on issues	Takes public stands on issues

*Proscriptive means the firm reacts when its action is called (or threatened to be called) to the public's attention.

havior up to a level where it is congruent with the prevailing social norms, values, and expectations."[25] Whereas the concept of social obligation is proscriptive in nature, social responsibility is prescriptive in nature. At the intermediate level an organization's approach to social responsibility acknowledges the importance of ethical and socially responsible behaviors. Thus, these managers voluntarily pursue their social responsibilities. They recognize that laws often change more slowly than society's expectations, and they try to make their actions keep pace with social norms, values, and expectations of performance.[26] Frequently seen as good corporate citizens, socially responsible organizations are willing to assume a broader responsibility than that prescribed by law and economic requirements. For example, these organizations are likely to take steps to reduce the pollution if they consider certain levels to be dangerous, even if these levels are acceptable by legal standards.

At the highest level of social commitment are organizations whose managers are socially responsive. Social responsiveness suggests that what is important is "not how corporations should respond to social pressure but what should be their long-run role in a dynamic social system."[27] Here business is expected to be "anticipatory" and "preventive." Managers in socially responsive organizations are proactive (leaders) in their dealing with social issues. They attempt to anticipate social issues. Organizations in this category, for example, take the lead in adopting new processes to protect the environment. Minnesota Power, like many other "environmentally conscious" organizations, has articulated its commitment to the natural environment in its Environmental Ethics statement. In a strategic policy statement, 3M formalized its commitment to environmental issues to (a) prevent pollution at the source, whenever possible; (b) solve its own pollution and conservation problems beyond compliance requirements; (c) assist regulatory and government agencies concerned with environmental activities; and (d) develop products that have a minimal effect on the environment.[28]

How do organizations in the United States measure up when they are rated on these criteria? Although organizations are still driven by the principle of social obligation, since the 1950s many have demonstrated a growing social consciousness. More and more are adopting attitudes of social responsiveness. Some of the most visible initiatives in recent years relate to environmental issues and the conduct of green business. Johnson & Johnson has one of the longest-standing commitments to social responsibility in environmentalism. During the 1940s, its credo stated, "We must maintain in good order the property we are privileged to use," which was revised in 1979 to also read "protecting the environment and natural resources." Part of this commitment is reflected by their creation of the position of Vice President for Worldwide Environ-mental Affairs.[29]

Our discussion of social responsibility would not be complete with-out acknowledging the fact that some firms take an obstructionist approach to social responsibility. Obstructionist managers choose to push the socially responsible envelope as far as they can.[30] They con-sciously engage in questionable and at times illegal acts, in the hope that they won't get caught, and in the hope that if they do get caught, the fine imposed will be less than the benefits incurred. These firms often work to prevent knowledge of their behavior becoming visible. Evidence revealed during the late 1990s suggests that many individuals in the tobacco industry concealed evidence as to the harmful health risks associated with tobacco.[31] Their sleight of hand was revealed during a congressional hearing, when several of the presidents and CEOs from the industry appeared to blatantly lie to Congress when asked if nicotine was addictive—all of them said that they did not believe that it was!

CORPORATE SOCIAL PERFORMANCE

The internal and external groups that emerged during the trustee-ship period have grown in strength and size. Today's manager must be aware of the needs of the stockholders, customers, suppliers, creditors, government, community, and all the women and men, managers and nonmanagers, who work full- or part-time for the organization. This philosophy is reflected in Johnson & Johnson's credo: "We believe our first responsibility is to the doctors, nurses, and patients, to mothers and fathers and all others who use our products and services. . . . We are responsible to our employees, the men and women who work with us throughout the world. . . . We are responsible to the communities in which we live and work and to the world community as well. . . . Our final responsibility is to our stockholders."[32]

Johnson & Johnson's credo reflects a relatively new concept—that a variety of individuals and groups are organizational stakeholders. These individuals, both inside and outside the organization, have a direct interest in the organization. The large number of stakeholders complicates management's social responsibility. An organization should be responsive to everyone; but there are many groups, each with its own particular set of needs, and these needs can, and often do, conflict. How, for example, can an organization meet the needs and interests of investors, while simultaneously meeting its community's needs for money to build a new library?

In an effort to respond to such questions in the past few decades there has been a trend toward making the concern for social and ethical issues more and more pragmatic. Increased attention placed on social responsiveness was part of this trend and has resulted in a focus on corporate social performance (CSP). The performance focus is intended to suggest that what really matters is what companies are able to accomplish—the result of their acceptance of social responsibility and adoption of a responsiveness philosophy.

A focus on CSP has resulted in more and more corporations acknowledging the link between nonfinancial areas and the bottom line. According to *Beyond the Numbers,* a white paper recently released by KPMG, corporate stakeholders, customers, and workers are pushing a trend toward nonfinancial performance reporting; their concerns about environmental management, worker relations, and social responsibility are gaining the attention of business executives worldwide.[33] The report indicates that business leaders are realizing that failure to address the demand for accountability of soft controls can negatively impact their product and credibility. Additionally, organizations that account for all aspects of their performance, not just financial indicators, enhance their reputation among investors, customers, and employees and therefore gain a competitive advantage.

CSP activities such as community involvement, philanthropy, and providing exemplary benefits to employees do not always have direct and tangible ties to firm operations, particularly when performance outcomes are market based. CSP can provide important information about the particular values embedded within the firm.[34] For example, firms that actively comply with environmental regulations signal that they have some degree of concern for the natural environment. Firms that provide their employees with exemplary benefits packages show that they are willing to devote resources to the development and welfare of their employees. Similarly, firms that support community service activities signal that they are in some manner committed to community concerns. Thus, socially responsible activities of the organization can be a strong signal of what the firm values and believes to be deserving of the attention, resources, and efforts of the organization.

If CSP is a signal of what is important to a firm, then it is reasonable to conclude that these signals could be used by individuals who are seeking to form impressions about the firm, its values, direction, and overall worth. These individual evaluations of firms are relevant in a variety of settings and circumstances. Individuals make decisions such as whether they want to work for a firm, whether they will purchase a firm's goods and services, and whether they want to invest in a firm. For each of these decisions, information about these various dimensions of a firm can often be variable and incomplete—leaving an individual with unclear expectations or perceptions of the firm's capabilities. A CSP signal has the potential to serve as an uncomplicated decision tool for individuals making decisions about a firm. For example, an individual deciding whether or not to work for an organization could focus on what he or she knows about how the organization has treated its employees in the past. A potential customer deciding whether or not to purchase an organization's goods can focus on what he or she knows about the organization's product liability record. And an investor deciding whether or not to invest in an organization can focus on what he or she knows regarding the organization's recent expensive product-recall crisis.

KPMG's findings also show that nonfinancial performance measurements allow companies to evaluate aspects of their operations that they wouldn't have investigated using traditional reporting standards.[35] For example, most business risks derive from nonfinancial factors; therefore, focusing on other aspects of the operation allows management to avert risk in areas traditionally overlooked. Such analysis, according to the paper, leads to improved performance in all areas, which ultimately impacts the bottom line.

The report highlights several corporations worldwide, such as BP Amoco, Body Shop International, and the Toyota Motor Corporation, that are taking a leading-edge approach to social and environmental reporting. For example, Toyota issues an annual environmental report at the urging of its shareholders. The company has discovered that keeping tabs on nonfinancial matters helps business. Kevin Butt, head of environmental affairs for Toyota, explains, "Reporting on our environmental performance increases awareness of what we're trying to do as a good corporate citizen. Over the long term, I think we'll see a continuous increase in market share as a result."[36]

Other stories in the business press and media show us that other benefits, not directly related to financial business, can also arise from an organization's strong social performance. For example, Mobil Oil has long held the belief that the time and money it spends on social duties results in an atmosphere of trust and confidence that engenders increased goodwill: "This sense of goodwill can be used to counter unfavorable media stories or negative events. The corporate image is carried like a shield into battle. It is useful to hide behind and often becomes an integral part of corporate efforts to influence political and economic issues."[37]

Similarly, Security Pacific National Bank recognized multiple nonfinancial benefits from being seen as a socially responsible company. The most important of the "intangible" benefits, according to the bank's president and CEO, is an enhanced self-image for employees: "You see people take pride in working for a company that is favorably perceived by the public. That sense of pride also results in improved morale, which reflects itself in dealings with the customer and community."[38]

These examples highlight just two of the nonfinancial benefits that can arise from CSP. They also represent two of the more salient nonfinancial benefits, an improved reputation and an enhanced employee self-image, both of which involve insider and outsider stakeholder perceptions of the organization. One need not ponder the stakeholder issues and perceptions that have evolved under the rubric of social responsibility to recognize how they have and will continue to change. The issues and perceptions, and especially the degree of organizational interest in the issues, are always in a state of flux. As times change, so does the emphasis on the range of social issues that business must address.

Also of interest is the fact that particular issues are of varying concern to businesses, depending on the industry in which they exist as well as other factors. A manufacturer, for example, is considerably more absorbed with the issue of environmental protection than is an insurance company. Likewise, a bank is not as pressed on environmental issues as a manufacturer.

CORPORATE CITIZENSHIP

In recent years, the use of the term *corporate citizenship* in reference to businesses' corporate social performance has been advocated by a number or business practitioners and academic alike. Corporate citizenship has been described by some as a broad, encompassing term that basically embraces all that is implied in the concepts of social responsibility, responsiveness, and performance. For example, one set of authors defined good corporate citizenship as "serving a variety of stakeholders well."[39] One author holds that corporate citizenship is composed of a three-part view that encompasses (1) a reflection of shared moral and ethical principles, (2) a vehicle for integrating individuals into the communities in which they work, and (3) a form of enlightened self-interest that balances all stakeholders' claims and enhances a company's long-term value.[40] Davenport's definition of corporate citizenship includes a commitment to ethical business behavior, and balancing the needs of stakeholders, while working to protect the environment.[41]

Carroll has recast his four categories of CSR as embracing the "four faces of corporate citizenship"—economic, legal, ethical, and philanthropic. Each face, aspect, or responsibility reveals an important facet that contributes to the whole. He poses that "just as private citizens are expected to fulfill these responsibilities, companies are as well." Altman speaks of corporate citizenship in terms of corporate community relations. In this view, it embraces the functions through which business intentionally interacts with nonprofit organizations, citizen groups, and other stakeholders at the community level.[42] Some definitions refer to global corporate citizenship; as well, companies are increasingly expected to conduct themselves appropriately wherever they are doing business.

The Conference Board provides an all-encompassing, yet practical definition of corporate citizenship, which includes "managing effectively a company's actual and potential economic, environmental and social impact on the communities in which it operates and on society as a whole, while enhancing corporate reputation and increasing profits."[43] Interactions with stakeholders—employees, environmental groups, community activists, and shareholders—are integral to this definition of corporate responsibility.

The benefits of good corporate citizenship to stakeholders is fairly apparent. But, what are the benefits of good corporate citizenship to the firm itself? A review of studies attempting to discern the benefits to companies of corporate citizenship, defined broadly, revealed empirical and anecdotal evidence supporting the following.[44]

- Improved employee relations (e.g., improves employee recruitment, retention, morale, loyalty, motivation, and productivity).
- Improved customer relationships (e.g., increased customer loyalty, acts as a tiebreaker for consumer purchasing, enhances brand image)
- Improved business performance (e.g., positively impacts bottom-line returns, increases competitive advantage, encourages cross-functional integration)
- Enhanced company's marketing efforts (e.g., helps create a positive company image, helps a company manage its reputation, supports higher prestige pricing, and enhances government affairs activities)

Clearly there are benefits to those businesses that are willing to act as good corporate citizens. These businesses must continue to find ways to be responsive to their various stakeholders, each with its own particular needs and interests, while still meeting its own needs to survive and thrive in the marketplace.

CSR is showing up in company mission statements. John Hancock, for example, concludes its mission statement with the following sentence: "In all that we do, we exemplify the highest standards of business ethics and personal integrity, and recognize our corporate obligation to the social and economic well-being of our community." John Hancock goes on to state its commitment to ethical behavior:

In order to exemplify the highest standards of business ethics, we conduct the Company's affairs in strict compliance with both the letter and the spirit of the law, and will at all times treat policyholders, customers, suppliers, and all others with whom the Company does business fairly and honorably. Recognizing that our reputation of unquestioned integrity and honesty is our most valued asset, under no circumstances will what we achieve be allowed to take precedence over how we achieve it.[45]

At Sempra Energy, a San Diego–based electricity and natural gas company, management has expressed a strong commitment to enhancing the quality of life in the communities where it does business and stated that it is not only good business for the company and its employees to be deeply involved in community activities, but also the right thing to do:

> We have a vested interest in ensuring that businesses thrive, community needs are met, the environment is protected, and our diverse human resources are engaged to their fullest potential.
> Our main focus is building and maintaining valuable relationships with communities and community leaders in markets where we do business. We also regularly encourage employee leadership and involvement in civic and community affairs, and make charitable contributions to community and civic organizations through both Sempra Energy and its key affiliates.[46]

Social Audit

One way in which organizations can identify and communicate issues of public interest to both internal and external stakeholders is through a social audit. A *social audit* is a detailed examination and evaluation of an organization's social performance. A thorough social audit involves sophisticated strategic planning and evaluation.

The majority of the top 500 corporations in the United States include information about their social performance in their annual reports. Triple-bottom-line reporting is an attempt to make public information on the organization's financial, social, and ethical performance. As early as the mid-1970s, the National Aeronautics and Space Administration (NASA) issued "spinoff" reports that detail the many ways in which technology developed by NASA has been applied to non-aerospace uses. Inspection of Grand Metropolitan's 1990 annual report shows the scope of their community involvement in such areas as inner-city regeneration, support for the disabled and young, education, and arts and culture. In recent years, public accounting firms like Ernst & Young have gotten into the business of preparing social and ethical audits. The Environmental Services Group for Ernst & Young has conducted a detailed inspection of BP Amoco's operations on the Alaskan oil fields at Prudhoe Bay. The results of this inspection went into BP Amoco's annual report describing the company's environmental behavior for the public.[47]

According to PricewaterhouseCoopers, the triple-bottom-line reports have particular meanings: The economic performance means that companies must go beyond a standard return to the bottom line, but they need also to provide economic benefit to the community— possibly by developing human capital. Environmental performance is determined by how the corporation fares with regard to global warming, emissions, and other ecological measures; and the social performance examines how a company acts with regard to gender and ethnic concerns, labor practices (including child labor), human rights, and other social investments.[48]

In effect, companies often need this independent verification of their good deeds in order to overcome earlier ethically irresponsible debacles. For example, Nike was widely criticized for its labor practices in Southeast Asia; it is feverishly working to overcome its image as a child labor exploiter. Accordingly, a social audit helps to validate Nike's claims that it no longer allows children under 18 to work in its sneaker factories.

The social audit may be used for more than simply monitoring and evaluating firm performance. Managers can also use social audits to scan the external environment, determine firm vulnerabilities, and institutionalize CSR in the organization. In addition, companies are not the only ones who conduct social audits; public interest groups and the media watch companies who claim to be socially responsible very closely to see if they practice what they preach. These organizations include consumer groups and socially responsible investing firms that construct their own guidelines for evaluating companies.

Royal Dutch Shell suffered two major public relations disasters in 1995: Environmentalists accused it of improperly disposing of an oil rig in the North Sea, and human rights activists charged the company with negligence regarding its humanitarian duties in Nigeria. Shell responded by admitting that despite the company's belief that it acted honorably, the accompanying results were not good enough; Shell has since published two triple-bottom-line audits and has been trying to reclaim its reputation.[49] During one month in early 2001, Shell's audit showed that they cancelled 106 agreements with contractors who were unable to meet Shell's business principles and that the company fired seven employees over four instances of bribery in the past year.[50]

Today's organizations must consider the impact of their operations on stakeholders. They must constantly be aware of the impact of CSP on multiple stakeholders' bottom lines. Failure to do so will likely ensure missed opportunities and a competitive disadvantage.

CORPORATIONS AS STAKEHOLDERS

One author reasons that the social responsibility of corporations is based on social power and that "if business has the power, then a just relationship demands that business also bear responsibility for its action in these areas."[51] He terms his view the "iron law of responsibility." "[I]n the long run, those who do not use power in a manner in which society considers responsible will tend to lose it." Davis discusses five broad guidelines or obligations business professionals should follow to be socially responsible:

1. Businesses have a social role of "trustee for society's resources." Since society entrusts businesses with its resources, businesses must wisely serve the interests of all the stakeholders, not just those of owners, consumers, or labor.
2. Business shall operate as a two-way open system, with open receipt of inputs from society and open disclosure of its operations to the public.
3. Social costs as well as benefits of an activity, product, or service shall be thoroughly calculated and considered in order to decide whether to proceed with it. Technical and economic criteria must be supplemented with the social effects of business activities, goods, or services before a company proceeds.
4. The social costs of each activity, product, or service shall be priced into it so that the consumer (user) pays for the effects of his consumption on society.
5. Business institutions as citizens have responsibilities for social involvement in areas of their competence where major social needs exist.[52]

These five guidelines provide a foundation for creating an organization that is committed to building socially responsible relationships with its corporate stakeholders.

DIVERGING VIEWS ON SOCIAL RESPONSIBILITY

Not everyone agrees that contemporary organizations should be driven by the principles of charity and stewardship. Proponents of CSR have suggested that firms that take a major role in tackling social issues are good investment risks and will eventually be more profitable than less socially responsive firms.[53] Other evidence, however, does not show a simple or a consistent relationship between social responsibility and profitability.[54] TIAA/CREF, a teacher retirement organization, reports that the rate of return among their list of "Social Choice" stocks was 10.8 percent for 1999, compared to 21, 36, and 33 percent for their Stock, Global Equity, and Growth accounts, respectively. A look at research focusing on the relationship between corporate social performance and financial performance reveals a very mixed picture, as some studies report a positive relationship, while others report a negative one.[55]

These mixed findings should not be interpreted as a contradiction, nor are they intended to confuse you. What they tell us is that although socially responsible behavior can favorably impact an organization's bottom line, unfortunately this is not always the case. At times the financial costs of being socially responsible force firms into an unfavorable financial position vis-à-vis firms that are not socially responsive.[56] What is not clear from the research at this point is when it will be financially profitable to be socially responsible and when it will not. A profitability claim cannot legitimately be used to argue either for or against social responsibility. Other arguments, however, need to be considered.

Arguments against CSR

Sociologists have suggested that because society has many needs, an organization can be categorized according to (1) needs it fulfills and (2) the benefits that society derives from the organization's existence.[57] Critics of CSR have, in essence, used the sociologists' analysis to propose that each type of organization in society should specialize. In their view, corporations exist solely to provide goods and services and to earn profits. Thus, curing society's social ills becomes the responsibility of other organizations, including governmental and charitable organizations. Among the major arguments against CSR are:

- The costs of socially responsible behavior are often passed along in the form of lower dividends to stockholders, lower wages for employees, or higher prices for consumers.
- The costs of socially responsible behavior lower a corporation's operating efficiency and thus weaken its ability to offer goods and services at the lowest possible competitive cost.
- Accepting social responsibility sends mixed signals about an organization's goals to both organization and community members. Organization members may have difficulty meeting goals if they do not know whether their primary mission is to make a profit

or to act responsibly. Community members may develop unrealistic expectations that the organization is unable to fulfill. For example, expecting an organization to keep a plant open to protect jobs in the community even when the plant becomes unprofitable may be asking too much of the organization.

- By assuming social responsibilities, corporations would become even more powerful, and many already exercise too much power over society.
- Business people are trained in such areas as marketing, finance, and manufacturing, not in how to deal with social problems.

One other argument that merits mention is that by encouraging business to assume social responsibilities we might be placing it in a deleterious position in terms of the international balance of payments. One consequence of being socially responsible is that business must internalize costs that it formerly passed on to society in the form of dirty air, unsafe products, consequences of discrimination, and so on. The increase in the costs of products caused by including social considerations in the price structure would necessitate raising the prices of products, making them less competitive in international markets. The net effect might be to dissipate the country's advantages gained previously through technological advances. This argument weakens somewhat when we consider the reality that social responsibility is quickly becoming a global concern, not one restricted to U.S. firms and operations.

Arguments for CSR

Those who argue in favor of organizations acting in socially responsible ways offer many reasons. Among them are:

- The assumption of social responsibility balances corporate power with corporate responsibilities.
- The voluntary assumption of social responsibility discourages the creation and imposition of government regulations.
- Acts of social responsibility by organizations help correct the social problems (such as air and water pollution) that organizations create.
- Organizations, as members of society, have a moral obligation to help society deal with its problems and to contribute to its welfare.

Two supporting arguments deserve mention:[58] "Business has the resources" and "Let business try." These two views maintain that because business has a reservoir of management talent, functional expertise, and capital and because so many others have tried and failed to solve general social problems, business should be given a chance. These arguments have some merit, because there are some social problems that can be handled, in the final analysis, only by business. Examples include a fair workplace, providing safe products, and engaging in fair advertising.

An additional argument is that "proacting is better than reacting." This position holds that "proacting" (acting in a proactive manner, anticipating and initiating) is more practical and less costly than simply reacting to problems once they have developed. Environmental pollution is a good example, particularly business's experience with attempting to clean up rivers, lakes, and other waterways that were neglected for years. In the long run, it would have been wiser to have prevented the environmental deterioration from occurring. A final argument in favor of CSR is that the public strongly supports it. A 2000 *Business Week*/Harris poll revealed that, with a stunning 95 percent majority, the public believes that companies should not only focus on profits for shareholders but also be responsible to their workers and communities, even if making things better for workers and communities requires companies to sacrifice some profits.[59]

These arguments for and against CSR have led to the emergence of two distinct sides in the social responsibility debate.

Most notable among arguments against CSR has been the classical economic argument. This traditional view holds that management has one responsibility: to maximize the profits of its owners and shareholders. Economist Milton Friedman argues that managers should not be required to earn profits for business owners while simultaneously trying to enhance societal welfare.[60] In his view, these two goals are incompatible and will lead to the demise of business as we know it. Friedman argues that social problems should be resolved by the unfettered workings of the free market system. Further, this view holds that if the free market cannot solve the social problem, then it falls upon government and legislation to do the job. Friedman has also suggested that forcing organizations to engage in socially responsible behavior may be unethical, because it requires managers to spend money that belongs to other individuals—money that otherwise would be returned to stakeholders in the form of higher dividends, wages, and the like.

Keith Davis provides another perspective, in favor of CSR.[61] To him, organizations are members of society. Because they take resources from society for their own use, they have a responsibility to return to society a value for those resources. Society should be able to determine the nature of the value to be returned and to expect organizations to assist in solving social problems. After all, organizations are social instruments that exist and operate at the discretion of society.

The strategy of public corporations having a broader appeal to many stakeholders has resulted in wider use of corporate performance measures that are both financial and social. As a result of these and other efforts, many stakeholders are increasingly concerned about the relationship between corporate social performance (CSP) and financial performance. This is especially the case as questions continue to rise about the financial performance of firms considered "Best Citizens." The same question is also raised about the Best Corporate U.S. Citizens that are also recognized as global leaders. Unbiased and rather conclusive empirical evidence demonstrates that organizations that are simultaneously committed to social and environmental issues important to their stakeholders also have superior financial performance and superior reputations as well.[62]

More specifically, although there appear to be mixed results on the relationship between socially responsible behavior and business performance, the empirical evidence for a positive correlation between stakeholder inclusive, socially responsible business practice and business performance—as defined by growth in sales or stock price—is quite compelling.[63] Similar evidence has emerged with respect to organizations and their "sustainability," that is, their combined social, environmental, and financial performance (cf. the Dow Jones Sustainability Index and Innovest's Eco-Value Rating system, both of which demonstrate reasonably consistent stock price premia for firms with superior environmental and social performance).

The importance of CSR and CSP is also evident in studies suggesting that both are important in the job choice process, as job seekers regularly perceive such organizations as more attractive than those who don't demonstrate a commitment to CSR and CSP. For example, job seekers consider CSP important to assessment of organizations and rate five specific CSP dimensions (environment, community relations, employee relations, diversity, and product issues) as more important than six other CSP dimensions. For instance, environment, community relations, and diversity dimensions have the largest affect on attractiveness ratings for job seekers.[64]

Thus we can see how organizations have developed a growing level of confidence in concepts such as corporate social responsibility and stakeholder responsiveness. Increasingly, they are argued from a pragmatic perspective, they are grounded in business language, and, perhaps most important, they reinfore the importance of and potential for enhanced financial performance. Peter Drucker's robust vision of CSR as a leverage opportunity for economic advantage and societal benefit has come of age.[65]

Despite clear evidence of a positive relationship between corporate social and financial performance, stagnant capital spending is impacting many organizations' corporate social responsibility (CSR) initiatives, even though many senior executives are aware of investors' positive bias in this area, according to a recent survey. Suprisingly, some three-quarters of the CEOs favored investing their own money in companies with demonstrable CSR policies, even though they would not spend money bolstering CSR practices at their own organizations, according to a recent survey conducted by Jericho Communications (Stock 2002).[66] Over one-third of the 264 Fortune 1,000 CEOs interviewed said they were more conscious of CSR since the September 11, 2001, attacks. The terrorism angle was important to many of the surveyed CEOs, over half of whom believed that global social responsibility programs could curtail support for terrorist groups. However, only 12 percent of companies were allocating more resources, and only 9 percent were committing more money to social issues.[67]

CONCLUSION

To act in a socially responsible way requires organizational leaders to consider the effect of their decisions on the well-being of society; thus, managers must ask themselves what their actions do *to* society and what their actions do *for* society. When similar considerations are made at a personal level, managers rely on their ethics to help them choose an appropriate course of action. More and more organizations have begun to take a more inclusive, more rounded approach, incorporating three important measures of how an organization is performing: financial, environmental, and social. Most of these organizations have accepted that to succeed in today's world, an organization needs to get all three right, not just one or even two. With that in mind, this chapter concludes by offering the following basic suggestions for those organizations interested in getting started on the CSR road, and a summary of the benefits of doing so. To start:

- Assign responsibility, and incorporate a structure, for reporting to senior management or board level.
- Conduct a baseline CSR review and produce a gap analysis.
- Review shareholders' and customers' perspectives and expectations.
- Write a policy statement, covering environmental, social, and community issues, that commits to action.
- Develop a set of corporate objectives and an action plan to implement the policies.
- Establish company-wide quantitative and qualitative targets and key performance indicators over a two- to five-year period, to-

gether with the necessary measurement, monitoring, and auditing mechanisms.

- Embed actions and strategies into core business strategies and processes.
- Communicate performance externally so that inquiries from fund managers and stakeholders do not take up too much internal management time.
- Benchmark environmental and social performance internally and externally.
- Monitor and report your progress in CSR and business improvement.

The benefits of CSR reporting will include:

- Improved operational and process efficiency.
- Competitive advantage from focusing on these key issues.
- Protected share liquidity.
- Positive engagement with investors, lenders, insurers and indexers.
- Protection against negative external scrutiny.

NOTES

1. V.E. Henderson, *What Is Ethical in Business?* (New York, McGraw-Hill, 1992).

2. P. Watts and R. Holme, "Meeting Changing Expectations: Corporate Social Responsibility" (WBCSD, Geneva, 1999). Available: http:// www.wbcsd.org/ publications/csrpub.htm (accessed 18 March 2001).

3. Talcott Parsons, *The Social System* (Glencoe, Ill.: Free Press, 1951); Parsons, *Essays in Sociological Theory* (Glencoe, Ill.: Free Press, 1954).

4. J. L. Paulszek, *Business and Society: 1976-2000* (New York: AMACOM, 1976).

5. Keith Davis, "Understanding the Social Responsibility Puzzle," *Business Horizon* (Winter 1967), 45–50.

6. J. W. McGuire, *Business and Society* (New York: McGraw-Hill, 1963).

7. E. M. Epstein, "The Corporate Social Policy Process: Beyond Business Ethics, Corporate Social Responsibility and Corporate Social Responsiveness," *California Management Review* 29, no. 3 (1987), 99–114.

8. Archie B. Carroll, "A Three-Dimensional Conceptual Model of Corporate Social Performance," *Academy of Management Review* 4, no. 4 (1979), 497–505.

9. Archie B. Carroll and A. K. Buchholtz, *Business and Society: Ethics and Stakeholder Management*, 5th ed. (Mason, O.: South-Western, 2003).

10. "After All the Smoke Cleared: An In-the-Trenches Look at How the War Against Big Tobacco Got Won," *Time* 98 (September 27, 1999). See: *http://www/time.com/*.

11. Carroll and Buchholtz, *Business and Society*, 31.

12. J. K. Pierce, D. G. Gardner, and R. B. Dunham, *Management and Organizational Behavior: An Integrated Perspective* (Mason, O.: South-Western, 2002).

13. W. C. Frederick, K. Davis, and J. E. Post, *Business and Society: Corporate Strategy, Public Policy, Ethics* (New York: McGraw-Hill, 1988).

14. Ibid.

15. J. W. McKie, "Changing Views," in *Social Responsibility and the Business Predicament* (Washington: The Brookings Institution, 1975), 22–30.

16. R. Hay and E. Gray, "Social Responsibilities of Business Managers," *Academy of Management Journal* 17 (1974), 135–43.

17. R. Ackerman and R. Bauer, *Corporate Social Responsiveness: The Modern Dilemma* (Reston, Va.: Reston Publishing Company, 1976), 6.

18. Epstein, "Corporate Social Policy Process, 103.

19. M. Wilson, *Corporate Reputation and the Triple Bottom Line: The Social Responsibilities of Business* (Washington, D.C.: Pricewaterhouse Coopers Management Consulting Services, 2000).

20. T. W. McAdam, "How to Put Corporate Responsibility into Practice," *Business and Society Review/Innovation* (Summer 1973), 8–16.

21. Keith Davis and R. L. Blomstrom, *Business Society and Environment: Social Power and Social Response* (New York: McGraw-Hill, 1971).

22. Ibid.

23. S. P. Sethi, "Dimensions of Corporate Social Performance: An Analytical Framework," *California Management Review* 17, no. 3 (1975), 58–64.

24. Ibid.

25. Ibid., 58.

26. Ibid., 62.

27. Ibid., 63.

28. D. A. Rondinelli and G. Vastag, "International Environmental Standards and Corporate Policies: An Integrative Framework," *California Management Review* (Fall, 1996), 106–22.

29. W. C. Rappleye, Jr., "From Apprehension to Comprehension to Leadership: How the Private Sector Has made Environmental Issues Its Own," *Across the Board* (March 2000), 32–57.

30. D. Dalton and R. Cosier, "The Four Faces of Social Responsibility," *Business Horizons* (May-June 1982), 19–27.

31. M. Obey, *Assuming the Risk: The Mavericks, the Lawyers, and the Whistle Blowers Who Beat Big Tobacco* (Boston: Little, Brown, 1999).

32. Our Credo, *Johnson & Johnson Annual Report*, 1999.

33. "Redefining Corporate Success," *The Internal Auditor,* 58, no. 1 (2001), 14–15.

34. B. R. Agle and C. B. Caldwell, "Understanding Research on Values in Business: A Level of Analysis Framework," *Business and Society* 38, no. 3 (1999), 326–86.

35. "Redefining Corporate Success," 15.

36. Ibid., 15

37. A. L. Page, "We're Good Guys: Image Propaganda from Mobil Oil," *Business and Society Review* 93 (1995), 33–35.

38. "Social Responsibility Helps Business, Involves Employees, Bank Head Says," *Southern California Business,* 33, no. 3 (1987), 11.

39. S. P. Graves S. Waffock and M. Kelly, "How Do You Measure Corporate Citizenship?" *Business Ethics* (March/April 2001), 17.

40. C. J. Fombrum, "Three Pillars of Corporate Citizenship," in N. Tichy, A. McGill and L. St. Clair (eds.), *Corporate Global Citizenship* (San Francisco: The New Lexington Press), 27–61.

41. Carroll and Buchholtz, *Business and Society*.

42. Ibid.

43. S. Muirhead and A. Tillman, *The Impact of Mergers and Acquisitions on Corporate Citizenship* (New York: The Conference Board, 2000).

44. Archie B. Carroll, K. Davenport, and D. Grisaffe, "Appraising the Business Value of Corporate Citizenship: What Does the Literature Say?" *Proceedings of the International Association for Business and Society* (Essex Junction, Vt., 2000).

45. John Hancock, Information posted on the company's website (*www.johnhancock.com*) (September 1999).

46. Sempra Energy, Information posted on the company's website (*www.sempra.com*) (September 1999).

47. T. K. Grose, "Called to Account," *Time* (October 4, 1999), 104–106. See: *http://www/time.com/*

48. M. Wilson, *Corporate Reputation and the Triple Bottom Line: The Social Responsibilities of Business* (Washington: Pricewaterhouse Coopers Management Consulting Services, 2000).

49. Ibid.

50. M. Jones, "Shell Audit Shows More Deals Ended," *Financial Times* (April 7, 2001), 15.

51. J. W. Weiss, *Business Ethics: A Stakeholder and Issues Management Approach* (Mason, O.: South-Western, 2003).

52. K. Davis and R. L. Blomstrom, *Business and Its Environment* (New York: McGraw-Hill, 1966).

53. Michael E. Porter and C. Van der Linde, "Green and Competitive: Ending the Stalemate," *Harvard Business Review* (Sept./Oct. 1995), 120–34.

54. *TIAA/CREF Variable Account Report*, TIAA/CREF, 1999.

55. P. A. Stanwick and D. Stanwick, "The Relationship Between Corporate Social Performance, and Organizational Size, Financial, Performance, and Environmental Performance: An Empirical Examination," *Journal of Business Ethics* 17, no. 2 (1998), 195–204.

56. Ibid.

57. P. M. Blau and W. R. Scott, *Formal Organizations: A Comparative Approach* (San Francisco: Chandler, 1962); Talcott Parsons, *Structure and Process in Modern Society* (Glencoe, Ill.: Free Press, 1960).

58. Keith Davis, "The Case for and against Business Assumption of Social Responsibility," *Academy of Management Journal* (June 1973), 312–22.

59. A. Bernstein, "Too Much Corporate Power," *Business Week* (September 11, 2000), 149.

60. M. Friedman, "The Social Responsibility of Business Is to Increase Profits," *New York Times Magazine* (September, 1970), 122–26; M. Friedman, "Does Business Have Social Responsibility?" *Bank Administration* (April 1971), 13–14.

61. Davis, op. cit.

62. *Curtis C. Verschoor* and Elizabeth A. Murphy, "Financial Performance of Large U.S. Firms and Those with Global Prominence: How Do the Best Corporate Citizens Rate?" *Business and Society Review* (Fall 2002), 371–80.

63. James C. Collins and Jerry I. Porras, *Built to Last: Successful Habits of Visionary Companies* (London: Century, 1995); S. A. Waddock and S. B. Graves, "The Corporate Social Performance—Financial Link," *Strategic Management Journal* 18 (1997), 303–19.

64. Kristin B. Backhaus, Brett A. Stone, and Karl Heiner, "Exploring the Relationship between Corporate Social Performance and Employer Attractiveness," *Business and Society* 41, no. 3 (2002), 292–318.

65. Peter Drucker, "The New Meaning of Corporate Social Responsibility," *California Management Review* (Vol. 26, 1982), 53-63.

66. Howard Stock, CEOs Scrimp on Social Programs Despite Investor Interest, "*Investor Relations Business* (Oct. 21, 2002), 1.

67. Ibid.

4

A Stakeholder Approach to Socially Responsible and Ethical Behavior

INTRODUCTION

No one would dispute that life in most business organizations was much simpler in years gone by. In reality, it was a less complex period, with minimal and clearly understood expectations among the various parties (investors who put up the money to start or finance the business, owners and their employees who needed to get and keep the business running, suppliers to make the raw materials available for production, and customers who purchased the product or services). Organizations face a much more complex state of affairs in today's society. The recognition by the public, or society, that today's business organization has evolved to the point where it is no longer the sole property or interest of the founder, the founder's family, or even a group of owner-investors has been a principal driving force behind this societal transformation.

Today's modern organization in many instances is the institutional centerpiece of a complex society made up of many people with a multitude of interests, expectations, and demands as to what organizations ought to provide. As discussed in more detail later in this chapter and in Chapter 11, the social contract between organizations and various parties has continually changed. Organizations that have been able to survive and thrive have found ways to respond to ever-changing expectations. These organizations have had to meet many assorted legal, ethical, and social responsibility or philanthropic expectations and demands and to be willing to change as a result of economic incentives.

Today organizations must be responsive to an increasingly diverse number of individuals and groups. Organizations may have been able to ignore certain individuals and groups in the past because they were powerless or unable to affect the organization. The growing importance of the role of stakeholders in the organizational equation over the past few decades has made it apparent that organizations must address the legitimate needs and expectations of stakeholders if they want to be successful in the long run. Some believe "stakeholder inclusion" to be the key to company success in the twenty-first century. Others have noted that business must also address stakeholders because it is the ethical course of action.[1] Clearly, stakeholders have claims, rights, and expectations that should be honored. We believe a stakeholder approach (or analysis) can help us to better understand why organizations' ethical lapses occur. The purpose of this chapter is to define what we mean by stakeholders, to clarify their importance in understanding organizational action and inaction, and to provide a foundation for further discussion of the role various stakeholders play in ethical debacles and the fall of giants.

ORGANIZATIONAL STAKEHOLDERS

Today's managers and employees must be aware of their organizations' various stakeholders. The term stakeholder is a variant of the more familiar and traditional idea of *stockholders*—investors in or owners of businesses. A stockholder owns a piece or share of one or more businesses. Thus, a stockholder is also called a stakeholder. However, stockholders are just one group of many legitimate stakeholders with which organizations must effectively interact.

Stakes and Stakeholders

Understanding the idea of a stake is important to appreciating the concept of stakeholders. A *stake* is an interest or share in an undertaking. Or as it relates to an organization, a stake is any interest, share, or claim that a group or individual has in the outcome of an organization's policies, procedures, or actions toward others. In the former definition a stake can range from simply an interest in an undertaking at one extreme to a legal claim of ownership at the other extreme. In between these two extremes is a "right" to something. This right might be a legal right to a certain treatment, rather than a legal claim of ownership.

Legal rights might include the right to fair treatment (e.g., not to be discriminated against at work) or the right to privacy (not to have one's privacy invaded or abridged). The right might be thought of as a moral right, such as that expressed by an employee: "I've got a right to be promoted to a position because my 25 years of work here give me that right." Or a consumer might say, "I've got a right to a quality product after what I've paid for this."

The stakes of stakeholders are not always obvious or explicit. The economic viability of competing organizations can be at stake when one organization threatens entry into or competition in a market. The physical health of a community can be at stake when a corporation decides to dump toxic wastes in nearby waterways illegally. Stakes also can be present, past, or future oriented. For example, stakeholders may seek compensation for an organization's past actions, as occurred when lawyers recently argued that certain organizations owed their employees monetary compensation for years of discriminating against them (i.e., denying them promotions and the like). Stakeholders may seek future claims, that is, they may seek injunctions against organizations that announce plans to close down a plant or move a baseball team, as Major League Baseball Commissioner Bud Selig recently tried to do in the case of the Minnesota Twins.

For our purposes, a stakeholder is an individual or a group that has one or more of the various kinds of stakes in a business. The individual or groups can affect or be affected by the actions, decisions, policies, practices, or goals of the organization.[2] With stakeholders, therefore, there is a potential two-way interaction or exchange of influence.

In today's complex global environment, many individuals and groups come under the umbrella of an organization's stakeholders. From the company point of view, certain individuals and groups have legitimacy in the eyes of management. That is, they have a legitimate interest in or claim on the operations of the business. The most obvious are stockholders, employees, and customers. From the point of view of a highly pluralistic society, stakeholders include not only these groups, but other groups like competitors, suppliers, the community, special-interest groups, the media, and society or the public at large as well. Others have also strongly argued that the natural environment, nonhuman species, and future generations should be considered among business's important stakeholders.[3]

Categorizing Stakeholders

There are various ways to categorize stakeholders. For example, one scheme for classifying stakeholders is to view them as being core, strategic, or environmental.[4] *Core* stakeholders are a specific subset of strategic stakeholders that are essential for the survival of the organization. *Strategic* stakeholders are those stakeholder groups that are vital to the organization and the particular set of threats and opportunities it faces at a particular point in time. *Environmental* stakeholders are all others in the organization's environment. The relationships among these three groups of stakeholders can be conceptualized by thinking of concentric circles with core stakeholders in the center circle and with strategic and environmental stakeholders in rings further from the center.

An older and more traditional scheme for categorizing stakeholders is to view them as falling into one of two categories: primary or secondary. *Primary* stakeholder groups typically are comprised of shareholders and investors, employees, customers, and suppliers, together with what is defined as the public stakeholder group: the government and communities that provide infrastructures and markets, whose laws and regulations must be obeyed, and to whom taxes and other obligations may be due.[5] Others have added both trade associations and environmental groups to this list of primary stakeholders.[6] Still others have highlighted the high level of interdependence between the corporation and its primary stakeholders.[7] For instance, it has been noted that without the continuing participation of primary stakeholders, an organization cannot survive as a going concern. Thus, the primary stakeholders of an organization include its owners/investors, customers, employees and managers, local communities, suppliers, and other business partners. Also of primary importance to an organization's survival are its shareholders and board of directors.[8]

Secondary stakeholders include all other interested groups, such as media, government and regulators, lobbyists, competitors, social pressure groups (such as environmental groups), civic institutions, and trade associations. Primary social stakeholders have a direct stake in the organization and its success and therefore are influential. Secondary social stakeholders may be extremely influential as well, especially in affecting reputation and public standing, but their stake in the organization is more representational of public or special interests than direct. The level of accountability to a secondary stakeholder tends to be lower, but these groups may wield significant power and quite often represent legitimate public concerns.

In addition to the classifications of primary and secondary social stakeholders, we can define stakeholders as social and nonsocial.[9] Primary nonsocial stakeholders include the natural environment, future generations, and nonhuman species. Secondary nonsocial stakeholders include: environmental pressure groups and animal welfare organizations. It is important to note that secondary stakeholders can quickly become primary ones. This may occur with special-interest groups or the media when the urgency of a claim (as in a boycott demonstration) takes precedence over the legitimacy of that claim. In today's complex global environment, the media have the power to instantaneously transform a stakeholders' status with coverage on the evening news. Thus, it may be useful to think of primary and secondary classes of stakeholders for discussion purposes, but we should not forget how easily and quickly those categories can shift.

The stakeholder approach is a pragmatic way of identifying and understanding multiple (often competing) claims of many constituencies. The varied group of different organizational constituents will have widely divergent and often conflicting expectations, obligations, and requirements for the actions and decision making of the company. As a result, any cohesive strategy or understanding of the implementation of an organization's strategy or decisions must consider a thorough and comprehensive stakeholder analysis.

To build an enduring and resilient competitive advantage, an organization must establish strong relationships with all of its key stakeholders. Organizations cannot afford to ignore certain other specialized and highly influential groups. These groups include government agencies that look at organization compliance with regulatory standards, financial-ratings agencies that monitor economic performance, corporate-conscience agencies that evaluate social performance, and consumer agencies that assess product quality. Most of these groups enjoy lots of analytic resources and often have access to better information than ordinary stakeholders. Their opinions significantly affect the way an organization is regarded by its less-informed observers. Indeed, a whole performance assessment and reputational-building industry has evolved that scrutinizes, evaluates, and champions organizations.

Most of these specialized agencies become skilled at articulating and defending the interests of a particular stakeholder group. The focused ratings that these specialized groups produce draw attention to different aspects of an organization's performance and affect its various images and its overall standing in the eyes of the organization's various stakeholders. Like the key stakeholders discussed in the remainder of this chapter, organizations must continually develop proactive responses to specialized stakeholder groups. While we recognize that the list of stakeholders that stake claims to organizations is extensive, as suggested in our discussion to this point, we will now focus only on boards of directors, management, non-management employees, investors/shareholders, analysts, auditors, and government.

BOARDS OF DIRECTORS

Because organizations may have hundreds of thousands of shareholders, they elect a smaller group, known as the board of directors, to govern and oversee the management of the business. The board is responsible for ascertaining that the manager puts the interests of the owners (i.e., shareholders) first. Directors advise management. They do not manage the actual corporation. The board, however, is charged with establishing the goals of the corporation, setting its direction, and evaluating how well its professional managers meet these objectives. A board provides leadership and oversight.

Typically, boards of directors are responsible for ensuring a company is managed in the best interest of the shareholders. Overseeing management is where the corporate system has a tendency to break down. For corporate governance (i.e., the method by which a firm is being governed, directed, administered, or controlled and to the goals by which it is being governed) to function appropriately, the board of directors must be an effective, potent body carrying out its roles and responsibilities in ascertaining that management pursues the shareholders' best interests.

Board independence from management is a crucial aspect of good governance. It is here that the difference between inside directors and outside directors becomes most pronounced. Outside directors are independent from the organization and its top managers. In contrast, inside directors have some sort of tie to the organization. Sometimes they are top managers in the organization; other times, insiders are family members or others with close ties to the CEO. To varying degrees, each of these parties is "beholden" to the CEO.[10] Insiders might also be professionals such as lawyers under contract to the organization or bankers whose bank does business with the organization. This can create conflict-of-interest situations. For example, a commercial banker/director may expect the company on whose board she or he is serving to restrict itself to using the services of her or his own organization and be willing to support the CEO in return for the business provided.

Questions on the extent to which boards are doing what they are supposed to be doing have existed for years, and problems in some organizations have been rather evident. For example, in March 2001, *Business Week* characterized the board of Xerox as being "asleep at the wheel" with a "host of governance problems." The board had too many members with ties to the firm, board members sat on too many other boards, and the directors owned little equity in the firm.[11]

Another problem is managerial control of the board processes. CEOs often can control board perquisites such as director compensation and committee assignments. Board members who rock the boat may find they are left out in the cold. As one corporate board member told *Fortune*, under conditions of anonymity, "This stuff is wrong. . . .What people understand they have to do is go along with management, because if they don't they won't be part of the club. . . .What it comes down to is that directors aren't really independent. CEOs don't want independent directors."[12]

MANAGEMENT

Management is the group of individuals given responsibility for running the organization and managing it on a daily basis. Along with the board, top management establishes overall policy. Middle- and lower-level managers carry out this policy and conduct the daily supervision of the operative employees. Most organizations function on at least three distinct but overlapping levels, each requiring a different managerial focus and emphasis. They include the *operations level*, the *technical level*, and the *strategic level*. Managers at each level must plan, organize, lead, and control.

Top management reflects a group of people responsible for establishing the organization's overall objectives and developing the policies to achieve those objectives. Titles typical of top management positions include chairman of the board, chief executive officer, president, senior vice president, and cabinet secretary. The corporate executives assist the board with setting the goals, strategies, and goals of the organization and then are tasked with implementing action plans, along with creating a culture that supports the company's core values and guiding principles. Most actions and strategies for the kind of ethical climate an organization develops derive from top management. It has become a cliché, but this premise must be established at the outset: The ethical tone of an organization is set by top management. All managers and employees look to their bosses at the highest level for cues as to what is acceptable practice. A former chairman of a major steel company stated it well: "Starting at the top, management has to set an example for all the others to follow."[13] Top management, through its capacity to set a personal example and to shape policy, is in the ideal position to provide a highly visible role model. The authority and ability to shape policy, both formal and implied, forms one of the vital aspects of the job of any leader in any organization. This aspect of becoming a moral manager has been referred to as "role modeling through visible action."[14]

Middle management includes all employees below the top-management level who manage other managers. These individuals are responsible for establishing and meeting specific goals in their particular departments or unit. Their goals, however, are not established in isolation. Instead, the objectives set by top management provide specific direction to middle managers regarding what they are expected to achieve. Ideally, if each middle manager met his or her goals, the entire organization would meet its objectives. Examples of job titles held by middle managers include division manager, district manager, vice president of finance, unit manager, commissioner, or division director.

First-level managers, like top and middle managers, are also part of the organization's management team. Because first-level managers oversee the work of operating employees they are often referred to as first-level or front-line managers. The kinds of job titles likely to identify someone as a first-level manager include shift manager, welding foreman, and receiving and warehousing manager, to name a few.

The information age and the Internet among other things are pushing organizations and their managers to adopt new business models, different or more intense uses of technologies, and information not seen before. As a result there has been an increased recognition that knowledge management (KM) is more important today than it was at the start of the fourth quarter of the twentieth century. KM is a formal, directed process of figuring out what information a company has that could benefit others in the company, then devising a way of making it easily available. In short, like quality management, process reengineering, and the Internet, organizations and their managers are confronted with the challenge of figuring out how to survive and thrive the "new economy," where speed and responsiveness are key to organizational success.

Because entry into and exit out of markets are increasing in volume and speed, the ability to participate in or retreat from markets has become a core skill essential for senior executives to exercise. Critical to that kind of skill is a profound understanding of market conditions and one's own organizational capabilities. Managers at all levels must effectively leverage knowledge to facilitate quick and sound decisions. KM ultimately calls for a management team to deploy its workforce in a way in which the firm can take advantage of what is in employees' heads.

Managers and their employees increasingly see organizations as collections of processes. The question must asked: Does one manage an enterprise or department differently in today's new economy or environment? The answer is both no and yes. No, in that much of what Peter Drucker taught us a generation ago about basic management responsibilities does not change. Roles and obligations remain the same. A manager is still responsible for setting direction and purpose, marshalling resources to implement those, and controlling the efficiency and effectiveness of such activities. Yes, in that process-centric companies are different than the most traditional hierarchical command-and-control world in which many of us grew up.

Clearly, the way managers and employees work together is changing, in part because of process management, but also as a result of the increased importance of knowledge. Just like the Internet is shifting power to customers beyond what they had before, because of access to information, so too employees with greater knowledge and skills are also acquiring greater say over their affairs at work.[15] As knowledge work increases, the role of management shifts from just leading in a direction to one in which they must create a fruitful environment and act as facilitators so that the "real work" of the enterprise can take place. Today's managers must take care of the KM needs of the firm, which means that they must increasingly balance the needs of the firm and those of employees.

NONMANAGEMENT EMPLOYEES

Employees are those hired by the company to perform the actual operational work. Managers are employees, too, but in this discussion we use the term *employees* to refer to nonmanagerial employees.

As employees, we ask that organizations we work for be trustworthy. While we demand that explicit contracts be honored, we also expect implicit contracts to be respected. We count on being treated fairly and honorably in job assignments, salary decisions, and promotions. We ask of organizations that they respect our fundamental rights as individuals and as citizens.

These expectations place tremendous pressure on organizations to develop policies and programs that support the well-being of all their employees, not just top management. Humane treatment involves not only concerns for health and safety but, also a growing regard for employees as partners in the work process. Over the last decade or so in many well-regarded organizations, employees have become part owners through their pension funds or stock-purchase plans. At a minimum, these employee-owners have earned the right to participate in the strategic decisions of the organizations they work for—and are demanding it.

Rapid developments in information technology continue to open up channels of communication and decision making, thereby enhancing employee involvement. Progressive organizations recognize this opportunity by creating programs that support employee endeavors. The commitment to the self-realization of all employees represents a genuine effort toward relationship-building with employees in better-regarded organizations. Well-regarded organizations work hard to establish trust with employees, whether those employees are unionized or not. By establishing trust with employees, those organizations sustain unyielding employee loyalty and commitment to the organization's mission.

Considerable attention is now being given to employee stakeholders—their status, their treatment, their rights, and their satisfaction. The development of employee stakeholder rights has been a direct outgrowth of the kinds of social changes that have brought other social issues into focus. The history of work has been one of steadily improving conditions for employees. Today's issues are quite unlike the old bread-and-butter concerns of higher pay, shorter hours, more job security, and better working conditions. These expectations still exist, but they have given way to other, more complex workplace trends and issues (e.g., changing social contract, changing workforce, and employee rights movement).

Changing Social (Employment) Contract

Three decades ago, employees stayed in the same company for years, and those companies rewarded that loyalty by offering job stability, a decent wage, and good benefits. Today's typical worker has had nine jobs by the age of 30.[16] The workforce of today is more mobile, less loyal, and more diverse. Their trust in their employers has eroded over the past twenty years to the point where, in 2001, only 38 percent of employees surveyed felt their employer was committed to them.[17] Today's employees aren't looking for a promise of lifetime employment. Instead, they are seeking competitive pay and benefits coupled with opportunities for professional growth. They want employers who provide them with opportunities, recognize their accomplishments, and communicate openly and honestly. These workforce changes have contributed to a newly emerging social contract between employers and employees. This new social contract—or set of reciprocal understandings and expectations regarding each party's role and responsibilities— represents a "revolution in America's workplace."[18] The revolution is basically this: The go-along-to-get-ahead culture of the past has been displaced by a high-risk environment in which Americas are being asked to give up the employment security they once took for granted for opportunities that are not longer clearly defined or guaranteed.[19]

The Changing Workforce

The workforce in the United Stated is changing in ways that also affect management practices and ethical issues. Several demographic trends predicted for "workforce 2000" have been and are being realized.[20] The workforce is aging; managerial positions are more difficult to fill; women entrants are increasing in number, with a mix of advances but with continued salary inequality; workforce cultures are mixing, as are values and potential value conflicts; the education gap in the workforce continues; the level of education lags in the United States compared to other countries; the number of workers with disabilities is expanding; and gay couples, still denied legal marriage in most states, are denied family healthcare insurance in most companies. More is said about the changing workforce in Chapter 11.

Employee Rights

As the booming economy that lasted through the latter part of the 1990s came to an end at the beginning of the twenty-first century, unemployment rose and in many instances new employees had job offers withdrawn before their jobs began, even though some companies did cushion the blow with creative compensation. At Intel, some new hires (who had letters of intent for jobs) were offered signing bonuses and two months' pay if they signed a voluntary separation agreement. Those who opted not to sign the agreement were given employment, but there was no guarantee what or where the job would be. Cisco Systems (and other companies like Dell Computers) gave three months' pay and career counseling services to people whose offers were withdrawn.[21] Like other workers these workers, expect to be treated with respect and, like all workers, deserve that consideration.

Employee stakeholders today are more sensitive about employee rights issues because of experiences like those of the new hires and the new social contract. Employee rights may be afforded on the basis of economic, legal, or ethical sources of justification. Failure to understand and effectively manage the rights of employees can create many ethical dilemmas for organizations and further strain the social contract with employees. Chapter 11 discusses employee rights in more detail.

INVESTORS/SHAREHOLDERS/STOCKHOLDERS

Investors represent an influential stakeholder groups. Under American corporate law, shareholders are the owners of the corporation. As owners, they should have ultimate control over the corporation. This control is manifested in the right to select the board of directors of the company. Generally, the degree of each shareholder's right is determined by the number of shares of stock owned. The individual who owns 100 shares of General Electric, for example, has 100 votes when the board of directors is elected. By contrast, the large public pension fund that owns 100 million shares has 100 million votes.

As investors, we expect organizations to be credible. We ask that managers live up to the claims and commitments they make in press releases, annual reports, and other communications. Having entrusted them with our hard-earned savings, we demand that they show good faith in their dealings with us. We want them to accurately convey risks of their strategies, warn us of impending problems, and disclose material facts that might influence our assessment of their performance.

Consider how the financial monitor Moody's Investors Services rates organizations. Its ratings depend heavily on how analysts interpret the organization's future prospects, the quality of its management, and especially the credibility of its plans:

> The rating process itself is . . . an opportunity for management to explain its business and its strategies to specialists who are trained to listen and to evaluate critically what they hear . . . Typically, Moody's asks to meet and spend some time with four to five senior representatives of the company's executive, financial, and operating management. A meeting with the chief executive officer is also desirable. We believe that management is critical to credit quality; therefore, Moody's likes to be briefed on management's philosophy and plans for the future.[22]

To investors, the currency of exchange is credibility. Therefore, organizations must do everything in their power to make credible claims that they act in good faith when interacting with investors.

There has been a dramatic increase in the number of people interested in supporting socially responsible companies through their investments. Historically, social responsibility investing can be traced back to the early 1900s, when church endowments refused to buy "sin" stocks—then defined as shares in tobacco, alcohol, and gambling companies. By the 1990s, self-styled socially responsible investing came into its own.[23] By the early 2000s, social investing was celebrating the fact that social or ethical investing was now part of the mainstream. Recent estimates suggest that social conscious investing in pension funds, mutual funds, and municipal and private portfolios now exceed $2.2 trillion.[24]

Many social investors are concerned about the ethics, social responsibility, and reputation of organizations in which they invest; and a growing corps of brokers, financial planners, portfolio managers, asset management, and mutual funds have made themselves available to help investors evaluate investments and purchase stock in ethical organizations for their social impacts. Whether it be called social investing, ethical investing, or socially conscious investing, it is clear that social investing has become part of the mainstream. *Business Ethics* magazine now gives annual social investing awards to mutual funds or investment firms that combine great financial returns with strong social impact.

More and more investors recognize that an ethical organizational climate or culture is the foundation of efficiency, productivity, and profits. On the other hand, investors also know that fines or negative publicity can lower stock prices, diminish customer loyalty, and threaten the long-term viability of the company. Witness the recent experiences of Global Crossing, Imclone, and Tyco International. Legal problems and negative publicity can have a strong adverse effect on the success of any organization. When the Securities and Exchange Commission (SEC) investigated Sunbeam for errors in accounting procedures that misrepresented sales and profits, the company's stock fell during several months from a high of $54 to less than $10. The negative publicity associated with the alleged wrongdoing had an enormous impact on the company and lender-investor confidence in Sunbeam, a previously trusted and respected American brand. Clearly, potential negative outcomes from perceived unethical or questionable decisions cause investors to take their investments elsewhere.

Investors are a stakeholder group that must be seen as a major concern for organizations that want to survive and thrive in the long term. To be successful, relationships with investors rest on dependability, trust, and commitment. Investors look at the bottom line for profits or the potential for increased stock prices. One CEO noted after a 21 percent increase in pretax profits that the bank's ethical and environmental stance enhanced customer loyalty and consequently profitability.[25] But investors also look for any potential crack, or flaws, in the company. Hence many smart company presidents spend a large amount of their time communicating with investors about the organization's reputation and financial performance and trying to attract them to the company's stock. The issue of drawing and keeping investors is a critical one for CEOs, as roughly 50 percent of investors sell their stock in companies within one year, and the average household replaces 80 percent of its common stock portfolio each year.[26] Gaining the stakeholder investors' trust and confidence is vital for sustaining the financial stability of the organization.

ANALYSTS

To investors the currency of exchange is credibility, and for organizations to protect credibility is no easy task. Indeed, organizations take great pains to maintain good relationships with financial analysts, especially those who toil in rating agencies. They spend considerable sums to promote themselves to those analysts and try hard to build good will.

A whole industry of "oracles" has come to the fore on Wall Street, the best of which are canonized annually as the "All America Research Team" by the industry bible, *Institutional Investor*. Since organizations know that many investors thrive on the "picks" of these star analysts, many are granted private audiences to discuss an organization's strategy with its top brass. Which is probably why those analysts are so highly paid; many earn more than $1 million a year.

The power that star analysts have to sway investors gives them a lot of influence over an organization's standing with investors, even though many of their predictions don't pan out. Some have suggested that on average following an analyst's recommendations proves to be no better than tossing a coin; even where an analyst is an expert with perfect estimates on the company, that expertise doesn't necessarily translate into good stock picks.[27]

Analysts should not be fooled by glossy organizational public relations (PR). The analyst's job is to explore the underpinnings of an organization's actions and projections—its credibility. Most will therefore keep detailed records of an organization's past claims and make systematic efforts to assess how well managers have lived up to them. Those who do gain credibility; those who don't, suffer. One senior analyst at Moody's, when asked how the organization rates firms, responded in this way: "We don't rate companies on their morality; we rate them on the credibility of their claims. We have to believe that they will do what they say they're going to do; that they will fulfill their commitments.[28]

If it's true that employees value trust, empowerment, and pride, investors seldom do. Indeed, most studies show that most investors are rather single-minded and look steadfastly to an organization's profitability, volatility, and indebtedness to gauge its future prospects and assess its attractiveness. John Whitehead, the former cochairman of Goldman Sachs, once put it this way: "What determines which companies sell at six times earnings and which companies sell at sixteen times earnings? It's a complex set of factors. But the principal ingredient is the perception of investors as to the quality of management, the quality of the people in the company. That is reflected in the record the company has established over a period of years. It's also reflected in a lot of intangible factors that have to do with . . . the quality of the company's products, and in a general perception of how the company comes across."[29]

In the end, what real value can we ascribe to analysts and their crystal balls? Those of us who dabble in the stock market would probably argue that, individually, analysts play a symbolic, comforting role that reduces our innate fears of uncertainty. Collectively, however, their effect is far greater. As a key stakeholder group their recommendations influence the movement of funds into and out of particular stocks and so affect an organization's market value and standing among other stakeholders.

AUDITORS

The federal government gave the accounting industry the valuable franchise to audit companies that sell shares to the public after the stock market crash of 1929. In return, auditors are supposed to do their best to make sure investors can trust corporate financial statements. With more than half of the nation's households owning stocks—directly or through pension or mutual funds—and a stagnant economy depressing stock values, the investing public has never needed a diligent accounting profession more.[30] The American system of accounting is still the gold standard for the world. In recent years, the U.S. accounting industry has changed markedly, consolidating into a handful of firms that have become global financial consultants. Formerly known as the Big Five (now the Big Three, after mergers) Arthur Andersen, Deloitte & Touche LLP, Ernst & Young, KPMG, and PricewaterhouseCoopers audit most of the companies whose shares trade on the nation's stock markets.

Licensed professionals are expected to do more than just make sure the numbers add up. They are supposed to check inventory, contact customers, and perform other tests before putting their stamp of approval on reports that fairly present the company's financial results. Increasingly, over the years the way these firms have done business is at odds with the accounting industry's public watchdog mission. For example,

- Major accounting firms often make more money from selling clients advice than they do from auditing their books. The accounting firms help businesses pick computer systems, lobby for tax breaks, and even evaluate takeover targets. Auditors have been graded and rewarded according to how much other business they win from their audit clients. Arthur Levitt, Jr., the former chairman of the SEC, which polices public companies, argued that such incentives could tempt accountants to go easy on an audit.[31]
- Auditors frequently leave their watchdog positions for jobs at the companies they audit. This career path can encourage auditors to make improper compromises, the SEC has warned. The route is so popular that auditors often find themselves dealing with former colleagues who are now their clients' executives (e.g., a number of former Arthur Andersen auditors left to work for Enron).

- The profession has sought to insulate itself from responsibility for false or fraudulent accounting. When things go wrong, firms typically decline to answer for their work, invoking client confidentiality.
- The system can discourage thoroughness. The fees companies pay their auditors are often set in advance, so the accounting firms' profit margins can diminish as their efforts increase. There are signs that accounting firms are putting fewer resources into audits, using inexperienced staff, or skimping on records checks.

These developments compound the more basic, underlying conflict: The auditors are hired, fired, and paid by the companies they are responsible for auditing.

"Too often, they operate under the principle that the customer is always right," said Nell Minow, an activist money manager and editor of the Corporate Library, a Web site on corporate governance. "They will give the answer that the customer wants . . . so they can continue to get the fees." Investment billionaire Warren E. Buffett put it this way in 1999: "Though auditors *should* regard the investing public as their client, they tend to kowtow instead to the managers who choose them and dole out their pay." Buffett quoted a proverb: "Whose bread I eat, his song I sing."[32]

Former SEC chairman Harvey L. Pitt, a lawyer who has represented the accounting industry, dismissed Buffett's observation as "a good sound bite" and "a nice thing for people who want to attack a profession to say." What prevents such obsequiousness, he said, is that "if an accounting firm has a reputation for being independent, for being professional and for doing its job, then everybody will flock to that firm."[33] Robert Kueppers, head of Deloitte's national office, said he and his colleagues know their highest priority: "The culture that I grew up with 25 years here is, your first responsibility is to get the audit done and get it done right."[34]

In 2000, an industry panel on audit effectiveness found that "both the profession and the quality of its audits are fundamentally sound." However, the number of corporations retracting and correcting earnings reports has doubled in the past three years, to 233, an Andersen study found. Major accounting firms have failed to detect or have disregarded glaring bookkeeping problems at companies as varied as Rite Aid Corp., Xerox Corp., Sunbeam Corp., Waste Management Inc., MicroStrategy Inc., Tyco International, Lucent Technologies, Enron, and Global Crossing.

Accounting firms cite a number of reasons for the rise in corrections. It's tough to apply standards that are nearly 70 years old to the modern economy, they say. Some believe that the SEC has made matters worse by issuing new interpretations of complex standards. "The question is not how does this reflect on the auditors," Arthur Andersen said in a written statement. Instead, the firm asked: "How is it that auditors are able to do so well in today's environment?"[35]

Corporate America's accounting problems raise the question: Can the public depend on the auditors? "Financial fraud and the accompanying restatement of financial statements have cost investors over $100 billion in the last half-dozen or so years," said Lynn E. Turner, who stepped down in summer 2001 as the SEC's chief accountant.[36] The shareholder losses resulting from accounting fraud or error could rival the cost to taxpayers of the savings-and-loan bailout of the early 1990s, he said. Enron investors, including employees who held the company's stock in their retirement accounts, lost billions.

Accounting industry leaders continue to deny that they are to blame. They say that the number of failed audits is tiny in relation to the many thousands performed successfully, and that it's often impossible for auditors to see through a sophisticated fraud. "The industry's record is strong," said Stephen G. Butler, chief executive of KPMG LLP. "I think the fundamental question is: Will you ever get to the point where there are no audit failures? In my view, you won't, just as you won't get to a point where there are no airplane crashes or no automobile crashes, no matter what the safety design or procedures."[37]

Despite the words of Butler and some of his colleagues, it is important that they not forget that in a 1984 ruling, the Supreme Court declared that auditors have an overriding duty to protect the public interest. "This 'public watchdog' function demands that the accountant maintain total independence from the client at all times and requires complete fidelity to the public trust," the court said.[38]

The leading industry trade group, the American Institute of Certified Public Accountants (AICPA), encouraged auditors to take a broad view of their role in a 1999 publication titled *Make Audits Pay: Leveraging the Audit into Consulting Services*. The book says the auditor should think of himself as a "business adviser" and promote his accounting firm's consulting services because "intense competition has reduced the audit to a mere commodity that is distinguishable to the consumer only according to price." The book notes that "conflicts may arise" in asking the auditor to perform two roles that are inherently at odds. "The business adviser is a client advocate," responsible for "acting in the owner's best interests." That is "completely different from the professional skepticism required of the auditor," the book says. But it suggests that the conflicts are manageable if the auditor errs on the side of looking out for the public interest.[39]

Within the accounting business, consulting is widely viewed as more glamorous and lucrative than auditing. The SEC's Pitt said the profession has faced "some difficulties in attracting the best and the brightest." Among the Big Five firms, U.S. consulting revenue totaled more than $15 billion in 1999—about half the firms' total revenue—the SEC reported last year. That was up from 13 percent in 1981. The AICPA has described the "certified public accountant" designation as a marketing liability. "The marketplace says the worst thing we have going for us is the 'A' in CPA," Barry Melancon, the trade group's president, wrote in 1998, referring to the word "accountant."[40] To reflect the variety of services accountants offer, AICPA leaders in fall 2001 proposed creating a new credential for "strategic business professionals," and AICPA members were given until December 28, 2001, to vote on the idea. (It was rejected.)

The continued rise in fees that companies pay to their auditors for non-auditing services like consulting are viewed as a major problem that will lead to more and more conflicts of interests which has been viewed as a major culprit in the rise and fall of both Enron and Arthur Andersen. However, many accounting executives still justify providing these other services to their clients since in their view providing consulting services improves audits because it helps an accounting firm get to know a client's business better.

GOVERNMENT

Over the past four decades, the depth, scope, and direction of government involvement in business has made the business-government relationship a hotly debated issue. The role of government, particularly in the regulation of business, has ensured its place among the major stakeholders with which business must establish an effective working relationship if it is to survive and thrive.

Business has never been fond of government's having an activist role in establishing the ground rules under which it operates. Government regulatory actions can often force significant changes in industry practices and strategic approaches. In some instances deregulation has proved to be a potent precompetitive force in the airline, banking, natural gas, telecommunications, and electric industries. Government efforts to reform Medicare and health insurance have become potent driving forces in the health care industry. In international markets, host governments can drive competitive changes by opening up domestic markets to foreign participation or closing them off to protect domestic companies.

Over the years the areas in which the government has chosen to initiate legislation has changed. For example, prior to the mid-1950s, most congressional legislation affecting business was economic in nature. Several illustrations of this include the Interstate Commerce Act of 1887, the Sherman Antitrust Act of 1890, the Clayton Antitrust Act of 1914, the Securities Act of 1933, the Securities and Exchange Act of 1934, and the 1935 Wagner Act. Since the 1950s, however, legislation has been concerned largely with the quality of life. Several examples include the Civil Rights Act of 1964, the Water Quality Act of 1965, the Occupational Safety and Health Act of 1970, the Consumer Product Safety Act of 1972, the Warranty Act of 1975, and the Americans with Disabilities Act of 1990.

The multiplicity of roles that government has assumed has also increased the complexity of its relationship with business. Several of the varied roles that government has assumed in its relationship with business suggest the influence, interrelationships, and complexities that are present.[41] These roles indicate that government:

1. Prescribes the rules of the game for business.
2. Is a major purchaser of business's products and services.
3. Uses its contracting power to get business to do things it wants.
4. Is a major promoter and subsidizer of business.
5. Is the owner of vast quantities of productive equipment and wealth.
6. Is an architect of economic growth.
7. Is a financier.
8. Is the protector of various interests in society against business exploitation.
9. Directly manages large areas of private business.
10. Is the repository of the social conscience and redistributes resources to meet social objectives.

Government is clearly a major employer, purchaser, subsidizer, competitor, financier, and persuader in the business-government relationship. Thus, government has a significant influence on business in both regulatory and nonregulatory ways. Broadly speaking, government regulations have been used for two central purposes: achieving certain economic goals and achieving certain social goals. These latter two types of regulation are customarily referred to as economic regulation and social regulation. Briefly, economic regulations focus on market conditions and economic variables (entry, exit, prices, services). Some selected industries affected by economic regulation include railroads, aeronautics, and communications; and government agencies that are relevant to these industries are the Civil Aeronautics Board (CAB) and the Federal Communications Commission (FCC). On the other hand, social regulation focuses on people in their roles as employees, consumers, and citizens. Virtually all industries are affected by social regulation. Organizations such as the Equal Employment Opportunity

Commission (EEOC), the Occupational Safety and Health Administration (OSHA), Consumer Product Safety Commission (CPSC), and the Environmental Protection Agency (EPA) are examples of the regulatory agencies that exist within the federal government that exist to address social regulation issues.

Possibly as a result of this charge, a clash of emphases partially forms the crux of the antagonistic relationship that has evolved between business and government over the years. Some have termed this problem as "a clash of ethical systems."[42] The two ethical systems of belief are the individualistic ethic of business and the collective ethics of government. Table 4.1 summarizes the characteristics of these two philosophies.[43]

The clash of these two ethical systems partially explains why the recent business-government relationship is adversarial in nature. In elaborating on this adversarial nature of the business-government relationship, Jacoby offered the following comments:

> Officials of government characteristically look upon themselves as probers, inspectors, taxers, regulators, regulators, and punishers of business transgression. Businesspeople typically view government agencies as obstacles, constraints, delayers, and impediments to economic progress, having much power to stop and little to start.[44]

The business-government relationship has been deteriorating. The goals and values of our pluralistic society have become more complex, more numerous, more interrelated, and, consequently, more difficult to reconcile. The result has been increasing conflicts among diverse interest groups, with trade-off decisions becoming harder to make. In this process, it has become more difficult to establish social priorities, and consensus has in many cases become impossible to achieve.

TABLE 4.1   The Clash of Ethical Systems between Business and Government

Business Beliefs	Government Beliefs
Individualistic ethic	Collectivistic ethic
Maximum concession to self-interest	Subordination of individual goals and self-interest to group goals and group interests
Minimizing the load of obligations society imposes on the individual (personal freedom)	Maximizing the obligations assumed by the individual and discouraging self-interest
Emphasizes inequalities of individuals	Emphasizes equality of individuals

Although business and government are intertwined in their functioning, in our socio-economic system business must never lose sight of the paramount role government plays as one of its key stakeholders. Government has become one of the citizenry's designated representatives charged with articulating and protecting the public interest, thus reinforcing the complex interactions among business, government, and the public.

As noted earlier there are other stakeholders (e.g., suppliers, competitors, unions) that organizations must be responsive to; however, for our purposes we will not offer a discussion of them at this point.

CONCLUSION

Information technology and the Internet continue to revolutionize business paradigms and processes. Industries and companies are downsizing, restructuring, merging, and reinventing their businesses. Mid-level management layers are diminishing. Functions are being eliminated and replaced by online automation and networked infrastructures. Knowledge workers with technological and people skills must manage processes and themselves in cyberspace with speed, efficiency, and accuracy.

Probably the most important component of an organization's external environment (e.g., natural and social conditions) is its stakeholders. These are the shareholders, customers, suppliers, governments, and any other groups with a vested interest. Stakeholders influence the organization's access to inputs and ability to discharge outputs. Some have suggested that each organization's distinctiveness depends on the stakeholders it emphasizes. Unless they pay attention to the needs of stakeholders, organizational leaders may find their business in trouble.

Because organizations operate in a much more complex and turbulent environment than a few decades ago, careful analysis of corporate decisions may be a waste of precious time.[45] Organizations remain responsive by giving employees more freedom to make decisions, allowing them to experiment, and viewing mistakes as learning opportunities. In other words, today's organizations are best prepared to change and meet the demands of an increasingly complex and turbulent environment when its employees are valued as key internal stakeholders and empowered to make decisions.

Today's organizations that are perceived as ethical and socially responsible often have a strong and loyal customer base, as well as a strong employee base, because of trust and mutual dependence in the organization-employee relationship.[46] When employees perceive their organizations as having an ethical climate, they are more likely to be committed to and satisfied with their work. This theme will become increasingly evident as we continue our discussion on ethics, social responsibility, and corporate citizenship in action in the remainder of this book.

NOTES

1. David Wheeler and Maria Sillanpää, *The Stakeholder Corporation: A Blueprint for Maximizing Stakeholder Value* (London: Pitman Publishing, 1997); Archie B. Carroll and Ann K. Buchholtz, *Business and Society: Ethics and Stakeholder Management*, 5th ed. (Mason, O.: South-Western, 2003).

2. R. Edward Freeman, *Strategic Management: A Stakeholder Approach* (Boston: Harper Collins, 1984), 25.

3. Mark Starik, "Is the Environment an Organizational Stakeholder? Naturally!" *International Association for Business and Society (IABS) Proceedings* (1993), 466–71.

4. Max B. E. Clarkson, "A Stakeholder Framework for Analyzing and Evaluating Corporate Social Performance," *Academy of Management Review* 20 (1995), 92–117.

5. Ibid., 106.

6. M. D. Cohen, James G. March and J. Paul Olsen, "A Garbage Can Model of Organizational Choice," *Administrative Science Quarterly* 17 (1972), 1–25; Thomas Donaldson and Lee E. Preston, "The Stakeholder Theory of the Corporation: Concepts, Evidence, and Implications," *Academy of Management Review* 20 (1995), 65–91; Freeman, *Strategic Management*, 25.

7. Donaldson and Preston, *Stakeholder Theory*, 69; Freeman, *Strategic Management*, 5.

8. Clarkson, *Stakeholder Framework*.

9. Wheeler and Sillanpää, *Stakeholder Corporation*, 167.

10. Murray L. Weidenbaum, *Strengthening the Corporate Board: A Constructive Response to Hostile Takeovers* (St. Louis: Washington University, Center for the Study of American Business, 1985).

11. Louis Lavelle, "The Gravy Train Is Slowing," *Business Week* (April 2, 2001), 44.

12. C. J. Loomis, "This Stuff Is Wrong," *Fortune* (June 25, 2001), 72–84.

13. L. W. Foy, "Business Ethics: A Reappraisal," Distinguished Lecture Series, Columbia Graduate School of Business (January 30, 1972), 2.

14. Linda Klebe Trevino, Laura Pincus Hartman, and Michael Brown, "Moral Person and Moral Manager: How Executives Develop a Reputation for Ethical Leadership," *California Management Review* 42, no. 4 (2000), 128–42.

15. James W. Cortada, *21st Century Business: Managing and Working in the New Digital Economy* (Upper Saddle River, N.J.: Prentice-Hall, 2001).

16. Michael Conlin, "Job Security, No, Tall Latte, Yes," *Business Week* (April 2, 2001), 62–64.

17. David L. Lewis, "Out in the Field: Workplace Want Loyal Workers? Then Help Them Grow," *Boston Globe* (July 15, 2001), H2.

18. Carroll and Buchholtz, *Business and Society*; "Revolution in America's Workplace," *Business Week* (October 17, 1994), 252.

19. "Revolution."

20. S. Shellenbarger, "Why Many Bosses Need to Alter Their Approach toward Older Workers," *The Wall Street Journal* (May 23, 2001), A6; J. Stuller, "Ready for the Other Millennium Bomb?" *Chief Executive* (July, 2000), 48–54.

21. L. A. Armour, "Who Says Virtue Is Its Own Reward?" *Fortune* (February 16, 1998), 186–89.

22. *Moody's Corporate Department, Moody's Rating Process* (New York: Moody's, 1989).

23. Keith H. Hammonds, "A Portfolio with a Heart Still Needs a Brain," *Business Week* (January 26, 1998), 100.

24. Carroll and Buchholtz, *Business and Society*, 200.

25. M. Doyle, "Ethics Pays—Says Co-op Bank Chief," *The Daily Telegraph* (Detroit) (April 19, 1998), C1.

26. D. Rynecki, "Here Are 8 Easy Ways to Lose Your Shirt in Stocks," *USA Today* (June 26, 1998), 3B.

27. S. Antilla, "Gang That Couldn't Pick Straight," *New York Times* (August 10, 1992), D1, D3; Charles J. Fombrun, *Reputation: Realizing Value from the Corporate Image* (Boston: Harvard Businesss School Press), 34.

28. Fombrun, *Reputation*, 65.

29. Lippincott and Marguiles, Inc., "Takeovers," *Sense 87*, 1985, 4.

30. D. S. Hilzenrath, "After Enron, New Doubts about Auditors," *Washington Post* (December 5, 2001), A01.

31. Ibid.

32. Ibid.

33. Ibid.

34. Ibid.

35. Ibid.

36. "Auditors, 'Public Watchdogs,'" *Washington Post* (December 5, 2001), A01.

37. Ibid.

38. Ibid.

39. American Institute of Certified Public Accountants (AICPA), *Make Audits Pay: Leveraging the Audit into Consulting Services* (Jersey City, N.J.: AICPA, 1999).

40. Ibid.

41. George A. Steiner, *Business and Society*, 2nd ed. (New York: Random House, 1975), 226.

42. L. E. Birdsell, "Business and Government: The Walls Between," in J. H. Jacoby (ed.), *The Business-Government Relationship: A Reassessment* (Santa Monica, Calif.: Goodyear, 1975).

43. J. H. Jacoby (ed.), *The Business-Government Relationship: A Reassessment* (Santa Monica, Calif.: Goodyear, 1975).

44. Ibid., 167.

45. Henry Mintzberg, *The Rise and Fall of Strategic Planning* (New York: Free Press, 1994).

46. O. C. Ferrell, J. Fraedrich, and L. Ferrell, *Business Ethics: Ethical Decision Making and Cases* (Boston: Houghton Mifflin, 2000).

5

Why Unethical Behavior Occurs in Organizations

INTRODUCTION

The potential for individuals and organizations to behave unethically is limitless. Unfortunately, this potential is too frequently realized, as suggested by our earlier discussion. Consider, for example, how Ford and Firestone failed to address problems in the Bridgestone/Firestone—Ford Explorer tire-separation controversy. Despite the more obvious examples of unethical organizational practices, many go on almost routinely unnoticed in a number of organizations. What accounts for the unethical actions of people in organizations? More specifically, why do people commit unethical actions, when individuals knew or should have known that they or the organization was committing an unethical act?

Many recognize self-interest as a strong motivating factor to explain why people behave unethically. Ethical behavior is influenced by characteristics of the individual, his or her social relationships, and the organizational system in which he or she is embedded. All this should be taken into consideration to help explain ethical behaviors when individuals are accountable to more than one audience. The divergent expectancies of multiple stakeholders may result in behavior that is less predictable and that, in the eyes of the organization, may be undesirable.

It is important to remember that the public at large is demanding that business executives, managers, government officials, workers in general, and the organizations they represent all act according to high ethical and moral standards. With each Salomon Brothers and Enron debacle, there is renewed concern with maintaining high standards of ethical behavior in organizational transactions and in the workplace.

To organizations and employees, acting ethically and legally means saving billions of dollars each year in theft, lawsuits, and settlements. Ethics matters in business because all the internal and external stakeholders stand to gain when organizations, groups, and individuals seek to do what is right, and to do things the right way.

The purpose of this chapter is to increase our understanding of why unethical behavior occurs in organizations. After first defining what is meant by unethical behavior our focus turns to individual and organizational factors contributing to unethical behavior. The chapter concludes with a look at the role of groupthink and stress as possible precursors to unethical behavior.

WHAT IS UNETHICAL BEHAVIOR?

Unethical behavior is defined as behavior that has a harmful effect upon others and is "either illegal, or morally unacceptable to the larger community."[1] Others note that unethical behavior is a social phenomenon and is influenced by social relationships, individual difference characteristics, the moral issue, and the organization.[2]

There is increasing concern that unethical behavior is a cancer continuing to destroy the fabric of society in too many of today's organizations and beyond. We daily face a crisis of ethics in the West that undermines our competitive strength and standing in the global marketplace. This crisis involves businesspeople, government officials, customers, and employees. Especially worrisome is unethical behavior among employees at all levels of the organization.

In academia, fraud has reached epidemic proportions. The intense desire to be successful has changed cheating in school from an anomaly into standard practice. At work, individuals cut corners on quality control, cover up incidents, abuse or lie about sick days, lie to and deceive customers, steal from employers, and put inappropriate pressures on others. Other unacceptable actions include cheating on expense accounts, discriminating against coworkers, paying or accepting kickbacks, fixing prices, and other forms of fraud. These types of unethical behavior cost industry billions of dollars a year and damage the images of corporations.

Recurring unethical behavior themes include managers lying to employees, office nepotism and favoritism, taking credit for others' work, receiving or offering kickbacks, stealing from the company, firing an employee for whistleblowing, padding expense accounts to obtain reimbursements for questionable expenses, divulging confidential information or trade secrets, terminating employment without giving sufficient notice, and using company property and materials for personal use. Other more visible examples over the years have included the H. B. Fuller Co. selling glue in Honduras that was being recklessly used for "sniffing" by Honduran street children, Beech-Nut Nutrition Company's practice of selling adulterated apple juice and passing it off to the public as "100% fruit juice," Dow Corning selling defective silicone breast implants, wrongdoings by Salomon Brothers in the Treasury auction scandal, Sears Roebuck & Co. engaging in sales abuses at its auto centers by pressuring customers to purchase unneeded or unwanted services, the tobacco industry manufacturing and marketing what an increased number of people consider to be an inherently dangerous product, pork-barreling by the U.S. Congress, and more recently Enron's questionable accounting practices and unethical partnerships.

These samples of both specific organizational and individual incidents typify the kinds of ethical concerns one finds today on television and in newspapers and magazines. These examples of questionable and unethical practices range from major laws being broken to whether or not organizations and individuals have been ethical (or socially responsible). Although such practices occur throughout the world, their presence nonetheless serves to remind us of the challenge facing organizations.

Standards for what constitutes ethical behavior lie in a grey zone, where clear-cut right-or-wrong answers may not always exist. As a result, unethical behavior sometimes is forced on organizations by the environment in which it exists and laws such as the Foreign Corrupt Practices Act. For example, if you were a sales representative for an American company abroad and your foreign competitors used bribes to get business, what would you do? In the United States such behavior is illegal, yet it is perfectly acceptable in other countries. What is ethical in this case? Similarly, in many countries women are systematically discriminated against in the workplace; it is felt that their place is in the home. In the United States, again, this practice is illegal. If you ran an American company in one of these countries, would you hire women in important positions? If you did, your company might be isolated in the larger business community, and you might lose business. If you did not, you might be violating what most Americans believe to be fair business practices.

Falling trade barriers and increased international business will continue to create opportunities for organizations to expand their operations internationally. The globalization of the economy increases and will continue to increase the complexity of dealing with ethical issues because of varying cultural perceptions of morality. Thus, many of these multinational businesses must find ways to address the difficult task of trying to decide the best ethical practices for one organization on a worldwide basis.

Effectively managing ethical issues as we continue to transition further into the twenty-first century will pose challenges for organizations and their employees. Compounding the ethical challenges are many economic, legal, and technological ambiguities, issues, and questions important to organizational success. There is every indication that this period of turbulence will continue to be characterized by significant changes in the economy, in society, in technology, and in global relationships. However, despite this continuing turbulence, organizations must continue to increase their understanding of why unethical behavior occurs in organizations.

WHY UNETHICAL BEHAVIOR OCCURS IN ORGANIZATIONS

Ethical pressures or issues occur on different level, which cascade out from the individual to the global. These levels include individual or personal, the organizational level, the industry level, the societal level, and the international level. Again, personal level ethical challenges include situations we face in our personal lives that are generally outside the work context. People in their roles as employees and managers also confront ethical issues at the organizational level that may carry consequences for the organization's reputation and success in the community and also for the kind of ethical environment or culture that will prevail on a day-to-day basis in the organization. An organization's managers can also influence ethics at the industry level (e.g., real estate, insurance) or at the professional level (e.g., pharmacy, accounting). It becomes rather difficult for an organization's employees to have any direct effect on business ethics at the societal or international levels. For our purposes, because organizational employees are quite removed from the industry, societal, and international levels, we will focus our discussion of why unethical behavior occurs in organizations primarily on the personal and organizational levels.

Individual Factors Contributing to Unethical Behavior

Every individual is confronted with ethical challenges in his or her personal or employee (work) situations, and each individual is a stakeholder of someone else. Someone else—a family member, a friend, an associate or other colleague—has a stake in each individual's behavior; therefore, an individual's ethics are important to them also. What we discuss here is aimed at increasing our understanding of those individual factors that contribute to the occurrence of unethical behavior and impact the ethical judgments individuals must make.

The ethical issues that individuals face at work are complex. A review of articles appearing in the *Wall Street Journal* more than a decade ago during one week revealed more than sixty articles dealing with ethical issues in business.[3] The themes appearing throughout the articles were distilled into twelve major ethical issues, as follows:

1. Stealing: taking things that don't belong to you.
2. Lying: saying things you know aren't true.
3. Fraud and deceit: creating or perpetuating false impressions.
4. Conflict of interest and influence buying: bribes, payoffs, and kickbacks.
5. Hiding versus divulging information: concealing information that another party has a right to know, or failing to protect personal or proprietary information.
6. Cheating: taking unfair advantage of a situation.
7. Personal decadence: aiming below excellence in terms of work performance (e.g., careless or sloppy work).
8. Interpersonal abuse: behaviors that are abusive of others (e.g., sexism, racism, emotional abuse).
9. Organizational abuse: Organizational practices that abuse members (e.g., inequitable compensation, misuses of power).
10. Rule violations: breaking organizational rules.
11. Accessory to unethical acts: knowing about unethical behavior and failing to report it.
12. Ethical dilemmas: choosing between two equally desirable or undesirable options.

You can see that few of these issues are clear-cut. All of them depend on the specifics of the situation, and their interpretation depends on the characteristics of the individuals examining them. For example, look at issue 2, lying. We all know that "white lies" are told in business. Is this acceptable? The answer varies from person to person. Thus, the perception of what constitutes ethical versus unethical behavior in organizations varies among individuals.

Making ethical decisions is part of each employee's job. It has been suggested that ethical decision-making requires three qualities of individuals[4]:

1. The competence to identify ethical issues and evaluate the consequences of alternative courses of action

2. The self-confidence to seek out different opinions about the issue and decide what is right in terms of a particular situation
3. Toughmindedness—the willingness to make decisions when all that needs to be known cannot be known and when the ethical issue has no established, unambiguous solution

What are the individual characteristics that lead to these qualities? Individual differences that affect ethical behavior are value systems, locus of control, Machiavellianism, and cognitive moral development.[5]

Individuals' Value Systems

Systems of beliefs that affect what the individual defines as right, good, and fair are referred to as values. Ethics reflects the way values are acted out. For the individual that means acting in ways consistent with one's personal values and the commonly held values of the organization and society.

Employees are exposed to many value systems: their own, their boss's, the organization's, the customers', and others'. In most instances, the individual's greatest allegiance will be to personal values. When the value system conflicts with the behavior the person feels must be exhibited, the person experiences a value conflict. Suppose, for example, that an individual believes that telling the truth is important in all situations. Yet this individual sees that those who get ahead in his organization bend the truth (e.g., fudge their numbers and deceive other people). Why should the individual tell the truth if telling the truth doesn't pay? It is the individual's values, a basic sense of what is right and wrong, that override the temptation to not tell the truth.

Locus of Control

Another individual difference on ethical behavior is locus of control, a personality variable that affects individual behavior. Individuals with an internal locus of control (internals) believe that they control events in their lives and that they are responsible for what happens to them. In contrast, individuals with an external locus of control (externals) believe that outside forces such as chance, fate, or other people control what happens to them.[6]

Internals are more likely than externals to take personal responsibility for the consequences of their ethical or unethical behavior. Externals are more apt to believe that external forces caused their ethical or unethical behavior. Internals make more ethical decisions than do externals. Internals are also more resistant to social pressure and are less willing to hurt another person, even if ordered to do so by an authority.[7]

Machiavellianism

Machiavellianism is another individual difference that affects ethical behavior. Niccolò Machiavelli wrote *The Prince*, a guide for acquiring and using power.[8] The primary method for achieving power that he suggested was manipulation of others. Machiavellianism, then, is a personality characteristic indicating one's willingness to do whatever it takes to get one's own way.

A high-Mach individual behaves in accordance with Machiavelli's ideas, which include the notion that it is better to be feared that loved. High-Machs tend to use deceit in relationships, have a cynical view of human nature, and have little concern for conventional notions of right and wrong.[9] They are skilled manipulators of other people, relying on their persuasive abilities. Low-Machs, in contrast, value loyalty and relationships. They are willing to manipulate others for personal gain and are concerned with others' opinions.

High-Machs believe that the desired ends justify any means. They believe that manipulation of others is fine if it helps achieve a goal. Thus, high-Machs are likely to justify their manipulative behavior as ethical. They are emotionally detached from other people and are oriented toward objective aspects of situations. And high-Machs are likelier than low-Machs to engage in behavior that is ethically questionable.[10]

Cognitive Moral Development

An individual's level of cognitive moral development also affects ethical behavior. Lawrence Kohlberg proposed that as individuals mature, they move through a series of six stages of moral development.[11] With each successive stage, they become less dependent on other people's opinions of right and wrong and less self-centered (acting in one's own interest). At higher levels of moral development, individuals are concerned with broad principles. Kohlberg's model focuses on the decision-making process and on how individuals justify ethical decisions. Kohlberg, drawing heavily on the work of developmental psychologists such as Piaget, formulated a theory of the development of moral reasoning about how people think about what is right and wrong and how the decision-making process changes through interaction with peers and the environment.

Cognitive moral development occurs at three levels, and each level consists of two stages. The stages of moral reasoning central to Kohlberg's theory are briefly summarized here.

Preconventional Level (Self-Orientation)—the person's behavior or ethical decisions are based on external rewards, punishments, and self-interest.

Stage 1: Punishment avoidance. The physical consequences of an act determine whether it is good or bad. The individual obeys rules to avoid punishment. The individual has little awareness of others' needs. Stage 1 is usually associated with the development of small children, but signs of Stage 1 development are also evident in adult behavior. For example, some organizations forbid their buyers to accept gifts from salespeople. A buyer in Stage 1 development might justify a refusal to accept gifts from salespeople by referring to the organization's rule that defines accepting gifts as an unethical practice, or the buyer may accept the gift if he or she believes that there is no chance of being caught.

Stage 2: Reward seeking. The individual follows the rules only if it is in her or his immediate interest to do so. The person has awareness of other's needs but not of right and wrong as abstract concepts. Fairness to the individual is of paramount importance in this stage. For example, a sales representative in Stage 2 development doing business for the first time in a foreign country may be expected by custom to give customers "gifts." Although gift giving may be against company policy in the United States, the salesperson may decide that certain organization rules designed for operating in the United States do not apply overseas. In the culture of some foreign countries, gifts may be considered part of a person's pay. In this instance, not giving a gift might represent an unfair deal for the salesperson. (Cultural differences in business ethics are discussed later in this chapter)

Conventional Level (Others Orientation)—The focus is on the expectations of others (parents, peers) or society (laws).

Stage 3: Good boy/good girl. The person tries to live up to the expectations of people close to them, not to fulfill any moral ideal. The individual considers the well-being of others, although motivation is still derived from obedience. An automobile production manager in this stage might follow the orders of his boss to speed up an assembly line if he believed that this action would generate more business and profits for the company and thus maintain employee jobs. In addition to considering his own well-being in following the boss' order, he also tries to put himself in his boss's position, as well as in the employees' situation.

Stage 4: Law and order. Respect for authority, order and doing one's duty determine what is right as individuals broaden their perspective to include the laws and norms of the larger society. They fulfill duties and obligations and want to contribute to society. For example, an employee may recognize that safety standards in the foreign country she is working in would be considered inadequate in her host country. The employee feels it is her duty to complain because the lower safety standards might endanger workers and eventually members of the public-at-large.

Postconventional Level (Universal Values, Humankind Orientation)—The individual sees beyond laws, rules, and the expectations of other people.
Stage 5: Social contract. Individuals are aware that people have diverse value systems and they uphold their own values despite what others think. The consensus of society, which can change, defines what is right. For an individual to be classified in Stage 5, decisions must be based on principles of justice and rights. The CEO of a company may decide to establish a social responsibility and ethics training program because it will provide a buffer to prevent ethical missteps or legal problems, and the organization will be a responsible contributor to society.
Stage 6: Universal ethical principle orientation. Right is defined in terms of self-chosen universal principles of good and bad. The individual follows self-selected ethical principles. If there is a conflict between a law and a self-selected ethical principle, the individual reasons and uses conscience and moral rules to guide actions. A person at this stage may be more concerned with social ethical issues and not only rely on the business organization for ethical direction. For example, a member of Ford Motor Company at this stage might have argued for discontinuing the use of Bridgestone/Firestone tires that had been linked to deaths and injuries several years ago because the inalienable right to life makes killing wrong, regardless of the reason. Therefore, company profits would not be a justification for the continued use of the product.

In the stages of moral development, right and wrong are successively defined in slightly different terms. In general, the stages proceed from self-oriented thinking and from a punishment-reward orientation to an abstract principle orientation. Each successive stage represents a higher level of reasoning regarding the definition and nature of right and wrong. A number of studies suggest that the moral reasoning of adults is similar to that described in Stage 4 of Kohlberg's theory[12] and that moral reasoning at Stage 5 or beyond is not common, even in educated groups such as managers.[13]

As individuals mature, their moral development passes through these stages in an irreversible sequence. All individuals are not going to pass through each of the stages in Kohlberg's model. Some do not even progress past Stage 1. Kohlberg argues that individuals cannot move to a higher stage without first going through the earlier stages. Individuals may have difficulty seeing the logic of moral reasoning more than two stages above their own. People tend to be attracted to the reasoning of the next highest level and will move when their present level proves inadequate to handle a complex moral dilemma.

Since it was proposed, more than thirty years ago, Kohlberg's model of cognitive moral development has received a great deal of research support. Individuals at higher stages of development are less likely to cheat, more likely to engage in whistle-blowing, and more likely to make ethical business decisions.[14]

Moral judgments are social judgments and are prescriptive or normative judgments about people's rights, obligations, and responsibilities, rather than their preferences. Critics, including Carol Gilligan[15] have argued that Kohlberg's theory is a theory of "justice reasoning" rather than a theory of moral judgment; however, Colby and Kohlberg dispute this, stating that:

> Although it is true that the dilemmas in the Standard Moral Judgment Interview pose conflicts of rights, the actual judgments made by respondents may focus on concern and love for another person, on personal commitments, on one's fellow human beings as well as rights, rules, and duties. As long as these concepts are used prescriptively, as defining what is morally right or good, the scope of the domain we assess is considerably broader than is conveyed by the term *justice reasoning*.[16]

Gilligan has also argued that the model does not take gender differences into account. Kohlberg's model was developed from a twenty-year study of eighty-four boys.[17]

Gilligan contends that women's moral development follows a different pattern—one that is based not on individual rights and rules but on responsibility and relationships. Women and men face the same moral dilemmas but approach them from different perspectives—men from the perspective of equal respect and women from the perspective of compassion and care. Researchers who reviewed the research on these gender differences concluded that the differences may not be as strong as originally stated by Gilligan. Some men use care reasoning and some women may use justice reasoning when making moral judgments.[18]

There is evidence to support the idea that men and women view ethics differently. A review of sixty-six studies found that women were more likely than men to perceive certain business practices as unethical. Young women were more likely to see breaking the rules and acting on insider information as unethical. Both sexes agreed that collusion, conflicts of interest, and stealing are unethical. It takes about twenty-one years for the gender gap to disappear. Men seem to become more ethical with more work experience; the longer they are in the workforce, the more their attitudes become similar to those held by women. There is an age/experience effect for both sexes: Experienced workers are more likely to think lying, bribing, stealing, and colluding are unethical.[19]

To understand Kohlberg's theory and its use as a mechanism for understanding why individuals might commit unethical acts, one must remember that it is a cognitive theory. What counts is the reasoning processes involved in a decision, not the decision itself. So, a stage 1 individual and a Stage 5 individual may make the same decision, but for very different reasons.

The process of developing a style of moral reasoning spans a person's entire childhood and much of adulthood. Kohlberg's theory describes a way of viewing the world that develops over a long period of time. It has been suggested that ethical behavior reflects both individual and situational influences; among the individual influences, the style of moral reasoning might not be the most important factor.[20] A variety of other individual characteristics, including locus of control and ego strength, might be important in determining whether an individual translates his or her judgment about what is right or wrong into ethical or unethical behavior at work.

Individual differences in values, locus of control, Machiavellianism, and cognitive moral development are important influences that must be considered when trying to understand why unethical behavior occurs in organizations. While these things are important to increasing our understanding of why unethical behavior occurs in organizations, we also need to consider other factors as discussed in the next section.

Moral (Ethical) Intensity, Ethical Sensitivity, and Situational Influences

Some other factors that can help us understand why unethical behavior occurs in organizations are the moral intensity of the issue, the individual's ethical sensitivity, and situational factors. Moral intensity is the degree to which an issue demands the application of ethical principles. The higher the moral intensity, the more that ethical principles should provide guidance to resolve the issue. Stealing from your employer is usually considered high on moral intensity, whereas taking a company pen for personal use is much lower on the scale. Several factors influence the moral intensity of an issue, such as the extent to which the issue clearly produces good or bad consequences, other in the society think it is good or evil, the issue quickly affects people, the decision maker feels close to the issue, and the person is able to influence the issue.[21]

Even if an issue has moral intensity, some employees might not recognize its ethical importance because they have low ethical sensitivity. Ethical sensitivity is a personal characteristic that enables people to recognize the presence and determine the relative importance of an ethical issue.[22] Ethically sensitive people are not necessarily more ethical. Rather, they are more likely to recognize whether an issue requires ethical consideration and can more accurately estimate the moral intensity of the issue. Ethically sensitive people tend to have higher empathy, and to have more information about the specific situation. For example, accountants would be more ethically sensitive regarding procedures than would someone who has not received training in this profession.

Another important factor explaining why good people do bad things is the situation in which the unethical conduct occurs. A few recent surveys have reported that employees regularly experience corporate pressure that leads to selling beyond the customers' needs, lying to the client, or making unrealistic promises. Other surveys have found that most employees believe they experience so much pressure that it compromises their ethical conduct. For instance, nearly two-thirds of the mangers in one study stated that pressure from top management causes people further down in the hierarchy to compromise their beliefs, whereas 90 percent of top management disagreed with this statement.[23] The point here is not to justify unethical conduct. Rather, we need to recognize the situational factors that influence wrongdoing so that organizations can correct these problems in the future.

Cultural Differences in Business Ethics

When Harry Gould, Jr., visited Gould's Paper's manufacturing plants in France, he asked his French counterpart to show him the books (financial statements). The French executive casually asked, "Which books do you want to see?" The executive kept three sets of records— one for his family, one for the revenue collector, and the real one. "[The French executive] didn't think anything about that," Gould recalls. "There's a cultural mind-set that has no bearing on the reality we are used to here in the United States."[24]

As Harry Gould discovered, organizational decision makers face a larger set of ethical dilemmas when they enter the global marketplace. As suggested in our discussion of Kohlberg's cognitive moral development theory, cultural differences can partially explain why some unethical practices occur in organizations. The French executive saw little wrong with having three sets of financial records, whereas most Americans would consider this practice of falsifying information highly unethical. This isn't an isolated example. Many years ago, the United States made bribery at home or abroad a criminal offense for American companies, whereas it was a legitimate tax deduction in Australia, Germany, Netherlands, and several other countries until a couple of years ago.[25] Various studies have identified differences across cultures regarding attitudes toward software piracy, résumé padding, and a host of other ethical issues.[26]

Do these studies suggest that people in some countries have fewer ethical values or are more prone to commit unethical acts? Not necessarily. Research indicates that fundamental ethical principles are fairly similar across cultures, but people interpret the ethical implications of specific situations differently.[27] False financial reporting may be more common in France than in the United States, for example, because French businesspeople might believe it is widely practiced and has little adverse effect on anyone. Americans, on the other hand, are more likely to view false financial reporting as unethical because they believe it has adverse consequences. Thus, financial reporting likely has higher moral intensity in the United States than in some other cultures.

ORGANIZATIONAL FACTORS CONTRIBUTING TO UNETHICAL BEHAVIOR

Now we shift our attention to the organizational level, where we find the context in which individual employee or managerial decision-making and unethical behavior occur. Actions and practices that take place within the organization's culture, or climate, are just as vital as decision making in bringing about ethical or unethical practices or results. To understand why unethical behavior occurs in organizations, we must understand what is meant by organization culture and appreciate that the organization's ethical climate is just one part of its overall organization culture.

Our focus in this section is on understanding factors that may come to bear on an organization's employees that contribute to the occurrence of unethical behavior. We will first define organization culture and then take a closer look at several key factors that lead to the development of an unethical climate. The question that needs to be considered in increasing our understanding of why unethical behavior occurs in organizations is: "What factors contribute to unethical behavior in the organization?"

Organizational Culture

Every company has a unique organizational culture. Each has its own business philosophy and principles, its own way of approaching problems and making decisions, its own work climate, its own embedded patterns of "how we do things around here," its own lore (stories told over and over to illustrate company values and what they mean to stakeholders), its own taboos and political don'ts—in other words, its own ingrained beliefs, behavior and thought patterns, business practices, and personality that define its organizational culture. The bedrock of Wal-Mart's culture is dedication to customer satisfaction, zealous pursuit of low costs, a strong work ethic, Sam Walton's legendary frugality, the ritualistic Saturday-morning headquarters meetings to exchange ideas and review problems, and company executives' commitment to visiting stores, talking to customers, and soliciting suggestions from employees.

At Microsoft, there are stories of the long hours programmers put in, the emotional peaks and valleys in encountering and overcoming coding problems, the exhilaration of completing a complex program on schedule, the satisfaction of working on cutting-edge projects, the rewards of being part of a team responsible for a popular new software program, and the tradition of competing aggressively. At McDonald's the constant message from management is the overriding importance of quality, service, cleanliness, and value; employees are drilled over and over on the need for attention to detail and perfection in every fundamental of the business. The organizational culture at American Express Company stresses that employees help customers out of difficult situations whenever possible. This attitude is reinforced through numerous company legends of employees who have gone above and beyond the call of duty to help customers. This strong tradition of customer loyalty might encourage an American Express employee to take unorthodox steps to help a customer who encounters a problem while travelling overseas. Such strong traditions and values have become a driving force in many other companies including IBM, the Procter & Gamble Co., Southwest Airlines, and Saturn, a division of General Motors, which has developed its own organizational culture, including values related to product quality, customer service, and fairness in pricing.

Culture serves four basic functions in organizations. First, culture provides a sense of identify to members and increases their commitment to the organization. When employees internalise the values of the company, they find their work intrinsically rewarding and identify with their fellow workers. Motivation is enhanced, and employees are more committed.[28]

Second, culture is a sense-making device for organization members. It provides a way for employees to interpret the meaning of organizational events.[29]

Third, culture reinforces the values in the organization. For example, during Jack Welch's tenure as CEO of General Electric, several cultural changes were undertaken to create a results-oriented atmosphere where all of GE's businesses were held to a standard of being number one or number two in their industries as well as achieving good business results: the concept of a boundaryless organization (where ideas, best practices, and learning flow freely from business to business); the reliance on "workout sessions" to identify, debate, and resolve burning issues; a commitment to six sigma quality; and globalization of the company.

Finally, culture serves as a control mechanism for shaping behavior. Norms that guide behavior are part of culture. At Westinghouse, employee suggestions increased fivefold following the emphasis on total quality. It became a norm to think of ways to improve processes at the division.

Unfortunately, some organizational cultures seem to support unethical purposes. Some organizations develop cultures or climates that do not promote ethical norms, which leads their employees to behave accordingly. For example, if an organization makes most of its profits froml unethical or illegal activities, then individuals who join the organization will have a hard time surviving unless they participate in these unethical activities. The ethical climate of the organization is a component of the organizational culture. Whereas organizational culture involves norms that prescribe a wide range of behavior for members of the organization, the ethical climate indicates whether organizations have an ethical conscience.

The ethical climate component of organizational culture can be thought of as the character or decision processes used to determine whether responses to issues are right or wrong.[30] The organizational culture and the resulting ethical climate may be directly related to the recognition of ethical dimensions of decisions, the generation of alternatives, and individual cognitive moral development. The more ethical the perceived culture of the organization, the less likely it is that unethical decision-making will occur.

Ethical Behavior and Organizational Culture

Do organizations vary in the "ethical climates" they establish for their members? The answer to the question is yes, and it is increasingly clear that the ethical tone or climate of organizations is set at the top. What top managers do, and the culture they establish and reinforce, makes a big difference in the way lower-level employees act and in the way the organization as a whole acts when ethical dilemmas are faced. This is a theme that we will revisit throughout this book. For example, there was no doubt in anyone's mind at Johnson & Johnson what to do when the infamous Tylenol poisoning took place. Company executives immediately pulled their product from the marketplace. They knew that "the J & J way" was to do the right thing regardless of its cost. What they were implicitly saying was that the ethical framework of the company required that they act in good faith in this fashion. On the other hand, as will be highlighted in later chapters, the scandal that rocked Salomon Brothers in 1991, in the investment banking division of Salomon, Inc., can be traced to its culture, which was directed by the controversial CEO John Gutfreund. Gutfreund's leadership style helped to mold a corporate culture that eventually resulted in unethical and illegal behavior by its members.

The ethical climate of an organization is the shared set of understandings about what is correct behavior and how ethical issues will be handled. This climate sets the tone for decision making at all levels and in all circumstances. Some of the factors that may be emphasized in different ethical climates of organizations are:

- Personal self-interest
- Company profit
- Operating efficiency
- Individual friendships
- Team interests
- Social responsibility
- Personal morality
- Rules and standard procedures
- Laws and professional codes

As suggested by that list, the ethical climate of different organizations can emphasize different things. In the Johnson & Johnson example just cited, the ethical climate supported doing the right thing because of social responsibility—regardless of the cost. In other organizations—perhaps too many—concerns for operating efficiency and the bottom line may outweigh social considerations when similarly difficult decisions are faced. When the ethical climate is not clear and positive, ethical dilemmas will often result in unethical behavior. In such instances, an organization's culture also can predispose its members to behave unethically. For example, it has been suggested that a relationship exists between organizations with a history of violating the law and continued illegal behavior.[31] Thus, some organizations have a culture that reinforces illegal activity. In addition, some organizations are known to selectively recruit and promote employees who have personal values consistent with illegal behavior; organizations also may socialize employees to engage in illegal acts as a part of their normal job duties. For instance, in an account of cases concerning price fixing for heavy electrical equipment, it was noted that General Electric removed a manager who refused to discuss prices with a competitor from his job and offered his successor the position with the understanding that management believed he would behave as expected and engage in price-fixing activities.[32] Such behavior by top management contributes to the development of a culture where doing the right thing is discouraged. Employees quickly learn what is and is not acceptable behavior.

It is important to understand organizational culture as ethical climate and in doing so organizational climates can be ranked by degrees of moral maturity. As in the similar, individual-level Kohlberg scheme discussed earlier in the chapter, with its preconventional morality types and its six stage types, the type names probably matter less than the maturity dimension as such (e.g., as a useful reference for benchmarking and ethical auditing).[33] Organizational climates can be described and compared by dominating ethics types and reference group levels (three ethics types and reference group levels can then be combined into nine theoretical "ethical climate types").[34]

The points in the previous paragraph suggest that ethical dilemmas will often result in unethical behavior if an organization's leadership furthers an immature, unclear, ambivalent, or negative ethical climate. Such unethical behavior is, of course, not only furthered by an unethical climate, but reproduces such an ethical climate in a system feedback fashion, being contagious and self-reinforcing (or perhaps provoking internal or external counterreactions, or norms). In such instances, an organization's culture predisposes its members to behave unethically. The Salomon Brothers fiasco (see Chapters 6 and 9) along with the Enron debacle (see Chapters 7 and 8) provide vivid examples of the extent to which organizations and their leaders create corporate cultures that encourage unethical practices.

Unethical behavior occurs in all areas of society: business, government, religion, education, and sports. Pressure, opportunity, and predisposition can all lead to unethical activities and all contribute to the development of counternorms, a bottom-line mentality, and groupthink, which are all precursors to unethical behavior.

What Behaviors Does the Organization Reward?

One answer to the question of why groups and individuals knowingly commit unethical actions is based on the idea that organizations often reward behaviors that violate ethical standards. Consider, for example, how many business leaders over the years have been expected to deal in bribes and payoffs, despite the negative publicity and ambiguity of some laws, and how good corporate citizens who blow the whistle on organizational wrongdoing may fear being punished for their actions. Organizations tend to develop *counternorms*, accepted organizational practices that are contrary to prevailing ethical standards. Some of the norms and counternorms that are shaped and maintained by the organization's reward system are as follows[35]:

Societal norms or ethics		Organizational counternorms
Be open and honest	vs.	Be secretive and deceitful
Follow the rules at all costs	vs.	Do whatever it takes to get the job done
Be cost-effective	vs.	Use it or lose it
Take responsibility	vs.	Pass the buck
Be a team player	vs.	Take credit for your own actions; grandstand
Maintain corporate loyalty	vs.	"Bad mouth" the company

The first pair is discussed next, to give the reader a sense of how norm-counternorm shifts can create ethical ambiguity that may lead to unethical behavior.

Openness and Honesty vs. Secrecy

One set of seemingly common organizational norms comprises openness, honesty, and full disclosure or, in Woodrow Wilson's terms, "open covenants, openly arrived at." Full disclosure acts, sunshine laws, and the Freedom of Information Act are indicators of the normative expectations surrounding honesty and openness.

The counternorms of secrecy, lying, and deceit clearly are more socially undesirable as well as ethically problematic.[36] Stonewalling indicates the counternorms of withholding and hiding relevant information. However, such counternorms may be necessary and functional, especially when "full disclosure" results in more inventive forms of secrecy. Secrecy may be made more socially desirable when presented in terms of confidentiality of sources. However, when a pattern of secrecy (and lying) begins to appear to be the normal appropriate action to take, then unethical behavior (or ambivalence) may occur if (a) the reward system supports secrecy (and lying) and (b) the withholding of information is harmful to the welfare of a group of stakeholders.

Organizational reward systems may punish honesty and reward dishonesty. The case of B. F. Goodrich in the classic aircraft brake scandal is one example: falsifying data required to win certification was rewarded by the company.[37] In this case like others the counternorm of secrecy, deceitfulness, and stonewalling toward important stakeholders (the government, press, and community) placed organizational actors in positions where unethical behavior was rewarded, even if for the short-term.

As suggested, there are many other organizational counternorms that promote morally and ethically questionable practices. That these practices are commonly rewarded and accepted suggests that organizations may be operating within a world that dictates its own set of accepted rules. This reasoning suggests another answer to the question of why organizations knowingly act unethically, namely, because managerial values exist that undermine integrity. That is, managers develop some ways of thinking (of which they may be quite unaware) that foster unethical behavior.

Managerial Values That Undermine Integrity

Another culprit contributing to why organizations knowingly act unethically is referred to as the *bottom-line mentality*. This line of thinking supports financial success as the only value to be considered. It promotes short-term solutions that are immediately financially sound, despite the fact that they cause problems for others within the organization or the organization as a whole. It promotes an unrealistic belief that everything boils down to a monetary game. As such, rules of morality are merely obstacles, impediments along the way to bottom-line financial success.

A similar bottom-line mentality, the *political bottom line*, is also quite evident in the public sector. For example, when it comes to spending money, the U.S. Congress has no equal. Although much of this expenditure is for purposes of national concern, a sizable portion is devoted to pork-barreling. Pork-barreling refers to the practice whereby a senator or representative forces Congress to allocate monies to special projects that take place in his or her home district. In many cases, the projects have little value and represent a drain on the taxpayers. They do, however, create jobs—and political support—in the home district. This practice is common, because many members of Congress believe it will help them get votes in the next election.

In some more extreme—and definitely ethically questionable—situations, such actions are designed to reward some large-scale campaign contributors in the home district. A case in point is the efforts of former Representative Les Aspin of Wisconsin to get the Defense Appropriations committee to include $249 million to continue making a certain ten-ton truck (in Wisconsin, naturally) that the army was trying to phase out. It was unneeded, but Aspin wanted the project for his home district. Was this legal? Yes? Was it ethical? That depends upon your point of view. Clearly, Aspin thought it was appropriate. Aspin was not, nor are others like him in Congress alone when one considers the political bottom line, given the realities of private and public organizations in recent years.

Leaders (and managers) also tend to rely on an *exploitative mentality*—a view that encourages using people in a way that promotes stereotypes and undermines empathy and compassion. This is a highly selfish perspective, one that sacrifices concerns for others in favor of benefits to one's own immediate interests. There is also the *Madison Avenue mentality*—a perspective suggesting that anything is right if the public can be convinced that it's right. The idea is that executives may be more concerned about their actions appearing ethical than about their legitimate morality—a public relations—guided morality. It is this kind of thinking that leads some companies to hide their unethical actions (by dumping their toxic wastes under cover of night, for instance) or otherwise justify them by attempting to explain them as completely acceptable.

It is not too difficult to recognize how individuals can knowingly engage in unethical practices with such mentalities. The overemphasis on short-term monetary gain and getting votes in the next election may lead to decisions and rationalizations that not only hurt individuals in the long run, but threaten the very existence of organizations themselves. Some common rationalizations used to justify unethical behavior are[38]:

- Pretending the behavior is not really unethical or illegal.
- Excusing the behavior by saying it's really in the organizations' or your best interest.
- Assuming the behavior is okay because no one else would ever be expected to find out about it.
- Expecting your superiors to support and protect you if anything should go wrong.

Some have suggested that conditions of opportunity and predisposition are antecedents of illegal behavior.[39] That is, rather than tightening conditions creating pressure for illegal acts, it may be that loosening ambiguous conditions create opportunities to behave illegally.

Predisposition indicates a tendency or inclination to select certain activities—illegal or unethical ones—over other activities because of socialization or other organizational practices. Some avoid the assumption that an organization's managers or agents subscribe to a different set of ethical standards than the rest of society. Instead, they recognize that organizations and industries can exert a powerful influence on their members, even those who initially have fairly strong ethical standards.

Organizations operating in certain industries tend to behave unethically. Certain industry cultures may predispose organizations to develop cultures that encourage their members to select unethical acts. If an organization's major competitors in an industry are performing well, in part as a result of unethical activities, it becomes difficult for organizational members to choose only unethical actions, and they may regard unethical actions as a standard of industry practice. Such a scenario results in an organizational culture that serves as a strong precipitant to unethical actions and lays the foundation for another precursor to unethical behavior: groupthink.

GROUPTHINK: A PRECURSOR TO UNETHICAL BEHAVIOR

Want to make a stupid decision? It's easier if you have help. Just gather a few like-minded colleagues together in an atmosphere that values getting along over getting things done, and you're on your way. As leader, be sure to voice your opinion early, often, and loudly. Make sure that everyone knows that challenging faulty thinking can cost one one's job. You're closer to trouble, but not there just yet. But if a few other factors fall into place, your group will likely embrace a plan that's so risky that no individual member of the group would ever even think of recommending it. Welcome to groupthink.

What Is Groupthink?

Groupthink is a process of rationalization that sets in when members of a team begin to think alike. It can be fostered by an organization's culture or managers who do not tolerate dissent, or it can develop under leaders who offer their employees so much encouragement and praise that pretty soon everyone begins to underestimate the seriousness of potential problems. Most of the time, groupthink pops up quickly and wreaks havoc before anyone realizes what's going on.

Part of the problem is that groupthink, once in motion, generates its own fuel. Kani, the supervisor, has deep misgivings about the boss's new proposal, but his fear keeps him from speaking up. Dangaia and Sieya misread Kani's silence as support and decide not to express their concerns. Before long, others simply accept the proposal on the basis of the support it has been given.

Usually, the more complex an issue, the more likely groupthink can take over; people are less likely to disagree when they don't have all the facts. Groupthink is also a high risk when membership in the group is valued.

Groupthink and Unethical Behavior

What guides the behavior of managers and employees as they cope with ethical dilemmas? What results in unethical behavior by some groups in organizations? One model suggests that individuals' (and groups') standards of right and wrong are not the sole determinant of their decisions.[40] Instead, these beliefs interact with other individual characteristics (such as locus of control) and situational forces (such as an organization's rewards and punishments and its culture). All of these factors shape individual and group decisions and behaviors that result from them. The model shows how people can choose to engage in acts they consider unethical when the culture of an organization and its prevailing reward structure overwhelm personal belief systems.

Organizational culture is a key component when looking at ethical behavior. A closer look at the work done on "groupthink"[41] may help explain why organizations develop cultures in which individuals and groups knowingly commit unethical acts or ignore them even though they believe the activities to be wrong. The presence or absence of ethical behavior in organizational members' actions is both influenced by the prevailing culture (ethical climate) and, in turn, partially determines the culture's view of ethical issues. The organization culture may promote the assumption of responsibility for actions taken by individuals and groups, thereby increasing the probability that both will behave in an ethical manner. Alternatively, the culture may diffuse responsibility for the consequences of unethical behavior, thereby making such behavior more likely. In addition, there is the increased potential for groupthink, a precursor or result of organizational counternorms and unethical behavior.

Our definition of groupthink introduced earlier is based on the work of Irving Janis,[42] who defines groupthink as "a mode of thinking that people engage in when they are deeply involved in a cohesive in-group, when the members' striving for unanimity override their motivation to realistically appraise alternative courses of action." Groupthink is viewed as a dysfunctional process by Janis, who further describes it "as a deterioration of mental efficiency, reality testing, and moral judgment" resulting in pressures within a group. During groupthink small groups develop shared illusions and related norms that interfere with critical thinking and reality testing. For our purposes, groupthink occurs when a group places a higher priority on organizational counternorms that lead to organizational benefits, thus encouraging and supporting unethical behavior. In addition, these counternorms are shaped and maintained by key organizational actors and the organization's reward system.

A group suffering from groupthink shows recognizable symptoms. Table 5.1 presents these symptoms.[43] Evidence of most of these symptoms appear in the unedited transcripts of the deliberations of the people involved in the Watergate cover-up [44]and records on discrimination violations, horizontal or vertical price-fixing, and intentional securities fraud.

TABLE 5.1   Symptoms of Groupthink

- *Illusions of invulnerability*. Group members feel they are above criticism. This symptom leads to excessive optimism.
- *Illusions of group morality*. Group members feel they are moral in their actions and therefore above reproach. This symptom leads the group to ignore the ethical implications of their decisions.
- *Illusions of unanimity*. Group members believe there is unanimous agreement on the decisions. Silence is misconstrued as consent.
- *Rationalization*. Group members concoct explanations for their decisions to make them appear rational and correct. The results are that other alternatives are not considered, and there is an unwillingness to reconsider the group's assumptions.
- *Stereotyping the enemy*. Competitors are stereotyped as evil or stupid. This leads the group to underestimate its opposition.
- *Self-censorship*. Members do not express their doubts or concerns about the course of action. This prevents critical analysis of the decisions.
- *Peer pressure*. Any members who express doubts or concerns are pressured by other group members, who question their loyalty.
- *Mindguards*. Some members take it upon themselves to protect the group from negative feedback. Group members are thus shielded from information that might lead them to question their actions.

The flaws in the groupthink decision-making process often result in several kinds of ethical decision-making defects and outcome variables.[45] The ethical decision-making defects are:

1. Few ethical alternatives perceived
2. No reexamination of preferred unethical alternative
3. No reexamination of rejected ethical alternatives
4. Rejection of dissenting opinions
5. Selective bias of new information
6. Win at all costs

The outcome variables are:

1. Unethical decisions
2. Lower quality decisions

Groupthink occurs in organizations that knowingly commit unethical acts when the group is cohesive, when a leader promotes solutions or ideas even if they are unethical, and when the group has no internal rules or control mechanisms to continually prescribe ethical behavior.

Groupthink can occur in decision making within almost any organization, as may have been the case at Beech-Nut, E. F. Hutton, Salomon Brothers, and more recently at Enron. The experiences provide examples of how even the most reputable of companies can suffer from an ethical breakdown through groupthink and subsequent poor judgment. Executives at Beech-Nut, E. F. Hutton, Salomon Brothers, and Enron showed group characteristics found in groupthink experiences; for example, they exhibited excessive or blind loyalty, a bottom-line mentality, arrogance and overconfidence, and a promotion of unethical solutions by its leaders. In addition, each of these organizations also showed clear symptoms of groupthink, decision-making defects, and outcome variables discussed earlier. In each organization individuals were willing to take the approach of "let's all close our eyes to this problem."

In a sense, individuals and groups in organizations commit unethical acts because of an overabundance of characteristics that don't allow them to operate ethically in a large, free-wheeling organization. The values of organization members in the organizations are important. That is, groupthink and the ensuing unethical behavior may be precipitated by arrogance. Arrogance is the illegitimate child of confidence and pride found in groups experiencing groupthink. Arrogance is the idea that not only can you never make a mistake, but no one else can ever be right.

In some organizations arrogance is an insurmountable roadblock to ethical behavior. The flipside of arrogance is the ability to shine, to star, while working within the limits of ethical policies and guidelines. Another reason why groupthink may occur in some organizations is that they lack the value of ethical commitment, that is, a willingness to commit to a goal that's bigger than they are—to keep acting ethically, even when there is a threat of failure, until they finally come up with ethical business decisions.

Another reason unethical acts are committed in some organizations has to do with another human value, loyalty. It's something valued in all organizations. No one wants to work with anyone who has no concern for anyone or anything else. Loyalty counts in organizations; however, it should not be an unwillingness to question the unethical behavior of a group or organization. Groupthink occurs when arrogance, overcommitment, and loyalty help a group to shine above the ethical interests of an organization.

When groupthink occurs, organizations are more likely to strive for unanimity, ignore the voices of dissenters and conscience, and make decisions that result in unethical behavior. But by ignoring voices of caution and conscience and working with a bottom-line mentality for short-term profit, the organizations end up severely damaging their reputation. The likelihood of unethical behavior increases when organizations fail to promote positive and ethical cultures and reduce the probability of groupthink by programming conflict into decisions.

The symptoms of groupthink thrive in the sort of climate outlined in the following critique of corporate directors in the United States, which is quite characteristic of Enron's board of directors before the company's fall:

> Many directors simply don't rock the boat. "No one likes to be the skunk at the garden party," says (management consultant) Victor Palmieri. . . . "One does not make friends and influence people in the boardroom or elsewhere by raising hard questions that create embarrassment or discomfort for management."[46]

Quite often groupthink is recognized only after a group has made a disastrous decision. When this occurs, the members are apt to ask, "How could we have been so blind? Why didn't anyone call attention to our errors?" Unfortunately, at the time the group was making its decision(s), it is unlikely that any criticism or questioning of its actions would have been given serious consideration.

Stress

Stress on the job has been found to be a major factor influencing unethical behavior.[47] Role stress is strain, conflict, or disruptive result of a lack of agreement on certain job-related activities. The role that an individual plays within a business, including the various tasks that have the potential to create conflict, may have a direct bearing on ethical decision-making behavior. Some tasks require a decision maker to make many more tradeoffs and to face many more ethical dilemmas than others. Salespeople, for example, are often confronted by customers who state or imply that they will purchase a product if given extra personal incentives that may be against company policy—that is, a bribe. Accountants who are working on the audit of a company may be called aside and asked not to report information in a way that might disclose discrepancies. A human resources manager may discriminate against a minority. Since there is little doubt that ethical decision-making is stressful for decision makers who face conflict, the tendency is for role-stress situations to increase the likelihood of unethical behavior.[48]

So, why does unethical behavior occur? As you might imagine, no one factor accounts for all the unethical things that people do. Rather, a wide variety of forces encourage ethically questionable behavior. Table 5.2 summarizes some of these factors.

A number of internal danger signs that commonly put any organization at ethical risk are worth noting.[49] The signs can be used as a quick way to assess the extent to which unethical behavior is likely to occur in an organization:

TABLE 5.2   Ethically Questionable Business Practices: Why Do They Occur?

REASON	COMMENT
Society places a high value on economic success.	People adopting a "bottom-line" mentality strive for financial success at any cost.
Some corporate mission statements emphasize profit as the sole objective.	In organizations cultures develop that encourage people to do whatever is necessary to be profitable.
Intense competition occurs between people, groups/teams, departments, or companies.	In the face of competition, people may lose sight of any goal other than winning, such as behaving unethically.
Management is concerned with "the letter of the law" rather than with "the spirit of the law."	Generally, laws dictate only what is permissible—not what is morally appropriate. As such, laws represent the minimum acceptable standards that people should follow.
Corporate policies regarding ethical behavior are ambiguous.	Many codes of ethics are vague and provide little guidance regarding appropriate and inappropriate behavior.
Inadequate controls allow people to get away with behaving unethically.	Lax accounting systems and the absence of security procedures make behaving unethically all too easy for some people.
Business leaders fail to comprehend the public's ethical concerns.	Some people forget the public at large is increasingly intolerant of unethical behavior by business leaders.

1. The organization normally emphasizes short-term revenues (bottom-line mentality) above long-term considerations.
2. The organization routinely ignores or violates internal or professional codes of ethics.
3. The organization tends to look for simple solutions to ethical problems and is satisfied with quick fixes.
4. The organization encourages ethical shortcuts because it is unwilling to take an ethical stand when there is a financial cost to a decision.
5. The organization ignores the consequences of the implicit messages sent by policy decisions that either directly or indirectly discourage ethical behavior.

6. The organization fails to see just how important the organizational culture is in shaping the values that determine how individuals will react to ethical dilemmas.
7. The organization fails to see that ethical analysis goes beyond mere compliance with the law, as it usually sends ethical problems to the legal department.
8. The organization focuses exclusively on the mileage to be gained by good media coverage, since it views ethics solely as a public relations tool to enhance its image.
9. The organization treats its employees differently than its customers, which reflects an arrogance that creates distrust and hostility within the organization.
10. The organization lacks standardization in its performance-appraisal and promotion practices, as merit is replaced by political influence, favoritism, and cronyism.
11. The organization has no clear procedures or policies for handling ethical problems, leaving employees with no guidelines to use as a reference.
12. The organization provides no mechanisms for internal whistleblowing in which potential problems can be brought to the attention of upper management and other interested parties
13. The organization lacks clear lines of communication within the organization, which allows problems to get out of hand before most managers realize there is a problem.
14. The organization attempts to cover up improprieties without realizing this strategy usually backfires.
15. The organization is only sensitive to the needs and demands of the shareholders and ignores other stakeholders.
16. The organization encourages employees to leave their personal ethical values at the office door as a sharp demarcation is drawn between personal values and work values.

CONCLUSION

Unethical acts continue to occur, as is evidenced by the recall of Firestone tires and the 103 deaths that forced it and by the Enron debacle. Is everyone who makes an unethical decision an unethical person, or are there organizational climates and counternorms that contribute to their actions? It is such questions that organizational leaders must continually answer for themselves if they are to better understand why unethical behavior occurs in organizations.

By understanding the dynamics of why unethical behavior occurs in organizations we are in a better position to create a more ethical environment or culture. Individual differences can help us understand why unethical behavior occurs in organizations. The best way to use the knowledge of individual differences may be to recognize that they help explain why ethical behavior differs among individuals and to focus organizational efforts on creating a work situation that supports ethical behavior.

Organizational factors influence ethical behavior. For example, the type of climate plays a major role in whether or not the organization develops counternorms, reward systems, and groupthink that can all result in unethical employee behavior. There is a strong relationship between the kind of culture, ethical climate, and employee performance that organizations and their leaders develop. Some organizations support financial success as the only value to be considered. Such an attitude will promote a bottom-line mentality and an unrealistic belief that everything boils down to a monetary game.

NOTES

1. Thomas M. Jones, "Ethical Decision Making by Individuals in Organizations: An Issue Contingency Model," *Academy of Management Review* 16, no. 2 (1991), 366–95.

2. D. J. Brass, K. D. Butterfield, and B. C. Skaggs, "Relationships and Unethical Behavior: A Social Network Perspective," *Academy of Management Review* 23, no. 1 (1998), 14–33.

3. J.O. Cherrington and D. J. Cherrington, "A Menu of Moral Issues: One Week in the Life of the Wall Street Journal," *Journal of Business Ethics* 11, (1992), 255–65.

4. Kenneth Andrews, "Ethics in Practice," *Harvard Business Review* (September–October 1989), 99–104.

5. Donna L. Nelson and James C. Quick, *Organizational Behavior: Foundations, Realities, and Challenges*, 4th ed. (Mason, O.: South-Western, 2003); Ronald R. Sims and Johannes Brinkmann, Leaders as Moral Role Models: The Case of John Gutfreund at Salomon Brothers," *Journal of Business Ethics* 35 (2002), 327–39; O. C. Ferrell, J. Fraedrich, and L. Ferrell, *Business Ethics: Ethical Decision Making and Cases* (Boston: Houghton Mifflin, 2000); J. W. Weiss, *Business Ethics: A Stakeholder and Issues Management Approach*, 3rd ed. (Mason, O.: South-Western, 2003).

6. J. B. Rotter, "Generalized Expectancies for Internal versus External Control of Reinforcement," *Psychological Monographs*, 80 (1966): 1–28.

7. H. M. Lefcourt, *Locus of Control: Current Trends in Theory and Research*, 2nd ed. (Hillsdale, N.J.: Erlbaum, 1982).

8. Niccolò Machiavelli, *The Prince*, trans. George Bull (Middlesex, England: Penguin Books, 1961).

9. R. Christie and F. L. Geis, *Studies in Machiavellianism* (New York: Academic Press, 1970).

10. R. A. Giacalone and S. B. Knouse, "Justifying Wrongful Employee Behavior: The Role of Personality in Organizational Sabotage," *Journal of Business Ethics* 9 (1990), 55–61; S. B. Knouse and R. A. Giacalone, "Ethical Decision-Making in Business: Behavioral Issues and Concerns," *Journal of Business Ethics* 11 (1992), 369–77.

11. L. Kohlberg, *The Psychology of Moral Development: The Nature and Validity of Moral Stages*, 2 vols. (New York: Harper & Row, 1984); L. Kohlberg, *Essays on Moral Development*. Vol. 2, *The Psychology of Moral Development: The Nature and Validity of Moral Stages* (New York: Harper & Row, 1969).

12. A. Colby, "Evolution of Moral Development Theory," in W. Damon (ed.), *Moral Development* (San Francisco: Jossey-Bass, 1978), 21–36.

13. Linda Klebe Trevino, "Ethical Decision Making in Organizations: A Person-Situation Interactionist Model, *Academy of Management Review* 11, no. 3 (1986), 601–17.

14. Ronald R. Sims and Johannes Brinkmann, "Leaders as Moral Role Models: The Case of John Gutfreund at Salomon Brothers," *Journal of Business Ethics* 35, (2002), 327–39.

15. Carol Gilligan, *In a Different Voice: Psychological Theory and Women's Development* (Cambridge, Mass: Harvard University Press, 1982).

16. A. Colby and L. Kohlberg, *The Measurement of Moral Judgment* Vol. 1 (New York: Cambridge University Press, 1987).

17. Gilligan, *In a Different Voice*.

18. S. Jaffe and J. S. Hyde, "Gender Differences in Moral Orientation: A Meta-Analysis," *Psychological Bulletin* 126 (2000), 703–26.

19. G. R. Franke, D. F. Crown, and D. F. Spake, "Gender Differences in Ethical Perceptions of Business Practices: A Social Role Theory Perspective," *Journal of Applied Psychology* 82 (1997), 920–34.

20. Trevino, "Ethical Decision Making." 613.

21. B. H. Frey, "The Impact of Moral Intensity on Decision Making in a Business Context," *Journal of Business Ethics* 26 (2000): 181–95; J. M. Dukerich, M. J. Waller, E. George, and G. P. Huber, "Moral Intensity and Managerial Problem Solving," *Journal of Business Ethics* 24, 29–38.

22. J. R. Sparks and S. D. Hunt, "Marketing Researcher Ethical Sensitivity: Conceptualization, Measurement, and Exploratory Investigation," *Journal of Marketing* 62, (1998), 92–109.

23. B. Stoneman and K. K. Holliday, "Pressure Cooker," *Banking Strategies* (January-February, 2001), 13; D. McDougall and B. Orsini, "Fraudbusting Ethics," *CMA Management* 73 (1999), 18–21.

24. P. Haapaniemi and W. R. Hill, "Not Just for the Big Guys!" *Chief Executive* (September 1998), 62–73.

25. M. Milliet-Einbinder, "Writing Off Tax Deductibility," *OECD Observer* (April 2000), 38–40; F. Rotherham, "NZ Moves to Curb Corruption by Ending Tax Deductible Bribes," *Independent Business Weekly* (June 30, 1999), 27.

26. T. H. Stevenson and C. D. Bodkin, "A Cross- National Comparison of University Students' Perceptions Regarding Ethics and Acceptability of Sales Practices," *Journal of Business Ethics* 17 (1998), 45–55; T. Jackson and M. C. Artola, "Ethical Beliefs and Management Behavior: A Cross-Cultural Comparison," *Journal of Business Ethics* 16 (1997), 1163–73.

27. P. F. Buller, J. J. Kohls and K. S. Anderson, "A Model for Addressing Cross-Cultural Ethical Conflicts," *Business and Society* 36 (1997), 169–193.

28. L. Smircich, "Concepts of Culture and Organizational Analysis," *Administrative Science Quarterly* 28 (1983): 339–58; U. Weiner and Y. Vardi, "Relationships between Organizational Culture and Individual Motivation: A Conceptual Integration," *Psychological Reports* 67 (1990), 295–306.

29. M. R. Louis, "Surprise and Sense Making: What Newcomers Experience in Entering Unfamiliar Organizational Settings," *Adminstrative Science Quarterly* 25 (1980), 209–64.

30. R. T. DeGeorge, *Business Ethics*, 3rd ed. (New York: Macmillan Publishing Company, 1990).

31. M. S. Baucus and J. P. Near, "Can Illegal Corporate Behavior Be Predicted? An Event History Analysis," *Academy of Management Journal* 34, no. 1 (1991), 9–36.

32. Ibid.; G. Geis, "The Heavy Electrical Equipment Antitrust Case of 1961, in G. Geis and R. Meier, (eds.) *White-Collar Crime: Offenses in Business, Politics, and the Profession* (New York: Free Press, 1977), 117–32.

33. S. Zadek et al. (eds.), *Building Corporate Accountability: Emerging Practices in Social and Ethical Accounting, Auditing and Reporting* (London: Earthscan, 1997).

34. Ronald R. Sims and Johannes Brinkmann, "Leaders as Moral Role Models: The Case of John Gutfreund at Salomon Brothers," *Journal of Business Ethics* 35 (2002), 327–39.

35. E. Jansen and M. A. Glinow, "Ethical Ambivalence and Organizational Reward Systems," *Academy of Management* 10, no. 4 (1985), 814–22.

36. S. Bok, *Lying: Moral Choice in Public and Private Life* (Vintage Books, New York, 1979); S. Bok, *Secrets: On the Ethics of Commitment and Revelation* (Vintage Books, New York, 1983).

37. K. Vandevier, "The Aircraft Brake Scandal: A Cautionary Tale in Which the Moral Is Unpleasant," in A. G. Athos and J. J. Babarro (eds.), *Interpersonal Behavior: Communication and Understanding Relationships* (Englewood Cliffs, N.J.: Prentice-Hall, 1978), 529–40.

38. S. W. Gellerman, "Why "Good" Managers Make Bad Ethical Choices," *Harvard Business Review* (July–August 1986), 85–90.

39. Baucus and Near, "Illegal Corporate Behavior," 12.

40. Trevino, "Ethical Decision Making." 603.

41. I. L. Janis, *Victims of Groupthink* (Boston: Houghton-Mifflin, 1972).

42. Ibid.

43. Ibid.

44. D. D. Van Fleet, *Behavior in Organizations* (Dallas: Houghton Mifflin, 1991).

45. G. Moorehead, "Groupthink: Hypothesis in Need of Testing," *Group and Organization Studies* 7, no. 4 (1982), 429–44.

46. L. Baum, "The Job Nobody Wants," *Business Week* (September 8, 1986), 60.

47. M. H. Cunningham and O. C. Ferrell, "Ethical Decision-Making Behavior in Marketing Research Organizations," working paper, School of Business, Queen's University, Kingston, Ontario, 1999.

48. O. C. Ferrell, J. Fraedrich, and L. Ferrell, *Business Ethics: Ethical Decision Making and Cases* (Boston: Houghton Mifflin, 2000).

49. R. A. Cooke, "Danger Signs of Unethical Behavior: How to Determine If Your Firm Is at Ethical Risk," *Journal of Business Ethics* 10 (1991), 249–53; R. R. Sims, "Linking Groupthink to Unethical Behavior in Organizations," *Journal of Business Ethics* 11, (1992), 651–62.

6

Unethical Behavior in Action: Beech-Nut, E. F. Hutton, and the Case of John Gutfreund at Salomon Brothers

INTRODUCTION

Unethical organizational practices are still embarrassingly commonplace. A variety of individual and organizational factors play a critical role in discouraging—or fostering—responsible behavior on the job. For example, the culture of an organization that often rewards behaviors that violate ethical standards is a source of unethical conduct. Further, organizations that place too much emphasis on managerial aggressiveness and corporate success at all cost, competitiveness, and profit are just as likely to stimulate unethical actions. Of course, probably nothing is more important to an ethical corporate atmosphere than the moral tone and example set by an organization's top leadership. Failure by top leaders to identify key organizational values, to convey those values by personal example, and to reinforce them by establishing appropriate organizational policies demonstrates a lack of ethical leadership that fosters an unethical organizational culture.

This and the next chapter take a closer look at unethical behavior in action. These case examples will examine how organizational culture and a lack of ethical leadership led to unethical missteps at Beech-Nut, E. F. Hutton, and Salomon Brothers. After first offering some discussion of the relationship between leadership, organizational culture and ethics, this chapter will discuss the ethical missteps at Beech-Nut and E. F.

Hutton. Then the focus turns to how a lack of ethical leadership created a culture that led to the bond trading scandal at Salomon Brothers. Five primary mechanisms available to leaders for embedding and reinforcing aspects of culture will be used to systematically analyze Salomon Brothers' culture and John Gutfreund's leadership, which led to Salomon's illegal bidding at U.S. Treasury auctions.

LEADERSHIP, ORGANIZATIONAL CULTURE, AND ETHICS

Leadership is a critical component of the organization's culture because leaders can create, maintain, or change culture. Thus, leadership is important to establishing an ethicallyoriented culture. The idea that corporate leaders are responsible for organizational ethics is not a new one. In 1938, management theorist Chester I. Barnard described the executive's role in "creating morals for others" in his book *The Functions of the Executive*.[1] Barnard suggested that the function of developing organizational morals is a distinguishing characteristic of executive work going far beyond the moral challenges faced by individuals generally. Besides superior technical skills, a high capacity for responsibility, and a complex personal morality, this task requires moral creativity in defining an organization's code of ethics and instilling the fundamental attitudes that support it.

According to a report from the Business Roundtable, a group of senior executives from major American corporations, leadership is crucial to organizational ethics. "To achieve results, the Chief Executive Officer and those around the CEO need to be openly and strongly committed to ethical conduct, and give constant leadership in tending and renewing the values of the organization."[2] In surveys of practicing managers, honesty and competence emerge as the most important qualities identified as essential to good leadership.[3] This view was echoed by Vin Sarni, former CEO of PPG Industries, a large multinational firm, in a 1992 speech to Penn State business school students. Sarni said that the title CEO stands for Chief Ethics Officer, a statement that recognizes how important it is for the organization's leader to set the firm's ethical standards.[4]

If the organization's leaders seem to care only about the short-term bottom line, employees quickly get that message too. John G. Rangos, Sr., the founder of Chambers Development Co., a waste management firm, demanded bottom-line results. When executives reported to him in 1990 that profits would fall short of projections, he is quoted to have said, "Go find the rest of it." And so they did, until an outside audit in 1992 found that the company had falsely reported strong profits in every year since 1985, although it was losing money all the time. Former employees say that, in the pursuit of growth, manipulated numbers were tolerated, or perhaps even encouraged. One former employee who found discrepancies in 1988 was told, "this is how the game is played."[5]

Leaders represent significant others in the organizational lives of employees, with significant power qua behavior role models or simply power, in the meaning of being able to force others to carry out one's own will. Leaders' example and decisions affect not only the employees who report to them, but also the stockholders, suppliers, customers, the community, the country, and even the world. Considerations of the ethical component in day-to-day decisions will set the tone for others who interact with the company. Thus, the image of the business leader will affect how others choose to deal with the company and will have long-term effects, as all managers and employees look to the highest level for their cues as to what is acceptable. Top executives must live up to the ethical standards they are espousing and suggest ethical behaviors in others. This book this position assumes that leadership can make a difference in creating an ethical or unethical organizational culture.

Work on ethical and unethical charismatic leaders also highlights the importance of the leader in the ethics equation. More specifically, charismatic leaders can be very effective leaders, yet they may vary in their ethical standards. Such differences determine the extent to which an organization builds an ethically oriented culture, the types of values followers will be exposed to, and the role models with whom employees will have their most direct personal contact.[6]

The following is an example of bad ethical leadership encountered in a small company where a long-time employee was identified as having embezzled about $20,000 over a fifteen-year period.[7] When the employee was approached and questioned as to why she had done this, she explained that she thought it was all right because the president had led her to believe it was. She further explained that any time during the fall, when the leaves had fallen in his yard and he needed them raked, he would simply get company personnel to do it. When the president needed cash, he would take it out of the company's petty cash box or get the key to the soft drink machine and raid its coin box. When he needed stamps to mail his personal Christmas cards, he would take them out of the company stamp box. The woman's perception was that it was all right for her to take the money because the president did it frequently.

Organizational Culture as Ethical Climate

One way to pull together the contributions about how organizational culture is shaped and reinforced by leadership style is to understand organizational culture as ethical climate. One could also ask to what degree the moral maturity of organizational cultures or climates, dominating reference group types, or dominating ethics types are interdependent or interacting with leadership styles. One could also ask if unethical leadership styles foster an unethical climate or vice versa, if the effect of unethical leadership is reinforced or neutralized by the organization's ethical climate.

Ethical dilemmas will often result in unethical behavior if an organization's leadership furthers an immature, unclear, or negative ethical climate. Such unethical behavior is, of course, not only furthered by an unethical climate, but also reproduces such an ethical climate, in a system feedback fashion, being contagious and self-reinforcing (or perhaps provoking internal or external counterreactions). In such instances, an organization's culture predisposes its members to behave unethically.

Beech-Nut

The admission by Beech-Nut, the second largest baby-food producer in the United States at the time, that it had sold millions of jars of "phony" apple juice shocked many company employees as well as industry executives. Since 1891, the concepts of purity, high quality, and natural ingredients had served as the foundation of its corporate culture and had been a consistent marketing theme. What had caused Beech-Nut to stray from its heritage and reputation?

Perhaps some portion of motive can be inferred from a report President Neils Hoyvald wrote to Nestle, the company that had acquired Beech-Nut in the midst of his cover-up. "It is our feeling that we can report safely now that the apple juice recall has been completed. If the recall had been effectuated in early June [when the FDA had first ordered it], over 700,000 cases in inventory would have been affected. . . . Due to our many delays, we were only faced with having to destroy 20,000 cases."[8]

Beginning in 1977, the company began buying a chemical concoction, made up mostly of sugar and water, and labeling it "apple juice." Sales of that product brought Beech-Nut an estimated $60 million between 1977 and 1982 while reducing material costs about $250,000 annually.

When various investigators tried to do something about it, the company stonewalled. Among other things, they shipped the bogus juice out of a plant in New York to Puerto Rico, to put it beyond the jurisdiction of federal investigators, and they even offered the juice as a giveaway to reduce their stocks after they were finally forced to discontinue selling it.

In the end, the company pleaded guilty to 215 counts of introducing adulterated food into commerce and violating the Federal Food, Drug and Cosmetic Act. The FDA fined Beech-Nut $2 million. In addition, Beech-Nut's president Neils Hoyvald and its vice president of operations John Lavery were found guilty of similar charges. Again, why did they do it?

The answer to this question is complex. However, underlying the company's ethical failure were strong financial pressures. Beech-Nut was losing money, and the use of the cheap, adulterated concentrate saved millions of dollars. Beech-Nut employees seemed to use two arguments to justify their actions: They believed that many other companies were selling fake juice, and they were convinced that their adulterated juice was perfectly safe to consume. In addition, some employees took refuge in the fact that no conclusive test existed to determine natural from artificial ingredients. With regard to this latter point, Beech-Nut seems to have shifted the burden of proof around. Other juicemakers had been known to cut off suppliers if the supplier could not demonstrate that their product was genuine. At Beech-Nut, senior management apparently told R&D that *they* would have to prove that an inexpensive supplier's product was adulterated before the company would switch to another supplier. Beech-Nut compounded its problems when government investigations began by stonewalling rather than cooperating, apparently in order to gain time to unload a $3.5 million inventory of tainted apple juice products. Thus, although at first Beech-Nut appeared to have been the innocent victim of unscrupulous suppliers, the company by its later actions changed a civil matter into criminal charges.

E. F. Hutton

In 1985, the E. F. Hutton Group Inc., one of the nation's largest brokerage firms, pleaded guilty to 2,000 counts of wire and mail fraud, paid a fine of almost $3 million, and put over $9 million into funds to pay back defrauded banks and investors. The court case focused the nation's attention on banks' overdraft policies, but it also provided an example of how leadership and a weak ethical culture can cause trouble and an eventual fall for even the mightiest institutions.

Hutton's crime involved a form of check kiting. A money manager at a Hutton branch office would write a check on an account in bank A for more money than Hutton had in that account. Because of the time lag in the check-collection system, these overdrafts sometimes went undetected, and Hutton could deposit funds to cover the overdraft in bank A's account on the following day. Even if the bank noticed the overdraft, it was unlikely to complain, because Hutton was such an important customer and because certain kinds of overdrafts are fairly routine.

In any case, the Hutton manager would deposit the check from bank A into an account in bank B, where the money would start earning interest immediately. In effect, the scheme allowed Hutton to earn a day's interest on bank A's account without having to pay anything for it. A day's interest may not sound like much, but Hutton was getting as much as $250 million in free loans every day, and a day's interest on such a sum is substantial.

Eventually, complaints from banks arrived at the desk of the vice president and money manager. It was not long before the media picked up the explanation. No contingency plan was in place. As the full tale unfolded, Hutton's senior executives debated whether the problem was internal or external. Defensive doubting gave way to aggressive anger. Had they actually done something drastically wrong or only pushed a common but dubious practice too far?

Hutton top management hired former attorney general Griffin Bell, Jr., to investigate their overdraft practices. He discovered that branch managers received a percentage of any interest earned from the overdrafting. The accounting practice failed to distinguish between the interest earned from cash management and commissions earned from brokerage transactions. This minor discrepancy was enough to inspire a new and easy way to hit gross revenue targets. Because of the Hutton culture, officers and company personnel either failed to grasp the implications of their system or simply took liberties with what was becoming a clearly enunciated ethic.

Hutton concluded that the officers were not basically at fault and rationalized that they were just overzealous. They supported this view even though it was found that the Hutton culture evidently provided supervisory slippage at all three levels, from branch manager to executive money manager to the chief financial officer. They reasoned that their real ethical problem was external and not internal—that is, how they were perceived by clients. Thus, they decided against an in-house ethical cleanup program that could have created a tighter organization with articulated standards. Instead, they hired Bill Cosby, at a cost of more than $1 million, to recapture their reputation.

Comments from victims of the Hutton caper indicate that they were most offended at the arrogance of the executives who expected special favors. They treated their banking colleagues as slaves rather than equals. The Hutton money managers seemed unmindful or unaware of any possible cost or inconvenience to others. They were imperialistic. Little if any consideration was extended to clients. Hutton executives abused a fine reputation. They expected to be treated differently. The overdrafts were neither casual nor occasional, but planned. Hutton was distinguished by these motives and methods that led to the decision to commit unethical acts.

Excuses for Hutton's behavior are easy to find if one wants to. The increased competition among brokerage firms and signals from Washington provided impetus for "ethical innovation," to put it politely. Increased pressure on the financial bottom line always puts pressure on the quality of group decision making and the ethical bottom line. In a sense, one might say "that something's got to give." The mounting deficits in Washington along with its pro-business attitude gave birth to an anything-goes mentality. Couple that with the Hutton organizational culture in particular, and it's easy to understand the resulting check kiting.

E. F. Hutton misread public reaction and treated the check kiting as a public relations issue. Although they understood the importance of public perception, they failed to see that their problems were internal and a result of failed leadership and an organizational culture that allowed an unethical behavior to occur.

Salomon Brothers

"We're not talking about the failure to cross a *t* or to dot an *i* in this kind of case. It is not an adequate ethical standard to aspire to get through the day without being indicted." Richard Breeden, SEC Chairman on charges against Salomon.[9]

Wrongdoings by Salomon Brothers in the Treasury auction scandal in the early 1990s provides a more detailed look at unethical behavior in action. A chronology of how the Salomon Brothers fiasco unfolded follows:

December 1990. Salomon submits bids, in the names of customers who hadn't authorized them, at an $8.57 billion auction of four-year notes. The bids enable the firm to buy 46 percent of the securities, breaching Treasury rules that bar individual bidders from buying more than 35 percent at any single sale.

February 1991. Through unauthorized customer bids, Salomon buys 57 percent of securities sold at an auction of $9.04 billion of five-year Treasury notes.

February. As a "practical joke" against a Salomon employee, a managing director persuades an unidentified customer to submit a bogus bid for $1 billion at the $11.01 billion auction of thirty-year Treasury bonds. The plan goes awry, and the bid is actually submitted.

April. In a $9.06 billion auction of five-year notes, Salomon exceeds the bidding limit with a 35 percent bid for its own account, in addition to a $2.5 billion bid for a customer and the repurchase of $600 million of that bid at the auction price.

Late April. Paul Mozer, managing director in charge of government bond trading, informs Salomon Chairman John Gutfreund, President

Thomas Strauss, and Vice Chairman John Meriwether about the illegal bidding in February. No immediate action is taken.

May 22. In the Treasury's $12.26 billion auction of two-year notes, Salomon effectively buys at least 44 percent of the issue. The firm bids $2 billion for a customer and repurchases $500 million from the customer at the auction price, in addition to "inadvertently" failing to disclose its own position of $497 million. Government investigators allege that Salomon may have controlled as much as 85% percent of the issue. Dealers charge that Salomon forced up prices to squeeze its competitors.

June. The SEC and the Justice Department issue subpoenas to Salomon and certain clients.

July. Salomon reviews its government bond operations and launches "full" investigation.

August 9. Salomon first discloses that it violated bidding rules in December, February and May and suspends Mr. Moser, his top aide, Thomas Murphy, trader Christopher Fitzmaurice, and clerk Henry Epstein.

August 14. Salomon discloses that Gutfreund, Strauss, and Meriwether knew of the violations in April and releases details of additional violations.

August 16. Gutfreund and Strauss announce that they will resign at August 18 board meeting. Warren E. Buffett is named interim chairman.

August 18. The Treasury Department bars Salomon from participating in government securities auctions for customers' accounts, but allows the firm to continue bidding for its own accounts. Deryck C. Maughan, former head of Salomon's Tokyo operations, is named chief operating officer in charge of day-to-day operations. Salomon board accepts resignations of Gutfreund, Strauss, and Meriwether and fires Moser and Murphy.[10]

The scandal that in 1991 rocked Salomon Brothers, the investment banking division of Salomon, Inc., can be traced to its culture, which was directed by the controversial CEO John Gutfreund. Gutfreund's leadership style helped to mold a corporate culture that eventually resulted in unethical and illegal behavior by its members.

In his book *Liar's Poker*, Michael Lewis[11] provides a hilarious but partially confirming and troubling description of the corporate culture at Salomon Brothers under Gutfreund's leadership. Lewis served as a bond salesman and detailed his impressions as a trainee and salesman in London and New York. The culture described by Lewis is characterized by the macho swaggering of the successful salesman and traders. The trading floor was the site of idiotic feats of gluttony (for example, guacamole was ordered in five-gallon drums), practical jokes and horseplay (such as throwing telephones at trainees), and childish (except for the scale) bravado. The book's title refers to a legendary game of liar's poker (a sort of card game played by using serial numbers on dollar bills) in which the stakes were $1 million. The organization described in Lewis' book is not one in which examples from the top discouraged unethical behavior by lower-level employees. There are movies that describe such cultures, too—for example, Oliver Stone's *Wall Street* of 1987, with a focus on the master-apprentice relationship between Gekko (Michael Douglas) and Fox (Charlie Sheen).

Gutfreund's leadership led to a culture that was tailor-made for greedy and power-hungry employees whose commitment to ethical behavior was suspect. Five primary mechanisms (attention, reactions to crises, role modeling, allocation of rewards, and criteria for selection and dismissal) by which a leader can both embed and reinforce aspects of an organization's culture[12] will be used here to describe the culture shaped and reinforced at Salomon Brothers under John Gutfreund's leadership.

Culture is the basic assumptions and beliefs shared by members of a group or organization. These assumptions and beliefs involve the group's view of the world and their place in it, the nature of time and space, human nature, and human relationships. Culture impacts employees' or group members' behavior because one of its major functions is "to help us understand the environment and determine how to respond to it, thereby reducing anxiety, uncertainty, and confusion."[13] Therefore, an organization's culture dictates to its members how situations are to be handled and what their expected behavior will be. A strong leader who has been in power for a substantial length of time can mold an organization's culture—a strong or weak culture that can exercise good or bad influence depending on an organization's goals, policies, structures, and strategies. Indeed, that was what John Gutfreund was able to do at Salomon Brothers.

What Leaders Pay Attention To

Leaders in an organization communicate their priorities, values, and beliefs through the themes that consistently emerge from what they focus on. These themes are reflected in what they notice, comment on, measure, and control (what is criticized, praised, or asked about).

If leaders are consistent in what they pay attention to, measure, and control, employees receive clear signals about what is important in the organization. If, however, leaders are inconsistent, employees spend a lot of time trying to decipher and find meaning in the inconsistent signals. If the organization's leaders seem to care only about short-term financial results, employees quickly get that message and act accordingly.[14]

Gutfreund's tenure at Salomon was marked by an absolute attention to a short-term business focus and what was happening that day or that week. Through this short-term perspective, Gutfreund forced his employees to produce profits immediately. Dedication to short-term revenues above long-term considerations creates a climate where unethical behavior thrives. The consequences of pushing ethical and legal boundaries are not immediately realized, and a short-term profit maximizer often ignores any possible long-term ramifications of his actions. This "bottom-line mentality" thinking supports the company goal of financial success as the only value to be considered. It promotes short-term solutions that are immediately financially sound, despite the fact that they cause problems for others within the organization or the organization as a whole. It promotes an unrealistic belief that everything boils down to a monetary game. As such, rules of morality are merely impediments along the way to bottom-line financial success.

There is no evidence that Gutfreund ever created a long-term strategy for Salomon's future. Decision making had been instantaneous for John Gutfreund as a trader, and he may have continued to agonize over long-term or complex management problems as CEO. He always had an executive committee to help make the crucial decisions of the firm. This should not, however, be confused with delegation of power. No one was allowed to forget who was in charge of the destiny of Salomon. Most of the daily decisions were made quickly, "on the fly," by two or three members of the executive committee, while they were on the floor. When a more difficult decision needed to be made, Gutfreund's preferred style was "to virtually overwhelm a problem with ideas and suggestions until they [the committee] find a solution."[15] One could surmise that Gutfreund was never comfortable making long-range or personnel-related decisions without group discussion and brainstorming.

A short-term mindset is often, but not necessarily unethical as such (nor is a long-term mindset necessarily ethical). The trading business seems to be a good illustration of how a short-term mindset can interact with unethicalness, in particular during Gutfreund's tenure at Salomon. When an organization's entire focus is on next quarter's profits, its future is in jeopardy. In these situations, paying attention to the most recent bottom-line profits often means disregarding long-term implications of employees' actions. Additionally, dedication to short-term profits usually means those profits will be gained at any cost, including breaking ethical standards or the law.

How Leaders React to Crises

A crisis situation allows followers to see what is valued by the leader, because its emotionality brings these values to the surface. The way leaders deal with crises communicates a powerful message about culture. Emotions are heightened during a crisis, and learning is intense.

An example of Gutfreund's crisis management strategy can be seen in the next paragraph in his reaction to the knowledge that someone at his firm had placed bids on Treasury bills in excess of the legal maximums. Salomon, Inc., released information in August 1991 that the firm had overextended themselves in several U.S. Treasury bill auctions. Securities laws limit the percentage of any one auction to 35 for each dealer, so that no one can secure the market and influence the pivotal T-bill interest rate. This auction is at the cornerstone of the American economy and the rest of the capital markets; as well, all other interest rates are guided by it. Many scandals rocked Wall Street in the late 1980s and early 1990s, but none touched so close to the foundation of the American financial system. By the end of the disclosures, it had been revealed that Salomon owned up to 94 percent of one Treasury auction and was well over the allowed limit in several other instances.

Gutfreund's reaction to unethical and illegal behavior in his organization was to try to cover it up. When the initial cover-up failed, he then lied and attempted to save his position as CEO. It is little wonder that employees of Salomon were motivated to commit unethical acts and break the law when they were shown the way by their leader. His management of crises indicated that ethical wrongdoing was to be hidden from the authorities at any cost. There is no evidence that Gutfreund took any actions against the transgressors. Gutfreund's inaction was doubly disturbing because the actions that led to the bond trading scandal violated the unwritten code of ethics among traders, "my word is my bond," a code so strong it was given the weight of a legal contract.[16] His inaction showed that Salomon was not committed to any sort of ethical or legal standard. Thus, resulting in the crisis situation Warren Buffett was confronted with when he temporarily took over Salomon Brothers following Gutfreund's tenure. (Chapter 9 provides a more detailed discussion of Buffett's tenure at Salomon Brothers.)

How Leaders Behave (Role Modeling)

A leader communicates strong messages to his employees about his values through his own actions. Through role modeling, teaching, and coaching, leaders reinforce the values that support the organizational culture. Employees often emulate leaders' behavior and look to the leaders for cues to appropriate behavior. Many companies are encouraging employees to be more entrepreneurial, that is, to take more initiative and be more innovative in their jobs. The Scientific Foundation reports a study that showed that managers who want to change the organization's culture to a more entrepreneurial one must "walk the talk"; in other words, they must demonstrate entrepreneurial behaviors themselves.[17] This is the case with any cultural value. Employees observe the behavior of leaders to find out what is valued in the organization.

Kent Druyvesteyn, former staff vice president, ethics, General Dynamics Corporation, made a similar point about leaders as ethical role models.

> People in leadership need to . . . set the tone by example of their own conduct. We could have had all the workshops in the world. We could have even had Jesus and Moses and Mohamed and Buddha come and speak at our workshops. But, if after all of that, someone in a leadership position then behaved in a way which was contrary to the standards, that instance of misconduct by a person in a leadership position would teach more than all the experts in the world.[18]

Clearly, the development of an ethical corporate culture depends on the tone set at the top.

Employees who wished to emulate Gutfreund's rise to power at Salomon saw that his hard work and aggression had paved the road to his success. Although aggressiveness is certainly desirable in the fast-paced investment banking community, Gutfreund's rise to power included the betrayal of his mentor, Salomon's owner, Billy Salomon, to further his career. He once again used "below-the-board" deals, which signaled that this type of maneuvering would be tolerated, and perhaps encouraged, at Salomon. To be like John Gutfreund, one could not hold to a strong sense of personal ethics. When leaders like Gutfreund make "special deals" it tells the whole organization that ethical behavior is not important.

In an unbelievable act of betrayal, John Gutfreund sold Billy Salomon's company to Philip Brothers (Phibro) in 1982 without even discussing it with the man whose name still appeared on the door. Employees looking on were being told that any one could be double-crossed at Salomon, even top managers. Gutfreund had decided, without consulting his mentor, that the changes in the investment banking industry necessitated that Salomon build up its capital base in order to remain competitive. Phibro was a giant commodities trading firm, and it bought the company for $554 million, which many considered to be well below what could have been obtained for the firm. Billy Salomon was understandably bitter and humiliated by the sale of his own company without his knowledge. Although he made just under $10 million on the sale (which pales in comparison to the $32 million made by Gutfreund), he did not even receive a premium for his shares. A case could be made that Gutfreund's betrayal of Billy Salomon to further his own ambition indicated that similar behavior would be tolerated, even rewarded, at Salomon.

Gutfreund's leadership style and the culture that he had shaped and reinforced were doomed to turn on him one day. Those who wanted to model themselves after Gutfreund saw that any opportunity for power should be seized and capitalized upon for personal gain. Adherence to a code of ethics would only be a deterrent if you wanted to get ahead at Salomon. Those who were like Gutfreund did not hesitate to twist a situation to their advantage, regardless of the ethical consequences.

How Leaders Allocate Rewards

The behavior displayed by people the leader decides to reward with pay increases or promotions signals to others what is necessary to succeed in an organization. Using rewards and discipline effectively may be the most powerful way for leaders to send signals about desirable and undesirable conduct. To ensure that values are accepted, leaders should reward behavior that is consistent with the values. Some companies, for example, may claim that they use a pay-for-performance system that distributes rewards on the basis of performance. When the time comes for raises, however, the increases are awarded according to length of service with the company. Imagine the feeling of a high-performing newcomer who has heard leaders espouse the value of rewarding individual performance and then receives only a tiny raise.

The reward system created by a leader indicates what is prized and expected in the organization. This view is in line with a basic management doctrine, namely: You get what you measure and pay for.[19] When an instance of ethical achievement occurs—for instance, when someone acts with integrity and honor—the organization's leaders must reward it. Such an effort sends as clear a message to the rest of the organization as when an organization rewards an employee who acts unethically. To stimulate competition and innovation, Salomon always paid extremely high bonuses. Vice Chairman Lewis Ranieri, for one, was paid $2.5 million a year in each of the golden years between 1982 and 1986. By 1990, 106 employees each took home $1 million or more. At $1.6 billion in 1992, compensation remained the heftiest expense on Salomon's books. Although consistent with the bank's trading outlook, these bonuses only tied pay to the bank's short-term performance, encouraging staffers to achieve quick results but discouraging them from appreciating how their actions might affect the bank's long-run ethical capital.

In early 1990, John Gutfreund made a secret deal with one of the bank's most profitable fiefdoms, risk arbitrage, to let them retain 15 percent of the group's profits that year. To everyone's surprise, the group's performance improved dramatically. By the year's end, that meant outsized bonuses for the group's top traders. One bond trader pocketed a cool bonus of $23 million, exceeding all prior compensation rules that unofficially denied paying commission. Not surprisingly, news of the extraordinary bonuses of the arbitrage group angered many managers within other areas of Salomon and infuriated traders like Paul Mozer, doubtless fueling his fraudulent bidding activity.

All of this occurred because Gutfreund couldn't see his way clear to disciplining the different businesses of the bank. As one observer noted:

> In John Gutfreund's Salomon, nobody much wanted to supervise departments that were making money; in Ronald Reagan's and George Bush's administrations, nobody much wanted to regulate anything that was making money. Greed was good; more greed was better. Fraud was undesirable but only a frictional inefficiency, and, after all, the best people were doing it.[20]

John Gutfreund continued in his mentor's tradition by rewarding aggressiveness. The people he promoted lived for Salomon. He said, "I'm addicted to this business,"[21] and he expected his employees to display a similar loyalty and commitment. A former employee said, "You have to learn to never say no, to always find a way to get the deal done, no matter what. Salomon people never give up."[22]

Could it be that the amount of aggression at Salomon created an atmosphere where getting ahead was the number-one priority, and the firm's commitment to ethical behavior was suspect?

After the scandal broke in 1991, a *New York Times* editorial put a moral caveat on the bank's aggressiveness. It characterized Salomon as a company that celebrated clever evasion of rules and trampled anyone standing in the way of profit and as a company governed by a "culture of greed, contempt for government regulations, and a sneering attitude toward ethics or any other impediment to earning a buck."[23] This is not an organization you'd necessarily want to do business with.

The consequences of unethical or illegal actions are not usually realized until much later than when the act is committed. In addition, the unethical or illegal route is often the most lucrative and, therefore, was the most attractive to Salomon's employees.

How Leaders Hire and Fire Individuals

Among powerful ways that leaders reinforce culture are through the selection of newcomers to the organization and the way it fires employees and rationalizes the firing. The criteria for selection and dismissal reveal how leaders' decisions about whom to recruit or dismiss signal their values to all their employees.

The selection of newcomers to an organization is a powerful way that the leader reinforces culture. Leaders often unconsciously look for individuals who are similar to current organizational members in terms of values and assumptions. Some organizations hire individuals on the recommendation of a current employee; this tends to perpetuate the culture because the new employees typically hold similar values. Promotion-from-within policies also serve to reinforce organizational culture.

Gutfreund's leadership style selected ambitious, aggressive young people and gave them the chance to create new departments and new products and to enjoy success they could not achieve at other firms. Gutfreund said, "We listen to young people. We give them responsibility."[24] Unfortunately, the criteria by which he dismissed employees were vague and led to ambiguous performance standards. When people are not sure what to do, unethical behavior may flourish as aggressive individuals pursue what they believe to be acceptable.

The way a company fires an employee and the rationale behind the firing also communicate the culture. Some companies deal with poor performers by trying to find them another place within the organization where they can perform better and make a contribution. Other companies seem to operate under the philosophy that those who cannot perform are out quickly.

Specific performance guidelines were lacking at Salomon; criteria for dismissal were vague. If Gutfreund decided that employees could not handle responsibilities they were given, he would dismiss them. His potential successor, Ranieri, was a great force within Salomon, and his mortgage-trading department "was the kind of fiefdom that challenged management's control."[25] Although Ranieri was thriving in Salomon's management system, he forgot the most important thing: Gutfreund insisted that he himself be "perceived as the brightest star in Salomon's galaxy. He will accept no competition."[26] When interest rates dropped in 1987, Gutfreund seized the opportunity to eliminate his "competition." On July 13, 1987, Gutfreund called Ranieri in to what seemed to be a normal meeting at their lawyers' offices. Much to Ranieri's surprise, his mentor demanded his resignation. When Gutfreund was interviewed about why he fired his former superstar, he compared the firing to a divorce. The causes, he claimed, were numerous—a series of things over the years, not one specific act.

While Ranieri's dismissal stands out (because he was so close to the top), many others were fired by John Gutfreund. When the company was downsized by 12 percent of his staff in 1987, the group was fired together, without focus on individual acts or any behavior of specific people. There are both ethical and legal risks associated with Gutfreund's chosen leadership style: "Reliance solely on subjective measures (e.g., "what my feelings tell me is right") can lead to vague and inconsistent management policies."[27] These ambiguities can also lead to crossing ethical and legal boundaries, as Salomon's employees proceeded to do.

No action of management has more impact on its operational ethics than the people it promotes, dismisses, or allows to stagnate. John Gutfreund seems to exemplify Kelly's Destructive Achiever (DA) who "has the charisma of a leader [ethical manager] but lacks his operational values; this achiever's net effect on the long-term welfare of the organization is negative."[28] Additionally, the promotion of employees who were like himself led Gutfreund to contaminate the entire Salomon Brothers organization. Kelly notes that "Every time a DA is promoted and the ethical difference between the DA and other candidates is apparent to the staff, the organization's value base is diminished and the way is opened to even faster deterioration."[29] John Gutfreund selected those employees who shared his aggressive, win-at-all-costs mentality. His short-term view may have prevented him from seeing what the long-term costs of this kind of personality could be on the organization as a whole.

How Gutfreund Exhibited the Five Primary Mechanisms

Gutfreund employed all of the five mechanisms to shape the culture within Salomon Brothers and leave his impression on the firm. (Figure 6.1 provides a visualization of the interaction between leadership, organizational culture, and unethical behavior.

Attention: Gutfreund looked at the most recent bottom-line profits and disregarded long-term implications of employee actions.

Reaction to crises: He lied, covered up ethical and legal transgressions, and tried to preserve his own position at any cost.

Role modeling: He set an example for secret deals and for unethical behavior being tolerated and hidden.

Allocation of rewards: He promoted those who were most like him, lacking any commitment to ethical principles.

Criteria for selection and dismissal: He had vague policies that confused employees and let them make their own decisions about how to "win" the internal Salomon competition.

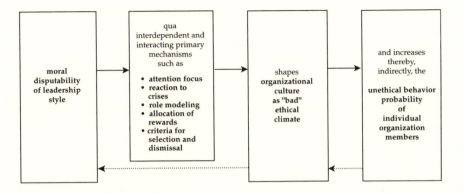

Figure 6.1 Leadership Style, Organizational Culture, and Unethical Behavior Model

WHAT WENT WRONG AT BEECH-NUT, E. F. HUTTON, AND SALOMON BROTHERS

Mr. Gutfreund, a one-time bond trader, kept this tough-guy image to the end. After formally offering to resign, Mr. Gutfreund told top executives at a closed-door meeting: "I'm not apologizing for anything to anybody. Apologies don't mean [expletive]. What happened, happened."[30] The same arrogance that enabled Mr. Gutfreund to build Salomon into the dominant force in the $2.3 trillion Treasury securities market also led to his becoming ensnared in a government trap that became his and other key company executives' undoing.

Everyone knows that selling jars of phony apple juice is unethical. In addition, everyone who has a checking account knows that bouncing checks is wrong, and you do not have to be a financial wizard to know that writing bad checks is illegal. Finally, everyone now knows that illegal bidding in Treasury auctions is wrong. How could some of the country's most sophisticated executives and money managers become involved in such unethical behavior? The answer in all likelihood may well be a combination of failed leadership and groupthink. That is, groupthink that may be fostered by the bottom-line mentality that supports financial success, short-term solutions, and a willingness to go outside the ethical lines.

Beech-Nut's employees were under a lot of financial pressures; instead of cooperating with government investigators, they compounded their problems by stonewalling rather than cooperating. Hutton's employees were under a lot of pressure to make money, and the company no doubt paid more attention to profit figures than to how those figures were achieved. The practice may have started accidentally, but once it got going, the money managers apparently wrote unnecessary checks solely to profit from the check-kiting scheme as the money passed from bank to bank.

Company employees evidently had the necessary company loyalty and commitment to enable groupthink to come into play. Most important, once it became clear that high-level executives were not going to stop the scheme, employees became very good at ignoring any information that might lead them to conclude that the practice was illegal. An internal Hutton memo recommended that: "if an office is overdrafting their ledger balance consistently, it is probably best not to request an account analysis."[31] Executives at Salomon showed group characteristics found in groupthink experiences; for example, they exhibited excessive or blind loyalty, a bottom-line mentality, arrogance and overconfidence, and a promotion of unethical solutions by its leaders. In addition, like Beech-Nut and E. F. Hutton, Salomon Brothers also showed clear symptoms of groupthink and decision-making defects that resulted in unethical activities. In each organization, individuals were willing to take the approach of "let's all close our eyes to this problem."

In a sense, individuals and groups in Beech-Nut, E. F. Hutton, and Salomon Brothers committed unethical acts because of an overabundance of characteristics that didn't allow them to operate ethically in a large, free-wheeling organization. The values of organizational members in all three organizations were important. That is, failed leadership, groupthink and the ensuing unethical behavior may have been precipitated by arrogance. Arrogance is the illegitimate child of confidence and pride that is found in groups experiencing groupthink. Arrogance is the idea that not only can you never make a mistake, but no one else can ever be right, a point quite evident in our look at the fall of Enron in Chapters 7 and 8.

In Beech-Nut, E. F. Hutton, and Salomon Brothers, arrogance was an insurmountable roadblock to ethical behavior. The flipside of arrogance is the ability to shine, to star, while working within the limits of ethical policies and guidelines. Another reason that groupthink may have occurred in these organizations is that they lacked the value of ethical commitment or moral courage, that is, a willingness to commit to a goal that is bigger than they are—to keep acting ethically or morally, even when there is a threat of failure, until they finally come up with ethical business decisions.

A third reason for the unethical acts committed by Beech-Nut, E. F. Hutton, and Salomon Brothers has to do with another human value, loyalty. Loyalty is valued in all organizations. No one wants to work with anyone who has no concern for anyone or anything else. Loyalty counts in organizations; however, it should not mean an unwillingness to question the unethical behavior of a group or organization. Group-think and unethical activities occur when arrogance, overcommitment, and loyalty help a group to shine above the ethical interests of an organization.

When groupthink occurs, organizations like Beech-Nut, E. F. Hutton, and Salomon Brothers are more likely to strive for unanimity, ignore the voices of dissenters and conscience, and make less than quality decisions, which results in unethical behavior. However, by ignoring voices of caution and conscience and working with a bottom-line mentality for short-term profit, all three companies' managers ended up severely damaging their own company's reputation. By not doing a better job of promoting positive and ethical organizational cultures (climates), these organizations increased the likelihood of unethical behavior, groupthink, and their fall from grace.

The lack of ethical leadership puts an organization at risk. Leaders who do not exercise ethical leadership will cause potential ethical problems to be ignored or will block efforts to fix them. They hamstring efforts to improve an unethical climate. They will not allocate the resources needed or will stop short of taking effective action. In the long run, their lack of leadership will come back to haunt their organization.

Too often organizational leaders believe that having personal values that underlie ethical leadership is enough, but it isn't. Their unwillingness to put their values into action brands them as unethical leaders. Having missed the opportunity to set the correct tone through their actions, like Gutfreund at Salomon Brothers, they fail themselves and their companies. Table 6.1 offers a final look at the comparison between the behaviors of ethical and unethical leaders.

CONCLUSION

Organizations that support financial success as the only value to be considered increase the likelihood of the accompanying employee attitudes, a bottom-line mentality and an unrealistic belief that everything boils down to a monetary game. By emphasizing short-term revenues above long-term consequences, organizations like Beech-Nut, E. F. Hutton, and Salomon Brothers create a climate in which individuals and groups understand that unethical behavior is acceptable. In addition, these same organizations are unwilling to take a stand when there is a financial cost to any group's decision, which contributes encourages ethical shortcuts by its members.

The scandal at Salomon Brothers highlighted a leadership style by Gutfreund that helped create a "win-at-all-costs" ethical climate that led to unethical and illegal consequences. His actions and behavior

TABLE 6.1   Ethical and Unethical Leader Behaviors

Ethical Leader Behaviors	Unethical Leader Behaviors
Is committed to high ethical standards which apply to everyone	Is willing to compromise standards based on the situation—top performers and executives are held to a different standard
Uses customer welfare, doing what's best for the public, as one of the primary standards	Uses the company's welfare, doing what's best for them, as the primary standard
Is willing to confront situations where ethics are questionable and confronts ethical issues openly and honestly	Is unwilling to confront ethical issues unless they are safe, uncomplicated, and lack risk, doesn't make ethics an issue, ignores ethical issues or deals with them in a covert or behind-the-scenes way
Takes timely and appropriate action on ethical issues	Avoids taking action on ethical issues in favor of expediency, or seeks to "soften" the blow by minimizing the impact, takes action only when forced to
Is proactive in heading off ethical problems	Does not deal with ethical issues until there is an obvious and significant problem
Sets an example for others, treats ethics as a priority	Downplays the importance of ethics, treats it as nice to do, not a must do
Treats ethics as a performance measure no different than sales, etc., actively supervises it	Seeks to minimize his/her personal responsibility for supervision of ethical issues and behavior
Learns about the legal and ethical aspects of the business and doesn't plead ignorance when asked a question	Ignores the legal and ethical aspects, "that's what attorneys are for," pleads ignorance of the issues and the regulations or rules
Does not use the excuse that other companies have lower standards	Sets his/her standard at the lowest level of the competition and uses as an excuse that other companies are not taking as high a standard

communicated important messages to others in the organization about the company's ethical climate. One author speculated at the beginning of the Salomon T-bill auction crisis that "the biggest casualty may well be Salomon's corporate culture. Despite inroads made in the more genteel investment banking business, Solly is at bottom a bond house run by and for traders . . . greed might have pushed them outside the rules."[32] Gutfreund's short-term horizon, his ability to make split-second decisions but not long-term plans, his aggressiveness and lack of tact all were strengths that allowed him huge success as a trader. By instilling such attributes in all of his employees, however, Gutfreund created a culture that pushed everything to the limit, with little thought for the long-term implications to the firm.

Again, leadership on ethics begins at the top. William C. Ferguson, former chairman and CIO of NYNEX Corporation, recently noted that "the shadow of the leader—the example that they set is the most important weapon in the ethics arsenal."[33] Leaders cannot shrink from their obligation to set a moral example for those they lead.[34] They must draw the line between, on the one hand, the perpetual push for higher profits and, on the other, actions antagonistic to the values of the larger society.

Ethical business leadership requires "not only harvesting the fruit we can pluck today, not only investing in the small trees and experimental hybrids that won't yield a thing in this quarter or the next, but also caring for the soil that allows us to produce such a rich harvest in the first place."[35] If leaders want to cast an ethical (or unethical) shadow, they need to practice what they preach. They need to cast an ethical shadow. They must make ethics the cornerstone of how they conduct business by practicing ethical behavior in their personal life, in their business, and in their relationships.

Organizations must create and maintain strong ethical organizational cultures that run counter to a "win at all cost" mentality. These same organizations must recognize how the organizations strategy and culture can lay the foundation for unethical behavior to flourish. This is especially the case when organizational leaders must undertake an ethical turnaround like the one undertaken by Warren Buffett following John Gutfreund's tenure at Salomon Brothers as (See Chapter 9.)

NOTES

1. Chester I. Barnard, *The Functions of the Executive* (Cambridge, Mass.: Harvard University Press, 1938), 272 ff.

2. Business Roundtable, *Corporate Ethics: A Prime Business Asset* (New York: Business Roundtable, 1988).

3. Barry Z. Posner and William H. Schmidt, "Values and the American Series," *The Wall Street Journal* (October 31–November 3, 1992), 33.

4. Linda K. Trevino and Karen A. Nelson, *Managing Business Ethics: Straight Talk about How to Do It Right* (New York: John Wiley & Sons, 1995).

5. Ibid.

6. J. M. Howell and B. J. Avolino, "The Ethics of Charismatic Leadership: Submission or Liberation?" *Academy of Management Executive* 6, no. 2 (1992), 43–54.

7. Archie B. Carroll, *Business and Society*, 2nd ed. (Cincinnati, O.: South-Western, 1992).

8. S. Kindel, "Bad Apple for Baby," *Financial World* (June 27, 1989), 48.
9. K. G. Salwen, "SEC Chief's Criticism of Ex-managers of Salomon Suggests Civil Action Likely," *The Wall Street Journal* (November 20, 1991), A18.
10. M. Siconolfi and L. P. Cohen, "Sullied Solly: How Salomon's Hubris and a U.S. Trap Led to Leaders' Downfall," *The Wall Street Journal* (August 19, 1991), A1, A4.
11. Michael Lewis, *Liar's Poker* (New York: Norton, 1989).
12. Edgar H. Schein, *Organizational Culture and Leadership* (San Francisco: Jossey-Bass, 1985).
13. Ibid., 86.
14. Trevino and Nelson, *Managing Business Ethics.*
15. B. McGoldrick, "Salomon's Power Culture," *Institutional Investor* (March, 1986), 67–76.
16. Lynn S. Paine, *Cases in Leadership, Ethics, and Organizational Integrity: A Strategic Perspective* (Chicago: Irwin, 1997).
17. Jon A. Pearce, T. R. Kramer, and D. K. Robbins, "Effects of Managers' Entrepreneurial Behavior on Subordinates," *Journal of Business Venturing* 12 (1997), 147–60.
18. Trevino and Nelson, *Managing Business Ethics.*
19. L. V. Larimer, "Reflections on Ethics and Integrity," *HRFocus* (April 1997), 5.
20. Siconolfi and Cohen, "Sullied Solly," A4.
21. McGoldrick, "Salomon's Power Culture," 70
22. Ibid.
23. *New York Times*, Editorial (August 22, 1991), A26.
24. McGoldrick, "Salomon's Power Culture," 81
25. J. F. Berry, "Under Siege," *Business Month*, (June 1988), 65–68.
26. McGoldrick, "Salomon's Power Culture," 72.
27. B. H. Drake and E. Drake, "Ethical and Legal Aspects of Managing Corporate Cultures," *California Management Review* (Winter 1988), 107–23.
28. C. M. Kelly, "The Interrelationship of Ethics and Power in Today's Organizations," *Organizational Dynamics* (Summer 1987), 5–18.
29. Ibid.
30. Siconolfi and Cohen, "Sullied Solly," A4
31. D. Goleman, "Following the Leader," *Science* 85 (October 1985): 18.
32. G. Weiss, "The Salomon Shocker: How Bad Will it Get?" *Business Week* (August 26, 1991), 54–57.
33. W. C. Ferguson, "Ethical Foundations," *Executive Excellence* (June, 1997), 15–16.
34. W. C. Butcher, "The Need for Ethical Leadership," *Executive Speeches* (April/May, 1997), 83–87.
35. Ibid.

7

Enron: How a Failure of Leadership, Culture, and Unethical Behavior Brought a Giant to Its Knees

INTRODUCTION

When people hear the word "Enron," most think of corruption on a colossal scale—a company where a handful of highly paid executives were able to pocket millions of dollars while carelessly eroding the life savings of thousands of unwitting employees. But earlier, the same people would have heralded Enron as a paragon of corporate responsibility and ethics—successful, driven, focused, philanthropic and environmentally responsible. Enron appeared to represent the best a twenty-first-century organization had to offer. How did Enron transition from that golden status to being equated with questionable accounting techniques and off balance-sheet financing transactions, misleading statements, unscrupulous executives, dishonest partnerships, and ill-gotten personal gain?

The roots of Enron's fall can be found in its failed leadership and culture. This chapter describes how executives at Enron created an organizational culture that put the bottom line ahead of ethical behavior. After a brief background on Enron and its rise and fall, like our analysis of the Salomon Brothers fall, the five primary mechanisms available to leaders to create and reinforce aspects of culture are used to analyze systematically the culture and leadership that led to the company's fall after shocking disclosures about the company's finances.

BACKGROUND

A company with humble beginnings, Enron began as a merger of two Houston pipeline companies in 1985. Although Enron faced a number of financially difficult years, the deregulation of the electrical power markets took effect in 1988, and the company redefined its business from "energy delivery" to "energy broker." Enron quickly changed from a surviving company to a thriving one.

Deregulation allowed Enron to become a matchmaker in the power industry, bringing buyers and sellers together. Enron profited from the exchanges, generating revenue from the difference between the buying and selling prices. Deregulation allowed Enron to be creative—for the first time, a company that had been required to operate within the lines could innovate and test limits. Over time, Enron's contracts became increasingly diverse and significantly more complex.

Customers could insure themselves against all sorts of eventualities—such as a rise or fall in interest rates, a change in the weather, or a customer's inability to pay. By the end, the volume of such financial contracts far outstripped the volume of contracts to deliver actual commodities, and Enron was employing a small army of Ph.D.s in mathematics, physics, and economics to help manage its risk.

As Enron's products and services evolved, so did the company's culture. In this newly deregulated and innovative forum, Enron embraced a culture that rewarded "cleverness." Now that formal regulatory limits had been removed, pushing the envelope was seen as the best way to operate particularly in Enron's Finance Corporation. Deregulation opened the industry up to experimentation and the culture at Enron was one that expected employees to explore this new playing field to the utmost. Pushing the limits was considered a survival skill.

Enron's former president and CEO Jeffery Skilling actively cultivated a culture that would push limits; "Do it right, do it now, and do it better" was his mantra. He encouraged employees to be independent, innovative, and aggressive. In the *Harvard Business Review's* case study, "Enron's Transformation," employees were quoted as saying, "You were expected to perform to a standard that was continually being raised," "The only thing that mattered was adding value," and "It was all about an atmosphere of deliberately breaking the rules."[1] While a culture that admires innovation and unchecked ambition and publicly punishes poor performance can produce tremendous returns in the short run, achieving additional value in the long run by constantly upping the ante becomes harder and harder. Employees are forced to stretch the rules further and further, until the limits of ethical conduct are easily overlooked in the pursuit of the next big success.[2] The culture that developed at Enron bore striking similarities to the culture at

Salomon Brothers in the early 1990s, when the investment firm faced its own ethical crisis. Each company demonstrated a lack of ethical leadership that fostered an unethical organizational culture.

INSIDE ENRON: A LOT OF SMOKE AND MIRRORS

Enron's spectacular success and the positive scrutiny the company was receiving from the business press and the financial analysts only added fuel to the company's competitive culture. The business community rewarded Enron for its cleverness, and Enron's executives felt driven by this reputation to sustain the explosive growth of the late 1990s, even when they knew that it was not possible. A negative earnings outlook would be a red flag to investors, indicating Enron was not as successful as it appeared. If investors' concerns drove down the stock price because of excessive selling, credit agencies would be forced to downgrade Enron's credit rating. Trading partners would lose faith in the company and trade elsewhere, and Enron's ability to generate quality earnings and cash flows would suffer. Enron executives wanted to avoid this scenario at all costs. As a result Enron entered into a deceiving web of partnerships and employed increasingly questionable accounting methods to maintain its investment-grade status. Enron executives were able to convince themselves that they were doing nothing wrong—they were pushing the envelope—but rather acting for the good of the organization, as evidenced by their foray into limited partnerships, keeping debt off the balance sheet, and conflicts of interests.

Partnerships

Partnerships are an easy and efficient way to raise money. However, in an effort to continue to push the value envelope, Enron took partnerships to a new level by creating "special purpose vehicles" (SPVs), pseudo-partnerships that allowed the company to sell assets and "create" earnings that artificially enhanced its bottom line. Enron exaggerated earnings by recognizing gains on the sale of assets to SPVs. In some cases, the company booked revenues prior to a partnership generating significant revenues. Project Braveheart, a partnership Enron developed with Blockbuster, was intended to provide movies to homes directly over phone lines. Just months after the partnership was formed, Enron recorded $110.9 million in profits prematurely; these profits were never realized, as the partnership failed after only a thousand-home pilot.

While premature booking of earnings seems very clearly unethical, it is easy to understand how a culture like Enron's could stimulate justification of such behavior. Enron was used to succeeding. Enron employees were the best and the brightest and were extremely clever. Clever people do not make business deals that fail; therefore, booking earnings before they are realized is not wrong, just "early." The culture at Enron was quickly eroding the ethical boundaries of its employees.

Keeping Debt off the Balance Sheet and Partnerships at Arm's Length

The SPVs not only allowed Enron to boost earnings, but also allowed the company to keep debt off its balance sheet. A highly leveraged balance sheet would jeopardize its credit rating, as its debt-equity ratio would rise and increase its cost of capital. To avoid this, Enron parked some of its debt on the balance sheets of its SPVs and kept it hidden from analysts and investors. When the extent of its debt burden came to light, Enron's credit rating fell and lenders demanded immediate payment of hundreds of millions of dollars in debt.

This is another example of the results of cultural ethical erosion; Enron's decision makers saw the shuffling of debt as a timing issue, not an ethical dilemma. Clever people would eventually make everything right, because the deals would all be successful in the long run. Moving debt was as easy as predating a check and would harm no one, and therefore it was not an ethical issue.

Each questionable partnership decision carried additional cleverness burdens. In order to keep information from the public, Enron had to guarantee that the SEC did not consider its partnerships Enron subsidiaries. If these partnerships were classified as such, in-depth disclosure and stricter accounting methods would have been required. To remain cleverer than the SEC, Enron enlisted help from its outside accountants and its attorneys (Arthur Andersen, and Vinson & Elkins). The accountants and attorneys all referenced the FASB rule that holds that partnerships are not considered subsidiaries as long as 3 percent of their equity comes from outside investors and they are managed independently of their sponsors. This is commonly known as being at arm's length. Enron crafted relationships that were, thanks to this ruling, de facto partnerships, although they were de jure subsidiaries. A close look at the partnerships revealed that the outside investments came from companies (like SE Thunderbird LLC) that were owned by Enron. The following paragraphs provide a more detailed look at Enron's efforts to keep debt off the balance sheets and at several of the partnerships.

Whitewing. Documents describing one of the largest such structures—a partnership called Whitewing, established by Enron and a still-unidentified party—illustrate how Enron favored outside investors while not fully informing shareholders of billions of dollars of potential liabilities.[3] Whitewing shows how Enron regularly financed growth without adding directly to the corporate debt shown on its books. In November 2001, Enron valued Whitewing's assets at $4.7 billion, but some Enron officials say that figure is significantly exaggerated.

Off-balance-sheet transactions are used by many companies. Federal and congressional investigations into Enron's collapse are trying to determine whether Enron used its labyrinth of partnership structures to hide key information about its financial condition. Whitewing's role was to buy an assortment of power plants, pipelines, and water projects in India, Turkey, Spain and Latin America that Enron had snapped up through the mid-1990s, when the Houston company was set on becoming a global energy supplier.

By 1999, Enron President Jeffery K. Skilling was refocusing the company as a global broker of energy, a trader of financial contracts rather than an operator of energy facilities. Whitewing was responsible for reselling the assets. But Enron also guaranteed to Whitewing's investors that if the power plants and other assets were sold at a loss, Enron would make up the difference with shares of its common stock, or with cash if necessary. As of November 2001, that requirement stood at more than $2 billion—an obligation that shareholders didn't know about.

A part of that hidden guarantee to Whitewing investors surfaced suddenly in October 2001, after Enron's credit rating was dropped to near junk-bond level by rating agencies. That triggered a requirement that Enron immediately pay $690 million of its obligations to Whitewing. Enron was able to delay the payment but had to disclose the problem, stunning investors and feeding the loss of confidence that led to the company's bankruptcy filing. Such arrangements were "designed to give the safer return to the outside investors and put substantially more risk on the [Enron] shareholders," said Clayton Vernon, an economist and manager at Enron who was fired by Enron after he wrote an e-mail criticizing Enron chairman Kenneth L. Lay in October 2001.[4]

From an accounting and a public-disclosure standpoint, the arrangement was "indefensible," said Vernon, who is among the former employees suing Enron. Whitewing was the center of an aviary of entities with bird names—Osprey, Condor, Egret, Peregrine, and Blue Heron were all linked to Whitewing.

Chewco. With its Star Wars name, its elusive origin, and its central role in the implosion of Enron Corp., the investment partnership named Chewco was one of the important mysteries as the Enron scandal unfolded in late 2001. Chewco was exposed in detailed pages of a report commissioned by Enron's board of directors.

In the Chewco story are examples of huge profits improperly claimed by Enron and individual enrichment by Enron insiders, according to the report by a special investigating committee. In three years, a $125,000 investment by a second-level financial executive and his domestic partner ballooned into a $10.5 million payoff, plus other lucrative fees.

On paper Chewco appeared independent; control was shared by Enron and outside investors in an arrangement that would permit Enron to keep some of its energy projects and debts off its books. Enron executives created Chewco in 1997 as part of a complex investment in another Enron partnership that owned stakes in natural gas projects.

But personal motives dominated Chewco's history, according to the report. First, then–chief financial officer (CFO) Andrew S. Fastow proposed that he be allowed to manage Chewco. Jeffery Skilling, then Enron's president, told the committee that Fastow also wanted to have members of his wife's family as Chewco's investors, but Skilling said he told Fastow no.

Because of his senior executive position, Fastow could not run Chewco without publicly disclosing his role, which Skilling did not want, the investigators said. So Fastow turned Chewco over to a friend, Michael J. Kopper, then–managing director of Enron Global Finance, whom Fastow supervised. Kopper's role did not have to be disclosed because of his lower rank. To remove any public appearance that Kopper might be seen as controlling Chewco, several more pieces were tacked on. An entity, Big River Funding, became Chewco's limited partner. Little River Funding was set up as the owner of Big River.

In December 1997, as Chewco was being created, Kopper transferred his ownership in both Big River and Little River to his domestic partner, William D. Dodson, an employee of an airline. That left Kopper with no formal ownership interest in Chewco. Kopper invested $115,000, and Dodson invested $10,000. Before Enron bought out their interests in March 2001, Fastow stepped in and pressured Enron to pay more. Kopper and Dodson ultimately shared a $10.5 million windfall from their $125,000 investment.

Kopper, in addition to collecting his regular Enron salary, was paid about $2 million in questionable management fees relating to Chewco from 1997 to 2000. According to the Powers report (named for William Powers, Jr., head of the special investigation committee that wrote it), Chewco required little management—mainly clerical work involving transferring funds. Much of that was done by another Enron employee on company time and occasionally by Fastow's wife, although the Powers report said it wasn't known if she was paid.

The outlines of Chewco's role in Enron's collapse emerged in newspaper reports and in investigations by lawyers representing shareholders. Enron, the report said, violated accounting standards when it created Chewco, enabling the company to claim $405 million of profits from 1997 through 2000 that it was not entitled to have, while also concealing more than $600 million in debt. Enron executives broke the rules a second time, the report said, using Chewco to report a profit on the increased value of Enron common stock held by a related partnership, Jedi.

Chewco was an early example of the Byzantine investment structures that were Fastow's specialty. Its roots go back to 1993, when Enron formed the Jedi partnership with the giant California Public Employees Retirement System (Calpers) to invest in natural gas projects. By 1997, company executives were eager to expand Jedi, but Calpers was reluctant. So Fastow and Kopper decided to buy out Calpers's share, which was then worth $383 million, and replaced it with their new creation, Chewco Investments LP.

Jedi was operating off Enron's books. To keep it there, Chewco, as Jedi's new half-owner, would have to meet certain accounting standards. It would have to be independent of Enron's control, and its owners had to put in a small but specific amount of real money. That investment requirement came to 3 percent of Chewco's capital, or about $11 million. Kopper was a successful executive, former associates say, but he didn't have $11 million. The solution was to borrow most of the money from a willing lender—in this case, Barclays Bank PLC. The remaining 97 percent included a loan from Jedi and another from Barclays. In another questionable part of the transaction, Enron guaranteed the Barclays loans.

But the creation of Chewco was hurriedly done, and there was a fateful slip. At the last minute, key details of the transaction changed, primarily because Barclays wanted more collateral for its loans. Accordingly, the size of Barclays' loan to Kopper and Dodson was trimmed by $6.6 million, making their investment less than 3 percent. If Fastow or Kopper had found another investor to make up the difference, Chewco would have met the standard. That was not done.

From its beginning then, as Chewco—and thus Jedi—didn't meet accounting requirements, Enron should not have kept Jedi's debt off its books or have segregated Jedi's profits and losses from Enron's results, the committee said. Belatedly, the company corrected the error in November 2001, with the devastating revision of its revenue and profits.

Conflicts of Interest

Although the partnerships were classified correctly according to the FASB, Enron officials obviously had close ties with them. This raised the question conflicts of interest. Andrew Fastow, Enron's former CFO, ran or was partial owner of two of the most important de facto partnerships: LJM Cayman LP and LJM2 Co-Investment LP. Michael Kopper, a former managing director at Enron, managed a third partnership, Chewco Investments LP.

The culture of cleverness at Enron started as a pursuit of excellence that devolved into the appearance of excellence as executives worked to develop clever ways of preserving Enron's facade of infallible success. Although Enron maintained that top officials at the company reviewed the dealings with potential conflicts of interest, Enron later claimed that Fastow earned over $30 million from Enron with his companies. At some point in the bending of ethical guidelines for the good of the company, Enron's executives also began to bend the rules for personal gain. Once a culture's ethical boundaries are breached, it becomes easier to justify more extreme ethical compromises.

Stock Shares as Guarantees

As with any interaction, Enron's executives could only "rob Peter to pay Paul" for so long. Within the Enron culture, the acts had seemed to be insignificant rule bending, but combined, these incremental ethical transgressions resulted in a business catastrophe. Although Enron's executives had believed that everything would work successfully in the long run, the questionable partnerships left the company vulnerable when financial troubles came to light. As partnerships began to fail with increasing regularity, Enron was liable for millions of dollars it had not anticipated losing. Promises began to come due, and Enron could not follow through on its financial obligations. For example, Enron had promised CIBC World Markets the majority of the profits from Project Braveheart for ten years, or in the event of failure Enron would be obligated to repay CIBC its entire $115.2 million investment. Not only did Enron book the earnings prematurely, but it was also forced to repay CIBC its full investment.

The Financial Implosion

The partnerships that once boosted earnings and allowed Enron to prosper became the misplaced card that caused the Enron house to collapse. The stability of Enron's house of cards had been eroded by the very culture that had allowed it to be built. Enron was forced to renounce over $390 million in earnings from dealings with Chewco Investments and Jedi, another partnership. The company was also forced to restate earnings back to 1997, and the restated earnings totaled only $586 million, a mere 20 percent of the initially reported figures. The very results Enron sought to prevent—falling stock prices, lack of consumer and financial market confidence—came about as a direct result of decisions that had been driven by Enron's culture.

But Enron's ethical failings did not stop with the unraveling of the company's questionable business dealings. At a time when strong company leadership was most needed, Enron's leader abandoned the company. In August of 2001, Jeffery Skilling resigned as president and CEO of Enron and sold shares of his company stock totaling $66 million dollars. Just two months later, Enron restated earnings, stock prices plummeted, and the company froze shares in an attempt to help stabilize the company. Enron employees, who had been encouraged to invest heavily in the company, found themselves unable to salvage their investments. The company culture of individualism, innovation, and aggressive cleverness left Enron without compassionate, responsible leadership. Enron's board of directors was slow to step in to fill the void, and individual Enron employees for the first time realized the ramifications of a culture with leaders that eschew the boundaries of ethical behavior.

Table 7.1 provides a timeline of important Enron events.

TABLE 7.1 Timeline of Enron's Collapse

July 1985: Houston Natural Gas merges with InterNorth to form Enron, originally an interstate natural gas pipeline company.

1989: Enron begins trading natural gas commodities.

June 1994: Enron trades its first unit of electricity.

Nov. 1999: EnronOnline is launched, the first global commodity trading Web site.

2000

Sept. 10, 2000: Enron Chairman Kenneth Lay contributes more than $290,000 to George W. Bush's election campaign.

Oct. 10, 2000: Enron hires Linda Robertson, from the Clinton administration, as vice president for federal government affairs to head its Washington office, infuriating Republican leaders who oppose business groups hiring Democratic lobbyists.

2001

Jan. 2001: Enron backer Patrick H. Wood III appointed Bush's chairman of the Federal Energy Regulatory Commission.

Jan. 3, 2001: Lay is one of the 474 people Bush names to advise his presidential transition team.

Feb. 2001: Jeffery Skilling takes over as chief executive. Lay remains as chairman.

TABLE 7.1   continued

March 2001: Karl Rove, President Bush's senior adviser, met privately with Intel officials, of which company he owned over $100,000 worth of shares. At the time, Intel was concerned with government approval of a merger between a Dutch company and an Intel supplier. The merger was later approved.

May 19, 2001: Congress begins implementing President Bush's energy plan into legislation.

June 5, 2001: Rove divests his stocks in energy, defense and pharmaceutical companies. Rove owned holdings in Enron, Boeing, General Electric, and Pfizer worth more than $100,000 in each.

June 30, 2001: The White House acknowledges Rove was involved in shaping the administration's energy policy at a time when he owned equities in energy companies.

Aug. 14, 2001: Lay takes over as CEO after Skilling resigns for personal reasons. Skilling had helped transform the company from a natural gas pipeline company to a global marketer and trader of energy.

Oct. 12, 2001: An in-house lawyer at Arthur Andersen e-mails the lead partner in the firm's Houston office to remind him of the firm's document-destruction policy.

Oct. 15, 2001: Lay talks to Commerce Secretary Donald L. Evans. Commerce officials say the call did not cover Enron's financial troubles.

Oct. 16, 2001: Enron reports a $618 million third-quarter loss and discloses a $1.2 billion reduction in shareholder equity, partly related to partnerships run by Chief Financial Officer Andrew Fastow.

Oct. 17, 2001: SEC sends a letter to Enron asking for information after the company reported hundreds of millions of dollars in third-quarter losses.

Oct. 20, 2001: A report filed with the Internal Revenue Service reveals that a political group allied with House Majority Whip Tom DeLay (R-Tex.) raised nearly $500,000. The Republican Majority Issues Committee (RMIC) was required to show, for the first time, how it raises and spends its money. One of the committee's largest donations included Enron's $50,000.

Oct. 22, 2001: Enron acknowledges a Securities and Exchange Commission inquiry into a possible conflict of interest related to the company's dealings with the partnerships. Shares of Enron sank more than 20 percent on the news.

Oct. 23, 2001: Lay reassures investors in a conference call.

Oct. 24, 2001: Enron ousts CFO Andrew Fastow.

Oct. 26, 2001: *Lay calls Federal Reserve Chairman Alan Greenspan to provide information.*

Oct. 28, 2001: Lay talks by telephone with Treasury Secretary Paul H. O'Neill to inform him of financial problems facing Enron. A Treasury spokeswoman says O'Neill did nothing to help the company.

Oct. 29, 2001: Lay talks by telephone with Evans. A Commerce spokesman says Lay asked Evans if he could do anything to influence a decision by Moody's Investors Service to downgrade Enron's credit rating. A commerce spokesman says Evans decided not to intervene.

TABLE 7.1 continued

Oct. 31, 2001: *Enron announces that the SEC inquiry has been upgraded* to a formal investigation.

Nov. 8, 2001: Andersen receives a federal subpoena for documents related to Enron.

Nov. 8, 2001: Enron files documents with the SEC revising its financial statements for the past five years to account for $586 million in losses. Lay speaks with O'Neill again about Enron's plight.

Nov. 8, 2001: Enron begins talks to sell itself to rival Dynegy for about $8 billion in stock and cash.

Nov. 9, 2001: The company discloses that it overstated its earnings by $567 million since 1997. Two company officials are fired.

Nov. 9, 2001: Dynegy announces an agreement to buy its much larger rival Enron for more than $8 billion in stock and cash.

Nov. 13, 2001: Lay turns down a $60.6 million severance payment that would be triggered at the completion of the Dynegy deal.

Nov. 19, 2001: Enron restates its third-quarter earnings and tries to restructure a $650 million obligation that could come due.

Nov. 21, 2001: Enron reaches agreement to extend a $690 million debt payment.

Nov. 22, 2001: Enron gets a 3-week loan extension on a $690 million note.

Nov. 28, 2001: Dynegy seeks to abruptly cut the amount of its buyout offer as Enron's credit rating is cut to junk-bond status.

Nov. 29, 2001: SEC investigation is expanded to include Arthur Andersen.

Nov. 29, 2001: Dynegy deal collapses.

Dec. 2, 2001: Enron, once one of the world's largest electricity and natural gas traders, files for Chapter 11 bankruptcy protection.

Dec. 3, 2001: Enron arranges up to $1.5 billion debtor-in-possession financing to keep operating while in bankruptcy and announces 4,000 layoffs.

Dec. 12, 2001: Joseph F. Berandino, chief executive of Arthur Andersen, appears before Congress, testifying Enron might have violated securities laws.

2002

Jan. 3, 2002: Senator Joseph Lieberman (D-Conn.) chairs the full Governmental Affairs Committee that heads the investigation of the White House's involvement in the collapse. Top executives and directors of Enron are subpoenaed by the Senate committee.

Jan. 10, 2002: The Justice Department confirms that a criminal investigation of Enron's collapse has begun.

Jan. 22, 2002: A former Enron employee claims she saw documents being shredded after the announcement of the Securities Exchange Commission investigation in October.

Jan. 23, 2002: Kenneth Lay resigns as Enron's CEO.

TABLE 7.1 continued

Jan. 23, 2002: The FBI begins its investigation of the document shredding.

Jan. 24, 2002: Congressional hearings begin. David Duncan, former partner at Andersen LLP, refuses to testify about the shredding of Enron-related documents.

Jan. 25, 2002: Former Enron Vice Chairman J. Clifford Baxter is found dead in his car, in an apparent suicide.

Jan. 28, 2002: Lay's wife defends him in a television interview.

Jan. 30, 2002: Enron names turnaround expert Stephen F. Cooper new CEO.

Jan. 31, 2002: Minutes of an Enron board of directors meeting show the board backed moving debt off of the company's books.

Feb. 1, 2002: The Justice Department instructs the White House to preserve any documents related to its dealings with Enron. The White House agrees to comply.

Feb. 2, 2002: A report prepared by a special committee of Enron's board of directors is released. The report details management failures in supervising partnerships.

Feb. 3, 2002: Arthur Andersen hires former Federal Reserve Chairman Paul A. Volcker to lead firm's reforms.

Feb. 3, 2002: Lay abruptly cancels testimony before a Senate panel.

Feb. 4, 2002: Senate panel votes to subpoena Lay.

Feb. 4, 2002: Lay cuts remaining ties to company, resigning from board of directors.

Feb. 4, 2002: Lay implicated in plot to inflate profits and hide losses, according to a report created by an investigative arm of Enron's board of directors.

Feb. 7, 2002: Documents show senior Enron lawyer Jordan Mintz was rebuffed while attempting to draw attention to corporation's partnerships more than a year earlier.

Feb. 8, 2002: Lay sells stake in NFL Houston Texans.

Feb. 8, 2002: Former chief financial officer Fastow takes the fifth before a House panel.

Feb. 8, 2002: Testimony from former chief executive Skilling contradicts previous statements made by Enron partners.

Feb. 12, 2002: Former Enron CEO Lay invokes Fifth Amendment right and refuses to testify after being forced by congressional subpoena to appear on Capitol Hill.

Feb. 14, 2002: Enron executive Sherron Watkins testifies before a House Committee, sharply disputing previous testimony and implicating Skilling and Fastow as culpable for Enron's demise.

Feb. 14, 2002: Documents reveal Enron executive offered Lay public relations advice on how to blame others for Enron's rapidly increasing financial troubles.

Feb. 14, 2002: Documents reveal Enron executive offered Lay public relations advice on how to blame others for Enron's rapidly increasing financial troubles.

TABLE 7.1   continued

Feb. 14, 2002: Enron fires chief risk officer Rick Buy and chief accounting officer Rick Causey.

Feb. 14, 2002: The Securities and Exchange Commission reveals plans to alter its policies on corporations' disclosure of financial information.

Feb. 15, 2002: Regents of the University of California are named as lead plaintiff in class-action lawsuit against senior Enron executives.

Feb. 17, 2002: Reports indicate Enron enlisted the aid of a Bush campaign advisor.

Feb. 21, 2002: Sources tell The *Washington Post* that accounting firm Arthur Andersen is willing to make a substantial payment to settle a class-action suit with Enron shareholders.

Feb. 22, 2002: Insurance companies move to revoke coverage for Enron.

Feb. 23, 2002: Arthur Andersen executives deny knowledge of Enron document destruction.

Feb. 23, 2002: GAO files unprecedented lawsuit against Vice President Cheney in the matter of interaction between Enron Corp. executives and the Bush administration's energy task force.

Feb. 27, 2002: Former Enron employees offer to testify in exchange for immunity from prosecution.

Feb. 27, 2002: Skilling appears before Congress a second time, maintaining claims that he knew nothing about corrupt accounting practices.

Feb. 28, 2002: Enron request for insurance payments to top executives is denied.

Mar. 1, 2002: House Democrats introduce legislation to impose more restrictions on auditors and Wall Street analysts.

Mar. 7, 2002: President Bush reveals detailed proposal to require corporate chief executives to vouch personally for their companies' financial statements.

Mar. 11, 2002: New documents collected by House committee conflict with sworn testimony given by former Enron executive Skilling.

Mar. 14, 2002: Enron's law firm faces House panel in the matter of the firm's off-the-book partnerships and accounting practices.

Mar. 20, 2002: The House and Senate offer pension reform plans to offer more legal protection to workers in the wake of the Enron controversy.

Mar. 21, 2002: Ratings agency officials say Enron lied to hide liabilities.

Mar. 23, 2002: Debate intensifies among former Enron partners and creditors' committee due to allegations of favoritism.

Mar. 23, 2002: Congress issues subpoenas to Enron executives to determine the fallen company's relationship with political contacts and influence over the presidential administration's energy policy.

Mar. 24, 2002: Reports show Lay's relationship to George Bush was a mix between close friend and nudging lobbyist.

TABLE 7.1 continued

Mar. 25, 2002: Army secretary Thomas E. White, a former Enron executive, lists 44 previously undisclosed phone calls made from his home to Enron executives prior to his decision to sell more than 200,000 shares.

Mar. 27, 2002: Reports show UBS Paine Webber broker was dismissed after advising clients to sell stock due to Enron's financial trouble.

Mar. 27, 2002: Army secretary Thomas E. White denies improper contacts with former Enron colleagues.

Mar. 29, 2002: Enron is given a 90-day ultimatum to turn over documents to investigators.

Mar. 29, 2002: Enron asks bankruptcy court judge for a new round of employee retention bonuses and severance packages.

Apr. 2, 2002: Sen. Joseph Lieberman calls for new laws and dramatic changes in American business executive behavior.

Apr. 2, 2002: Sources say former Enron advisor Carl E. Bass was removed from his position after voicing concerns regarding accounting policies.

Apr. 3, 2002: Internal memos reveal accounting firm Arthur Andersen was overruled after questioning Enron methods used to hide losses.

Apr. 4, 2002: Congressional subcommittee announces date for public Enron hearing.

Apr. 4, 2002: Investigators push hard to obtain plea deals from ex-Enron lieutenants who made profits from illegitimate business deals.

Apr. 4, 2002: The Securities and Exchange Commission supports need for an outside examiner with special powers to investigate Enron's fall.

Apr. 4, 2002: The Labor Department's plan to replace the overseers of Enron's retirement plans falls apart after disagreements with Enron executives.

Apr. 4, 2002: Thomas White reveals Enron showed significant support prior to his nomination as army secretary, fueling rumors of Enron influence over the Bush administration.

Apr. 4, 2002: Employment contract approved for Enron's interim CEO Stephen Cooper. Executives are hired as Enron executives, not independent contractors, to ensure legal responsibility to the company.

Apr. 8, 2002: Lawyers for Enron shareholders seek to put on trial Wall Street practices of banks and brokerages, which played a crucial role in Enron's fraud on investors.

Apr. 9, 2002: David Duncan, Arthur Andersen's lead Enron auditor, pleads guilty to obstruction of justice in destroying Enron-related documents.

Apr. 11, 2002: House of Representatives passes Bush's new pension reform bill in the wake of Enron scandal.

Apr. 11, 2002: Suicide note left by Baxter, former Enron vice chairman, is released.

Apr. 12, 2002: The Securities and Exchange Commission rejects Enron's bonus and severance plan, saying the firm did not reveal enough information about recipients of the proposed package.

TABLE 7.1 continued

Apr. 12, 2002: Accounting firm Arthur Andersen continues to seek deferred prosecution in exchange for an admission of wrongdoing in the destruction of Enron-related documents.

Apr. 17, 2002: Arthur Andersen breaks off settlement talks with the Justice Separtment in the matter of the destruction of Enron-related documents.

Apr. 17, 2002: A House committee approves legislation passing a new auditor oversight board.

Apr. 18, 2002: Enron's post-collapse President and COO Jeffrey MacMahon announces his resignation, calling for outside leadership of the company.

Apr. 24, 2002: The House passes accounting reform package, calling for stricter oversight and stricter disclosure policies in wake of the Enron scandal.

May 6, 2002: Jury selection begins Monday in the criminal trial of the once-vaunted Arthur Andersen accounting firm in connection with the Enron implosion.

May 7, 2002: Enron directors spread blame around by telling Congress that executives of the company and its auditors, Arthur Andersen LLP, deprived them of information they needed to deal with problems.

May 8, 2002: Suit accuses UBS Paine Webber of serving Enron rather than investors.

May 13,2002: Federal regulators expand trading probe amid damaging Enron memos.

May 14, 2002: Enron's former lead auditor continues his testimony against Arthur Andersen.

May 15, 2002: Senate investigations focus on whether energy regulators should have seen Enron warning signs sooner.

May 23, 2002: Senate Panel Subpoenas White House for information on Enron contacts.

May 24, 2002: Enron's strong ties to the White House are detailed. Papers show aides seeking to limit bankruptcy's damage. As Enron slid toward a bankruptcy filing, the White House's top economic, policy, and communications officials mobilized to minimize the damage to financial markets and to the Bush administration, according to new disclosures to Congress.

June 1,2002: McMahon quits. He assumed the post January 24 in the wake of the resignation of Skilling in August 2001.

June 6,2002: Arthur Andersen Investigation: Criminal Case Goes to Jury

June 11, 2002: Former Enron workers reach a historic severance agreement with Enron; the settlement offers real and immediate severance pay to former employees.

June 25, 2002: Rabobank files a lawsuit claiming that three U.K. bankers colluded with former Enron executives in setting up off-balance sheet deals that ultimately led to the U.S. energy group's demise.

July 11, 2002: Senate panel says Enron directors were largely responsible for firm's demise.

TABLE 7.1 continued

July 18, 2002: U.S. Army secretary Thomas White is due to testify before a Congressional panel. Thomas White denied any knowledge of the manipulation of California electricity markets by Enron Corp.

July 23, 2002: Bankruptcy: Congress probes banks' role in fraud. Officials from leading investment banks Citigroup Inc. and J. P. Morgan Chase under investigation. The U.S. Senate subcommittee on investigation panel focused on $8.5 billion in loans that Enron had received from Citigroup and J. P. Morgan between 1992 and 2001.

July 24, 2002: Officials for two of the nation's largest financial institutions, Citigroup and J. P. Morgan Chase, told Senators today that they did not improperly help Enron disguise portions of the enormous debt that contributed to the company's collapse last fall.

July 29, 2002: A Senate panel last week said a seven-month probe unearthed evidence demonstrating that J. P. Morgan Chase and Citigroup funneled more than $8 billion to Enron disguised as contracts for natural gas and oil, allowing the financially troubled energy giant to hide its enormous debt from credit rating agencies and the investing public for years.

Aug. 1, 2002: Senate panel questions Merrill Lynch on its financial dealings with Enron. Merrill Lynch tried to defend its relationship with Enron before a Senate panel that raised questions about whether the financial firm purchased electricity-generating barges in Nigeria from Enron.

Aug. 2, 2002: Former executive Michael J. Kopper pleaded guilty Wednesday to defrauding Enron and its shareholders using schemes created with ex-chief financial officer Fastow and others. Kopper becomes the first Enron executive to be charged; he could get up to 15 years in prison and be fined millions of dollars when sentenced.

Aug. 24, 2002: Court freezes accounts of relatives of former Enron executive Fastow.

Aug. 26, 2002: U.S. wins first Enron guilty plea; federal authorities delivered their strongest signal yet to the power industry on how tough they intend to play in prosecuting Enron officials.

Aug. 28, 2002: Bankruptcy Court Approves historic settlement between Enron and employee committee. The settlement provides for additional severance pay for eligible severed Enron employees, and authorizes the Employee Committee to investigate and potentially recover sizable bonuses paid to select Enron employees prior to the company's filing for bankruptcy in December 2001.

Aug. 29, 2002: Enron creditors call for $12 million from former Enron executive Kopper. A committee of unsecured Enron creditors has asked the U.S. Bankruptcy Court in New York for the $12 million former Enron executive Michael Kopper has promised to repay the federal government.

Sep. 2, 2002: Enron started the formal process under which it intends to sell its interests in the assets, ranging from Portland General Electric to an electricity distribution company in Brazil to a U.S.-based oil and gas exploration and production company.

TABLE 7.1   continued

Sep. 13, 2002: Three former British bankers have been indicted on wire fraud charges connected to an alleged $7.3 million scheme involving Enron Corp. The indictment, filed Thursday in the U.S. District Court for the Southern District of Texas, alleges the former bank officers secretly invested in an Enron entity, Southampton LP, through a series of financial transactions.

Sep. 16, 2002: In a class action brought by Enron shareholders in the United Astates law firms, Vinson & Elkins and Kirkland & Ellis are, along with Enron executives, the accountants, and a number of banks, named as co-defendants.

Oct. 1, 2002: The University of California filed a motion in U.S. District Court that would prevent documents relating to the University of Californina–led lawsuit against Enron from being sealed.

Oct. 3, 2002: Ex-CFO Fastow charged with fraud and released on $5 million bail. Fastow, who allegedly masterminded schemes to hide $1 billion in debt while reaping $30 million in shadowy profits for himself, became the highest-ranking Enron executive to face charges in the collapse of the energy-trading giant.

Oct. 9, 2002: Senate report blasts SEC for failing to rein in Enron.

Oct. 16, 2002: Arthur Andersen sentenced for its part in Enron scandal. Andersen LLP was fined $500,000 and sentenced to five years probation Wednesday for obstruction of justice in the Enron Corp. investigation.

Oct. 18, 2002: Enron's top West Coast energy trader pleaded guilty Thursday to playing a major role in manipulating the wholesale electricity market during California's power crisis, proving for the first time that criminal fraud contributed heavily to the state's energy woes.

Oct. 31, 2002: Former Enron Corp. chief financial officer Fastow is indicted on 78 federal counts alleging he masterminded a scheme to artificially inflate the energy company's profits.

What did the Enron executives do to mold a corporate culture that resulted in unethical behavior and the collapse of the company? The remainder of this chapter offers some answers.

LEADERSHIP MECHANISMS AND THE ORGANIZATIONAL CULTURE AT ENRON

With corporate leaders who encouraged rule-breaking, fostering an intimidating, aggressive environment, it is not surprising that the ethical boundaries at Enron eroded away to nothing. Leadership is a critical component of the organization's culture because leaders can create, reinforce, or change the organization's culture. In addition, the following five primary mechanisms can be used by a leader to create, direct, manage, or change organization's culture: attention, reaction to crises, role modeling, allocation of rewards, and criteria for selection and dismissal. These five criteria reinforce and encourage behavioral and cultural norms at an organization. The Enron executives used the five mechanisms to reinforce a culture that was morally flexible, opening the door to ethics degeneration, lying, cheating, and stealing.

Attention

The issues that capture the attention of the leader (what is criticized, praised, or asked about) will also capture the attention of the greater organization and will become the focus of the employees. If the leaders of the organization focus on the bottom line, employees believe that financial success is the leading value to consider. Donald M. Wolfe even suggests that a focus on profit, "promotes an unrealistic belief that everything boils down to a monetary game."[5] As such, rules or morality are merely obstacles, impediments along the way to bottom-line financial success.[6] One former executive of Enron described Jeffrey Skilling as a leader driven by the almighty dollar. "Skilling would say all that matters is money. You buy loyalty with money."[7]

Enron executives' attention was clearly focused on profits, power, greed, and influence. They wanted their employees to focus on today's bottom line and to be more clever than the competition. Skilling communicated his priorities to his employees overtly in both word and deed; his intent was unmistakable. Consistently clear signals told employees what was important to leadership—"Profits at all costs."[8]

A quote from a former Enron employee says it best: "There were no rules for people, even in our personal lives. Everything was about the company and everything was supposed to be on the edge—sex, money, all of it."[9] In Sherron Watkins' testimony before the House Subcommittee, she said, "Enron is a very arrogant place, with a feeling of invincibility." Another Enron employee noted about the company's environment, "It was all about creating an atmosphere of deliberately breaking the rules. For example, our official vacation policy was that you could take as much as you wanted whenever you wanted as long as you delivered your results. It drove the human resource department crazy."[10]

Another example of self-promotion and today's bottom-line mentality is former Enron CFO Andrew Fastow's network of questionable partnerships. These partnerships provided profit for Fastow personally, as well as for some of his more favored employees, who were aware of his actions. Fastow demanded that Enron grant permission for him to invest in and personally profit from the partnerships, and he passed on some of his earnings to associates who aided him. In addition, his colleagues within Enron's top ranks were jealous of his profit-taking.

These actions sent a clear message that management's attention was focused on the bottom line for the company as well as personal gain, regardless of the means. Ethics were pliable, as evidenced by Fastow's special-interest dealings. The board of directors suspended the company's code of ethics at least twice, which made Fastow a wealthy man at the expense of Enron.[11] If an organization's leaders seem to care only about the short-term bottom line, employees quickly get the message too.

How else could employees read the tea leaves at Enron as focused on anything other than the short-term when CEO Kenneth Lay both blessed the relaxation of conflict-of-interest rules designed to protect Enron from the very kinds of transactions (self-dealing) that brought the company down and participated in board meetings allowing the creation of the off-balance-sheet partnerships that were part of those transactions? By late summer 2001, when Lay was reassuring investors and employees that all was well, he had already been informed that the company had problems with some investment vehicles that could cost it hundreds of millions of dollars.[12]

The bottom-line mentality supported the goal of financial success as the only value to be considered. Ethical questions have been raised since the collapse of Enron. What about morality? What about the long-term implications of employee's actions? Will profits be gained at any cost? "Everyone was just too excited about the stock price and how rich we were getting. The company sold its soul for a higher stock price," according to a senior executive.[13]

Reaction to Crises

A crisis allows followers to see what the leader values, because emotionality brings these values to the surface. With each impending crisis, leaders have an opportunity to signal throughout the organization about the company's values. Enron's reaction to crisis provides further evidence of the company's unethical bent.

Enron was facing a crisis: how could they sustain their phenomenal growth rate? Leaders reacted to that by creating a culture that valued profitability, even when it was at the expense of everything else. The off-balance-sheet partnerships they got into were tremendously risky. However, since normal growth of the stock price would have fallen short of expectations anyway, the only thing they could do was to pursue the target profitability of the unrealistic expectations. The leaders should have had the vision to recognize this was an accident waiting to happen.

Once the Enron situation came to light, the reaction from the Enron executives was very telling. The executives became busy shifting the blame and pointing fingers. Jeffery Skilling even went as far as tellling an incredulous Congress that despite his Harvard Business School degree and business experience, he neither knew of nor would understand the intricacies of the Enron accounting deals. Skilling also was quoted on CNN saying if "he knew then what he knows now—he *still* would not do anything differently."

Even before the issues came to light, it appears that Skilling was willing to abandon the company to save his own skin as evidenced by his mysterious resignation in August 2001, giving only "personal reasons" as an explanation for his sudden departure (and he still sold significant amounts of company stock at a premium). Both Kenneth Lay and Sherron Watkins also sold stock before prices began to dramatically plummet. Kenneth Lay sold stock, he says, because he had some personal debts to pay off. Sherron Watkins claims she sold hers after the September 11, 2001, terrorist attacks. Watkins also sold stock while she was making allegations of deceptive accounting practices.

Enron began systematically firing those it could lay blame on before it declared bankruptcy. A self-serving exoneration committee was employed to explain (or excuse?) the current situation.[14] After Skilling resigned his post, Kenneth Lay returned as CEO, promising that there were no "accounting issues, trading issues, or reserve issues" at Enron. Congressional testimony, news accounts, and federal investigations have since shown that wasn't the case. Throughout October 2001, Lay insisted that Enron had access to cash and that the company was "performing very well," while he failed to disclose that Enron had written down shareholders' equity by $1.2 billion, or that Moody's was considering downgrading Enron's debt.[15] Company insiders also referred to Loretta Lynch, the Yale-educated litigator who was among the first to question Enron's practices, as "an idiot." They called Bethany McLean, the *Fortune* magazine journalist who first broke the story, "a looker who doesn't know anything."[16]

Next consider the crisis of having to admit accounting irregularities. At first, the leaders of the company tried to deny there was a problem. They next tried to cover up any evidence of a problem or any wrongdoing. They even tried to seize the computers of anyone they thought was trying to expose them, as well as to destroy many files thought to be guilt-proving. Many executives tried blaming each other, saying that they didn't know what was going on or that it was someone else's responsibility to know about the problems and do something about it. Both Kenneth Lay and his wife proclaimed his innocence. Lay claimed to have been unaware of the sweetheart deals, which were entirely the brainchildren of Skilling and Fastow. Watkins also blamed them for the debacle, while shifting any blame from herself.

"I take the fifth."[17] This was the response Kenneth Lay gave to the Senate Commerce Committee when asked to explain Enron's failure. Although all but one of Enron's officers (curiously, Skilling) invoked the Fifth Amendment right not to self-incriminate, the story has played out much like that of the Salomon Brothers and John Gutfreund fiasco in the early 1990s. Document shredding and lies, both overt and by omission, had become the preferred strategy for Enron's management.[18] These bold acts from Enron leadership show a poor reaction to crisis.

From anonymous whistle-blowing to hiding behind the 5th Amendment, to declaring bankruptcy, to document shredding, to committing suicide (Cliff Baxter), the leaders at Enron have run the gamut of responses in their reaction to the company's crisis. Willet and Always (2002) noted that "the mantra at Enron seems to be that ethical wrong-doing is to be hidden at any cost; deny, play the dupe, claim ignorance ('the ostrich instruction') lie, quit."[19] It appears that the truth and its consequences have never been a part of the Enron culture.

Role Modeling (How Leaders Behave)

Actions speak louder than words. Role-modeling behavior is thus a very powerful tool that leaders have to develop and influence corporate culture. Through role modeling, teaching, and coaching, leaders reinforce the values that support the organizational culture. Employees often emulate leaders' behavior and look to the leaders for cues to appropriate behavior. Many companies are encouraging employees to be more entrepreneurial, that is, to take more initiative and be more innovative in their jobs. The Scientific Foundation reports a study that showed that managers who want to change the organization's culture to a more entrepreneurial one must "walk the talk"; in other words, they must demonstrate entrepreneurial behaviors themselves.[20] This is the case with any cultural value. Employees observe the behavior of leaders to find out what is valued in the organization. Arguably, this was the most significant shortcoming of Enron executives.

According to the values statement in Enron's annual report, the company maintains strong commitments to communication, respect, integrity, and excellence. However, there is little evidence to show management modeling of these values. For instance, while the first pillar of the values statement addresses an obligation to communicate, Sherron Watkins describes a much different pattern of behaviors, taken from hearing transcripts:

> I continued to ask questions and seek answers, primarily from former coworkers in the Global Finance Group or in the business units that had

hedged assets with Raptor. I never heard reassuring explanations. I was not comfortable confronting either Mr. Skilling or Mr. Fastow with my concerns. To do so, I believe, would have been a job-terminating move.[21]

Enron's leaders sent a strong message about their values through their own actions. They broke the law as they concentrated too specifically on financial measures and the creative partnerships described earlier. For example, on October 16, Mr. Lay announced to analysts that Enron had eliminated $1.2 billion in shareholder equity by terminating a partnership created by former CFO Andrew Fastow. This arrangement allowed Enron to buy and sell assets without carrying the debt on its books. This was an effective method of keeping Enron's credit clean and the stock price high. These actions clearly show the self-serving attitude of Enron leadership. The executives not only condoned such unethical behavior, they initiated it and were rewarded for it. These partnerships were used to deceive investors about the enormous debt Enron was incurring. It also sent a message to employees that full and complete disclosure is not a requirement, or even recommendation. If the company achieved short-term benefits by hiding information, it was acceptable.

Enron's leaders also ignored, then denied serious problems with their business transactions and were more concerned about their personal financial rewards than those of the company. For example, when the company's stock price began to drop as the problems were becoming public, the company was "coincidentally" transitioning from one investment program to another. Employees were unable to sell their stock, but the executives were quickly selling off many of their shares. Another abhorrent example is the executives' lack of integrity in communicating to the employees and investors. They maintained that the company was financially stable and that many of their emerging problems really were not too serious, even though they knew the truth and were making financial decisions to protect their personal gain.

In retrospect, the leadership of Enron almost certainly dictated the company's outcome through their own actions by providing perfect conditions for unethical behavior. Michael Josephson, president of the Josephson Institute of Ethics, aptly described these conditions as they relate to the character of leadership. "People may produce spectacular results for a while, but it is inevitable that techniques depending so heavily on fear as a motivator generate survival strategies that include cheating, distortion, and an internal competitive ethos characterized by a look-out-for-number-one attitude."[22] Josephson might argue that Enron's leaders not only lacked the ethical courage to prevent the demise of the company, but also lacked the character to know the difference. "Just as the destiny of individuals is determined by personal character, the destiny of an organization is determined by the character of its leadership. And when individuals are derailed because of a lack of character, the organization will also be harmed."[23]

Allocation of Rewards

The behavior displayed by people the leader decides to reward with pay increases or promotions signals to others what is necessary to succeed in an organization. Thus, to ensure that values are accepted, leaders should reward behavior that is consistent with the values. Some organizations, for example, may claim that they use a pay-for-performance system that distributes rewards on the basis of performance. When the time comes for raises, however, the increases are awarded according to length of service with the company. Imagine the feelings of a high-performing newcomer who has heard leaders espouse the value of rewarding individual performance and then receives only a tiny raise—a violation of the social contract.

The reward system created by a leader indicates what is prized and expected in the organization. This view is in line with a basic management doctrine: You get what you measure and pay for.[24] When an instance, of ethical achievement occurs—for instance when someone acts with integrity and honor—the organization's leaders must reward it. Such an effort sends as clear a message to the rest of the organization as when an organization rewards an employee who acts unethically.

Enron's reward system established a "win-at-all-costs" focus. The company's leadership promoted and retained only those employees who produced consistently, with little regard to ethics. In 2000, according to the *New York Times,* Skilling singled out one of his vice presidents, Louise Kitchen, for her results-oriented approach to Enron's online business. Kitchen started the company's Internet-based trading business even though Skilling repeatedly turned down her requests to begin such a program. Kitchen ignored the former CEO's decision and instead used already allocated funds to pull the new network together. A former vice president who attended the meeting described it best. "The moral of this story is break the rules, you can cheat, you can lie, but as long as you make money, it's all right."[25]

The company's compensation structure was one of several questionable policies and procedures that fostered an unethical work culture. The compensation structure promoted self-interest above any other interest, which produced a deterioration of the team approach once used by Enron associates. Performance reviews were public events, and poor performance was ridiculed (or employees were fired through a "rank and yank" process that encouraged employee/coworker sabotage). The strongest performing units even went as far as to ignore company policy—granting unlimited vacation time, as noted earlier, as long as the work got done; no one would listen to Human Resources' complaints.[26]

Extremely high bonuses were doled out to executives who behaved in desirable ways. Ridiculously large bonuses were paid in the form of stock options to executives, who were thereby incited to keep the stock price up at any cost. Annual bonuses were as high as $1 million for traders, for executives it was even more. Enron developed a reputation for both internal and external ruthlessness, as employees attempted to crush the competition wherever it lay, and was considered extremely aggressive for a non-investment bank. Additionally, the executives at Enron played favorites, inviting top performers to spend weekend vacations with the executive staff. The best workers (determined through day-to-day bottom-line results) received staggering incentives and exorbitant bonuses. One example of this was Car Day. On this day, an array of lavish sports cars arrived for the most successful employees.[27]

Retention bonuses that were paid to about 500 executives shortly before the company declared bankruptcy ranged in value from $1,000 to $5 million. Some believe that these bonuses were granted to Enron's inner circle and to people who helped in setting up the problematic financial partnerships that led to the company's downfall. Overall, Enron's system for allocating rewards rewarded individuals who embraced Enron's aggressive, individualistic culture and were based on short-term profits and financial measures.

Criteria of Selection and Dismissal (How Leaders Hire and Fire Employees)

The criteria for hiring and firing employees describes how leaders' decisions about whom to recruit or dismiss signals their values to all their employees. The selection of newcomers to an organization is a powerful way in which leaders reinforce culture. Leaders often unconsciously look for individuals who are similar to current organizational members in terms of values and assumptions. Some companies hire individuals on the recommendation of a current employee; this tends to perpetuate the culture, because the new employees typically hold similar values. Promotion-from-within policies also serve to reinforce organizational culture.

Ken Lay placed an immediate focus on hiring the best and smartest people, those who would thrive in a competitive environment. Skilling shared Lay's philosophy. Skilling hired only Ivy League graduates with a hunger for money that matched his. He hired people who considered themselves the best and the brightest and were out to forward their own causes. Stanford and Harvard graduates, who would otherwise have worked on Wall Street, these people were paid well to work in Texas and to build the Enron culture. Their reward for giving up the allure of Silicon Valley and Wall Street was a high salary and a large bonus opportunity.

Skilling perpetuated a focus on short-term transactional endeavors from the very beginning by hiring employees who embodied the beliefs that he was trying to instill: aggressiveness, greed, a will to win at all costs, and an appreciation for circumventing the rules. This was the same culture of greed that brought turmoil to Salomon Brothers on Wall Street in the early 1990s. Office sexual relations were fairly common, even among married employees. Divorce rates among senior executives were skyrocketing as well. Instant gratification, both personally and professionally, was part of the Enron culture. Skilling did everything he could to surround himself with individuals who had similar values and assumptions and fit into the Enron culture.

The way a company fires an employee and the rationale behind the firing also communicates the culture. Some companies deal with poor performers by trying to find them a place within the organization where they can perform better and make a contribution. Other companies seem to operate under the philosophy that those who cannot perform are out quickly.[28]

Enron carried out an annual "rank and yank" policy, whereby the bottom 15 to 20 percent of producers was let go or fired after a formal evaluation process each year. Associates graded their peers, which caused a great amount of distrust and paranoia among employees. Enron's employee reviews added to the competition by reviewing job performance in a public forum and sending the bottom 5 percent to the redeployment office—dubbed the "office of shame."[29] What better way to develop a distrustful work environment than to pit employees against one another and as Larry Bossidy, CEO of AlliedSignal, recently noted "forced ranking promotes bad employee morale,"[30] a win-at-all costs mentality, and a willingness to cross the ethical line.

According to Enrongate.com, employees who tried to blow the whistle were punished. Whistle-blowers received career setbacks and hostility. It did not pay to tell the Enron secrets. The most popular whistle-blower, Sherron Watkins, recounted how her fears about being fired for speaking out led her to reach out to Kenneth Lay through anonymous warnings. She even publicly stated that Andrew Fastow tried to have her fired once he found out that she was the author of the anonymous memo to Lay.[31] Watkins reported that her computer was confiscated and she was moved to another office after she submitted her letter to Lay. Another employee, Jeff McMahon, also spoke up against the conflicts of interest seen in the off-book partnerships. As a reward for his actions, he was reassigned to a new job.

On the other hand, those who closed their eyes to the wrongdoings were rewarded. Chief Accounting Officer Richard Causey renegotiated his contract for a large gain. Mr. Causey received $425,000 per year along with a $300,000 signing bonus. He was eventually fired by the board and received no severance pay. A former Enron employee said, "It was very clear what the measures were and how you got promoted at Enron. That absolutely drives behavior . . . getting the deal was paramount at Enron."[32] In fact, a Houston headhunter described the freedom given by Skilling when he was Enron's CEO to loyal employees, "Once you gained Jeff's trust, the leash became really long."[33]

The selection and rewards system was consistent with the culture at Enron. It promoted greed, selfishness, and jealousy within the organization. These are the same values that those at the top espoused and promoted. Like Salomon Brothers, Enron's lifeblood was young people (youth was not considered a barrier to success, but almost a prerequisite). Enron was also guilty of promoting Destructive Achievers?[34] According to Kelly, "No action of management has more impact on its operational ethics than the people it promotes, dismisses, or allows to stagnate." Lay and Skilling seemed to exemplify Kelly's Destructive Achiever (DA), who "has the charisma of a leader [ethical manager] but lacks his operational values; this achiever's net effect on the long-term welfare of the organization is negative."[35] Kelly notes that "Every time a DA is promoted and the ethical difference between the DA and other candidates is apparent to the staff, the organization's value base is diminished and the way is opened to even faster deterioration."[36] Enron's executives selected those employees who shared their aggressive, win-at-all-costs mentality. Their short-term view may have prevented them from seeing what the long-term costs of this kind of personality could be on the organization as a whole.

MADISON AVENUE MENTALITY AT ENRON

Also evident was the *Madison Avenue mentality*—a perspective suggesting that anything is right if the public can be convinced that it's right. There should be no doubt that Jeffrey Skilling and others at Enron had convinced the public that their model was right. As advocated by Skilling and Fastow, anyone who couldn't understand its business "just didn't get it." Let us not forget how many Wall Street analysts were so willing to believe what so few understood about the Enron model. The analysts took the company's word on its numbers because they delivered the growth earnings—and that's what mattered most. Michigan's congressman John Dingell's words offer an insightful view of this situation: "Here is an example of superbly complex financial reports.

They didn't have to lie. All they had to do was to obfuscate it with sheer complexity—although they probably lied too."[37]

At Enron it appeared that senior leadership was more concerned about their actions appearing ethical than by their legitimate morality—a public relations–guided morality. It is this kind of thinking that leads companies like Enron to create an environment in which unethical behavior can occur, while also hiding their unethical actions (e.g., Andrew Fastow's network of questionable partnerships) or otherwise justifying them by attempting to explain them as completely acceptable. Rather than disclose the rampant conflicts of interest within the company, Enron hired countless lawyers and accountants to help it meet the letter of the law while ignoring its intent. Further, it was common knowledge at Enron that if you didn't ask the right questions you didn't get the right answers. The latter point is most evident in the following comments offered by Skilling in a February 2001 interview with *Fortune* magazine: "Our business is not a black box. It's a very simple model. People who raise questions are people who have not gone through it in detail. We have explicit answers, but people want to throw rocks at us."[38] However, once Enron was exposed, Jeffery Skilling found himself unable to provide the requisite explicit answers.

Enron was a human refinery, where managers wrung their hands over their advancing age and feared their superiors would deem them too meek. Some worried that not giving enough to the chairman's favorite political candidate could send their careers into a dive. Some even detected a menacing tone in letters urging them to offer large contributions to United Way. Other employees noted that one day you were viewed with favor and the next day you were not. Employees knew who was in the in-crowd and who was not; and many wanted to continue to be liked in the organization and would do everything they could to ensure that they would be liked.

Enron regularly bragged about its pressure-cooker culture. This was most evident in an Enron annual report: "When Enron no longer needs someone they are removed and replaced." "We insist on results." Some former Enron employees said they embraced the competition. Others, however, said loyalty required a sort of groupthink. You had to "keep drinking the Enron water," or more sardonically, "drink the Kool-Aid," a reference to the poisoned drink used in the Jonestown massacre of 1978.

The entire cultural framework of Enron not only allowed unethical behavior to flourish, it almost guaranteed it. Enron thrived in an atmosphere of arrogance and invincibility, where risk-taking was encouraged and a relative lack of supervision existed. Performance reviews were crucial, and people were reluctant to criticize anyone who might have an influence on their own evaluations. Like other employees,

Enron employees looked to their leaders for the behavior to model. Since Enron's leadership openly encouraged short-term profitability, autonomy, risk taking, and innovation, without ever explicitly stating or exhibiting that they believed ethical behavior was a value of the organization, it is no wonder that ethical violations continued to build during Enron's period of prosperity. Enron's internal culture provided an ethical void, and the support and push it was given by numerous exogenous stakeholders rapidly culminated in its momentous downfall.

The story of Enron sounds so smart it was stupid. Deeply defective leadership from Lay and Skilling played a significant role in creating the company's culture, which led to its undoing. We may never know whether it was hubris, greed, psychological shock or just plain stupidity that let them to behave in the way they did.[39] Consequences of unethical or illegal actions are not usually realized until much later than when the act is committed.[40]

Despite the formation of Enron in 1985 from the union of Houston Natural Gas and Omaha-based InterNorth, its true culture did not actually emerge until 1988, when it went from a "stodgy but safe gas pipeline company" to the "World's Leading Company," capitalizing on the deregulation of both gas and energy and pioneering the swapping of natural gas. The new culture at Enron, headed by founder Lay, started out as a culture of challenge and confrontation. When Skilling and Fastow joined the company in 1990, the culture quickly evolved into one of arrogance, aggressiveness, greed, cockiness, secretiveness, and ruthlessness.

Unfortunately, the leaders at Enron were textbook examples of the behaviors leaders should attempt *not* to model. Table 7.2 offers a comparison between the behaviors of ethical and unethical leaders and corresponding examples exhibited by Enron's leaders.

Enron's house of cards collapsed as a result of a decision process that evolved from the erosion of ethics within the company. The culture at Enron, little by little, ate away at the company's ethical boundaries, allowing more and more questionable behavior to slip through the cracks. This deterioration did not go entirely unnoticed. Individual employees at Enron, auditors at Andersen and even some analysts who watched the financial markets noticed aspects of the Enron situation that did not seem right, long before the public became aware of Enron's transgressions. Even though these whistle-blowers existed, no leaders at Enron wanted to listen. For example, Enron appeared on short-seller Jim Chanos's radar screen in October 2000. According to Chanos, "It has been our experience that gain-on-sale accounting creates an irresistible temptation on the part of managements heavily incentivized with options and heavy stock ownership to create earnings out of thin air."[41] Despite this warning, no one listened. Sherron Watkins warned CEO

TABLE 7.2 Ethical and Unethical Leader' Behaviors and Enron Examples

Ethical Leader Behaviors	Unethical Leader Behaviors	Enron Examples
Is committed to high ethical standards which apply to everyone	Is willing to compromise standards based on the situation—top performers and executives are held to a different standard	Lay recommended to the board and Skilling to waive the ethics rules in 1999 and allow Fastow to lead private partnerships, while maintaining his position at Enron.
Uses customer welfare, doing what's best for the public, as one of the primary standards	Uses the company's welfare, doing what's best for them, as the primary standard	A handful of high-paid individuals pocketed millions of dollars while simultaneously eroding away the life savings of thousands of unwitting employees. To accomplish this, senior executives promoted the use of aggressive accounting techniques, entered into several questionable off-balance-sheet financing transactions, and misled analysts, investors, and the public alike.
Is willing to confront situations where ethics are questionable and confronts ethical issues openly and honestly	Is unwilling to confront ethical issues unless they are safe, uncomplicated, and lack risk, doesn't make ethics an issue, ignores ethical issues or deals with them in a covert or behind-the-scenes way	Mr. Odom, a partner in Andersen's Houston office, encouraged the destruction of Enron documents.
Takes timely and appropriate action on ethical issues	Avoids taking action on ethical issues in favor of expediency or seeks to "soften" the blow by minimizing the impact, takes action only when forced to	Baxter reportedly told Skilling that "We are headed for a train wreck and it's your job to get out in front of the train and try to stop it" ("CEO was Misserved," Washington Post). No one stopped the train wreck, and Baxter committed suicide.
Is proactive in heading off ethical problems	Does not deal with ethical issues until there is an obvious and significant problem	Same as above.
Sets an example for others, treats ethics as a priority	Downplays the importance of ethics, treats it as a nice to-do, not a must do	Same as above.
Treats ethics as a performance measure no different than sales, etc., actively supervises it	Seeks to minimize his/her personal responsibility for supervision of ethical issues and behavior	Once this debacle was called to attention, the reaction from the Enron executives was and continues to be shameful. They seem to blame one another or feign complete ignorance about the illegality of Enron's conduct.
Learns about the legal and ethical aspects of the business and doesn't plead ignorance when asked a question	Ignores the legal and ethical aspects, "that's what attorneys are for," pleads ignorance of the issues and the regulations or rules	Both Lay and his wife proclaim his innocence. He claims to have been unaware of the sweetheart deals, which were entirely the brainchildren of Skilling and Fastow. Watkins also blames them for the debacle, while shifting any blame from herself. Skilling and Fastow are not talking at all, with brief statements being made only by their lawyers. No one will accept responsibility for his or her actions.

TABLE 7.2   continued

Ethical Leader Behaviors	Unethical Leader Behaviors	Enron Examples
Does not use an excuse that other companies have lower standards	Sets his/her standard at the lowest level of the competition and uses as an excuse that other companies are not taking as high a standard	No example found.

Lay about the accounting irregularities, and a letter from an Arthur Andersen auditor predicted the magnitude of the accounting scandal, but still no one listened.

What existed in Enron's culture that kept individual employees from outing the executive wrongdoers, and what about the Enron way permitted the executives to behave the way they did? First, Enron's culture is an excellent example of groupthink at work. Although very individualistic, the culture at Enron was one that promoted conformity. Employees were loyal and wanted to be seen as part of the star team and to partake in its benefits. Employees were focused on the bottom line and "promoted short-term solutions that were immediately financially sound despite the fact that they would cause problems for the organization as a whole . . . rules of ethical conduct were merely barriers to success."[42]

Enron's top executives set the tone for this culture. Personal ambition and greed seemed to overshadow much of their corporate and individual lives. They strove to maximize their individual wealth by initiating and participating in scandalous behaviors. Jeffrey Skilling, former President and CEO, made $15.5 million; and Lay, chairman and CEO, made $16.1 million. Although Fastow's total was not available, we can make an educated guess that he also made millions, because options' strike prices were usually low and Enron's stock was trading at sixty times earnings.

How did Enron's top executives partake in fraudulent behavior and not get caught? The answer is quite simple—a failure of ethical leadership and corporate culture. According to Watkins, Enron's corporate culture was "arrogant" and "intimidating" and discouraged employees from reporting the partnerships the executives used to hide debt. In her testimony to the House subcommittee, she made the following statement:

There were swindlers in the emperor's new clothes discussing the fine material that they were weaving. I think Mr. Skilling and Mr. Fastow are highly intimidating individuals and I think they intimidated a number of people into accepting the partnerships and accounting schemes they concocted.[43]

CONCLUSION

The debacle at Enron, like the scandal at Salomon Brothers under John Gutfreund's leadership in the early 1990s, highlights a leadership style by Lay, Skilling, and Fastow that helped create a break-the-rules and win-at-all-costs culture or ethical climate that resulted in unethical and illegal consequences. The Enron executives' actions and behavior communicated important messages to others in the organization about the company's ethical climate. Enron's culture seems to have created an atmosphere ripe for the unethical and illegal behavior that occurred.

At Enron, it was clear that the stock price was the only thing that mattered. Executives at Enron didn't care how you got your numbers up—that was up to you; as long as you were successful, you would be rewarded. Short-term gains were the name of the game, and personal gains increased Enron's employee's motivation. In both words and deeds senior leadership communicated their priorities to employees: short-term gains and profits at all costs. Enron executives wanted their employees to focus on today's bottom line and to be more clever than the competition. Short-term transactional endeavors were an important part of organizational success, and employees were only as good as their last performance.

Personal ambition and greed seemed to overshadow much of the Enron top executives' corporate and individual lives. As evidenced by their 2001 stock trades Enron's executives were committed to maximizing their individual wealth, and rules of ethical conduct were merely barriers to success.

The counternorms of secrecy and deceitfulness were accepted and supported by the Enron organization; it did not pay to tell the Enron secrets. Many other organizational counternorms promoted morally and ethically questionable organization practices. If time and space permitted, discussing them would further help our understanding of how Enron's organizational culture was developed and reinforced.

Lay's resignation and the firing of individuals like Fastow will not be enough to change the fabric of the company. The leadership and culture that brought Enron to its knees makes hopes for improvement look bleak. The company filed for bankruptcy, and former and current employees of the company will continue to go through court hearings. This will be a lengthy process, with the outcome being only a guess. Enron will survive if it implements a genuine cultural turnaround strategy based on sound ethical practices.

Cultural change or an ethical turnaround for a company is a long and complicated process that cannot happen overnight or by simply firing unethical senior executives. However, such action is a good first step in clearing out the vestiges of the old unethical culture and creating, shaping, and maintaining a new culture committed to ethics. The company's new leaders could learn a great deal from the discussion in the next chapter of the actions taken by Warren Buffett during his interim leadership role at Salomon Brothers following the bond trading scandal.

NOTES

1. C. A. Bartlett and M. Glinska, *Enron's Transformation: From Gas Pipeline to New Economy Powerhouse* (Boston: Harvard Business School Press, 2001).

2. M. Josephson, "Character: Linchpin of Leadership," *Executive Excellence* 16, no. 8 (1999), 13–14.

3. P. Behr, "Enron Raised Funds in Private Offering: Shareholders in Dark, Documents Show," *Washington Post* (January 22, 2002), A01.

4. Ibid.

5. D. Wolfe, "Is There Integrity in the Bottomline: Managing Obstacles to Executive Integrity," in S. Srivastva (ed.), *Executive Integrity: The Search for High Human Values in Organizational Life* (San Francisco: Jossey-Bass, 1988), pp. 140–171.

6. R. R. Sims, "Changing an Organization's Culture Under New Leadership," *Journal of Business Ethics* 25 (2000), 65–78.

7. W. Zellner, "Jeff Skilling: Enron's Missing Man," *Business Week Online* (February 11, 2002).

8. R. Tracinski, "Enron Ethics," *Capitalism Magazine* [On-line] (January 28, 2002). Available: *http://www.capitalismagazine.com/2002/january/rwt.enron.htm*.

9. P. D. Broughton, "Enron Cocktail of Cash, Sex and Fast Living," *News.* Telegraph.co.uk (On-line journal). (February 13, 2002).

10. Op.cit, Bartlett and Glinska, *Enron's Transformation*, 11.

11. J. Landers, "'Enron Exec's Silence Is No Shock: Testimony Would Have Followed Hard-hitting Report on Activities," *The Dallas Morning News*, 2002 [On-line], Available: *http://www.kmsb.com/business/news/506152 enron.html*

12. B. Gruley and R. Smith, "Anatomy of a Fall: Keys to Success Left Kenneth Lay Open to Disaster," *The Wall Street Journal* (April 26, 2002), A1, A5.

13. G. Hansell, "The Fall of Enron Pressure Cooker Finally Exploded," 2002. *The Houston Chronicle [On-line]. Available: http://www.russreyn.com/news/news-item.asp?news=235.*

14. K. Brown and H. Sender, "Enron's Board Fires Arthur Andersen: Questions Arise about Auditor's Actions," *The Wall Street Journal*, 2002 [On-line]. Available: *http://wsjclassroomedition.com/tj 011802 enron.htm*; K. Eichenwald, "Report Lays Out Troubles at Enron: Internal Investigation Finds Profits Overstated to Executive's Enrichment," *New York Times*, 2002 [On-line]. Available: *http://www.austin360.com/aas/business/020302/3enrong.html*.

15. "Explaining the Enron Bankruptcy," CNN.com. (January 12, 2002). Available: *http://www.cnn.com.html*.

16. M. Dowd, "Enron, Hollywood Version," *The Roanoke Times* (February 10, 2002), 1.

17. *U.S. Congressional Hearing* (February 6, 2002), Washington: Oversight and Investigations Subcommittee Hearing on the Financial Collapse of Enron Coporation.

18. Brown and H. Sender, "Enron's Board."

19. B. Willet and T. Always, "For Investors, X Marks the Spot, Whether They Choose to See It or Not," FallStreet.com, 2002 [On-line]. Available: *http://www/ fallstreet.com/Spotlight/jan2502/htm.*

20. J. A. Pearce, II, T. R. Kramer and D. K. Robbins, "Effects of Managers' Entrepreneurial Behavior on Subordinates," *Journal of Business Venturing* 12 (1997): 147–60.

21. U.S. Congressional Hearings

22. Josephson, "Character," 11.

23. Ibid.

24. L. V. Larimer, "Reflections on Ethics and Integrity," *HRFocus* (April, 1997), 5.

25. J. Schwartz, "Darth Vader, Machiavelli, Skilling Set Intense Pace," *New York Times* (February 7, 2002), 1–2.

26. Bartlett and Glinska, *Enron's* Transformation, 13.

27. Broughton, "Enron Cocktail."

28. R. R. Sims and J. Brinkmann, "Leaders as Moral Role Models: The Case of John Gutfreund at Salomon Brothers," *Journal of Business Ethics* 35 (2000), 327–39.

29. J. Frey and H. Rosin, "Enron's Green Acres," *The Washington Post* (February 25, 2002), 1.

30. Ibid.

31. T. Hamburger, "Watkins Tells of 'Arrogant' Culture; Enron Stifled Staff Whistle-Blowing," *The Wall Street Journal* (February 15, 2002), A3, C1.

32. Hansell,

33. Zellner,

34. C. M. Kelly, "The Interrelationship of Ethics and Power in Today's Organizations," *Organizational Dynamics* (Summer 1987), 5–18.

35. Ibid.

36. Ibid.

37. B. McClean, J. Sung Revell, and A. Helyar, "Why Enron Went Bust: Start with Arrogance. Add Greed, Deceit, and Financial Chicanery. What Do You Get? A Company That Wasn't What It Was Cracked Up to Be," *Business 2.0, 2001* [On-line]. Available: *http://www.business2.com/articles/mag/print/0.1643.36124.FF .html.*

38. Ibid.

39. P. Eavis, "Enron Reaps What Its Cowboy Culture Sowed," TheStreet.com, 2001 [On-line]. Available: *http://www.thestreet.com/markets/detox/10004675.html*

40. R. R. Sims, "Leadership, Organizational Culture and Ethics," *Teaching Note,* 2002 Graduate School of Business, College of William and Mary, Williamsburg, Va.

41. Hamburger, "Watkins Tells," C1.

42. Sims, "Leadership," 3.

43. Hamburger, "Watkins Tells," C1.

8

Making Sense of Stakeholder Culpability in the Enron Demise

INTRODUCTION

Stakeholder theory and the accompanying stakeholder concept has become a central idea and commonly used framework for understanding business ethics. The five mechanisms available to a leader to develop and maintain an organization's culture have been explained (Chapters 6 and 7). We can gain further understanding of why giants like Enron take ethical falls by looking at the roles various stakeholders may have played in contributing to the company's fall. This chapter is concerned with gaining greater understanding of the various stakeholders responsible for or impacted by Enron's ethical wrongdoings. In particular, the chapter highlights some of the focal stakeholders and their culpability in the fall of Enron.

A STAKEHOLDER ANALYSIS OF ENRON

An important key to a stakeholder approach to understanding the Enron or any other organizational situation is to recognize that an organization has responsibilities in their relationships with all stakeholders (see Chapter 4). These responsibilities can be categorized according to corporate social responsibility and classified as economic, legal, ethical, and philanthropic.

Many different stakeholder groups either contributed to the development of Enron's ethical problems or have been affected by the resulting bankruptcy. As noted earlier, stakeholders have a tremendous capacity to influence situations and to drive outcomes. Therefore, it is important to examine the affected individuals and groups to evaluate their interests and levels of involvement when trying to make sense of such debacles. Obviously, Enron's employees and the Enron executives represent two primary groups. However, other groups have also played roles of significant influence. Understanding the interests of each affected group is helpful in identifying the goals and desires of the groups as well as accurately assessing the situation as a whole. A company failure the size of Enron's has the ability to impact many people indirectly. Obviously, legislation or business policy changes that are developed as a result will have an impact on not only the stakeholders of today, but members of the business community for years to come.

As a focal stakeholder, Enron management necessarily faced a need to balance the interests and objectives of many different stakeholders in the course of guiding the firm. Although these stakeholders face different consequences from Enron's fall, a common theme with these different stakeholders is that all displayed behaviors consistent with maximizing their own welfare. Many of these stakeholders—and especially the focal stakeholder, Enron management—were inclined to make short-term decisions to maximize their own wealth despite the potential consequences..

Enron and its subsidiaries had a wide variety of stakeholders: the board of directors, executives, employees, investors/stockholders, auditors (Arthur Andersen), bankers/analysts, law firms (Vinson & Elkins), and government—regulatory agencies, legislators, politicians, and community/public-at-large.

ENRON'S BOARD OF DIRECTORS

During a Senate subcommittee hearing May 7, 2002, key senators said, "Enron Corp.'s board of directors ignored a series of red flags about the company's risky accounting strategies for years."[1] The subcommittee was seeking to determine what the directors knew of Enron's complex financial dealings, including a web of thousands of off-balance-sheet partnerships used to hide some $1 billion in debt from investors and federal regulators. "The board had ample knowledge of the dangerous waters in which Enron was swimming and it didn't do anything about it," said Senator Carl Levin (D-Mich.).[2]

At the time, five current and former Enron board members appeared before the Senate permanent subcommittee on investigations to answer questions about what they knew of the company's complex financial partnerships before it went into bankruptcy in December 2001 and why they did not scrutinize Enron managers more carefully. In a surprise development, one of the witnesses testified that Enron's former chief financial officer, Andrew S. Fastow, told him he had made more than $45 million from some of the partnerships set up by Fastow to help Enron move debt off its books. Charles LeMaistre, who had headed the board's compensation committee, said that the board became concerned after the *Wall Street Journal* reported in October 2001 that Fastow had earned more than $7 million in compensation from the partnerships. Along with another board member, LeMaistre called Fastow on October 23, 2001, to ask about his investments and income from the partnerships. LeMaistre said Fastow told him that he had committed approximately $5 million to the partnerships and earned $45 million in income.

"I do not believe that the Board of Directors would ever have approved Mr. Fastow's participation in the partnerships if we had known he would be generating such compensation," LeMaistre said in prepared testimony.[3] Senator Levin was critical about the board's reluctance to seek such information earlier. "The point is you didn't get it and you didn't ask to get it," he said. "To me that is an approach which is totally unacceptable. That is what characterized the board. It was deferential to management." "Board members are charged with protecting the interests of average shareholders," said Senator Susan Collins (R-Maine), "yet Enron investors lost $60 billion when the company fell."[4]

Senators (along with many others) said the board should have been on alert as early as 1999, when auditors at Arthur Andersen LLP told them that the company employed accounting strategies that "push the limit." Senators asked why the board did not pay more attention to partnerships known as Whitewing and LJM, which Enron used to move debts off its books.

In response to questions from the Senate investigative panel, board members said that executives of the company and its auditor Arthur Andersen hid from them the information they needed to exercise oversight and deal with problems. "We cannot, I submit, be criticized for failing to address or remedy problems that were concealed from us," Herbert Winokur, a director and chairman of the Enron board's finance committee, testified at a hearing by the investigative panel of the Senate Governmental Affairs Committee.[5] Further, John Duncan, former chairman of the board's executive committee, said the directors "thoroughly executed their duties" and that management withheld significant financial problems from them. "I do not believe that Enron's fall would have been avoided" if the directors had asked more questions, Duncan told the hearing.[6]

Senators however insisted that the directors shared responsibility for Enron's stunning collapse and failed in their duty to protect shareholders of the energy-trading company. "The board must exercise independent judgment," committee chairman Senator Levin, told the five directors sitting before him. "The board is not supposed to be a rubber stamp for auditors or attorneys." Levin produced a document presented to the board's audit committee in February 1999 by David Duncan, Andersen's lead auditor for Enron. Duncan, referring to a series of complex financial transactions, wrote by hand in the lower right-hand corner of the document: "Obviously, we are on board with all of these, but many push limits and have a high . . . risk profile." Robert Jaedicke, who headed the audit committee, told Levin in response to questions that he did not recall seeing Duncan's note or his use of the words "push limits."[7]

Levin said directors approved complex financial arrangements knowing that Enron's management "handed out bonuses like candy at Halloween" — some $50 million for closing a deal for an electric power project in India that subsequently failed, for example. In addition, many of the directors themselves had conflicts of interest, said Senator Joseph Lieberman (D-Conn.) citing consulting contracts worth millions that some directors had with Enron and ties they had with charities that received large donations from Enron. The directors "must accept some of the blame for failing to uncover the crookedness in the company's behavior and books," Lieberman charged.[8]

Many of the directors, along with executives of Houston-based Enron, were named in a lawsuit by shareholders. The directors—and top Enron executives—have been criticized by lawmakers for reaping hundreds of millions of dollars from selling their company stock in 2000 and 2001. Many ordinary employees lost nearly all their retirement savings as Enron stock fell over a period of several months; they were blocked from selling it for about three weeks in fall 2001. Four of the five directors appearing at the Senate committee's hearing—Duncan, Winokur, Jaedicke and Charles LeMaistre—headed, respectively, the executive, finance, audit and compensation committees of the board. Also testifying was Norman Blake, a member of the finance and compensation committees, who was considered especially knowledgeable about the company's financial transactions. Texas Senator Phil Gramm's wife Wendy, who sat on the Enron audit committee, did not appear before the committee.

The *Powers Report* found that Enron directors failed to ask skeptical questions or provide sufficient oversight. William Powers, Jr., revealed that only after reading the report would the board members become aware of numerous past events for the first time. This raises the question of whether the Enron board members, and especially the internal auditing committees, violated a duty to shareholders by not keeping themselves informed, either purposefully or negligently. The board approved Fastow's role in the partnerships, and the procedure implemented to monitor this was not followed. Additionally, the practice of paying directors with stock, ostensibly to align directors' interests with those of shareholders, may also have created a motive for board members to not ask hard questions to which they did not want to hear the answers.

Conflicts of interest were also an issue for several auditing committee members.[9] For example, board member John Wakeham received $72,000 in 2001 from Enron, in addition to his director's fee, for some consulting advice. Enron also contributed to George Mason University, where another board member headed the regulatory studies program. "Charles O'Reilly, a Stanford University business school professor, said that while such donations rarely 'buy' the cooperation of directors, they do indicate the problem when chief executives and directors develop a 'pattern of reciprocity' in which they do favors for each other and gradually become reluctant to rock the boat, particularly on complex accounting matters."[10]

An important question still asked about the board of directors (clearly an important stakeholder asleep at the wheel) is: How much did Enron's board of directors know about the company's investment decisions? As the board continues to come under scrutiny as more and more of Enron's financial records are examined, the situation points to the importance of fiduciary responsibility and full disclosure.

ENRON'S EXECUTIVES

As stakeholders, Enron's executive officers must be the first targets for blame in the company's demise. They, after all, set the pattern by which the rest of the company operated. The following is a list of the Enron executives as of the latter half of 2001:

- Kenneth L. Lay—COB/CEO (C.E.O., Chairman)
- Mark Frevert—Vice COB (Chairman)
- Greg Whalley— President/COO (C.E.O.)
- Andrew Fastow—Executive VP/CFO (Finance)
- Rick Causey—Executive VP/CAO (Finance)
- Ben Glisan—Managing Director/Treasurer (Finance)
- Michael Brown—COO, Enron Europe (International Sales & Marketing.)
- James Derrick, Jr.—Executive VP/General Counsel (Legal)

- Steve Kean—Executive VP/Chief of Staff (Administration, Personnel)
- Mark Metts—Executive VP of Corporate Development (Corporate Development)
- Mark Koenig—Executive VP of Investor Relations (Investor Relations)
- Richard Buy—Executive VP/Chief Risk Officer

These and other executives who left the company were responsible, like Jeffery Skilling, for crafting the deals that resulted in the company's disgrace. They were also the individuals who were achieving great personal financial gains, powerful reputations for business cunning and acuity, honor, admiration, and fame within the business world before the company's collapse. They were the role models inside the company who were respected and emulated by other Enron employees. The culture of the business community at large and the culture within Enron encouraged these leaders to push the limits. The cult of personality and popularity (especially in the Houston area) was compelling and helps to explain, although not to justify their unethical behavior. These individuals thought they could do no wrong and that they would never be caught even if they did break a rule or two.

During the company's heyday, Enron executives behaved like shopaholics maxing out their credit cards on lavish shopping sprees. The company threw its money around to impress employees and clients, almost to the very end. Enron called off a $1 million Christmas party at Houston's Enron Field in mid-November 2002 just weeks before filing for bankruptcy.

Since Enron's financial difficulties came to light, it appears that the company's executives still have the most to fear from the various investigations of the firms' business practices, explaining their denial of any wrongdoing, silence, and finger pointing. As many of the company's executives have left (or been asked to resign), it seems that they have nothing to gain from full disclosure; some continue to believe they have little left to lose. In addition, to this, many of these executive stakeholders still identify so closely with reputations as "masters of the universe" that even to this day they deeply believe that they have done no wrong.

Kenneth Lay, former chairman and CEO, and more specifically Jeffery Skilling, former CEO and president, created a work environment in which making money was the top priority. One high-level Enron executive commented that the company's performance review and compensation systems were designed to foster creativity. Analysts, who once crowed about the incentive structure at Enron, have since criticized the company for "promoting greed and financial impropriety at the expense of long-term profitability." Risk taking and deal making were richly rewarded, with little oversight or control by management or the board of directors. When Enron executives began forming and approving off-balance-sheet partnerships, they knowingly inflated the company's earnings, which, in turn, led to higher stock prices. "Enron employees involved in the partnerships were enriched, in the aggregate, by tens of millions of dollars they should never have received," reads the *Powers Report*.[11] The report commissioned by Enron's own board of directors revealed that the company's executives reaped millions of dollars from the partnerships in question while Enron violated basic rules of accounting and ethics.

Once Skilling and other executives committed to the partnerships that made them so much money and brought such impressive short-term success to the company, they had very little motivation to cooperate with regulators to minimize potential damage to the company and its stockholders. Skilling resigned from Enron in August 2001, after a decade at the company, saying that his reasons were "personal." Later, in a *New York Times* interview, the ex-CEO continued to deny any wrongdoing, stating that he "had no idea the company was in anything but excellent shape" and that he was "stunned by the company's rapid descent after his departure."[12] Another company executive, former vice chairman J. Clifford Baxter, made nearly $22 million selling his inflated Enron stock options over a four-year period. He was later found dead in his car in a Houston suburb, the victim of an apparent suicide and the improprieties that he and the other Enron executives sowed so freely.

The Enron executives stated philosophy was to "get in early, push to open markets, position ourselves to compete, compete hard when the opening comes."[13] Enron's executives seemed to support a culture of innovation, which often included doing whatever was necessary in order to meet the financial goals. One author recently noted that "Enron's executives seemed to believe that there was a winner-take-all society—that there was a culture behind them saying, 'You're worth nothing if you're not a centi-millionare.'"[14] Many of them became very rich from the company's success, but they lost sight of the other stakeholders' interests.

One of the most outlandish aspects of the Enron debacle is that people at the top seemed to have gotten their money out of the company, leaving their fortunes intact. In fact, their claim that they were running one of the great risk-seeking enterprises of the new economy was rather hollow. Enron's executives were running a risk-free company for themselves, while the real risks were assumed by the company's lower-level employees and other stockholders.

Another outlandish aspect of the Enron debacle is the fact that shortly before hundreds of Enron employees were laid off and the company declared bankruptcy in December 2001, about 500 of the energy giant's executives were awarded hefty bonuses, according to a list reported by Salon.com.[15] The list of so-called retention bonuses, which was independently obtained by CNN, showed bonuses ranged from $1,000 to $5 million. The bonuses sparked anger among laid-off employees, who said the money should have been used to give them severance packages.

Many also questioned the motivation for the payments. One former executive told CNN the bonuses were awarded to Enron's inner circle and to people who worked at setting up the questionable financial partnerships that led to the company's demise. Enron officials disagreed. "The notion behind the retention payments," said then Enron president Jeffrey McMahon during a congressional hearing, "was one that if we were to go into bankruptcy is that these key individuals would remain with the company to protect the businesses' and assets' values for the creditors."[16] McMahon's bonus was $1.5 million. Two executives—John Lavorato and Louise Kitchen, who both worked in Enron's highly profitable energy trading company—received the biggest payments. Lavorato got a $5 million bonus, and Kitchen received $2 million. After leaving Enron, both went to work for UBS Warburg, which got Enron's trading unit in a bankruptcy auction in January 2002.

America's trust in the business world has been further eroded by the Enron incident. A *BusinessWeek*/Harris poll found that some 79 percent of Americans believed corporate executives put their own personal interests ahead of those workers and shareholders, as Enron's management is alleged to have done. It will take a long time for Enron's ripple effect to subside.[17]

The unfortunate irony in the Enron situation is that the company's executives would have been better off (still employed and not under criminal investigation) had they remembered the interests of the other stakeholders. Enron's corporate executives were a key stakeholder group that had too much power and influence. They provide a vivid example of how leaders' actions and behavior communicated important messages to others in the organization. While not knowing what to do, most employees look to the behavior of leaders for their cues as to what conduct is acceptable. Along with Enron's board of directors, the company's executives failed to demonstrate moral courage or to either model ethical leadership or create a climate of moral consciousness.

ENRON'S EMPLOYEES

As of October 2001, Enron had 20,600 employees to help carry out the mission of the organization. The employees at Enron play two distinct stakeholder roles. On the one hand, there are the employees that accepted and encouraged a corporate culture that eroded ethical boundaries. These employees were happy to accept Enron stock and profit from the successes that were generated through the executives' questionable business practices. They worked for the company, accepting the financial successes of the executives because each hoped to become the next big Enron success story. On the other hand, most of the rank-and-file employees of Enron were unaware of the dealings that their executive leadership was executing.

For the many Enron employees who were not aware of the choices that the executives were making, their stake in this matter was a career that provided them a salary, benefits, and opportunities for advancement. Few were in a position to see what Enron was doing, and because their managers seemed to be leading the company on a path to prosperity, fewer still thought to question the company's methods. One who did approach management, then company treasurer Jeff McMahon, was transferred when he complained to Skilling about the secrecy surrounding many of the company's deals.

Most of Enron's mid-level managers and nonmanagement employees worked in blissful ignorance, many pumping their hard-earned dollars into 401(k) retirement plans that were 62 percent invested in Enron stock. During the 1990s, the stock price soared 1,400 percent, and employees watched their nest eggs swell, confident that they would have a comfortable retirement. In a typical case, employee Bill Quinlan accumulated more than $1 million, only to watch it plunge to $10,000 when Enron declared bankruptcy. "I just kept my money in stock. It was such a good company that I stuck with it," said Quinlan, 65. "I just didn't keep track of the business end." In all, some 11,000 Enron employees lost not only their jobs, but also about $1 billion in equity value.[18]

As a direct result of executive misconduct, many innocent Enron employees are now without jobs and pensions. Thousands of employees who did nothing wrong have been laid off from the company since the problems were made public. Some may believe that those employees who were knowledgeable about what was going on in the company should have done more to put a stop to it. It has been said that instead of just doing what they were told to do, they should have reported wrongful acts to their superiors. If their superiors did not act to remedy the situation, they should have continued up the chain of command until everyone was aware of the situation. If this still did not resolve the issues, perhaps they should have gone to the regulatory agencies. To say so assumes that the organization's leaders created a culture where whistle-blowing was encouraged or employees viewed whistle-blowing as an option (see Chapter 10)

Another option for Enron employees was to personally quit the company before the downfall. But what about all the employees who had no idea such risky activities were happening? As the Enron employees invested themselves in the company, they deserved a reciprocal bond of trust from the company's executives in exchange for their commitment. What they got was the exact opposite.

Reactions from Enron employees have run the gamut of shock, anger, rage, acceptance, and hope. Employees started Web sites to share their experiences and feelings with others while many others have sought legal counsel. The subsequent employee reactions to a much smaller Enron will be pivotal to the ongoing changes the company must make and in its efforts to pick itself up from its fall. Early and ongoing signs have not been good. Low morale coupled with expectations of an uncertain future frayed employee loyalty. In the end, the Enron employees, like employees in any organization, represent a stakeholder group that should have been given more consideration.

ENRON INVESTORS/SHAREHOLDERS/STOCKHOLDERS

The stockholders include many different types of investors with Enron in their 401(k)s, mutual funds, and portfolios. Stockholders represent an important stakeholder because they had invested in Enron expecting to receive a return for their investment, which is affected by the profitability of the company. The overall risk picture changed dramatically for Enron when it entered these questionable partnerships, and the stockholders should have been made aware of this and perhaps even voted on it. Publicly owned company requirements insist on it, yet since they were not informed, the sustainable good of the company was once again put into jeopardy.

America's trust in the business world and in government has been further eroded by the Enron incident. One of the largest and seemingly most successful corporations in the world declared bankruptcy, despite being under the watch of supposedly able corporate leaders, skilled accounting experts, and government officials. Like the Enron employees who lost money through their 401(k) plans, investors saw hundreds of millions of dollars in equity evaporate when Enron self-destructed.

Depending on how you look at the issue, investors are either the victims in the Enron case or the perpetrators of the crime. Investors, then, are stakeholders on two levels: their greed helped to drive up the stock price, as they kept their money in the stock in the hopes that they would reap the rewards of the capital gains. However, they were also some of the biggest losers, because many employees and other investors had their entire life's savings in Enron stock—an enormous act of investor ignorance.

Many investors (and by investors, we mean both institutional investors and employees who were 401(k) contributors) were guilty of ignorance. "They (investors) were so in awe of the company's stock performance that they didn't seem to care how it worked. Instead, investors focused on growing trading volumes and revenues. . . . The lesson here is that when a company stock looks too good to be true, it probably is. Investors and analysts need to be more watchful and wary."[19] The exuberance that the stock market created in the late 1980s and 1990s gave first-time investors the impression that this was a way that ordinary people could get rich—and for some, it worked. Analysts, who loved the company almost to the bitter end, hyped shares of Enron so that their value climbed 88.6 percent in an otherwise brutal market. Institutional investors and individuals alike made Enron stock a mainstay of their portfolios, many not really understanding how the company made money.

But those who were unlucky and uninformed lost their life's savings in the Enron debacle. "Enron stock options were making the employees rich and helped the company attract the best and brightest. Not wanting to miss out on a sure thing, Enronites stuffed company shares into their 401(k) plans. The company required most employees to have a chunk of their 401(k)'s in Enron stock—but many employees had far more stock than Enron required, and far less diversified investments, such as mutual funds."[20]

Clearly, investors can also be viewed as victims in this scenario, as thousands of Enron employees lost effectively all their savings when the price of the stock plummeted. When a stock as strong as Enron's loses all of its value in a short period of time, the market loses confidence in investments. As a result of the actions of Enron's executives and the company's Chapter 11 filing, Enron's stock lost almost all value. The stock was delisted, and investors have no hope of recovering their investment. Small investors, understandably, are frightened when a giant, well-regarded company collapses overnight.

As a result of fear and distrust generated by the Enron fiasco, wary investors have in some instances punished any company that gave the slightest hint of accounting irregularity. For example, Tyco Corporation saw billions of dollars of market value evaporate overnight when questions arose about bookkeeping issues. K-Mart Corporation's January 2002 bankruptcy filing was triggered in part by Enron-inspired fears.[21] These companies, in turn, are forced to lay off employees to reduce their expenditures, thereby involving more people in the suffering caused by Enron.

Stakeholders, in this case, include so many investors—companies, retirees, pension funds, individual investors, insurance companies—the list goes on and on. Society (as a whole) and free markets domestically and abroad suffer when people can't trust the companies in which they invest. The Enron situation has clearly eroded America's trust in the business world and in government.

End results that would effectively end the problem at hand might be legislation that prohibits a certain percentage of a company's stock in pension funds (for example, more than 30 percent). Tighter regulation on financial disclosure (including fuller disclosure on Special Purpose Entities) might make companies more transparent and therefore more accountable to their shareholders. Finally, greater public awareness on the importance of portfolio diversification would prevent many investors from putting all of their eggs in one basket, so to speak. "The cult of share prices seduced managerial elites, ordinary investors and workers alike."[22] Although investors need to understand that they, too, are ultimately responsible for their own investments, legislation should protect investors from preying on the ignorance of ordinary investors.

The obvious lesson from the Enron debacle for the investor stakeholder groups is, don't keep too many eggs in one investment basket, especially in the company you work for. Utilities deregulation has suffered a severe blow: If a huge company like Enron can disappear overnight, how can you trust new market players to provide you with essentials like electricity, gas, and water?

In the end, the reaction of investors was swift and devastating. Enron's stock hit rock bottom. The danger to the organization from stockholders became reality in two ways. First, speculative panic drove massive sell-offs, destroying the company's market value. In turn, the loss of value not only increased the company's cost of capital—its borrowing power—but completely destroyed the company's credibility with customers and paralyzed its ability to function as it had in the past. The second reality was that the loss of reputational capital has fueled shareholder lawsuits against the company.

In some instances, a case can be made that this stakeholder group did not actively participate in the actions that caused Enron's fall and as a result has a right to be quite angry with the outcome of Enron's business practices. The investor stakeholder group is an important one—it has the ability to influence lawmakers who can alter the regulations and the punishments for transgressions that govern business practices.

ANALYSTS, BANKS, AND ENRON

On February 20, 2002, NBC's Lisa Myers reported that "Congressional investigators have Wall Street in their sights, and some of this country's biggest and best-known banks and brokerage houses may have a lot of explaining to do."[23] Congressional investigators demanded information from a dozen of the most prestigious investment firms—including Citigroup, Merrill Lynch, and J. P. Morgan. The idea has been to follow the money.

Cash from many of these Wall Street firms enabled Enron to set up controversial partnerships to hide debt, which contributed to Enron's collapse. The question Congress and others have continued to try to find answers to is "Did Wall Street know what Enron was really doing?" "If the bankers knew that these deals were risky, if the bankers knew that this information was being hidden from the investing community, then in my mind they are complicit in what went wrong," said Rep. James Greenwood (R-Pa.) of the House Energy and Commerce Committee.[24] Investigators believed that there was an incestuous relationship between Enron and some of Wall Street's elite. Here's some of what Congress said they knew:

- Banks or investment firms invested in high-risk partnerships that Enron used to hide debt.
- Banks then could earn huge profits on that investment, plus tens of millions of dollars in other fees from Enron.

Representative Greenwood said, "There is lots of evidence that there was a 'You scratch my back and I'll scratch your back' arrangement here."[25] Whistleblower Sherron Watkins testified that some banks complained to her they were pressured to invest in one partnership—LJM2—by Enron's Chief Financial Officer Fastow. "Mr. Fastow was almost somewhat threatening — that if you didn't invest in LJM, Enron would not use you as a banker or an investment banker again," Watkins testified. Documents showed that another Enron executive also reported complaints from banks in fall 2002, with First Union complaining it didn't get a bond deal it was promised for investing in the partnership.[26]

Some banks actually met with top Enron management in late October 2002 on the company's crisis. Sources who attended the meeting told NBC News that the banks pushed Enron to get rid of Fastow. It did.

In the Enron situation, analysts failed profoundly on several levels because of their inability (or perhaps their refusal) to report accurate information to investors and potential investors. In some cases, analysts were hampered by pressure to report favorably on stocks in which their parent companies had large investments and investment banking relationships. In other cases, analysts admittedly didn't understand Enron's accounting system; in either case, analysts were guilty of a lack of attention to potential problems, perceived inaccuracies, and outright fraud.

At issue in the case of analysts is the potential for fraud. As a result of the 1999 repeal of the Glass-Stegal Act, "Questions have been raised about the objectivity of security analysts who are pursuing investment banking business; about the way investment banks allocate underwritings of hot new issues among their clients; and about the activities of banks . . . acting simultaneously as lenders, underwriters, financial advisors, and principal investors in some transactions."[27] The firms failed to regard the long-term implication of analysts' bad recommendations: that investors would lose confidence in the market's ability to accurately predict stock growth.

If analysts weren't blatantly guilty of fraud, then they were guilty of not admitting that they couldn't understand Enron's complicated accounting. Analysts failed to follow one of the basic principles of democracy—"paying attention."[28] Inattention applies to negligence.[29] SEC chairman Harvey Pitt admitted that "there were legitimate concerns about the way analysts were performing their function and the extent to which the public was aware of what they were getting when there was an analyst report."[30] If the analysts themselves weren't guilty of outright fraud, then their companies were certainly guilty of contributing to the systematic abuse of the stock ratings game.

John Olson, the Houston analyst with Sanders Morris Harris Group who gained near-celebrity status for his early warnings about Enron, spotted the trouble with Enron early on. He stated at the North American Energy Conference of the Independent Petroleum Assocation Mountain States, "I thought Enron stock was gloriously overvalued for the last 12 years."[31] Olson pointed out with pride a memo Enron chairman Lay sent in June 2001 to his boss, Donald Sanders: "Don, John Olson has been wrong about Enron for over 10 years. And is still wrong. But he is consistent." Unlike other analysts, Olson said he could never match Enron's financials with the way it performed on Wall Street. "The company's transactions were so complicated—mired in several layers of partnerships, options and derivatives—that analysts couldn't figure out that one-third of the company's assets were nonperforming," he said. "And all of Enron's diversifications turned to mud," Olson said. "They'd just bury the bodies inside their trading operations."[32]

Olson placed much of the blame for Enron's "clever and contrived" house of cards squarely on investment bankers. "If you have analysts sitting on the same side of the table as investment bankers, you're in big trouble," Olson said. "We need to get investment banking out of research."[33]

Prior to Enron's collapse, New York and international banks such as J. P. Morgan & Chase, Citigroup, Deutschebank, and Merrill Lynch made millions of dollars underwriting debt and equity issues for Enron. The directors and fund managers of these banks also made private investments into the joint ventures and partnerships that led to the collapse of Enron. These investments are regarded as contributing to the deception of Enron's off-balance-sheet financing, as these banks are the masterminds behind the partnerships and "special-purpose vehicles" (specialized debt and equity instruments) used to hide astronomical amounts of debt and obligations from investor scrutiny.[34] It is ironic that these banks, which underwrote and sold Enron debt and equity in the open market, were also responsible for the fair and impartial analysis of the company. When questioned about these risky and speculative investments in Enron, the bankers almost unanimously state that it was necessary to engage in these activities in order to retain the possibility of future Enron business.

Bank analysts report on the financial health and viability of a company as it moves across the landscape of capital markets. As Enron investigations progress, numerous potential conflicts of interest have been revealed regarding the role of the banks and the actions of their brokers and analysts. When Enron was doing well, analysts stood to experience financial and reputation gains as their predictions were acknowledged and acted upon by their banks and investors. However, a line was crossed when analysts were instructed to remain bullish on Enron stock despite their knowledge to the contrary. Consequences have been severe; as a result of the Enron collapse, many of these analysts have lost or will lose their jobs and reputations.

A focal stakeholder in this blame game then is the investor, who cannot make informed decisions without perfect information. The investor, whether institutional or individual, must believe that the analyst is impartial in his or her recommendations and is making a good-faith recommendation on stocks based solely on facts. If the basis for trust, impartiality, is broken, then the market doesn't work freely. "Wall Street analysts are supposed to dig through the company's numbers to divine what's really happening—but almost none of them managed to do that. Regulators didn't regulate. Enron's board of directors didn't direct."[35]

As stakeholders, banks and their analysts, like Enron's management, profited from the rise in Enron stock. If anyone outside of Enron was in a position to question their activities, it was the analysts. However, raising red flags about Enron's financial statements simply was not a wealth maximizing action.

Shortly after the Enron story became front-page news, Congress began work on the regulation of analysts and their recommendations. "The proposals would require Wall Street research analysts to explain their stock rating systems and limit stock ownership in companies they recommend. The proposals would also require analysts to prominently disclose their firms' investment banking relationships in research. . . .At issue are conflicts between analysts and investment bankers—who have long known that negative research will hurt their chances of winning lucrative corporate-finance work."[36]

A resolution to the perceived problem with analysts that have come out of the Enron debacle (at least in the short run) is the legislation that would rein in analysts and hold them to a different standard. The proposals at hand would do the following:

- Require firms to disclose in a research report if they were compensated by the company within the past year or if they expected to be compensated within the next three months.
- Require analysts appearing on television to disclose if they own even one share of stock in a company they are discussing, or if their brokerage firm owns at least 1 percent share of a company's stock.
- Prohibit analysts from directly or indirectly promising favorable ratings.[37]

These and other proposed rules would mitigate the temptation (and the pressure) for analysts to recommend favorable ratings for companies that are current clients of brokerage houses and financial services firms (which are often one and the same).

At the center of the Enron debacle is trust. All of the stakeholders relied on relationships of trust among one another: investors to analysts, analysts to the accounting firms, analysts to Enron management analysts to financial institutions (and to the companies that they covered), financial institutions to Enron's leaders. The reliance on analysts' information is crucial to holding this whole system together. If investors can't trust analysts, then they have no basis on which to judge their investments, which affects the bank accounts of millions of ordinary citizens. The intertwined stakeholder relationships broke down because of the lack of trust in Enron's reporting.

ENRON AND ITS AUDITOR ARTHUR ANDERSEN

The collapse came swiftly for the Enron Corporation when investors and customers learned they could not trust its numbers. Six weeks after Enron disclosed that federal regulators were examining its finances, the global energy-trading powerhouse became the biggest bankruptcy in U.S. history. Like all publicly traded companies in the United States, Enron had an outside auditor scrutinize its annual financial results. In this case, blue-chip accounting firm Arthur Andersen had vouched for the numbers. But Enron, citing accounting errors, had to correct its financial statements, cutting profits for the past three years by 20 percent—about $586 million.

A case study posted on Arthur Andersen's Web site under "Success Stories" shows how the firm saw itself in 2001. As auditor for TheStreet.com Inc., a financial news service, Arthur Andersen said, it helped its client prepare for an initial public offering of stock, develop a global expansion strategy and secure a weekly television show through another client, News Corp. One of Arthur Andersen's "greatest strengths . . . is developing full-service relationships with emerging companies and then using all of our capabilities to find inventive ways to help them continue to grow," auditor Tom Duffy is quoted as saying.[38]

TheStreet.com chief executive Thomas J. Clarke Jr. said the accounting firm "become[s] a business partner because they're right there with you." He said the auditors answer to a committee of outside board members, not TheStreet.com executives, to provide checks and balances.[39]

As an independent auditor for Enron, Arthur Andersen was expected to ensure the company's financial statements represented the true financial picture of the company. Because the firm was responsible for auditing Enron's financial records, many are of the opinion that Andersen should have not only been aware of the company's off-balance-sheet partnerships, but that the firm also had a duty to bring these dealings to light to alert other stakeholders. Andersen also served as a consultant to Enron (a more lucrative role than simply being an auditor; Enron paid Anderson $52 million in fees in 2000 alone). It has been surmised that the firm played along with Enron's bookkeeping games so that it could keep its business partnership intact.

Clearly, a major stakeholder in the Enron downfall was its auditor, Arthur Andersen. At issue are two different ethical compromises: the Andersen stamp of approval on Enron's books when the financing was bogus and the Andersen consultation in helping to structure several of Enron's questionable deals. Even more egregious an act was the shredding of material documentation by the Andersen audit staff after Enron declared bankruptcy.

Arthur Andersen (and the auditing industry) put itself in a precarious situation by accepting auditing work as a way to parlay that business into more lucrative consulting contracts from the same clients. Although unethical and potentially misleading, it seems pointedly self-interested that Big Five firms would be dispensing financial advice and auditing the financial statements of the same company. It would obviously be in the best interest of the auditors to approve financial statements (fraudulent or not) if that meant that more lucrative work would follow. From the auditing side, the Andersen staff served as more of an enabler than a culprit, authorizing that Enron's financial statements were clean. Andersen staff members must have known about the tenuousness of the Special Purpose Entity financing and the overstated earnings. If healthy financial statements send a signal to Wall Street that translates into strong stock prices, then Andersen helped to defraud and mislead the American investing public by putting their seal of approval on bogus books. From the consulting side, Andersen appears to not only to have known about the questionable off-balance-sheet financing but also to have helped structure it. The *Wall Street Journal* suggested that "Arthur Andersen helped structure Andrew Fastow's partnerships. Most of the major transactions were designed to accomplish favorable financial statements, not to achieve bona fide economic transactions or to transfer risk. Many served to conceal from the market the very large losses resulting from Enron's merchant investments by creating an appearance that those investments were hedged. Andersen's billings reached $5.7 million beyond normal audit fees for the advice on only two of the partnerships."[40]

This type of ethical breach is not particular to Andersen; it is part of a systemic ill that infected any company that used the Big Five for auditing work. These auditing firms have had a lock on most major companies in the United States. The Big Five represent the closest thing to a cartel that U.S. antitrust law allows. Andersen, Deloitte & Touche, Ernst & Young, KPMG, and Pricewaterhouse Coopers often work as a marketing and PR unit, backing the same policies and defending each other's practices.[41]

In a manner similar to that used by Enron's executives, Arthur Andersen's leadership compounded the seriousness of its situation when its wrongdoings began to become public. Employees of the firm were reportedly ordered to destroy documents related to Enron, even after it was known that the SEC was in the process of running an investigation on the company's actions. Later, after the *Powers Report* stated that Andersen was "seemingly complicit in its maneuverings," Joseph Berardino, them the company's CEO, focused on protecting the image of the firm, without regard to other stakeholders. He and other executives quickly claimed that Enron had withheld information about the partnerships, and then moved to place all blame for the destruction of auditing documents on David Duncan, the Andersen partner who had been in charge of the Enron audit. Duncan was then summarily fired, found himself in court, and eventually pleaded guilty to related charges and began cooperating with the government on the fall of Enron.

Still desperate to save the tarnished image of Arthur Andersen, Berardino first publicly claimed that his company had been technically discharged from its relationship with Enron in December 2001 when the company filed for bankruptcy protection, then made an appeal for sympathy.[42] At that point, with the firm under investigation for possible misconduct and engulfed by lawsuits, Berardino admitted to serious errors in judgment when Enron-related documents were destroyed, but insisted that it was not company policy. "It was wrong. There's no other word for it. But 85,000 people did not work on the Enron engagement. 85,000 people did not destroy documents. And 85,000 people did not encourage anyone to destroy those documents."[43] Unfortunately for Andersen and its employees, as a result of loose morals among the firm's leadership, many of those 85,000 employees have suffered as if they had been accomplices.

As Enron's outside auditor, Arthur Andersen had an obligation to pass judgment on the fairness and accuracy of Enron's financial statements. This is a very important stakeholder role for as many other stakeholders (e.g., investors) rely upon a "clean opinion" when considering investment in a company. The failure of Arthur Andersen to help prevent or warn anyone about the largest bankruptcy in history creates a serious problem for audit firms in general and Arthur Andersen in particular. The reputation of an audit firm for being fair and unbiased in its work is its most valuable asset. Without it, the firm may not be viable going forward. This is certainly true of Arthur Andersen. Clearly, like the bank and analysts stakeholders discussed earlier, a conflict of interest was in place where a stakeholder had an incentive, in this case $100 million in annual consulting fees, to avoid decisions that did not maximize their own wealth. Enron management could have hired anyone in the Big 5 to be their outside auditor and consultant. Arthur Andersen was simply too close to Enron to be impartial.

Post-Enron bankruptcy has led to Congress and others taking a look at SEC policies and practices regarding the conflicts of interest surrounding both auditing and consulting work. One proposed idea was that companies would be forced to change auditing firms every five years, so that one firm doesn't have too much invested in the client as to blur the distinction between ethical and fraudulent. Finally, tighter regulation of the regulators should be part of the solution. Members of the accounting industry have dominated the boards and advisory councils that oversee regulation. When outsiders are present, they are normally finance executives at corporations that stand to benefit from favorable decisions or accounting professors whose endowed positions are financed by the Big Five accounting firms.[44]

Others on Capitol Hill have also questioned why the Federal Accounting Standards Board (FASB) is a private rather than a publicly funded oversight board. In the end, Congress may go too far in over regulating the industry—after all, politicians seem always to be thinking of the next election. But the Enron scandal has helped to uncover some systemic unethical practices, and stricter standards for auditors may help to put investors' faith back in the system.

ENRON'S LAW FIRM: VINSON & ELKINS

Enron's law firm, Vinson & Elkins (V&E), was also an important stakeholder in the Enron situation. For example, after Kenneth Lay requested that it investigate Sherron Watkins' allegations, V&E stated it did not think that further investigation was required. V&E faces lawsuits from shareholders, creditors, and former Enron employees on the grounds that it helped Enron prepare misleading financial reports. A further charge is that the firm failed to stop any of the questionable transactions that were brought to its attention. It has also been criticized for not seeking a third-party review of its work in the Watkins memo matter.[45]

On April 9, 2002, V&E, the second-largest law firm in Texas, was accused of participating in a fraudulent scheme that cost Enron shareholders and employees as much as $28 billion. The allegations against the Houston-based firm were spelled out in more than 800 pages of filings in two class-action lawsuits in federal court in Houston. The filings, submitted on behalf of Enron shareholders and employees, sought to add numerous defendants to claims against Enron and accounting firm Arthur Andersen LLP in connection with the collapse of what had been the world's largest energy trader. Besides V&E, the plaintiffs named the Chicago-based Kirkland & Ellis law firm, as well as nine prominent investment banks, including Citigroup, J. P. Morgan Chase & Co. and Merrill Lynch & Co. According to the suits, the law firms and banks helped Enron and Andersen disguise loans as income, hide debt, and arrange sham sales of overvalued assets, according to the amended lawsuits. In the process, the shareholders' complaint said, Enron became "a hall of mirrors inside a house of cards."[46] James Holst, general counsel of the lead shareholders' plaintiff, the University of California Board of Regents, said, "These prestigious banks and law firms" helped Enron executives "shore up the company's stock price and create a false appearance of financial strength and profitability."[47]

In her missive to Enron chairman and CEO Lay, Watkins suggested that the law firm wrote so-called opinion letters vouching for the legality of some of the deals now under scrutiny. According to two ex-Enron executives, V&E played a creative role in structuring and managing some of the company's controversial "special purpose" part-nerships. One former executive in the company pointed out that em-ployees would approach V&E lawyers "and say, 'this thing needs to work. How do we make it work?'" The executive added that the firm also gave Enron advice on how much information it had to disclose about its financial machinations in its 10K and 10Q reports to the SEC.[48]

Since the Enron debacle became public, there have been growing indications that Watkins' claims were true. Legally speaking, the key issue will be whether V&E blessed activities that it knew to be fraudulent. If so, it could be in trouble, according to University of Illinois law professor Ronald D. Rotunda, an expert in legal ethics: "Under those fact scenarios, they could have real problems."[49]

The allegations brought in the suit turned up the flame on V&E, which already was in the spotlight over its role in advising Enron on the various partnership transactions. V&E's lawyers have had to testify before Congress on Enron matters. In addition, the firm sent letters to clients assuring them that it did nothing wrong. The expanded lawsuits rely heavily on findings from congressional investigations and the powers' report. Powers recused himself from the sections dealing with V&E, which has been a major donor to the law school.

The shareholders' complaint mentioned earlier accused the firm of participating in structuring illicit partnerships that hide debt and inflated Enron's stock price. The lawsuit offers as a "prime example" Mahonia Ltd., a company in the Channel Islands off England that was used to conceal $3.9 billion in debt. According to the shareholders' lawsuit, "V&E issued opinions to Enron, Mahonia and J. P. Morgan representing that billions of dollars in forward sales contracts of natural gas and oil by Enron were legitimate commodities trades when, in fact, as V&E knew, the trades were bogus—manipulative devices to disguise loans from J.P. Morgan to Enron so those loans would not have to be shown as debt on Enron's balance sheet. No physical delivery of product was required or contemplated."[50]

The lawsuits contend that the partnership transactions amount to a massive Ponzi scheme. A Ponzi scheme is a type of illegal pyramid scheme using the "rob-Peter-to-pay-Paul" principle, in which money from new investors is used to pay off earlier investors until the whole arrangement collapses. The filings further described the V&E investigation of Enron's accounting practices as a "whitewash."[51]

There seems to be little that the firm can say to justify some of its legal involvement in the Enron downfall. For example, over five years, as Fastow structured ever-more-complex deals for the big energy and trading company, Ronald Astin and other V&E lawyers sometimes objected, saying the deals posed conflicts of interest or weren't in Enron's best interests. Unfortunately, V&E didn't blow the whistle. Again and again, its lawyers backed down when rebuffed by Fastow or his lieutenants, expressing their unease to Enron's in-house attorneys but not to its most senior executives or to its board. And when asked to assess Enron manager Watkins' warning to Lay last summer of potential accounting scandals, V&E delivered to Enron a report that largely downplayed the risks.

Enron asked the firm to investigate after Watkins raised concerns to then-chief executive Lay. The law firm's report, submitted in mid-October 2001, found "bad cosmetics" and "a serious risk of adverse publicity and litigation," but said further investigation was not warranted.[52] Seven weeks later, Enron plunged into the largest bankruptcy in U.S. history.

As evidenced by the lawsuits filed against V&E since the Enron debacle became front-page news, deals that troubled some V&E lawyers have been central to investigations of the fall of Enron. But while the mantle of heroine has fallen on Watkins, V&E has found itself on the defensive. A report of a special investigation done for Enron's board criticized the law firm for an "absence" of "objective and critical professional advice."[53]

The firm's bind casts a stark light on the central issue law firms face when they represent large corporations: Just what are their obligations to the client and the client's shareholders? In terms of legal ethics, outside lawyers have a clear ethical duty to withdraw from transactions in which clients are obviously breaking the law. But many situations are murkier. At what point should the lawyers speak up, and to whom, when the legality of planned corporate moves is merely questionable? And what about when individual executives are planning steps that appear not in the interests of the client company itself?

V&E's managing partner, Joseph Dilg, told a congressional panel probing Enron that so long as a transaction isn't illegal and has been approved by the client company's management, outside lawyers may advise on the transaction. "In doing so, the lawyers are not approving the business decisions that were made by their clients," he said.[54] Others, such as Boston University law professor Susan Koniak, say lawyers must do more. They have a duty to make sure a client's managers aren't "breaching their duties to the corporation," says Koniak, who testified before a Senate hearing on Enron and accountability issues in February 2002. Koniak believes V&E lawyers should have taken their concerns to Enron directors. However, she adds that what the firm actually did "is not any different from what most lawyers in most big firms would have done. This is how law is practiced. . . . It's a game of musical chairs, and Vinson & Elkins got caught standing up."[55]

Exactly what V&E did and when in the Enron matter isn't easy to determine, however some details can be gleaned from interviews done for the special report to Enron's board, conducted by the Washington law firm Wilmer, Cutler & Pickering. For example, the stakes for V&E were high. The firm's partners and Enron were intertwined in

Houston's corporate community. They shared causes ranging from the United Negro College Fund to electing George W. Bush. Kenneth and Linda Lay traveled the Houston social and charity circuit with Harry Reasoner and his wife, Macey. The friendship dated from a case Reasoner handled in 1976 for a former Lay employer, Florida Gas. Enron was V&E biggest client, pouring roughly $35.6 million into the firm's coffers in 2001, 7.8 percent of its revenue.

But by 1997, when Enron proposed the first of its now-notorious partnership deals, V&E's hold on Enron business was weakening as the company increasingly used other law firms as well. It was retaining Houston's Andrews & Kurth and Bracewell & Patterson. New York powerhouse Skadden, Arps, Slate, Meagher & Flom also did work for Enron and won even more after it opened a Houston office. Enron General Counsel James Derrick was interested in giving work to a lot of different firms.[56]

They needed little persuading. One Enron staffer noted: "Every large law firm in the country in one form or another tried to get Enron's business." "Enron became innovative and sexy and a nice client to have in your stable."[57] Enron planned to buy out the 50 perrcent stake that California Public Employees' Retirement System, or Calpers, held in an Enron investment partnership called Jedi—and then immediately sell that stake to a new entity called Chewco described in Chapter 7. Remember, Chewco was designed to be independent, so that several hundred million dollars of debt associated with Jedi wouldn't have to appear on Enron's balance sheet.

Enron "management and the board relied heavily on the perceived approval by V&E of the structure and disclosure of the transactions (i.e., partnerships like Jedi, Chewco, LJM, and LJM2)," according to the report to Enron's board.[58] According to one former Enron employee, the company might not have been able to pull off many of the transactions now under investigation without V&E's opinion letters. The company "opinion-shopped for what it needed." "If it hadn't gotten the opinion letters, it couldn't have done the deals."[59]

When Enron's board allowed Fastow to manage and invest in the LJMs, V&E should have made sure the directors understood the legal implications. They should have said to the board, "This is a big legal risk you're taking. Let's be clear about this. If anything starts going wrong, that's going to be evidence" in any resulting court fight.[60] Others like Roger Cramton, professor and former dean of Cornell Law School, says that with some of the deals Enron did, lawyers should have started "to be suspicious about whether these transactions are legal in the sense of fiduciary responsibility to the shareholders, to the board of directors and whether they are illegal in other senses."[61] But Cramton also points out that a lawyer can not substitute his or her business judgment for the client's, and whether to take legal concerns up a client's chain of a command is a complex judgment call. If the client is at material legal risk, the lawyer should "go to managers first and try to get them to listen. If they sugar-coat it over and they clearly don't want to know about them," going to the board or a board committee could be appropriate."[62]

V&E's share of Enron's legal pie continued to shrink—to 20 percent of work Enron farmed out in 2001. But V&E remained the firm Enron went to first with its most sensitive project. After Enron filed for bankruptcy in early December 2001, the firm stopped representing the company. At a congressional hearing in March 2002, Dilg, who oversaw the Enron account for V&E, deflected many questions, prompting an exasperated Representative Clifford B. Stearns of Florida to ask, "You're saying that you, as counsel for Enron, never saw anything egregious about anything they did during the entire relationship you had with Enron?" Dilg answered, "Yes, sir."[63]

A firm's legal representatives are supposed to ensure that the company follows the rules. However, when they are willing to help the organization bend the rules when it is convenient for them some of the time, then they do little to avoid ending up as co-conspirators in betraying the trust of other stakeholders.

OTHER STAKEHOLDERS AND ENRON

The remaining stakeholders to discuss (business associates and public associates) are not as directly involved as some of the ones already mentioned. However, they help explain the rest of the overall environment Enron was operating in and suggest some considerations that might have made those in power think harder before making such poor decisions.

The company's customers and vendors had a stake in Enron because they are affected by Enron's sales and their ability to stay in business. As Enron collapsed, many power companies lost money when Enron defaulted on trades that had been made but not settled. Competitors are also stakeholders because they had to compete against Enron. Since Enron was very successful, they too faced pressure to also be very successful. Many companies in the industry did not fully understand what Enron did and how it made money. Because of this, it was hard for them to follow Enron's lead, but that may have been a good thing for them after all. The final business associate is the Wall Street analysts who also added pressure on Enron to continue to show increasingly impressive results. As Enron continued to grow and prosper, the analysts continued to raise the bar for them. This may have helped give the executives an added incentive to try to put a positive spin on the company's financial status even as it was becoming increasingly tenuous.

Another major stakeholder in the troubles at Enron is the federal government. As pointed out in Chapter 4, both regulators and legislators are charged with the duty of protecting the public by making and enforcing rules designed to prevent corporate misdeeds. Unfortunately, elected officials often depend on campaign contributions to stay in office, and regulatory bodies are often rife with people who have close relationships within the industry they monitor. It appears now that the early success of Enron played some role in veiling government's eyes to the wrongdoings of the company, thus contributing to the catastrophic effects of Enron's bankruptcy. Consider the Securities and Exchange Commission (SEC).

The SEC plays a critical role in any issue facing the U.S. capital markets. Prior to the Enron debacle, the SEC kept a half-closed eye on Enron and its financial issues. Much of this can be attributed to the confusing distribution of responsibility among numerous agencies for oversight of financial reporting and compliance, including the SEC, the Department of Justice, and the FASB. Prior to the collapse, the SEC experienced the same Enron and bull-market-induced euphoria as many investors, evidenced by their failure to thoroughly (within published standards) review Enron's financial reporting for at least the three years prior to the bankruptcy.[64] Since the Enron debacle came to light, the current administration has been working with numerous agencies to develop new methods and oversight techniques to prevent similar occurrences in the future. Additionally, the SEC must regain confidence from the investing public. Lack of attention from organizations such as the SEC could encourage a company facing financial difficulties to attempt to skirt the law and regulations. Enron, a favored entity with the government and its agencies, engaged in questionable practices with the expectation that it would not fall under intense scrutiny that other less favored companies would.

The credibility of the regulatory agents is threatened since they should have policed Enron more effectively to ensure compliance. Government is also a stakeholder because the government enacts laws that restrict how companies can operate and manage their businesses. Politicians were in regular communication with Enron executives before and after the company filed for bankruptcy, and the media has made this a large issue.

Some politicians also received very large campaign donations from Enron. Congress has tried to determine if Enron exchanged legislative favors for money at all levels of the federal government. *Time* magazine reported that half of the House of Representatives, three-quarters of the

Senate, the head of the Justice Department, and both the president and vice president received money from Enron. Indeed, a total of $5.7 million of the company's money has found its way to Washington since 1989. President George W. Bush's campaigns alone received $623,000 over the course of his political career. Republican John McCain, who acknowledged receiving $9,500 from Enron in two campaigns, publicly stated, "We're all tainted by the millions and millions of dollars that were contributed by Enron executives."[65]

Finally, because Enron contributed extensively to the local Houston community, many charities, and other charities in the United States and internationally, these organizations are also stakeholders. They had prospered by the presence of this corporate giant, especially since it made a regular and active commitment to contributing money in its role as a corporate citizen. Enron's philanthropic contributions to the community must be acknowledged despite its failure to be socially responsible in legal, ethical and economic areas. Enron contributed to the quality of life and to the welfare of the Houston community.

After the December 2, 2001, bankruptcy filing, Enron cut back on its many commitments to social and political organizations. The company was a major contributor to nonprofit organizations in the area, and many of them received a substantial portion of their budget from Enron. Not only have these nonprofits experienced ongoing effects of the fallen energy company, but local businesses have also suffered. Some local eateries used to be filled with Enron employees during the lunch hour. Now, they have since experienced decreased capacity, because so many Enron people were laid off.

THE U.S. CAPITAL MARKET

Prior to the collapse, the U.S. market was in the midst of a slowing bull market and considered Enron to be one of its exceptional performers. Many investors and interests profited greatly from Enron's success. As Enron, one of the largest companies in the market collapsed, many companies that depended on Enron for business and capital began to feel the strain. Enron's creditors panicked as Enron's free fall became apparent, and the already tightened credit markets constricted even further. Enron's impact has been felt market wide as inquiries and investigations began daily concerning financial reporting accuracy, off-balance-sheet financing, and special purpose vehicles.

Debt rating services are scrambling to implement devices to signal early warning about impending collapses such as Enron's. The negligence of these agencies has contributed to decreased confidence in the markets.[66] Many believe the markets are partially to blame for the rise and fall of Enron. Market fixation on earnings growth encouraged Enron officials to engage in allegedly fraudulent activities in order to meet unrealistic expectations and to sell their integrity for inflated share prices. It is possible that these external expectations led the Enron executives to engage in questionable activities; however, a more ethical company would not have let the markets make its decisions.

CONCLUSION

In viewing the Enron situation from a stakeholder perspective, it is clear that there was an atmosphere of conflicting goals, which appears to be all to typical of many corporations. But what one must also recognize are unsound stakeholder prioritization, disproportionate risk bearing, and unjust decisions that ignored many of the primary but non-focal stakeholders. No concessions or notifications were made when the partnerships increased the risk for stockholders. Additionally, there was tremendous pressure to grow (from shareholders, employees, Wall Street, and others) and the result of poor judgment in decision making and not telling the truth.

Clearly, Enron along with other stakeholders were vulnerable on the issue of truth telling. Its board of directors and executives failed to fulfill their responsibilities in numerous ways. For example, board members were not doing their jobs because the company was not being operated and reported in a legal manner and it was their responsibility to perform due diligence. Enron's executives perhaps mesmerized by the tremendous potential for profitability and rapid innovations found themselves unable to do the right thing. Enron's accountants and most Wall Street analysts ratified and legitimized the company's scenarios and statements regarding its prospects. Were the accountants misled and otherwise, in Justice Cardozo's classic formulation (applied to an accounting firm), "skilled and careful in their calling?" The accountants and analysts certainly make the case for Enron deception, but "if the truth is not expected to be spoken," which certainly is the case, then it is their job to pierce the veil. No potential client thinks otherwise. The role of accountants and analysts is to serve shareholders and potential shareholders in rectifying the information asymmetries that exist when shareholders deal directly with the company. Investors, to include many of Enron's employees and government agencies responsible for oversight, responded to the hype of the analysts and media that the company could do no wrong and played their part in helping to reinforce the unreality that "the emperor had clothes."

Enron was deemed for some years to be the company of the future but Enron was not really a particularly modern business organization. Like Pius IX, the company rejected progressive innovation. Enron sought to circumvent or avoid systems that were designed to protect the company and its shareholders and to bolster the credibility of its dealings. Enron's corporate behavior does indeed constitute unethical practices and clearly is not the overall behavior one would expect from a socially responsible corporation.

In the end, there appears to be more than enough blame to go around for all of the stakeholders involved in the fall of the once giant Enron. An important question that must still be answered in more detail is why such unethical behavior occurs in organizations. The next few chapters will provide some answers to this question.

NOTES

1. C. Johnson, "Enron Directors Appear before Senate Subcommittee," *Washingtonpost.com* (May 7, 2002).

2. Ibid.

3. Ibid.

4. Ibid.

5. D. Kaufman, "Corporate Governance Insights," *The Corporate and Securities Law Advisor* 16, no. 3 (2002), 5–8.

6. Ibid.

7. Ibid.

8. Ibid.

9. L. Lavelle, "Enron: How Governance Rules Failed," *Business Week* (January 21, 2002), 28–29.

10. Anonymous. "Enron's Woes: Who Knew?" *Association Management* 54, no. 1 (January 2002), 28.

11. *CNN.comLawcenter*, "Enron Paid Hefty Bonuses before Bankruptcy" (February 10, 2002). See *http://www.cnn.com*.

12. "Ex-Enron CEO: Not Me" *CNNMoney*, (January 22, 2002). See: *http://www.money.cnn.com/*

13. Gale Group, Business Company Resource Center, *Enron Company History* (Farmington Hills, Minn: Thomson, 2002).

14. Markula Center for Applied Ethics, "What Went Wrong with Enron? A Culture of Evil?" Panel to Discuss the Enron Scandal (March 5, 2002).

15. *CNN.comLawcenter*, op. cit.

16. Ibid.

17. "Bracing for a Backlash," *Business Week* (February 4, 2002), 34–36.

18. M. Costello, "Company Stock Slams 401(k)s," *CNNmoney* (January 10, 2001). See: *http://www.money.cnn.com/*.

19. H. Wee, "Enron in Perfect Hindsight," *Businessweek.com* (December 17, 2001). See: www.businessweek.com/.

20. "Enron's Employees' 401Ks," *Msnbc.com* (February 11, 2002). See: *http://www.msnbc.com/*.

21. "Bracing for a Backlash," 35.

22. Wee, "Enron in Perfect Hindsight."

23. NBC News, "Enron: The Wall Street Connection: Banks, Investment Firms under Congressional Investigation" (February 20). See: *http://www.msnbc.com/news/*

24. Ibid.

25. Ibid.

26. Ibid.

27. The Betrayal of Capitalism, *New York Review of Books* (February 28, 2002), 2.

28. R. N. Bellah, *The Good Society* (New York: Knopf, 1991).

29. Edgar H. Schein, *Organizational Culture and Leadership* (San Francisco: Jossey-Bass, 1985).

30. "Rules Would Reel in Analysts," *NewYorkTimes.com* (February 12, 2002). See: *http://www.nytimes.com/*.

31. H. Draper, "Analyst: Enron Was Overvalued for 12 Years," *Msnbc.com* (March 15, 2002). See: *http://www/msnbc.com*.

32. Ibid.

33. Ibid.

34. A. Raghavan, J. Sapsford and M. Schroeder, "SEC Opens Inquiry into Links between Enron and Its Banks," *The Wall Street Journal* (January 15, 2002), A1, A5.

35. J. Emshwiller and R. Smith, "Murky Waters: A Primer on the Enron Partnerships," *The Wall Street Journal* (January 21, 2002), A1, A3.

36. "Wall Street Analysts Vilified to Get Stricter Regulations," *NewYorkTimes.com* (February 12, 2002). See: *http://www.nytimes.com/*.

37. "Rules Would Reel in Analysts."

38. "Auditors, 'Public Watchdogs,'" *Washington Post* (December 5, 2001), A01.

39. Ibid.

40. "Enron: First Apply the Law," *The Wall Street Journal* (February 11, 2002), A3.

41. "Lawmakers Plan More Financial Oversight," *The Wall Street Journal* (February 11, 2002), A5.

42. "Ex-Enron CEO: Not Me," *CNNMoney.com* (January 22, 2002). See: *http://www.money.cnn.com/*.

43. M. Tran, "Arthur Andersen Appeals for Sympathy," *Guardian Unlimited* (January 29, 2002). See: *http://www.guardian.co.uk*.

44. "Big Five Win Little Respect from Smaller Companies," *The Wall Street Journal* (February 12, 2002). See: *http://online.wsj.com/*.

45. "Is Enron's Law Firm Vulnerable to Law Suits? *Associated Press* (February 11, 2002). See: *http://www.ap.org/*.

46. R. K. M. Haurwitz, "Houston-Based Law Firm Vinson & Elkins Had Role in Fraud, Say Enron Foes," *Knight-Ridder/Tribune Business News* (April 9, 2002), 2.

47. R. Deger, "Leaning on the Lawyers in the Enron Case," *Daily Business Review* (Miami, Fla.) (April 19, 2002), A12.

48. M. France, W. Zellner, and C. Palmeri, "One Big Client, One Big Hassle," *Business Week* (January 28, 2002), 38–39.

49. Ibid.

50. Ibid.

51. Deger, Leaning on the Lawyers, A12.

52. "Enron Report Ties the Company's Ruin to Executives Who Formed Partnerships," *The Wall Street Journal* (February 1, 2002), A2.

53. M. C. Bender, "Lawmakers Accuse Enron Lawyers of Hiding Employee's Claims," *Knight-Ridder/Tribune Business News* (March 15, 2002), 2.

54. E. J. Pollock, "Limited Partners: Lawyers for Enron Faulted Its Deals, Didn't Force Issue," *The Wall Street Journal* (May 22, 2002), A1, A18.

55. Ibid.; "Enron Report Ties the Company's Ruin to Executives Who Formed Partnerships."

56. Bender, "Lawmakers Accuse," 2.

57. Pollock, "Limited Partners," A18.

58. Ibid., "Enron Report Ties the Company's Ruin to Executives Who Formed Partnerships."

59. Ibid.

60. Ibid.

61. Ibid.

62. Ibid.

63. A. Sloan and M. Hosenball, "No Accounting for It," *Newsweek* (February 25, 2002), 34–35; "Vinson & Elkins Attorneys Testify They Didn't Know All the Facts about Enron," *Knight-Ridder/Tribune Business News* (March 15, 2002), 2, 7.

64. M. Schroeder, "Enron Reports Weren't Reviewed Fully by SEC for Many Years before Collapse," *The Wall Street Journal* (January 18, 2002), A1, A7.

65. F. Pelligrini, "For Enron, Washington May Have Been a Bad Investment," *Time.com* (January 15, 2002). See: *http://time.com/*.

66. Schroeder, "Enron Reports," A7.

9

Ethical Turnaround in Action: Warren Buffett at Salomon Brothers

INTRODUCTION

Over the past 15 years, "culture" has become a common way of thinking about and describing an organization's internal world—a way of differentiating one organization's "personality" from another. An organization's culture socializes people, and ethics is an integral part of the organization's culture. Therefore, building and reinforcing an ethical organization means systematically analyzing and managing all aspects of the organization's culture so that they support ethical behavior. However, often an organization's culture subtly (and other times not so subtly) conveys to members that certain actions are acceptable, even though they are unethical or illegal. For instance, when executives at General Electric, Westinghouse, and other manufacturers of heavy electrical equipment illegally conspired to set electrical prices in the early 1960s, the defendants invariably testified that they came new to their jobs, found price-fixing to be an established way of life, and simply entered into it as they did into other aspects of their job. One GE manager noted that every one of his bosses had directed him to meet with the competition: "It had become so common and gone on for so many years that I think we lost sight of the fact that it was illegal."[1] To get back on the ethical road, an organization must change.

212 Ethics and Corporate Social Responsibility

Change is an organizational fact of life. If an organization has any chance of transforming themselves from an unethical culture and experience, it must be able to handle change positively—to alter policies, structure, behavior, and beliefs—and do it with a minimum of resistance and disruption. It is far better to deal with the need for change—to modify it, redirect it, or disarm it—than to ignore or fight it. However, for organizations like Salomon Brothers and Enron a successful ethical turnaround does not just happen spontaneously; proper change management is the key to achieving this goal. But, in reality, can an organization turn itself around ethically? If so, what needs to happen for an organization to make a successful ethical turnaround? Offering some answers to that question is the focus of this chapter.

TOWARD AN ETHICAL TURNAROUND

Turning around an unethical organizational culture implies decision making. Such change means that the status quo is to be abandoned and something new has been selected to take its place. In turning around an unethical organizational culture, decision making is the mechanism by which the need for abandoning the status quo is evaluated and, if change is needed, the means by which a new direction is selected. It is the premise of this book that to accomplish a successful ethical turnaround, the organization must understand the scope of the problem and be willing to make the decisions to undertake drastic measures.

Organizations like Beech-Nut, E. F. Hutton, Salomon Brothers, Enron, and others have found themselves faced with the challenge of accomplishing a successful ethical turnaround. No matter what resulted in the organization's culture leading to the unethical act(s), top leaders, managers and employees who are accustomed to more "normal" conditions usually lack an appreciation of the perspective, skills, and special actions that are necessary to accomplish a successful ethical turnaround. As a result, many efforts fail as the organization never recovers from its fall. Although achieving an ethical turnaround may seem to be an impossible task, many organizations that fail do so needlessly.

Inexperience in handling an ethical turnaround situation is the first problem For most organizational leaders. Organizational leaders and managers may incorrectly assume that business as usual can continue. In fact, drastic cultural, psychological, and behavioral changes within the company are invariably necessary. Some employees who have worked for the organization for many years will have to be fired (as evident in the case of Salomon Brothers discussed later in this chapter), trusting relationships with customers and other key stakeholders that have been developed over the years will have to be rebuilt, and policies and procedures will need to be replaced. All too often, the people responsible for the past cannot bring themselves to make such sweeping changes. In cases where the ethical turnaround is entrusted to the older top management, employees, customers, suppliers, government, and legal interests may be dubious and suspicious of top management's actions and motives. This problem may be overcome, in time, if the organization can afford to wait that long. However, achieving an ethical turnaround in this way becomes a far more difficult and risky task.

Establishing a New Ethical Culture

A successful ethical turnaround often requires that leadership be put in the hands of someone new, often someone without a past history in the company. This person must have the freedom and ability to make changes. If he or she cannot act decisively and quickly, the company is probably doomed. The top leader may determine that some members of the existing company management (assuming they were not involved in any organizational wrongdoings) are ethically competent and adaptable to the changing circumstances. In some situations, some of these managers should be retained, as they provide continuity, insight, and knowledge.

Those who cannot provide help to the organization during the transition will have to be recognized and, if necessary, replaced. However, the new leadership should not adopt an attitude of change merely for change's sake; it is foolish and needlessly expensive to replace the entire management structure. Members of existing management who are retained should form a link between new management and the rest of the organization, as the organization must still produce products or provide services during the turnaround period.

People are at the heart of a successful ethical turnaround. Employees of the organization must be committed to the ethical turnaround and feel personally involved in achieving it. A sense of urgency, cooperation, and participation must permeate the environment. Measures must be instituted to convert dispirited employees into believers, confident that the new leadership is committed to changing, that the company will survive, and that they will have a future as employees. The new ethical goals will be achieved through the actions of all employees, not just the few in upper management. Top management should not lose sight of this fact. In addition to motivating, training, and properly directing the activities of its current employees, management must ensure that new employees will be successfully oriented on the appropriate ethical behavior.

A successful ethical turnaround is not accomplished by reaching a consensus on what needs to be changed or which painful actions need to be taken; a major ethical change first requires the commitment and direction of top management. Although orders given by new leadership may contradict decades-long practices and ways of doing business, the process is necessary; it is futile to entrust the ethical turnaround to someone without the will or authority to impose radical change. An ethical turnaround needs a leader, not a caretaker. However, in this situation, a strong leader is not a dictator. Middle-level managers must be able to assist in this process, not just carry out the leader's orders. In a situation as complex as an ethical turnaround, too many decisions must be made for one person to make them all and ensure that they are effectively carried out.

Reinforcing the New Ethical Culture

Since a culture is a system of shared beliefs and responses that conditions people how to behave in the organizational environment. As noted in our discussion of Salomon Brothers and Enron, the ethical culture of an organization is defined by those things it rewards, and an employee's ethical behavior is dependent on both his or her values and the ethical climate within the organization. Further, both the content and the strength of an organization's culture have an influence on the ethical behavior of its managers and employees. Good people can be encouraged to do bad things when their organization's reward system positively reinforces wrong behaviors. When an organization praises, promotes, gives large pay increases, and offers other desirable rewards to employees who lie, cheat, and misrepresent, its employees learn that unethical behaviors pay off. In these situations, regardless of what management says is important, people in organizations pay attention to how actual rewards are handed out. Thus, top management should establish new values and priorities and strive to create an organizational culture that permeates the new ethical environment.

However, top management may not realize that the old ethical culture will not instantly die. Because of the strength of the previous culture, it often lies submerged in the subconscious of employees and may quickly reappear if the new culture is not reinforced. The potential for returning to old behaviors is often high. In addition, "automatic responses" that reflect the old culture can be very detrimental. As in any change effort, the organization must use positive reinforcement and direct feedback to show employees what is expected in the new ethical culture. Employees need to be informed on why the change in attitude is necessary; any regression to previous unethical behavior must be brought to everyone's attention and swiftly dealt with in the appropriate manner. Unlike any other organizational culture change, in which one can afford to take up to five years to replace the old culture the new ethical culture must completely replace the unethical practices of the past in a very short period of time.

The key acceptance of any change is effective communication. That involves intensive efforts to promote trust and ensure that management shares information honestly and on a timely basis with employees. Therefore, the new leadership must immediately set up an employee communications program that makes employees part of the effort to solve the organization's problems; people need information if they are to respond appropriately and be properly motivated to make the ethical turnaround successful.

The Importance of Open Communication

An ethical turnaround situation is a highly stressful environment for all concerned. All people fear the unknown, and the loss of their jobs is even paramount, when customers, government, and other stakeholders have been affected by the unethical behavior (as was the case in both the Salomon Brothers and Enron situations). Successful communications with employees can help reduce the level of personal stress. Employees should be kept informed on the status of the organization; how bad the unethical behavior affecting the organization is (for example, how bad sales and losses are); and what employees are expected to do. A sense of personal involvement and urgency will exist only if employees feel that they are part of the change team.

Communicating an explicit position on the importance of ethical behavior of employees and explaining the philosophy and values that are to guide the organization is a logical starting point for new leadership in turning around unethical or creating an ethical culture. This can take the form of policy statements, speeches, and the like and can set the stage for more open discussion on ethical behavior and related questions.

Three suggestions can be made about these communications. First, ambiguity about organizational priorities has to be eliminated. Somebody has to to say straightforwardly that the long-term vitality of the organization rests on the ethical integrity of its employees, that obeying the law and respecting the ethical standards of society come before immediate economic objectives, and that these priorities will be maintained even when the pressure is on for short-term sales and profits.

Second, these communications have to move from the "do good and avoid evil" level of abstraction to open discussion of concrete problems that would be obvious to anyone in the organization and in the industry. To avoid mentioning and taking a specific position on the very problems with which employees in the organization are confronted not only misses an opportunity to deal with those problems but also introduces a note of ambiguity into the communication.

Third, these communications should not only point to the value of "good conversation" (an interchange of ideas where organizational members talk and listen and learn from one another) but also make demands that it take place routinely and regularly. In getting employees to do something, a place to start is to ask them to do it. In considering questions of ethical behavior, there is a perverse tendency to focus on the bad guys and ignore the good guys. Good conversation creates the opportunity for discussions on examples of employees who exhibit ethical behavior in the organization, employees who in most instances far outnumber those who exhibit unethical behavior.

There are good reasons to believe that these communications of the new leadership's ideology are best viewed as necessary but not sufficient. First, there are problems of change and inertia. If an organization has not been operating with unambiguous corporate policies on ethical behavior and good conversation, it will take some concerted effort to break old patterns and establish new ones. Second, initial communications by the new leadership on the companies may be difficult for employees if they don't have some appreciation or understanding of the new ethical expectations and the employees may be tentative at first.

New leadership must also recognize that they face a number of powerful stakeholders who have much influence on key elements in the organizations and the success of an ethical turnaround initiative. Dealing successfully with these parties is a critical element in an ethical turnaround. Three or more stakeholders can complicate the situation.

The first stakeholder is the board of directors or the parent company, in cases where a subsidiary is experiencing ethical problems. The board of directors must be convinced that the proper actions, programs, and reorganizations are being implemented and must be confident that the new management is competent and will be successful in the ethical transformation. Of course, members of the board of directors must be changed if they failed to perform their duties during the organization's unethical misdeeds.

Banks or lenders are the second stakeholders; they are most concerned with the financial resources available and such aspects as asset disposition and use of the proceeds. Unfortunately, lenders often demand leadership that is critically needed elsewhere.

Government is the third stakeholder group. If an organization is involved with the government like both Salomon Brothers and Enron were, this will be a key and very time-consuming stakeholder. The new leadership may have to convince government to hold back on taking legal proceedings against the organization, especially if such behavior would put the organization out of business. However, this is not a sufficient reason for government not to take legal actions against the guilty organization.

Major customers are another stakeholder group. If customers cannot be convinced to stick with the organization during its ethical turnaround, all may be lost. Lastly, major suppliers are an additional constituency. They also must be reckoned with since they must also protect their interests.

Regardless of the internal or external stakeholders the new leadership responsible for the ethical turnaround of an organization must continue to communicate a consistent message on the expected ethical standards. While there will always be some degree of resistance to change or a period of doubt or uncertainty about the new ethical direction of the organization the new leadership must commit to increased visibility and activity with respect to expected ethical standards. The next section offers a practical description of how Warren Buffet, as the new leader at Salomon Brothers, attempted to turn Salomon's culture around by emphasizing both institutional and individual processes.

TOWARD AN ETHICAL CULTURE AT SALOMON BROTHERS: WARREN BUFFETT AS LEADER ROLE MODEL

Turning around or changing an organization's culture does not happen by chance. What is needed for an organization to successfully transform support for individual ethical behavior? Building on our discussion of the bond trading scandal at Salomon Brothers in Chapter 6, this section demonstrates that a successful ethical turnaround does not just happen spontaneously. In particular, new leadership, altering policies, structure behavior, and beliefs are paramount to success a successful ethical turnaround. The five primary mechanisms available to leaders for embedding and reinforcing culture introduced earlier will be used to systematically describe Warren Buffett's efforts to change Salomon Brothers' culture.

The public admission by John Gutfreund, CEO and chairman of Salomon Brothers, in the summer of 1991 that its government desk had placed illegal bids in thirty of the 230 auctions of government securities in which it had participated since 1986 provides a more recent example of the role an organization's culture plays in encouraging unethical behavior. Shortly thereafter, both Gutfreund and Thomas Strauss, Salomon's president, resigned, and the U.S. Treasury Department suspended Salomon from bidding for its clients at future Treasury auctions.

At the time, Salomon was without a doubt the most powerful broker on Wall Street and a top-gun trader of government securities. The disclosure threatened not only to shatter the firm's hard-won franchise and pristine reputation but to eviscerate its culture by striking at the heart of the bank's character and identity. This was surely the worst scandal to hit the company in its eighty-one-year history, and it would take exquisite managerial skill and timing to weather the storm.

Although no one could have predicted the precise form that a crisis would take—or it's timing—most industry observers believe that something like this was bound to happen to Salomon Brothers someday. Among the preconditions that made a crisis likely were, on the one hand, the firm's aggressively "macho" culture and, on the other, the lax regulatory and increasingly competitive environment that Salomon's traders faced. Like kindling, these two sets of factors helped to ignite unethical and illegal behavior in the bank.

A *New York Times* editorial put a moral caveat on the bank's aggressiveness. It characterized Salomon as a company that celebrated clever evasion of rules and trampled anyone standing in the way of profit and as a company governed by a "culture of greed, contempt for government regulations, and a sneering attitude toward ethics or any other impediment to earning a buck."[2] Not someone you'd necessarily want to do business with.

We can conclude from the Salomon bond trading scandal that ethics at work is greatly influenced by the organization's culture. More specifically, the lack of an organizational culture that explicitly promotes and encourages ethical decision making results in unethical conduct. To get back on the ethical road an organization must change.

CHANGING THE ETHICAL CULTURE AT SALOMON BROTHERS: NEW LEADERSHIP

Changing an organization's culture is an extremely difficult process. This view is consistent with an idea basic to organizational change and development efforts that changing individual and group behavior is both difficult and time consuming. The human tendency to want to conserve the existing culture is referred to as "cultural persistence" or inertia. Culture has an addictive quality, perhaps because culture members are aware that culture components cannot be altered without affecting other, cherished values and institutions. Also, an organization's culture that supports unethical behavior tends to feed on itself. Why would successful (but unethical) managers want to change? They wouldn't. They would tend to hire people like themselves and perpetuate the culture that exists.

Leaders that wish to change their organization's ethical culture must attend to the complex interplay of formal and informal systems that can support either ethical or unethical behavior. Thus, quick-fix solutions are not likely to succeed. A broad, multipronged approach to changing organizational ethics must be used in diagnosing and changing an organization's ethical culture.

The five primary mechanisms—attention, reactions to crises, role modeling, allocation of rewards, and criteria for selection and dismissal—emphasize institutional as well as individual processes. In each area, Buffett drastically altered the system and culture that led to the Salomon bond fiasco under former CEO John Gutfreund's leadership. Buffett placed a commitment to ethical standards as his top priority, and his first actions indicate this commitment. When Buffett had just become acting chief executive officer (CEO) of Salomon, he immediately began to carefully craft a new corporate culture.

Attention

Our goal is going to be that stated many decades ago by J. P. Morgan, who wished to see his bank transact "first-class business . . . in a first-class way." We will judge ourselves in fact not only by the business we do, but also by the business we decline to do. As is the case at all large operations, there will be mistakes at Salomon and even failures, but to the best of our ability we will acknowledge our errors quickly and correct them with equal promptness. (Warren Buffett, October 1991).[3]

Again, attention is what the leader focuses his employees to concentrate on (what is criticized, praised, or asked about), which communicates his and the organization's values about them. For example, John Gutfreund's tenure at Salomon was marked by an absolute attention to a short-term business focus and what was happening that day or that week. Through this short-term perspective (which may simply be a function of being in the trading business), Gutfreund forced his employees to produce profits immediately. Dedication to short-term revenues above long-term considerations creates a climate where unethical behavior thrives.

Buffett and Deryck Maughan (chief operating officer under Buffett and chairman and CEO following Buffett's resignation) set out to quickly focus attention on the urgency and severity of Salomon's situation. With their fate in the hands of government regulators, the firm had to be prepared for an onslaught of bad publicity and, possibly, huge legal fines. Almost immediately, Buffett introduced changes in formerly accepted individual and institutional practices by eliminating many perks of Salomon employees: magazine subscriptions were canceled; cars, drivers, and secretaries were discharged; and long-distance phone services and health benefits were cut. Signals were being sent that

Salomon Brothers under Buffett would be very different than it had been under Gutfreund's leadership. Buffett's initial actions demonstrated that it was important and necessary to focus employees on the fact that the culture they had been working within was simply not a feasible way to continue to do business.

The new Salomon would be committed to upholding ethical principles and purging those who had a past history of and/or knowledge of unethical or illegal behavior. Buffett displayed his commitment to high ethical and legal standards by immediately issuing a memo to all Salomon senior executives declaring they should report any but the smallest legal infractions to him directly. The full text of this memo is as follows:

> Unless and until otherwise advised by me in writing, you are each expected to report, instantaneously and directly to me, any legal violation or moral failure on behalf of any employee of Salomon Inc. or any subsidiary or controlled affiliate. You are to make reporting directly to me your first priority. You should, of course, report through normal chain of command when I am unavailable and, in other cases, immediately after reporting to me.
>
> Exempted from the above are only minor legal and moral failures (such as parking tickets or nonmaterial expense account abuses by low-level employees) not involving significant breach of law by our firms or harm to third parties.
>
> My private office telephone number in Omaha is (402) [rest of telephone number left out intentionally so Mr. Buffett would not be contacted at home by non-Salomon employees] which reaches me both at the office and at home. My general office number in Omaha is (402) 346-1400. The Omaha office can almost always find me. When in doubt, call me.
>
> Warren E. Buffett
> Chairman and Chief Executive Officer [4]

As noted in the memo, Buffett demanded that the executives "report, instantaneously and directly to me, any legal violation or moral failure" of any Salomon employee. This was to be their "first priority." The memo should have left no doubt in the senior Salomon executives' minds that new procedures and policies were taking shape within the company.

In addition to modifying compliance procedures, the new leadership turned its attention to Salomon's culture. Although confident that the firm was not "endemically corrupt" as charged by some outsiders, Maughan believed that certain aspects of the culture needed to be modified. Maughan continued,

> Mozer's behavior was out of the ordinary, but still we had to reassert the traditional values of the firm. In some way, in some fashion, we had

lost our way. A certain permissiveness had entered in the air. A bravado was attached to the taking of risk and the making of money. As a result, we were inattentive to shareholders and external constituencies, and not as customer-oriented as we should be."[5]

Maughan pointed to control and compliance as functions needing additional support. "This has nothing to do with the individuals involved, but with the culture and the system," he said. Accordingly, he took steps to reassert the significance and independence of the general counsel and chief financial officer.

Maughan's view of managing ethics was a mixture of disciplining and leadership.

> I lead by example. But when things go wrong, you can't turn a blind eye. Leadership must enforce values through punishment. If they don't exercise the power, then the values can't be upheld. People begin to believe the behavior is okay. I don't think anyone doubts that current management would act forcefully if someone does something wrong. And I don't just mean compliance with the law I also mean issues of diversity, the treatment of women, putting customer interests first, not cutting corners. These things are communicated to employees in the speeches we make and in our daily routine. And the vast majority of employees are glad to hear it because they want to work in a quality place.[6]

Reactions to Crises

A crisis situation allows followers to see what is valued by the leader because its emotionality brings these values to the surface. John Gutfreund reacted to crises by using arbitrary dismissal criteria, executing firing decisions ruthlessly, using "sneaky" tactics to secure his own job, and covering up and lying about ethical indiscretions. When a legal violation by the firm was brought to his attention, he reacted by attempting to cover up, not disciplining violators or providing full disclosure to the Salomon regulators. This, resulted in the crisis situation Buffett was confronted with when he temporarily took over Salomon.

Buffett's tenure as interim chairman at Salomon Brothers began in a crisis situation. As market developments were sending Salomon into a tailspin, government investigators were swooping in to determine the extent of wrongdoing. The Securities Exchange Commission (SEC), the Treasury Department, the Justice Department, the Federal Reserve Board, the Federal Bureau of Investigation (FBI), and the Manhattan District Attorney were all looking into potential rule violations by Salomon. Depending on the results of the investigations, Salomon faced a variety of potential sanctions in addition to criminal fines and civil damages: censure, suspension, or debarment from acting as a broker/dealer and as a primary dealer in government securities; administrative probation; modification of its operations; and required appointment of board members or managers acceptable to the SEC. Some were putting the chance of criminal indictment as high as 80 percent in the early days of the crisis.

John Gutfreund had purposefully withheld information from the government regulators, and Salomon was temporarily barred from its bread-and-butter business of dealing in the U.S. Treasury auction. Buffett's reaction to the crisis was swift. He began to set the tone for a new corporate culture, in preparation for a hearing before the regulators. During that hearing, Buffett's testimony and his preliminary damage control efforts were rewarded with Salomon being allowed to return to the Treasury securities market.

As Buffett and Maughan faced the press during a break in the August 18 board meeting, no one knew the full extent of the firm's misconduct. Creditors, customers, employees, Salomon's insurers, and the markets were all waiting to see what management would say and do. Authorities were moving forward to investigate fully. Of great concern was whether Salomon would face a criminal indictment. Recalling the demise of E. F. Hutton and Drexel, Burnham, many feared that Salomon could not survive a criminal conviction. Buffett explained his role to the assembled group: "My job is to clean up the sins of the past and to capitalize on the enormous attributes that this firm has." "Salomon," he said, "has to earn back its integrity."[7]

Immediately after the press conference, Buffett convened an executive committee meeting where he made it clear that Maughan was in charge. Buffett sought to draw the curtain on Salomon's past and to lay the groundwork for a fresh start on Monday. Henceforth, noted one executive, Salomon's history would have two parts: BC, "before crisis," and AD, "after Deryck."[8]

Unlike Drexel Burnham Lambert, Salomon did not hire a public relations firm to generate favorable stories in an attempt to influence the government investigation. Salomon cooperated fully with the authorities. Buffett and Maughan took the approach that the company had done something wrong, had lost the confidence of the government, and had an obligation to the government to explain what had happened.

On September 4, Buffett sent letters of apology to the firm's major customers, promising to do business in the future with honesty and candor. On the same day Buffett answered questions before a congressional committee investigating Salomon and the Treasury securities market. Buffett characterized Mozer's improprieties as "almost like a self-destruct mechanism . . . not the act of a rational man at all."[9] Buffett also said that the former management's delay in coming forward was one of the most troubling aspects of the situation, raising the questions of whether there was a climate within Salomon that appeared to tolerate or even encourage wrongdoing. At the hearing, Buffett unveiled changes in Salomon's compliance system intended to "make Salomon a leader in setting new standards in regulatory behavior in the financial industry." Buffett also described Salomon's new board-level compliance committee, to be chaired by Lord Young, a British executive who had preciously served in the Thatcher cabinet.

A final example of how Buffett reacted to the crisis at Salomon occurred in late October 1991 when he spent $600,000 publicizing his third-quarter letter to the shareholders. On October 31, the two-page ads displaying the letter appeared in the *Wall Street Journal*, the *New York Times*, the *Washington Post*, and the *Financial Times*. Buffett trumpeted the firm's new compliance procedures, noting his directive that Salomon's 9,000 employees

> be guided by a test that goes beyond rules: contemplating any business act, an employee should ask himself whether he would be willing to see it immediately described by an informed and critical reporter on the front page of his local paper, there to be read by his spouse, children and friends. At Salomon we simply want no part of any activities that pass legal tests but that we as citizens, would find offensive.

It is clear that Buffett's reaction to the crisis at Salomon was to provide full disclosure of the firm's wrongdoing and not to cover it up as Gutfreund had tried to do. Buffett's management of crises indicated that ethical wrongdoing would not be tolerated or hidden from the authorities at any costs. Not only did Buffett take action against transgressors, his action showed that Salomon was committed to a new ethical standard. There should be no doubt that Buffett's reactions to crises was effective in demonstrating to both the firm's employees and its key stakeholders that ethical behavior would be a cornerstone of Salomon's new culture.

Role Modeling

Leaders communicate strong messages to their employees about their values through their own actions. For example, employees who wished to emulate John Gutfreund could not hold to a strong sense of personal ethics. Greed is a quality that can push people to break ethical standards to further their cause and make money. And greed was a seed that Gutfreund planted in Salomon's culture, contributing to its employees ignoring ethical and legal standards and resulted in the bond trading scandal.

If Salomon had searched for an upstanding and seemingly ethical investor, they could not have found a better role model than Warren

Buffett. Perhaps the most important thing that Warren Buffett brought to the Salomon table was his image. For many, Buffett was an inspired and logical choice (especially since his Berkshire Hathaway firm was the major investor in Salomon). However, to this day, newspapers report that he went in to protect Berkshire's $700 million, but Carol Loomis suggests that this explanation seems awfully simplistic.[10] Loomis, a friend of Buffett for about thirty years, notes, "Sure, he wished for the safety of that investment. But beyond that he was a director of a company in deep trouble and, in a way that few directors do, he felt an obligation to all of its shareholders." Gutfreund says he asked Buffett to take the job. Buffett thinks he volunteered. Loomis recently indicated that Buffett did not in any case immediately decide to take the job at Salomon and only decided to take the job "until things got straightened out" after reading a fax of a *New York Times* story. The front-page headlines said: Wall Street Sees a Serious Threat To Salomon Bros.; High-level Resignations and Client Defections Feared.[11]

Regardless of how Buffett came to temporarily take over the helm of Salomon, the vaunted "sage of Omaha" has a solid reputation for conservative, long-term investing; he was a custom-made antidote to the get-rich schemes Salomon was being charged with. He was also known as a master at manipulating the media, something he had done skillfully in building his own image as a nice, down-to-earth, grandfatherly sort of guy, and definitely "Mr. Clean." That personal reputation for integrity proved extremely useful to Salomon.

Although there are numerous examples of contradictions to this image, it is only important that government officials, Salomon's customers, and the investment community in general perceived him to be a paragon of America's heartland virtues—almost a mythical figure riding in from Omaha on his white horse to rescue the pitiful New York bankers from their ethical downfall. At the time experts stated that they believed that one of the main reasons Salomon would survive their prosecution is because of Buffett himself. During the Capitol Hill hearings on Salomon's trading violations, Ohio Representative Dennis Eckart, referring to fictional financial villains, said, "Gordon Gekko and Sherman McCoy are alive and well on Wall Street. Mr. Buffett . . . get in there and kick some butt,"[12] Thus, there were those who saw Buffett as the "ideal" role model to get Salomon back on track.

One aspect of this Buffett image—being a "penny pincher"—may be the most important one to regulators and others watching the Salomon recovery. Buffett's Berkshire Hathaway employs 22,000 people, who are directed by only eleven people at its Omaha headquarters, which resembles a doctor's office more than the nucleus of a billion-dollar operation. Their offices are located in one corner of only one floor at the end of a hall that has "industrial carpet and plastic weave wall paper."[13]

Berkshire Hathaway's image is in stark contrast to the one Buffett took over at Salomon.

All of the evidence indicates that Warren Buffett, or at least the public image of Warren Buffett, was an exemplary ethical role model for Salomon employees to follow. It is drastically different from the image and the reality of John Gutfreund. Buffett usually sticks with a company's current management and invests for long-term, not just short-term gains. Buffett's philosophy was in stark contrast to Gutfreund and his "trader mentality" of going for short-term profit, no matter what the cost. In addition, Buffett did not share Gutfreund's hunger for personal cash flow. He is interested, instead, in maximizing long-term Salomon shareholder wealth.

Maughan's appointment as chief operating officer (COO) under Buffett (and eventually as the chairman and CEO of Salomon) also reassured Salomon's internal and external constituents. Dubbed "Mr. Integrity" in the press, Maughan had served ten years in the Treasury Department of the United Kingdom and had worked for four years in the London office of Goldman Sachs. In testimony before the U.S. Congress, Salomon highlighted Maughan's "strong understanding of the proper relationship between financial institutions and government authorities." On assuming his new position, Maughan pledged "an absolute insistence on the correct moral as well as legal behavior," though he added, "I don't think we want to remove all the elements of our success."[14]

Buffett successfully provided a role model for which Salomon's employees could emulate and still be successful in the process. Buffett and Maughan wanted Salomon's employees to move away from modeling their behavior after that of John Gutfreund where they saw an opportunity for power and seized and capitalized upon it for personal gain without giving any thought to the ethical and legal implications of their behavior. As a result of Buffett's tenure at Salomon, there were no more reported incidents of wrongdoing on the firm's part. No longer were the firm's employees twisting a situation to their advantage, regardless of the ethical consequences.

Allocation of Rewards

The behavior exhibited by people the leader decides to reward with pay increases or promotions signals to others what is necessary to succeed in an organization. The reward system created by a leader indicates what is prized and expected in the organization. John Gutfreund rewarded aggressiveness, greed, and short-term performance at Salomon. Unlike Wall Street firms of the past, promotion at Salomon was certainly not dependent upon your background (educational, family, or otherwise). Promotion and pay were based primarily on performance, but, unfortunately, only on recent performance.

Arguably the most controversial step Buffett took to force cultural change was his concerted attack on the pay structure. Clearly, Buffett favored a closer link between pay and performance. Buffett criticized the prevailing "egalitarian, share of the wealth" method of compensation as more suitable for a private partnership than for a public company dependent on shareholder capital. Thus began Buffett's "pay for performance" philosophy at Salomon. In addition, Buffett took the unusual step of taking out a two-page newspaper advertisement, which declared in part, "Employees producing mediocre returns for owners should expect their pay to reflect this shortfall. In the past that has neither been the expectation at Salomon nor the practice."[15]

To correct what Buffett termed "irrationalities" in the compensation system overall, compensation was reduced and departmental compensation was linked more closely to department performance in October 1994. It should be noted that Buffett was under increased pressure from Salomon's key stakeholders to impose a new compensation system designed to limit pay levels that were among Wall Street's grandest. With Buffett "performance" means return on equity for the stockholders, not each manager's divisional profits. In 1990, more than 106 employees earned over $1 million in salary and bonuses, but Salomon, Inc. had a return on equity of 10 percent, which was deemed "mediocre" by Buffett. Moreover, although operating profits remained relatively flat from 1989 to 1990, compensation increased by $120 million. To address this "irrationality," Buffett promptly took back $110 million that had been earmarked for employee bonuses for the third quarter. Although employees certainly were upset with the change, investors were delighted, and the stock jumped 8.6 percent a share on the day of the announcement.

Interestingly, it appeared that Buffett was also taking steps to return to an employee-owned philosophy, which existed at the firm before Gutfreund sold out to Phibro—that is, he intended to force the bankers and traders at Salomon to take more of their pay in Salomon common stock that would not be redeemable for at least five years. This would help to re-instill a long-term focus to Salomon employees and increase their interest in its future. Although individual performance would still be recognized, special arrangements like ones that Gutfreund and certain key managers had made which paid huge bonuses to some traders will be gone. Buffett vowed that top performers would, however, "receive first class compensation."

Inside Salomon, some saw Buffett's compensation reforms as a gesture of appeasement toward regulators who believed that Wall Streeters made too much money. They warned that the changes could drive away some of the firm's best people. Others saw Buffett's aim as shifting some of the financial impact of the scandal from shareholders to employees.

In his letter to shareholders, Buffett addressed the possibility that some employees would leave the firm because of the announced changes. However, he indicated that the changes were just as likely to induce top performers to stay. He went on, "Were an abnormal number of people to leave the firm, the results would not necessarily be bad. Other men and women who share our thinking and values would then be given added responsibilities and opportunities. In the end we must have people to match our principles, not the reverse."[16] The emphasis on certain principles and the long-term focus was key to encouraging employees to consider all ramifications of their actions, not just what these actions will mean to their department's profits this quarter.

Warren Buffett wanted to soften the swashbuckling image of the Salomon of old. To do that, he prodded the bank to sell off some big blocks of stock and take losses. The $391 million sale of the bank's shares of ConAgra recorded a $10 million loss, while the sale of Sun-Micorsystems produced a 17 percent loss. It sent to all traders a signal that Salomon was no longer interested in high-risk wait-outs, that the bank would no longer act as a bully trader, and that it would assume a less aggressive stance in the market. If the old Salomon had been like John Wayne, known for its swagger, the new Salomon was to become more like Ozzie Nelson, nice and low key, neither so strong nor so effective.

Buffett's efforts to rein in the excessive executive pay at Salomon by reallocating rewards (i.e., introducing a new compensation system) proved to be the most frustrating, controversial, and disastrous when one considers the five mechanisms for changing an organization's culture. In theory, the plan was eminently reasonable. Excessive compensation was one of the main reasons Salomon had been floundering—in 1994 it paid out $1.4 billion to employees, or $277 million more than it collected in net revenues. But the managing directors rebelled against the new plan, fearing they'd pocket a lot less money. Some jumped ship to high-paying European banks, and others to rival Wall Street houses. In all, more than twenty managing directors left Salomon in the year following the firm's introduction of the new compensation system.

In June 1995, Buffett and his hand-picked CEO Deryck Maughan scrapped the calamitous plan. While Buffett was working to change the culture at Salomon by reallocating rewards the firm was slipping in its rankings on the investment-banking-deal tables in 1995, partly reflecting the losses of key personnel.

Criteria for Selection and Dismissal

Criteria for selection and dismissal describes how a leader's decisions about whom to recruit or dismiss signals his or her values to all of the organization's employees. Gutfreund's leadership style selected ambitious, win-at-all-cost, aggressive young people and gave them the chance to create new departments, new products, and enjoy success they could not achieve at other firms. Gutfreund's and his hand-picked employees' short-term view prevented them from seeing what the long-term costs of this kind of personality and behavior could be on the organization as a whole.

Specific performance guidelines were lacking at Salomon under Gutfreund. The criteria by which Gutfreund dismissed employees was vague and led to ambiguous performance standards. When people are not sure what to do, unethical behavior may flourish as aggressive individuals pursue what they believe to be acceptable behavior. There are both ethical and legal risks associated with Gutfreund's chosen leadership style: Reliance solely on subjective measures (e.g., "what my feelings tell me right now") can lead to vague and inconsistent management policies. These ambiguities can also lead to crossing ethical and legal boundaries as Salomon's employees proceeded to do.

To further distance Salomon from the old way of life Buffett made efforts to ensure that anyone who was even remotely connected with the scandal was no longer employed by the company. This disciplining violators of ethical standards was one of the positive steps Buffett took to improve the ethical behavior of Salomon's employees. Upon taking control, Buffett severed all relations with Mozer and Murphy, terminated their employment, and declined to pay their legal expenses. Maughan named Eric R. Rosenfeld, previously co-head of U.S. fixed income arbitrage, and a former assistant professor at Harvard Business School, interim head of the government trading desk, an area in which he had no previous experience.

Salomon's former top legal advisor, Donald M. Feuerstein, knew of trading violations in April and had persistently advised senior officials to report them to the proper authorities. He was fired anyway. The law firm of Wachtell, Lipton, Rosen and Katz, which had conducted an internal investigation of Salomon in July, also stepped aside. Martin Lipton, a partner at the firm and a close friend of John Gutfreund, had helped to craft the August 9 and August 14 news releases. Robert E. Denham, a long-time associate of Buffett, replaced Feuerstein. Denham made it his personal goal to make sure Salomon operates according to the highest of ethical principles. Creating an ethical advocate's role can also improve an organization's ethics, and it appears that Denham was to serve such a role at Salomon.

Two weeks later, the Salomon board met and announced that it would not pay compensation and future legal or other expenses of Gutfreund, Strauss, Meriwether, or Feuerstein, except to the extent that the firm was legally obligated to do so under pre-existing agreements. Not surprisingly, signals of a new emphasis away from stocks and the traders toward bonds, as well as a change in culture, led to many defections in the firm. Such a drastic shift in strategic course necessitated similarly drastic changes in personnel. More conservative, less brash bond employees would be the new rulers at Salomon; the traders' role in upper management would be limited. In November of 1991, Buffett created a nine-man executive committee, primarily comprised of bond executives, to replace Gutfreund's office of the chairman and board of directors. The former office of the chairman had seven vice chairmen as members, and four of them were already gone by this time.[17] Traders no longer rule at Salomon. The former head of stock trading, for example, Stanley Shopkorn, was excluded from the committee and subsequently left the firm. Mr. Shopkorn had a history of "questionable" ethical behavior. His department had caused the firm to be fined $1.3 million on charges that it cheated customers during the crash of October 1987. He kept a handful of black-jack cards encased in Lucite to remind visitors of his skill at gambling with Salomon's money. Shopkorn's exodus signaled to others that the new Salomon will be a more cautious and leaner organization committed to ethical principles.

Firings and resignations have extended past senior employees closely connected to the old regime. Approximately 15 percent of Salomon's senior investment analysts, as well as many stock traders and analysts, were fired. Buffett was criticized for firing so many people so quickly. Alan Bromberg, a securities law professor at Southern Methodist University claimed, "This whole thing may have been an overreaction . . . sacking and condemning highly talented people for the sake of crisis containment . . . [Buffett] may have done more damage to Salomon's morale and its ability to conduct its business than it was worth."[18]

Bromberg's comments would be on target in most organizations, but ignores the fact that Salomon's unique culture seems to have created an atmosphere ripe for the unethical and illegal behavior that occurred. Firing Gutfreund was not enough to change the fabric of the company. Cultural change or an ethical turnaround for a company is a long and complicated process that cannot happen overnight, or simply by firing an unethical CEO. Gutfreund had been at Salomon his entire working career and had made his impact on every part of the organization. He had surrounded himself with people who shared his ethical principles, and the same people cannot abide by Buffett's new rules. Munger argued, "When the final chapter is written, the behavior evinced by Salomon will be followed in other, similar cases. People will be smart enough to realize this is the response we want—superprompt—even if it means cashiering some people who may not deserve it."[19] By bringing in Denham as an ethical champion and by dismissing those Salomon employees most like Gutfreund, Warren Buffett began to pave the way for a new culture. Although it was too soon to tell if this new culture would maintain its current commitment to ethics, by clearing out the vestiges of the previous one, Buffett was taking the first step.

Warren Buffett's ideas about whom to recruit or dismiss sent strong signals to Salomon's employees about the values important to him as a leader. Buffett successfully introduced clearer criteria for selection, dismissal, and performance standards in Salomon, thus eliminating many of the ambiguities that existed under his predecessor John Gutfreund.

SUMMARY OF HOW BUFFETT TURNED AROUND SALOMON'S CULTURE

Through Buffett's efforts, Salomon was able to survive both the negative publicity and the federal penalty. In a sense, one could say that the government needed access to Salomon's massive capital base and was also willing to put its faith in Warren Buffett and the new management philosophy. John Gutfreund's culture was so deeply ingrained in the fiber of Salomon, Inc., however, that simply removing him and other top managers was not enough. Further steps were taken to kill the culture and return the firm's ethical credibility.

Warren Buffett was ready to accept this challenge and took many of the necessary steps (through the mechanisms by which a leader can influence a corporate culture) to ethically turn around Salomon's culture:

Buffett began to focus attention on improving the moral fiber of the firm. Buffett's efforts were in stark contrast to what occurred under John Gutfreund's tenure where Gutfreund looked at the most recent bottom-line profits and disregarded long-term implications of employees' actions.

Buffett swiftly reacted to the crises facing the company by complying with authorities and firing ethical wrongdoers. Gutfreund lied, covered up ethical and legal transgressions, and tried to preserve his own position at any cost.

As a role model, Buffett conveyed the image of one of the country's most ethical investors. Gutfreund set an example of secret deals and for tolerating and hiding unethical behavior.

Buffett allocated rewards according to employees' performance. It can be assumed that a lack of commitment to ethical principles would ensure that employees would not be promoted. Gutfreund promoted those who were most like him, lacking any commitment to ethical principles.

Buffett brought in employees who proclaimed their commitment to ethical principles and ushered out all old employees connected to ethical misconduct. Gutfreund had vague policies that confused employees and let them make their own decisions about how to "win" the internal Salomon competition that thrived under his leadership.

Of the mechanisms used to make sense of Buffett's efforts to turn around Salomon's culture, the allocation of rewards under the guise of the new compensation system seemed to have proved to be the most difficult to introduce and sustain by Buffett. While Buffett's efforts to influence the organization's culture by reining in the excessive executive compensation was the right thing to do, it seems to have had mixed results, as Salomon lost many of its best performers. The criteria for selection and dismissals mechanism brought in a new type of employee to Salomon while eliminating those who possessed the traditional "trader win-at-all costs mentality," which many believe is necessary to be successful in the trading arena. Like Buffett's use of the new compensation system, it can be said that the new criteria for selection and dismissal had mixed results in changing Salomon's culture. More specifically, many of the individuals who made Salomon what it was in its heyday were either fired or left the firm on their own, which resulted in additional losses for the company.

The point should not be missed that while the allocation of rewards and reactions to crises had mixed results that led to a large number of employees being fired or voluntarily leaving the firm, Buffett's efforts were aimed at changing Salomon's culture. Ultimately, Buffett did so. Additionally, Buffett's use of the other three mechanisms (attention, reactions to crises, role modeling) had clear positive affects on moving Salomon's culture to one that supported ethical behavior.

While dramatic change is necessary, any organization trying to change its culture through an ethical turnaround goes through a difficult readjustment period. Buffett had to realize that once he had removed all of the employees who were thriving in the old culture, the remaining employees needed to be assured that their positions were safe. Stabilization had to be an important next step for Buffett.

In the end, Mr. Buffett proved that it was wiser to take tough measures early and suffer in the short run than to run the risk of losing the hard currency of a good reputation. Had John Gutfreund acted forcefully in April 1991 when he was informed of Paul Mozer's violations of auction rules, there would probably not have been a scandal. Although no company will ever eliminate the possibility of rogue members breaking the law, under Buffett's leadership, Salomon has shown us how to deal with them in a way that protects the company's most valuable asset—its reputation.

THE AFTERMATH

Less than two years after the trading scandal brought Salomon to the brink of collapse, the bank was back with a vengeance. In 1992, Salomon Brothers earned $1.4 billion before taxes, an all-time peak and a 34 percent gain over 1991. By March 1994, the company's stock price had jumped to a high of $50 per share from its low of $24 in June 1991, and its market value had grown to a healthy $5.5 billion.

In May 1992, Salomon agreed to pay $290 million in civil fines and damages, in return for which it would not face the kinds of criminal charges that had felled E. F. Hutton and Drexel. Instead, the company agreed to dole out $122 million for civil securities law violation, to pay $68 million in forfeitures to the Justice Department for settlement of antitrust and other claims, and to create a $100 million fund for restitutions in private damage claims. With considerable relief, the company also agreed to a two-month suspension of its primary dealership, to payment of legal costs of $12.5 million for private claims, and to $54.5 million in payments to holders of the company's stock and bonds. In March 1994, Salomon settled the remaining class-action lawsuits brought by rival bond traders claiming injury for an estimated $30 million in additional payments.

The joint investigation initiated by thirty-three individual states largely followed the lead of the federal agencies. Although these actions had the potential to be devastating, they did not amount to much in either fines or penalties, and no state had permanently banned Salomon from operating in its jurisdiction.

In December 1992, John Gutfreund agreed to never again run a securities firm and to pay a $100,000 fine as part of a settlement of civil charges stemming form the firm's illegal bidding. Thomas Strauss, Salomon's former president, agreed to a fine of $75,000 and suspension from associating with a Wall Street firm for six months. John Meriwether, a former vice chairman, agreed to a three-month suspension and a fine of $50,000.

In September 1993, Paul Mozer, the trader at the center of the Treasury scandal, was allowed to plead guilty to two felonies stemming from his submission of illegal bids when he was head of government bond trading for Salomon. He faced a maximum prison term of ten years and a $500,000 fine. By December 1993, he had been sentenced to a four-month term in a minimum-security prison and fined a mere $30,000. In justifying his lenient sentence, U.S. District Court Judge Pierre Leval praised Mozer's "valuable cooperation" in testifying against others. He also called Mozer's crime an "extremely foolish, arrogant, insouciant offense."[20] The closing chapter on the 1991 bond auction scandal was written on July 15, 1994, when Mozer agreed to pay a $1.1 million fine and accepted a permanent ban from the securities industry.

On June 3, 1992, in a surprise move, Salomon named its general counsel, Robert Denham, to replace Warren Buffett as chairman of Salomon, Inc. An outsider, Denham had been brought in only nine months before to shepherd the company through the long investigation that culminated in the $290 million settlement. Deryck Maughan was subsequently named chairman and chief executive of Salomon Brothers, while Buffett remained on the parent company's board and continued to chair its executive committee.

Competitors took advantage of the diminished role Salomon was forced to play. Shortly after the crisis broke, Salomon ranked fifth among investment banks, down from the first just before the crisis. Buffet's skillful handling of the crisis and revitalized reputation made long-term effects less clear. Salomon was still Wall Street's largest bank and among its most influential players.

Shortly before the scandal broke, John Gutfreund was asked about the future culture of Salomon. The man who throughout the 1980s personified Salomon's culture of aggressive bullying and who inspired fear and respect on Wall Street had this to say: "I'd like to see a return to more collegiality, more camaraderie. And I think this will come about, because I expect over the next few years that more ownership will revert to employees. Then there will be a community of interest that will change the interpersonal relationships again."[21]

AVOIDING FUTURE UNETHICAL ACTIONS

We've never been able to figure out how to reliably prevent the cyclical decline of great civilizations, religions, armies, or corporations. But if we cannot bring ourselves to believe that man and his organizations are perfectible, at least we must believe that we can improve our own areas of responsibility according to some set of ethical standards. To do otherwise is to abdicate to the natural entropy of power.[22]

The Salomon example is particularly difficult because so drastic a change was needed to retain the organization's viability—planned change was not an option. However, the Salomon saga presents a vivid example of how an organization under the right leadership can actively return from the brink and rebuild ethical capital damaged by a scandal. Like Johnson & Johnson before it, Salomon's adroit efforts under

Buffett's leadership demonstrates that an unethical culture need not be permanent.

While Salomon never achieved its previous ranking and notoriety in the investment banking arena, eventually being bought, it must be acknowledged that had not Warren Buffett temporarily taken over the helm at Salomon there may not have been a firm to acquire. In the end, an important lesson to be learned from this look at Warren Buffett and Salomon is that no matter whom the leader they must work to eliminate any inherent abstractness or the conflicting nature of the organizations ethical standards if they are going to be successful at an ethical turn-around. An understanding of the organization's culture (and subcultures) is a must first step for the new leader that should quickly be followed by proactive steps to communicate an explicit position on the importance of ethical behavior that will guide the future organization.

The following steps for restoring reputation are particularly helpful to leaders like Warren Buffett and Enron's CEO Stephen Cooper who are responsible for ethical turnarounds in organizations. The steps are as follows:

Step 1: Take immediate and public responsibility for what happened.

Step 2: Convey concern to all stakeholders.

Step 3: Show full and open cooperation with authorities.

Step 4: Remove negligent incumbent managers.

Step 5: Appoint credible leaders that represent all interests.

Step 6: Dismiss suppliers and agents tied to the incumbent managers.

Step 7: Hire independent investigators, accountants, accountants, counsel, PR.

Step 8: Reorganize operations to ensure greater control.

Step 9: Establish strict procedures.

Step 10: Identify and target the practices that stimulated infractions.

Step 11: Revise internal practices and pay systems.

Step 12: Monitor compliance.[23]

The goal of today's and tomorrow's leaders should be to ensure that they build and maintain a strong ethical organizational culture from the start so that they won't have to undertake the challenges of turning around an unethical culture. Following the guidelines to determine if a firm is at ethical risk can also be an effective first step by an organization interested in countering unethical behavior.[24] Cooke warns of organizational ethics becoming trivialized, because it is such a hot topic. By recognizing his warning signs early, an unethical experience, such as that of the Salomon Brothers, may be avoided. Several of the danger signs were exhibited by the culture created by John Gutfreund, including short-term revenue emphasis, arbitrary performance-appraisal standards, an internal environment discouraging ethical behavior, and ethical problems being sent to the legal department. Unfortunately, at least one danger sign—primary concern for shareholder's wealth—appeared in Buffett's new culture. Once any or all of these signs have been recognized, it is imperative that an organization take corrective measures.

Although Warren Buffett took several necessary steps through his leadership—establishment of a code of ethics, discipline of violators, and creation of an ethical advocate's role—it is also important that leaders committed to ethical turnarounds create a long-term strategic and ethical plan. The plan should emphasize a whistle-blowing mechanism and, most important, a training program in business ethics to ensure that there is little ambiguity when employees face ethical and/or legal dilemmas in the future. In a sense, what is needed at companies like Salomon Brothers and Enron is to ensure that ethics becomes paramount in the organization. As a way of concluding our discussion on Warren Buffet's ethical turnaround efforts at Salomon Brothers, Table 9.1 provides a brief update on activities towards the end of his tenure and beyond.

TABLE 9.1 Salomon Brothers: The Aftermath

1. May 1992—Salomon agreed to pay $290 million in civil fines and damages, in return for which it would not face the kinds of criminal charges that felled E. F. Hutton and Drexel.
2. None of the thirty-three individual states that jointly investigated Salomon permanently banned the company from operating in its jurisdiction.
3. June 1992—in a surprise move, Salomon named its general counsel, Robert Denham, to replace Warren Buffett as chairman of Salomon, Inc. Deryck Maughan was subsequently named chairman and CEO.
4. Dec. 1992—Gutfreund agreed never again to run a securities firm and to pay a $100,000 fine. Strauss (former president) agreed to a fine of $75,000 and suspension from associating with a Wall Street firm for 6 months. Merriwether (former vice chairman) agreed to a three-month suspension and a fine of $50,000.
5. Dec. 1993—Mozer had been sentenced to a four-month term in a minimum-security prison and fined a mere $30,000. In July 1994 he agreed to pay a $1.1 million fine and a permanent ban from the securities industry.
6. In 1992 Salomon Bros. earned $1.4 billion before taxes, an all-time peak and a 34 percent gain over 1991.
7. By March 1994, the company's stock price had jumped to a high of $50 per share from its low of $24 in June 1991. However, the firm lost nearly $1 billion, primarily in bond trading in 1994.

TABLE 9.1—continued

8. A 1994 revolt against efforts to rein in the pay of its high-priced traders and bankers left Buffett's handpicked team of Maughan & Denham hemorrhaging as droves of talented people walked out the door to work for other firms willing to pay their multimillion-dollar salaries.

9. By 1995, Salomon had still not recovered its top position among Wall Street firms and continued to experience losses. Its return on equity remained the lowest among the large Wall Street brokerage firms.

10. Spring 1995—Maughan sliced the powerful operating committee from fourteen to five, brushing aside rivals and naysayers even as he and the board publicly backed down on what one former official called "the compensation plan from hell."

11. From Oct. 1995 to Oct. 1996 Salomon's bond traders—who remained the heart of the firm—made a spectacular $2 billion.

12. The firm opened several new offices and hired 275 bankers, traders and research analysts worldwide from Oct. 94 to Oct. 96.

13. Salomon's compensation expenses were 47.3 percent of its net revenue, well below the average of 50.5 percent for its peers in Oct. 1996.

14. Perhaps the biggest beneficiary of Salomon's turnaround has been Buffett's holding company, Berkshire Hathaway, Inc. Buffett has more than $1 billion invested in Salomon and controls about 18 percent of its shares.

15. Salomon Bros. changed its management, attitude, and values but still suffers from the reputation it gained from illegally cornering the bond markets. However, the firm seems to be on the rebound.

16. Salomon Bros. was purchased by SmithBarney in December 1997.

CONCLUSION: WHAT CEO COOPER MUST DO AT ENRON

Pressure, opportunity, and predisposition can all lead to unethical activities; however, Enron's new CEO Stephen Cooper (an expert in organizational turnarounds) must take a proactive stance to promote an ethical climate. As CEO he must be the chief ethics officer of the organization, creating a strong ethics message that gets employees' attention and influences their thoughts and behaviors. Cooper must find ways to focus the organization's attention on ethics and values and to infuse the organization with principles that will guide the actions of all employees. Cooper's reputation for ethical leadership is more important now than ever in this new organizational era for Enron. New values must be the glue that holds things together at Enron, and these values must be conveyed from the top of the organization. Employees must understand that any single employee who operates outside of the organizational value system can cost the organization dearly in legal fees and can have a tremendous, sometimes irreversible impact on the organization's image and culture.

Cooper and the organization's other leaders need to talk about ethics and values, not in a sermonizing way, but in a way that explains the values that guide important decisions and actions. It will not be clear to employee that ethics and values are important, if they do not hear about ethics and values from the top. It means talking about the values that are important to Enron's leaders and the organization.

Cooper must take a number of steps (by using the mechanisms by which a leader can influence a company culture) to ethically turn around Enron's culture:

Attention—Cooper must focus attention on improving the moral fiber of the organization by not disregarding the long-term implications of employee's actions in favor of the most recent bottoms line profits.

Reaction to Crisis—Cooper must swiftly react to the crisis facing the company by complying with authorities and firing ethical wrongdoers. The company must stop lying, covering up ethical and legal transgressions, and trying to preserve those ethical wrongdoers at any cost.

Role Modeling—Cooper must convey the image of the moral manager. He must set the example of honesty and integrity for the rest of the organization.

Allocation of Resources—Using rewards and discipline effectively may be the most powerful way to send signals about desirable and undesirable conduct. That means rewarding those who accomplish their goals by behaving in ways that are consistent with stated values Cooper must allocate awards according to employees' performance and it must be assumed that a lack of commitment to ethical principles will ensure that employees will not be promoted.

Criteria for Selection and Dismissal—Cooper must bring employees into Enron who are committed to ethical principles and usher out all old employees connected to ethical misconduct. The company must have clear policies on the criteria for selection and dismissal that employees understand.

In conclusion, at the minimum Cooper must do the following to get back to an ethical organizational culture:

- Encourage ethical consciousness from the top, down showing the company supports and cares about ethical practices.

- One of the most basic of management principles states that if you desire a certain behavior, reinforce it. Formal processes must be used to support and reinforce ethical behavior.
- Provide rewards for ethical behavior and avoid providing rewards for unethical behavior.
- Punish unethical behavior and avoid punishing unethical behavior.
- When placing employees into competitive situations, be sensitive to the potential for unethical behavior and take appropriate steps to avoid it.
- Pay particular attention to principled organizational dissent. Principled organizational dissent is the effort by individuals in the organization to protest the status quo because of their objection, on ethical grounds, to some practice or policy.

NOTES

1. Jerald Greenberg and Robert A. Baron, *Behavior in Organizations* (Needham Heights, Mass.: Allyn and Bacon, 1993).
2. *New York Times,* editorial (August 22, 1991), A26.
3. Lynn S. Paine, *Cases in Leadership, Ethics, and Organizational Integrity: A Strategic Perspective* (Boston, Mass.: Irwin, 1997).
4. Ibid.
5. U.S. Securities and Exchange Commission. From the testimony of Richard S. Breeden, SEC Chairman, Washington, September 4, 1991.
6. Ronald R. Sims, "Changing an Organization's Culture under New Leadership," *Journal of Business Ethics* 25 (2000), 65–78.
7. L. Malkin, "5 Top Officers Leave Salomon as Buffett Takes Control of Firm," *International Herald Tribune* (August 19, 1991), 2; M. Siconolfi, "Salomon's Buffett Moves to Slash Sky-high Paychecks," *The Wall Street Journal* (October 30, 1991), C1.
8. Paine, *Cases in Leadership,* 48.
9. K. Salwen, "Buffett Gives Details to Inquiry by House," *The Wall Street Journal* (September 5, 1991), C1.
10. Carol Loomis, "Warren Buffett's Wild Ride at Salomon," *Fortune* (October 27, 1997), 114.
11. Ibid., 115.
12. L. N. Spiro, "How Bad Will It Get?" *Business Week* (October 7, 1991), 122–23; R. Suskind, "Warren Buffett's Aura as Folksy Sage Masks Tough, Polished Man," *The Wall Street Journal* (November 8, 1991), Al.
13. Suskind, "Buffett's Aura," A1.
14. W. Power, and M. Siconolfi, "Mr. Integrity Is Promoted to a Top Post," *The Wall Street Journal* (August 19, 1991), A2.
15. M. Siconolfi, "Salomon's Buffett."
16. Paine, *Cases in Leadership,* 50.
17. Siconolfi, "Salomon's Executive Panel Tilts to Bond Sector," *The Wall Street Journal* (November 7, 1991), C1.
18. L. P. Cohen, "Buffett Shows Tough Side to Salomon—and Gutfreund," *The Wall Street Journal* (November 8, 1991), A6.

19. Ibid.

20. Susan Antilla, "Ex-Salomon Trader Gets Four Months," *New York Times* (December 15, 1993), D2.

21. John Gutfreund, interviewed by Gilbert Kaplan in *Institutional Investor,* February 1991, 54.

22. C. M. Kelly, "The Interrelationship of Ethics and Power in Today's Organizations," *Organizational Dynamics* (Summer, 1987), 5–18.

23. Charles J. Fombrun, *Reputation: Realizing Value from the Corporate Image* (Boston, Mass.: Harvard Business School Press, 1996).

24. Robert A. Cooke, "Danger Signs of Unethical Behavior: How to Determine If Your Firm Is at Ethical Risk," *Journal of Business Ethics* 10 (1991), 249–53.

10

Institutionalizing Ethics: A Proactive Approach to Countering Unethical Behavior

INTRODUCTION

An important premise of this book is that if an organization institutionalizes ethics, it is unlikely to find itself trying to recover from a fall or having to undertake an ethics turnaround, as did Salomon Brothers and Enron. Institutionalizing ethics may sound ponderous, but its meaning is straightforward. It means getting ethics formally and explicitly into daily business life. It means getting ethics into company policy formation at the board and top management levels and through a formal code, getting ethics into all daily decision making and work practices down the line, at all levels of employment. It means grafting a new branch on the corporate decision tree—a branch that reads "right/wrong."[1]

Institutionalizing ethics is an important task for today's organizations if they are to effectively counteract the increasingly frequent occurrences of blatantly unethical and often illegal behavior within large and often highly respected organizations. The institutionalization and management of ethics is a problem facing all types of organizations—educational, governmental, religious, business, and so on.

THE PROCESS OF INSTITUTIONALIZING ETHICS

It would seem to be good strategy for an organization to be concerned about and adopt institutional ethics. An organization that is truly interested in bringing about a long-term ethical system, must first define institutionalization, while increasing their understanding about why some organizations and their employees remain ethically viable while others decline. This section focuses on defining institutionalization and presents some currently accepted mechanisms organizations may use to institutionalize ethics.

Institutionalization Defined

The approach emphasized in this chapter is to understand the existence of an ethical system via the concept of institutionalization. The institutionalization of ethics means getting ethics formally and explicitly into daily business life. Institutionalization should be examined in terms of specific behaviors or acts. A basic premise of this chapter is that the persistence of an ethical organization can be understood and studied by analyzing the persistence of the specific behaviors associated with an organization and its employees behaving ethically. An institutionalized act is defined as a behavior that is performed by two or more individuals, persists over time, and exists as a part of the daily functioning of the organization. It should be clear from this definition of institutionalization that an act is not all-or-nothing. An act may vary in terms of its persistence, the number of people in the organization performing the act, and the degree to which it exists as part of the organization.

Ethical principles can be institutionalized within organizations in a variety of ways by considering both long- and short-term factors. For the long term, organizations should develop their organization's culture so that it supports the learning—and, if necessary, relearning—of personal values that promote ethical behavior. For example, when decisions are made, managers should explicitly and publicly explain the ethical factors that accompany each alternative considered. An organization should create and continue to nurture an organizational culture that supports and values ethical behavior. This can be done, for example, by encouraging organization members to display signs of ethical values through whistle-blowing. In the short term, organizations can make public statements that ethical behavior is important and expected. The goal of such activities is to ensure that ethical concerns are considered in the same routine manner in which legal, financial, and marketing concerns are addressed.

Permanent board-level committees can also be created to monitor the ethical behavior of the organization. These committees, often called "social responsibility" or "public policy" committees, serve two functions within an organization. First, they lend legitimacy to the consideration of an ethics agenda at the highest level of organizational decision making. Second, they symbolically communicate to the employees and external stakeholders of the organization its commitment to ethical principles in conducting business.

Another mechanism for the institutionalization of ethics within an organization is the use of a code of ethics, discussed in more detail later in this chapter. Within an organization, this code describes the general value system of the organization, defines the organization's purpose, and provides guidelines for decision making consistent with these principles.

Another method that has gained in popularity in recent years is the implementation of ethics training programs, including seminars or workshops to reinforce good ethics. Organizations that have not been guilty of wrongdoing have recently initiated formal ethics programs in an effort to avoid public-relations problems, raise employee morale and productivity, and make their organizations more honest.

KEYS TO INSTITUTIONALIZING ETHICS

Organizations can enhance the institutionalization of ethics by first recognizing and then managing the importance of a number of key variables, such as organizational commitment, strong ethical culture, management's role, creating an environment that encourages whistle-blowing, and structuring an ethics enforcement system.

Organizational Commitment

Individuals react in very different ways to the organizations in which they work. Some employees give little thought to the organization, whereas others have very strong feelings, ranging from contempt and disgust to a high degree of loyalty to and identification with the organization. Social scientists and organizational researchers have devoted considerable attention to the concept of organizational commitment and to understanding its nature, causes, and consequences.

Upon entering an organization, employees are given opportunities to become schooled in and committed to the organization's goals, objectives, values, and ways of conducting business. Simply defined, *organizational commitment* is the relative strength of an individual's identification with and involvement in a particular organization.

It usually includes three factors: (1) a strong belief in the organization's goals and values, (2) a willingness to exert considerable effort on behalf of the organization, and (3) a strong desire to continue as an organizational member. Organizational commitment, then, is not simply loyalty to an organization. Rather, it is an ongoing process through which organizational actors express their concern for the organization and its continued success and well-being.

There are many reasons why an organization should want to increase the level of organizational commitment among its members. For example, the more committed the employee is to the organization, the greater the effort expended by the employee in performing tasks. In addition, highly committed workers are likely to remain with the organization for longer periods of time—that is, there is a positive relationship between the level of organizational commitment and job tenure. Finally, given the contribution a highly productive, trained employee can make to organizational productivity, keeping such an employee should be a high priority for the organization. Because highly committed employees wish to remain associated with the organization and advance organizational goals, they are less likely to leave.

What is it about employee experiences that leads them to be more or less committed to the organization? Ee must first consider exactly what leads to the phenomenon of commitment. Four factors for understanding the concept of organizational commitment are offered in the next few sections. The visibility, explicitness, and irreversibility of one's behavior and personal volition for one's behavior are the factors that commit individuals to their acts (to include ethical behavior).

Visibility. One major determinant of how committing a particular behavior may be is how observable that behavior is to others. Behaviors that are secret or unobserved do not have a committing force behind them because they cannot be linked to a specific individual. One of the most simple and straightforward ways to commit individuals to ethical behavior in an organization is to make their association with the organization public information. If they are part of the organization, they (by association) support that organization and its goals. Many organizations are already taking advantage of this visibility notion to increase employee commitment. When a new employee joins an organization, the employee's photograph and a formal announcement are sent to the local newspapers, in-house publications, and other such outlets to inform others of the new arrival. The same vehicles can be used by organizations to educate its new (and old) employees on its expectations on ethical behavior.

Maintaining visibility on expected ethical behavior is not a difficult task. Very little additional effort is required to associate individuals with their work, their accomplishments, and their organization. Organizations can follow the lead of General Electric in the late 1970s, for example, by annually issuing a booklet listing employees who have done socially good works both within and outside the company. In addition, might not a code provide for similar recognition of employees who have acted ethically? The more visible the organizations and individuals and their ethical contributions, the more committed they are likely to be to the organization's incentives for positive ethical behavior. The simple presence of an ethical code and a corporate ethics committee can increase the visibility of expected ethical behavior and the institutionalization of ethics within an organization.

Explicitness and irreversibility. Visibility alone is not sufficient to commit individuals to ethical behaviors. It must be combined with explicitness; the more explicit the expected behavior, the less deniable it is. Thus, explicitness is the extent to which the individual cannot deny what behavior is expected by the organization. How explicit the behavior is depends on two factors: its observability and its unequivocality. When a behavior cannot be observed but only inferred, it is less explicit. Equivocality is the difficulty of pinning down the act or behavior. It can be seen in the way people qualify the statements they make (such as "It sometimes seems to me that . . ." versus "I think . . ."). Explicitness is indeed a key component for the institutionalization of ethics. Explicitness can be enhanced by having all executives, managers, and employees sign a letter affirming their understanding of an organization's ethics policy and stating that they will (a) review the policy annually and (b) report all cases of suspicious (unethical) behavior.

Irreversibility. Irreversibility, on the other hand, means that the behavior is permanent; it cannot easily be revoked or undone. The importance of irreversibility can be observed in the circumstances that committed Great Britain and France to building the Concorde. Minister of Aviation James Avery included a clause in the 1961 agreement with France that both France's and Britain's decision to produce the Concorde were virtually irreversible. The clause required that if either partner withdrew from the collaboration, the entire development cost up to that point would be borne by the withdrawing party. Interestingly, the more rational it became to withdraw (because of escalating costs), the more committed the parties were to continuing. This type of commitment is typically referred to as behavioral commitment or escalation.

Organizations also are aware of the committing aspect of irreversible acts. Many organizations have developed benefit packages that are not transferable from one firm to another. The irreversible loss of these benefits should an individual choose to leave the organization commits the individual to continued employment. In addition, the orientation and training of employees on expected ethical behavior may reassure employees that an ethical stand will be supported and rewarded by the organization.

Organizational attempts to assimilate the individual in organizational relationships increases organizational commitment. For example, creating a network of relationships at work that become important to an employee is a primary way of connecting workers to the organization. Employees' perceptions of the irreversibility of their positions in an organization develop naturally over time. The longer they are employed by an organization, the more their skills are tailored to the unique demands of that organization. What they know and how they think about an organization become, in reality, what they know and how they think about the particular way their organization does business. The irreversibility of behavior is important because it influences the social contract (see Chapter 11). An organization can use both explicitness and irreversibility as tools for institutionalizing ethics through the creation of incentives and reinforcers (for example, by encouraging and rewarding organization members to display signs of ethical values through whistle-blowing).

Volition. To this point the importance of irreversibility in the commitment process has been emphasized, but a piece of the puzzle is still missing. Volition, with its observable equivalent—personal responsibility—is the fourth mechanism available to organizations for binding individuals to ethical behaviors. Without volition, behaviors are not committing. "Since I have no choice," one might reason, "I really cannot be held responsible for the consequences of my behavior." When individuals try to separate themselves from their actions, they might protest that they did not like what they were doing, but the money was too good to refuse. Another way in which individuals try to distance themselves from certain behaviors (usually those associated with unpleasant circumstances, like the consequences of committing an unethical act) is to insist that they have little personal responsibility for the behavior or the outcome. The classic example is a student trying to explain why he or she did not turn in a homework assignment: "because the dog ate it." Because the student could not control the dog, he or she believes that failing to turn in the homework was not volitional.

Enhancing employees' personal responsibility for their actions is critical to establishing their commitment to the organization, the accompanying expectations of ethical behavior, and the institutionalization of ethics within the organization. At this point, there should be no question that visibility, explicitness and irreversibility, and volition are important in the creation of organization members' commitment to ethical behavior. Further, commitment to an organization's ethical expectations and its goals is important because individuals will adjust their attitudes and expectations in situations to which they are committed. While enhancing organizational commitment to ethical behavior is an ongoing process, it is probably most critical early in an employee's association with an organization.

A number of factors that may lead to greater organizational commitment early in an employee's tenure with an organization and that can be used to institutionalize ethics are (1) personal factors such as the employee's initial level of commitment (deriving from initial job expectations, the social contract, and so on), (2) organizational factors such as an employee's initial work experiences and subsequent sense of responsibility, and (3) non-organizational factors, such as the availability of alternatives after the initial choice has been made (for example, jobs). Each of these three factors can serve as mechanisms for the organization to institutionalize and manage ethics. Individuals who are ethically committed to an organization's values and ethical policies at entry are likely to remain committed throughout their tenure with the organization. Consistency between organizational, work-group, and individual goals (expectations) on ethics will increase commitment to those goals. Finally, when the organization provides disincentives for unethical behavior and accepts no alternatives to ethical behavior, then organization members will behave in an ethically responsible manner.

Commitment to the organization and its goals is a major factor in predicting ethical behavior. Thus it is critical that organizations have mechanisms to enhance the development of organizational commitment among new employees. In fact, one way in which organizations with high levels of employee commitment differ from organizations with low levels of employee commitment is that the former tend to be "strong culture" organizations. For employees to be part of such an ethical culture, they must be educated as to the expectations and practices of the organization. The extent of their commitment to the organization may well hinge on their ability to understand, accept, and become a part of the organizational culture—"The way we do things around here."

STRONG ETHICAL CULTURE ORGANIZATIONS

A strong organizational culture founded on ethical business principles and moral values is a vital driving force behind countering unethical behavior, institutionalizing ethics, and continued overall success. An organization's culture can be strong and cohesive in the sense that the organization conducts its business or operations according to a clear and explicit set of principles and moral values, that management devotes considerable time to communicating these principles and values to organization members and explaining how they relate to its organizational environment, and that the values are shared widely across the organization by senior executives and rank-and-file employees alike.

Strong ethical culture organizations (SECOs) typically have creeds or values statements, and senior leadership regularly stress the importance of using these values and principles as the basis for decisions and actions taken throughout the organization. In SECOs, values and behavioral norms are so deeply rooted that they don't change much when a new CEO takes over—although they can erode over time if the CEO ceases to nurture them. They may not change much as an organization evolves and the organization acts to make organizational adjustments, either because the new organizational direction or focus is compatible with the present culture or because the dominant traits of the culture are organizational direction neutral and can be used to support any number of plausible organizational strategies.

Some factors that contribute to the development of SECOs are (1) a founder or strong leader who establishes values, principles, and practices that are consistent and sensible in light of customer needs, competitive conditions, and organizational requirements; (2) a sincere, longstanding organizational commitment to operating the organization according to these established traditions, thereby creating an internal environment that supports ethical decision making and organizational strategies based on cultural norms; and (3) a genuine concern for the well-being of the organizations' three biggest stakeholders—employees, customers, and stockholders.

SECOs are built on the premise that the organization must constantly find ways to ensure that unhealthy or unethical cultural characteristics are identified and eliminated. For example, one unhealthy trait that can contribute to unethical behavior is a politicized internal environment that allows influential managers to operate autonomous fiefdoms and resist staying true to the organization's accepted values, principles, and practices. In politically dominated cultures, many issues and decisions get resolved and made on the basis of turf—vocal support or opposition by powerful executives, personal lobbying by a key executive, and conditions among individuals or departments with vested interest in a particular outcome. What's best for the organization plays second fiddle to personal aggrandizement. Remember, how executives and others at Salomon Brothers and Enron lost sight of what was in the best interest of the organization because they were in powerful positions and the decision-making process was driven by a politically dominated culture that saw numerous individuals' vested interest in particular outcomes supersede the right thing to do for the larger organization.

MANAGEMENT'S ROLE IN INSTITUTIONALIZING ETHICS

A SECO founded on ethical organizational principles and moral values is important to organizational success. Senior leaders must be convinced that the organization must care about how it does business; otherwise an organization's reputation and ultimately its performance as put at risk. Organizational ethics and values programs are not window dressing; they are typically undertaken to communicate and create an environment of strongly held values and convictions and to make ethical conduct a way of life. Moral values and high ethical standards nurture the organization culture in a very positive way—they connote integrity, doing the right thing, and genuine concern for stakeholders. Value statements serve as a cornerstone for culture building; a code of ethics serves as a cornerstone for developing an organizational conscience. Table 10.1 indicates the kinds of topics such statements cover.

Organizations establish values and ethical standards in a number of different ways. These ways, used properly, lead to the institutionalization of ethics in the organization. Tradition-steeped organizations with a rich folklore rely heavily on word-of-mouth indoctrination and the

TABLE 10.1 Topics Frequently Covered in Value Statements and Codes of Ethics

Topics Covered in Values Statements	Topics Covered in Codes of Ethics
• Importance of customers and customer service • Commitment to quality • Commitment to innovation • Respect for the individual employee and the duty the organization has to employees • Importance of honesty, integrity, and ethical standards • Duty to stockholders • Duty to suppliers • Corporate citizenship • Importance of protecting the environment	• Honesty and observance of the law • Conflicts of interest • Fairness in selling and marketing practices • Using inside information and securities trading • Supplier relationships and procurement practices • Payments to obtain business/ Foreign Corrupt Practices Act • Acquiring and using information about others • Political activities • Use of company assets, resources, and property • Protection of proprietary information • Pricing, contracting, and billing

power of tradition to instill (or institutionalize) values and enforce ethical conduct (more will be said about enforcing ethical conduct later in this chapter). But many organizations today convey their values and codes of ethics to stakeholders and interested parties in their annual reports, on their Web sites, and in documents provided to all employees. In these situations, efforts to institutionalize or build ethics into the organization's culture are quite obvious as the values and codes of ethics are hammered in at orientation courses for new employees and in refresher courses for managers and employees. Making stakeholders aware of an organization's commitment to ethical business conduct is also important to the institutionalization of ethics. The trend of making stakeholders more aware of the organization's commitment to ethical organizational conduct is partly attributable to greater management understanding of the role these statements play in culture building and partly attributable to a growing trend by consumers to search out "ethical" products, a greater emphasis on corporate social responsibility by large investors, and increasing political and legal pressures on organizations to behave ethically.

Top Management's Role

Organizations committed to institutionalizing ethics recognize that there is considerable difference between saying the right things (having a well-articulated organizational value statement or code of ethics) and truly leading an organization in an ethical and socially responsible way. Organizations that are truly committed to ethical conduct make ethical behavior a fundamental component of their organization culture. They put a stake in the ground, explicitly stating what the organization intends and expects. Values statements and codes of ethical conduct are used as a benchmark for judging both organization policies and individual conduct. They don't forget that trust, integrity, and fairness do matter, and they are crucial to the bottom leaders.

In the late 1980s, Stack's Springfield ReManufacturing Corporation emerged as a model of how management and labor could successfully work together in a culture of trust and ownership. Leaders like Jack Stack were known for taking concepts like ethics and fairness seriously. As the dot.com era took hold in the late 1990s Stack and others never forgot that trust, integrity, and fairness were important to the bottom line. Stack made sure his organization was transparent—not only for investors, but also for employees, customers, and suppliers. The interests of shareholders, employees, customers, and Springfield ReManufacturing's surrounding community all continued to be treated as equals in the organization's eyes. While the pressure from Wall Street and the dot.com mania of the 1990s were leading to corporate excess,

Stack stuck with the "open-book management" culture that had made him something of a celebrity years earlier as many gathered to hear him during his annual trek to the Massachusetts Institute of Technology's Sloan School of Management for its Birthing of Giants program for new CEOs. By sharing all of the company's financial information with all employees and giving them an ownership stake in the company, Stack had built a level of mutual trust and respect unusual in business.

Other organizations like Southwest Airlines Co. and Harley-Davidson held similar beliefs and maintained comparable organizational cultures. These organizational cultures have not veered out of control over the last two decades or fallen victim to the bottom-line or "profit at any cost" mentality evident in too many of today's leaders and organizations. Like other beliefs and attitudes espoused by organizations and their members, top executives set the tone. The values they espouse, the incentives they put in place, and their own behavior provide the cues for the rest of the organization. As emphasized several times throughout this book, "The CEO sets the tone for an organization's culture or moral tone." This is because all managers and employees look to top management for their cues as to what is acceptable practice. A former executive of a major steel company stated it well: "Starting at the top, management has to set an example for all the others to follow."[2] Top management, through its capacity to set a personal example and to shape policy, is in the ideal position to provide a highly visible role model. The authority and ability to shape policy, both formal and implied, forms one of the vital aspects of the job of any leader in any organization. This "role modeling through visible action" is an important aspect of becoming a moral manager one who recognizes that managers live in a fishbowl and that employees are watching them for cues about what's important.[3]

John Gutfreund, Ken Lay, and Jeffery Skilling are examples of weak leadership (or role modeling); their behaviors sent cues to employees that unacceptable practices were acceptable. Such role modeling is guaranteed to increase the likelihood that unethical practices become a part of the organizational fiber. An example of positive ethical leadership may be seen in the case of an organization that was manufacturing vacuum tubes. One day the plant manager called a hurried meeting to announce that a sample of the tubes had failed a critical safety test. This meant that the batch of 10,000 tubes was of highly questionable safety and performance. The plant manager wondered out loud, "What are we going to do now?" The vice president for technical operations looked around the room at each person and then declared in a low voice, "Scrap them!" According to a person who worked for this vice president, that act set the tone for the corporation for years, because every person present knew of situations in which faulty products had been shipped under pressures of time and budget.[4] The vice president clearly exhibited the kind of leadership (role modeling) that is necessary to build and institutionalize ethics in an organization.

Gutfreund, Lay, and Skilling, and that vice president of operations provide vivid examples of how a leader's actions and behaviors communicate important messages to others in the organization. In the absence of knowing what to do, most employees look to the behavior of leaders for their cues as to what conduct is acceptable. In the case of the vice president of operations another point is illustrated. When we speak of management providing ethical leadership, it is not just restricted to top management. Vice presidents, plant managers, frontline managers, and, indeed, all managerial personnel carry the responsibility for role modeling ethical leadership.

In a period in which the importance of a sound ethical organization culture is strongly being advocated, ethical leaders must stress the primacy of integrity and morality as vital components of the organization's culture. In general, management needs to create a climate of moral consciousness. In everything it does, it must stress the importance of sound ethical principles and practices. A former president and chief operating officer for Caterpillar Tractor Company suggested four specific actions for accomplishing this:

1. Create clear and concise policies that define the company's business ethics and conduct.
2. Select for employment and partnerships only those people and organizations whose characters and ethics appear to be in keeping with corporate standards.
3. Promote people on the basis of the performance and ethical conduct and beliefs.
4. Company employees must feel safe enough to meet the obligation and the opportunity to report perceived irregularities in ethics or in accounting transactions. [5]

The leader must infuse the organization's climate with values and ethical consciousness, not just run a one-person show. This point is made vividly clear by the following observation: "Ethics programs which are seen as part of one manager's management system, and not as a part of the general organizational process, will be less likely to have a lasting role in the organization."[6]

Top management's commitment is crucial but not sufficient. Champions are also needed at lower organizational levels, especially key line managers. Many organizations are addressing the leadership requirement by forming of task or advisory committees on ethics, often headed by a senior manager. Some organizations also have a standing committee that oversees ethical behavior companywide. This chapter advises using the standing ethical behavior committee in addition to, rather than as a substitute for, a broader involvement team such as an ethics task force. This is especially important when an organization has been involved in illegal or unethical behavior and is committed to not making the same mistakes (as was the case in Salomon Brothers after Buffett took over for Gutfreund, as discussed in Chapter 9).

Citicorp has developed ethical principles to guide the company and create open communications. In order to promote communication at different levels of the organization, Citicorp has instituted a committee on good corporate practice whose aim is to institutionalize ethical standards and eliminate conflict of interest.

The Board of Directors' Role

Traditionally, directors have functioned as guardians of the financial interest of stockholders, with a specific concern for earnings and dividends. Even this role has been performed in a largely passive manner. Now, in the aftermath of major business scandals, the system of corporate governance and the role of directors have become subjects of special interest.

To help counter unethical behavior and to help in the institutionalization of ethics process, boards must extend their oversight beyond traditional matters of profits to areas of ethics. A concern for ethical performance is not necessarily consistent with stockholder interest, of course, but directors should recognize that there is a connection between ethics and profits.

The board of directors should demand moral leadership, because as directors they presumably have power to require ethical performance by management. The overall institutional impact of a board that demands ethical performance is greater than that of a president or vice-president who does the same.

Recognition of the growing responsibility and accountability of directors as a result of Salomon Brothers and Enron's scandals by the courts and the Securities Exchange Commission (SEC) should also serve as an impetus to increasing directors' involvement in the institutionalization of ethics process. In holding board members responsible, the SEC has taken the position that anyone in a position to know what is going on and to do something about it will be held liable. Overt action or direct participation in a fraud is not necessary for a judgment of liability. Directors presumably have access to the facts, or they should probe sufficiently to get the facts. Boards of directors must recognize that they have a responsibility for playing a significant role in an organization's efforts to institutionalize ethics.

Middle Management's Role

In order for an organization to institutionalize ethics (develop sound ethical practices) middle managers must also assume responsibility for convincing employees and for influencing their concern for moral values and ethical practice. Middle management must make certain that every department and employee fosters compliance with corporate ethical standards. They must ensure that ethical policies are followed in their department, focusing on things that are likely to crop up as moral or ethical dilemmas in connection with the activities of their departments. They must see that their people clearly and explicitly understand what is expected of them in the way of ethical behavior. They must tell employees not only what to do and what not to do but also how violations will be dealt with. They must encourage employees to spot and report potential ethical problems. They must develop a radar system that keeps them in touch with the ethical climate of their department and the organization (for example, ensuring that climate and attitude surveys are conducted).

The following analogy illustrates this requirement. In talking of the international environmental situation, one can conceive of the world as a ship commanded by fifteen different captains, all of whom speak different languages and all of whom, being nearsighted, can see only five feet in front of the ship. Yet the ship must have ten feet of clearance in order to maneuver. This dilemma can easily face middle managers. By the time they have identified potential ethical problems they are upon them. They need something comparable to radar to inform them of potential ethical obstacles. If they fail to anticipate obstacles, they will surely bump into them. They must be willing to get as much help and input as possible—to ask their people for recommendations for changes in policies and procedures. They must ensure that the organization has a hotline (as discussed later) for anonymously reporting unethical behavior.

The Organization's Value System

Both top and middle management have responsibility for developing the organization's value system, which is a cornerstone to institutionalizing ethics. According to the president of a consulting firm that specializes in individual and organizational performance, "Our experience with scores of clients correlates excellence most closely with consistent, clear and serious management value systems."[7] One company with a clearly defined value system is Merck & Co., a pharmaceutical firm. The effectiveness of its value system is reflected in Merck's consistently high-quality performance. For three successive years, Merck was voted America's most admired company in *Fortune* magazine's polls of chief executive officers.

In many organizations over the years, managers and employees tend to be self-serving, more concerned with protecting themselves and their interests than with any kind of ethics. Not so at Merck. For example, the company's field marketing representatives try to determine what's right for the doctor and the patient instead of how a particular sale might affect total sales volume. Such a focus is unusual in a highly competitive field like pharmaceuticals.

Merck's example shows that a positive approach is one key to success. When management compromises on quality, worker morale suffers and production slows down. It's easy for management to pay lip service to ethics and values, but what's more important is to put them into action and to act as examples.

Managers should keep in mind the following guidelines for establishing values that can help institutionalize ethics:

- Values cannot be taught, they must be lived. Employees do what they've seen done, not what they're told. If their superiors engage in unethical behavior, they will become lax in their own work habits.
- Values must be simple and easy to articulate. Managers should ask themselves whether the values are realistic and whether they apply to daily decision making.
- Values apply to internal as well as external operations. In other words, managers can't expect workers to treat customers well if they in turn don't treat their workers well in terms of honesty, frankness, and performance-based rewards.

Values are first communicated in the selection process. It is easier to hire people who share the corporate values than it is to train someone who doesn't identify with them to begin with. One executive recruiter said, "The best run organizations place a premium on the candidate's approach to issues of ethics and judgment. Anyone can read a balance sheet, but not everyone can handle a product quality or conflict of interest problem."[8]

An organization should constantly monitor its value system and make efforts to revise it when appropriate. Such a revision would be necessary from time to time, especially when:

- Downsizing, layoffs, decline in performance, attrition, or redeployment of the workforce is necessary.
- Significantly different groups are combined.
- Traditional values are inappropriate for the new climate.

- There has been a transgression of ethics, morals, or the law.
- There has been a significant strategic redirection.

Four principles that high-ethics organizations (HEOs) can employ to help develop values that support a culture of moral consciousness are:

- Principle 1: HEOs are at ease interacting with diverse internal and external stakeholders groups. The ground rules of these organizations make the good of these stakeholder groups part of the firm's own good.
- Principle 2: HEOs are obsessed with fairness. Their ground rules emphasize that the other person's interests count as much as their own.
- Principle 3: In HEOs, responsibility is individual rather than collective, with individuals assuming personal responsibility for actions of the organization. These organizations' ground rules mandate that individuals are responsible to themselves.
- Principle 4: The HEO sees its activities in terms of a purpose. This purpose is a way of operating that members of the organization value. Purpose ties the organization to its environment.

In private sector businesses, when embedding values into the organization's culture and operating practices, especially in the case of codes of ethics, special attention must be given to sections of the organization that are particularly vulnerable—procurement, sales, and political lobbying. Employees who deal with external parties are in ethically sensitive positions and often are drawn into compromising situations. Organization personnel assigned to subsidiaries in foreign countries can find themselves trapped in ethical dilemmas if bribery and corruption of public officials are common practices or if suppliers or customers are accustomed to kickbacks of one kind or another.

Communicating Ethical Standards or Expectations

Communication by the organizations top leaders is important to the building or the institutionalization of ethics into the culture, which keeps the organization on its ethical course. Management also carries a heavy burden in terms of providing ethical leadership in the area of effective communication. In the last section we saw the importance of communicating through acts, principles, and organizational climate. In this section we stress the importance of communication principles, techniques, and practices.

Conveying the importance of ethics or acceptable practices through communication includes both written and verbal forms of communication. In each of these settings, management should operate according to certain key ethical principles. *Candor* is one very important principle that requires that a manager be forthright, sincere, and honest in communication transactions. In addition, it requires the manager to be fair and free from prejudice and malice in the communication. A related principle is fidelity. *Fidelity* in communication means that the communicator should be faithful to detail, should be accurate, and should avoid deception or exaggeration. *Confidentiality* is a final principle that ought to be stressed. The ethical manager must exercise care in deciding what information he or she discloses to others. Trust can be easily shattered if the manager does not have a keen sense of what is confidential in a communication.

The organization's senior leaders must ensure that the ethical climate is consistent with the organization's overall objectives, as suggested by the behaviors of Jack Stack at Springfield ReManufacturing Corporation in our earlier discussion and Alfred P. West, Jr., at SEI Investments Company, discussed next. Communication is important in providing guidance for ethical standards and activities that integrate the functional areas of the organization. The vice president of marketing, for example, must communicate and work with regional sales managers and other marketing employees to make sure that all agree on what constitutes certain unethical practices, such as bribery, price collusion, and deceptive sales techniques. Senior organizational leaders must also communicate with managers at the operations level (in production, sales, and finance, for instance) and enforce overall ethical standards within the organization. For example, when Wendy's International was facing allegations of discrimination from one of its franchisees, Wendy's top management used this opportunity to enforce Wendy's ethical standards throughout the corporation. As a result, nearly a third of Wendy's new franchisees are minority, more than a quarter of the sold-back company-owned units have gone to minorities, and *Black Enterprise* magazine has recognized Wendy's as a top black franchiser.[9] Because of the communication efforts of Wendy's top executives and outside media, the internal and external understanding of Wendy's diversity initiatives has been strengthened.[10]

Alfred P. West, Jr., founder and CEO of financial-services firm SEI Investments Co. spends a lot of time emphasizing his vision of the company to the people who work there. His goal of building an open culture of integrity, ownership, and accountability is a harbinger for what organizations must look like if they are committed to developing organizational values and a strong culture where ethics are indeed institutionalized. Such institutionalization requires the constant communication and reinforcement of the values and behavior that are important to the organization. Values and behavior can most often be found in the organization's code of ethics, which is important to building, communicating, and sustaining ethics in an organizations culture.

Codes of ethics. As suggested earlier, top management has the responsibility for establishing standards of behaviors and for effectively communicating those standards throughout the organization. One classic way in which organizations have fulfilled their responsibility to communicate ethical standards or expectations is through the use of codes of ethics, or codes of conduct. Codes of ethics are a phenomenon of the past two decades, and most of the major corporations in the United States have them today.

The articulation and communication of ethical expectations (rules and standards) through written codes and standards is a must in the institutionalization of ethics process (i.e., building, sustaining, or transforming an unethical organization into an ethical one). Codes of ethics should not be confused with statements of values. Indeed, in some organizations the two may be the same, or at least overlap. However, they fill different roles. Rather than stating broad values held by the organization, written codes of ethics should be a series of clear, specific, positive, and direct statements from the top leadership of the organization and should be well circulated throughout the organization.

Both successes and failures have been reported with organizational codes of ethics, but the acid test seems to be whether or not such codes actually become "living documents," not just platitudinous public relations statements that are filed upon dissemination. Codes may not be a panacea of management, but, when properly developed and administered, they serve to raise the level of ethical behavior in the organization by clarifying what is meant by ethical conduct and encouraging ethical behavior.

No universal code of ethics or oath exists for business as the Hippocratic oath does for medicine. However, Paul Harris and four business colleagues, who founded Rotary International in 1904, made an effort to address ethical and moral behavior right from the beginning. They developed the following four-way test, which is now used in more than 160 nations throughout the world by the 1.2 million Rotarians in 29,000 Rotary clubs:

The Four-Way Test *OF WHAT WE THINK, SAY, OR DO*
1. Is it the TRUTH?
2. Is it FAIR to all concerned?
3. Will it build GOODWILL and better friendships?
4. Will it be BENEFICIAL to all concerned?

The test focuses the questioner on key ethical and moral questions.

Once values and ethical standards have been formally set forth, they must be institutionalized and ingrained in the organizations policie's, practices, and actual conduct. Several accepted actions important to implementing the values and codes of ethics are:

- Incorporation of the statement of values and the codes into employee training and educational programs.
- Explicit attention to values and ethics in recruiting and hiring to screen out applicants who do not exhibit compatible character traits.
- Communication of the values and ethics code to all employees and explaining compliance procedures.
- Management involvement and oversight, from the CEO down to frontline supervisors.
- Strong endorsements by the CEO.
- Word-of-mouth indoctrination.

Ethics officers and programs. In recent years, many organizations have begun creating ethics programs. These programs are often headed up by an ethics officer who is in charge of implementing the array of ethics initiatives of the organization. In some cases, the creation of ethics programs and designation of ethics officers have been in response to the 1991 Federal Sentencing Guidelines, which reduced penalties to those organizations with ethics programs that were found guilty of ethics violations. Other organizations started ethics programs as an effort to centralize the coordination of ethics initiatives in those organizations. Typical initiatives of organizations include codes of conduct (or ethics), ethics hotlines, ethics training, and ethics audits.

Over a decade ago NYNEX created one of the country's most impressive ethics programs. The program was initiated partially in anticipation of stiffer government penalties for white-collar crime and partially in response to a troubling pattern of ethical problems the company had faced in prior years. The NYNEX program included ethics training initiatives, a company code of conduct, and an Ethics Policy Committee. An ethics hotline was also installed whereby company employees could phone in their ethics questions and concerns.[11] BellSouth, Texas Instruments, Xerox, Boeing, Sears, and McDonnell Douglas are other companies with ethics programs.

The number of ethics officers occupying important positions have proliferated in recent years, just as ethics programs have grown significantly in major firms. In 1992 ethics officers created the Ethics Officers Association (EOA) to help define their profession and its possibilities. The three major objectives of the EOA, which are consistent with the quest to institutionalize ethics and improve organizations' ethical climates, are to:

- Provide multiple opportunities for wider acquaintance, understanding, and cooperation among ethics officers
- Provide a structure for sharing practical approaches to specific issues of common concern
- Foster the general advancement of research, learning, teaching, sharing, and practice in the field of business ethics[12]

The Ethics Officers Association claims members in over half of the Fortune 100 firms represented. Ethics officers in major companies provide ethics programs the best chance of succeeding and continuing to be integral parts of top management programs.

CREATING AN ENVIRONMENT THAT ENCOURAGES WHISTLE-BLOWING

Whistle-blowers are employees who inform authorities of wrongdoings by their organizations or coworkers. Whistle-blowers can be perceived as either heroes or "vile wretches" depending on the circumstances. Creating a culture where whistle-blowing is encouraged and whistle-blowers are safe is important to institutionalizing ethics in an organization. This means that the organization takes the time to manage whistle-blowing by communicating the conditions that are appropriate for the disclosure of wrongdoing. Clearly delineating wrongful behavior and the appropriate ways to respond are important organizational actions.

Before discussing how organizations can create cultures where whistle-blowing is encouraged and whistle-blowers are safe, let us briefly consider several recent high-profile examples of whistle-blowing. Dr. Jeffrey Wigand, head of research at Brown and Williamson Tobacco Company from 1989 to 1993, testified that his company knew and controlled nicotine levels in its products. His testimony, along with that of others, helped the government initially win a substantial lawsuit against the tobacco industry. As the film *The Insider* accurately documented, Wigand paid an enormous personal price as a witness.

FBI whistle-blower Coleen Rowley launched a bombshell memo in May 2002 accusing her bosses of ignoring warnings of the September 11, 2001, terrorist attacks. She angrily blasted agency director Robert Mueller and others for "a delicate and subtle shading/skewing of facts" and for making a rush to judgment to protect the FBI at all costs.[13] She sharply criticized the bureau for rewarding careerism and promoting a "culture of fear."

Just a few months before, Enron executive Sherron Watkins had penned another incendiary memo. She sent it to then chairman Kenneth Lay, detailing the firm's dire financial problems. Her candor was hardly rewarded. Management factions intent on squelching bad news admonished her and tried to get her fired for telling the truth. Since the giants fall in late 2001 Watkins has talked publicly about what she calls Enron's culture of intimidation. She has stated that there was widespread knowledge within the organization of controversial off-the-books partnerships and shaky finances, but that no one was confident enough to confront company officers.

Some whistle-blowers, like Michael Haley, a federal bank examiner, have not undergone such fates as the two examples offered here, as he won $755,533 in back pay, future loss of income, and compensatory damages under the federal whistle-blower statue and another amended federal statute. He had worked as a bank examiner for the Office of Thrift Supervision (OTS), starting in 1977. He inspected OTS-regulated banks, evaluating the soundness of their operations. He was terminated after he reported violations in federal banking laws and regulations regarding a forced merger.

As the impact of principled whistle-blowers is increasingly recognized by many in organizations who are responsible for matters of ethical conduct in the workplace, some important questions they all must answer are: Why do so few employees come forward to report that something is amiss? What more should organizations be doing to counter such behavior? While many rank-and-file employees wouldn't have the same access to information that Wigand, Rowley, and Watkins had, it is no leap of logic to assume that many employees in employees see red flags. Why don't they talk? What should organizations do to protect whistle-blowers and others who voice complaints, internally and externally? How do you create an environment where employees aren't ostracized or forced to commit career suicide if they report what they know?

Perhaps one of the most important things an organization can do to create an environment that encourages whistle-blowing and protects whistle-blowers begins with top management's acceptance that to silence a whistle-blower or to muzzle a watchdog is very likely to result in further compounding problems. When an organization fails to create a culture in which employees don't feel safe and have to conceal and distort information, the consequences can be catastrophic.

Whistle-blowing is contrary to our cultural tradition that an employee does not question a superior's decisions and acts, especially not in public. The traditional view holds that loyalty, obedience, and confidentiality are owed solely to the organizational employer. However, the more recent or emerging view holds that the employee has a duty not only to the employer but also to the public and their own conscience. Whistle-blowing, in this latter situation, becomes a viable option for the employee should management not be responsive to expressed concerns.

Organizational leaders must establish a culture where it is possible for employees to complain and protest and to get heard. An organization's Human Resources Management (HRM) department should take a leadership role in creating an atmosphere or culture that will not tolerate concealment and distortion of information, or discourtesy to and harassment of whistle-blowers. HRM is ideally set up for the task to ensure that employees right to speak out in cases where they think the company or management is engaging in an unacceptable practice. This is because HRM runs throughout the organization and is in a the position to work across the organization with lots of different employees.

Whistle-blowers are employees who often risk everything by taking public some malfeasance. They can also be those who come forward internally to report wrongdoing. Some are people of high moral character; others are not. It is imperative that a whistle-blower's information is taken seriously. An organization cannot make good decisions based on incomplete and often bad information. Employees who bring complaints must be treated with respect and even gratitude if an organization is truly committed to encouraging a culture supportive of whistle-blowing.

Setting up channels and other mechanisms that not only allow but also promote healthy, open communication involves HRM in sorting through a great deal of information. This can also mean training managers throughout the organization to fully understand and encourage candid employee comments. It should also entail implementing more effective solutions for receiving feedback, such as conducting anonymous employee surveys and setting up confidential help lines. HRM has the job of ensuring that the organization listens to what employees have to say and to weed out people who can not be relied on to make direct reports comfortable. That's why HRM has to conduct internal surveys to find out which managers are "kill-the-messenger managers." When such managers are identified, they must be retrained and they must be treated the same way the organization would treat any employee who misbehaves.

Creating an environment where whistle-blowers are safe means that the organization has developed an honest, open culture. Organizations have increasingly followed a trend to create departments that specifically deal with ethical matters. For example, Sears, Roebuck and Co. established an ethics program in 1994 to deal with standards and conduct and to develop effective lines of communication for receiving candid information from its employees, known as "associates." The company has an ombudsman and several programs related to ethics, including an annual seventy-question survey titled "My Opinion Counts." Sample questions include "Do you believe unethical issues are tolerated or not tolerated here?" and "Do you know how to report an ethical issue?"

The survey was developed as a way for employees to report problems without fear of reprisal. Like many other companies, particularly large corporations, Sears also offers toll-free anonymous help lines to its 330,000 employees. For example, the Sears Office of Ethics and Business Policy employs an "Ethics Assist" program in which employees call with a variety of questions. Questions come up about how to interpret company policy, how an employee wasn't treated fairly, what to do about an associate who is misusing a discount or misringing the register, or how Jesse backed up a truck to a loading dock and a TV disappeared.[14]

At Northrop hotlines are used whereby employees may phone in their inquiries about the company's ethics code or report suspected wrongdoing. Like Northrop, NYNEX receives thousands of calls per year. Xerox Corporation has a complaint resolution process to handle reported wrongdoing. Xerox employs a four-step process.[15] First, the company receives and examines a complaint. The complaint, or allegation, may come from its hotlines; from outside sources such as vendors, customers, or former employees; from whistle-blowers; or from law-enforcement agencies. Second, the company conducts an investigation. The investigation is completed by a team—a senior manager, a legal counsel, and a human resources management executive. Third, there is a management review of the team's report. Finally, step four involves the resolution. Part of the resolution is an attempt to determine why and how the reported incident occurred in the first place. Xerox thinks that the essential elements of the ethics investigation include adherence to a plan, good management communications, and a dedicated interest in ensuring a fair and impartial investigation.

An important task in building an organizational culture that institutionalizes ethics and creates a safe environment for whistle-blowers is to conduct an organizational assessment to look at existing standards. Areas to examine include the level of commitment from the organization's top management, the nature of training programs, communication tools such as help and hot lines, and the magnitude of organizational risks in matters ranging from internal harassment to product safety. What is most important is integrating standards and ethical values into everything from hiring to firing training, compensation, etc and so on.

While the task of developing an open culture is laborious, it requires constant role modeling by the organization's top leaders. This role modeling also has to be transferred into HRM performance processes. HRM must be proactive in intervening when management "shoots the messenger." That is why it is important that organizations offer employees toll-free help lines to report personal and organizational concerns. It shouldn't be surprising that Kenneth Lay, a featured speaker at ethics conferences and a man who waxed poetic about moral standards, did not offer Enron employees a help line—nor did Arthur Andersen.

An organization can do several things to work with its employees to reduce their need to blow the whistle. Five considerations that should be kept in mind are:

1. The company should assure employees that the organization will not interfere with their basic political freedom.
2. The organization's grievance procedures should be streamlined so that employees can obtain direct and sympathetic hearings for issues on which they are likely to blow the whistle if their complaints are not heard quickly and fairly.
3. The organization's concept of social responsibility should be reviewed to make sure that it is not being construed merely as corporate giving to charity.
4. The organization should formally recognize and communicate respect for the individual consciences of employees.
5. The organization should realize that dealing harshly with a whistle-blowing employee could result in needless adverse public reaction.

Increasingly, organizations are learning that whistle-blowing can be averted if visible efforts are made on the part of management to listen and be responsive to employees concerns.

In the end, an organizational climate which encourages whistle-blowing is an environment where the organization develops and promotes strong ethical values, where the ethical tone of the organization comes from the top, where the organization broadcasts an open-door environment that is highly receptive to employee input—no matter how bad the news. Management must be receptive to the subject of organizational wrongdoing. Organizations must put in place structures designed to support ethical behavior at every turn. Organizational systems must not militate against ethical behavior. Finally, organizations need internal courts that have the power to implement internal justice. Organizations such as TWA and Federal Express have developed good internal-justice programs. FedEx's open-door policy specifies that employees can discuss any work issue or problem with any manager—not just their own supervisor.

Managers have a responsibility to listen to and respond to their employees, especially regarding observations of and reporting of illegal and immoral acts. Mechanisms such as ethics offices are part of an organization's responsibility to provide due process for employees to report personal grievances, to obtain effective and just resolution of them, and to report the wrongdoings of others, including the employers. Four straightforward and simple steps management can take to eliminate the need for whistle-blowing are:

1. Develop effective internal grievance procedures and processes that employees can use to report wrongdoings.
2. Reward people for using these channels.
3. Appoint senior executives and others whose primary responsibilities are to investigate and report wrongdoing.
4. Assess large fines for illegal actions. Include executives and professionals who file false or illegal reports, who knowingly market dangerous products, or who offer bribes or take kickbacks.

Organizations cannot expect employees to be loyal to an organization that promotes or allows wrongdoing to its stakeholders and fails to create a safe environment for whistle-blowers, an environment in which employees feel they have to conceal and distort information on unethical wrongdoings. Whistle-blowers should be perceived as heroes rather than vile wretches. Organizations can manage whistle-blowing by communicating the conditions that are appropriate for the disclosure of wrongdoing. Clearly delineating (and punishing) wrongful behavior and the appropriate ways to respond are important organizational actions.

STRUCTURING AN ETHICS ENFORCEMENT SYSTEM

The institutionalization of ethics also requires the development of procedures for enforcing ethical standards and handling potential violations. In increasing numbers, organizations today are beginning to appreciate the need to follow up on their ethics initiatives and programs if they are truly committed to the institutionalization of ethics. Ethical audits are intended to carefully review such ethics initiatives as ethics programs, codes of ethics, hotlines, and ethics training programs. In addition, they are intended to examine other management activities that may add to or subtract from the organization's initiatives. This might include management's sincerity, communication efforts, incentive and reward systems, and other management activities. Ethics audits may employ written instruments, committees, and employee interviews.

More and more organizations will assess and attempt to institution-alize ethics as instruments, methods, and services are made available for conducting such programs. For example, the WalkerInformation research company has developed various methodology and resources like the "Business Integrity Assessment" program that organizations can use to assess their ethical culture and measure their ethics or compliance programs' effectiveness. Companies may then compare their results with national benchmark data established by Walker.

An organization that is really serious about institutionalizing ethics needs to conduct an annual or semi-annual audit of each leaders or manager's efforts to uphold ethical standards and formal reports on the actions taken by them to remedy deficient conduct. Consider the recent actions taken by Lockheed Martin when it was fined nearly $25 million for an ethics violation and its status as a major U.S defense contractor was put in jeopardy

Lockheed Martin's Comprehensive Ethics Compliance Program

In 1999, Lockheed Martin Corporation (LMC) was among the world's leading producers of aeronautics and space systems, with sales of over $25 billion. Since 1914, when the company first delivered aircraft to the U.S. Army Signal Corps, LMC had designed and built military aircraft and spacecraft for the U.S. military and its allies. LMC was a major contractor on the Mercury, Gemini, Apollo, Skylab, and Shuttle pro-grams. In 1999 the company's sales to the U.S. government accounted for more than 70 percent of its annual revenues.[16]

In 1995 LMC's status as a U.S. government contractor was jeopard-ized when company officials admitted that the company had conspired to violate U.S. anti-bribery laws in 1990, when LMC paid an Egyptian lawmaker $1 million to help the company secure a contract to supply Egypt with C-130 cargo planes. LMC was fined $24.8 million by the U.S. government and placed on a three-year probationary period, during which further ethics violations could bar the company from bidding on government contracts.

Following the conviction, LMC's CEO and other senior executives engineered the development of a comprehensive ethics compliance program that used the company's computer systems and Internet capa-bilities to guard against subsequent violations. Software programs al-lowed employees to go online to complete mandatory ethics training related to LMC's Code of Ethics and Business Conduct. The system records when employees complete online sessions on such topics as gratuities, insider trading, labor charging, software-license compliance, security, and sexual harassment. The Internet-based training program also allows the company to conduct up-to-the-minute ethics audits to determine how many hours of training have been completed by each of LMC's 17,000 employees.

LMC's ethics software programs also provide company managers with a variety of statistics related to ethics violations that do occur at the company. The system compiles data and prepares reports concerning detected violations like misuse of company resources, conflicts of interest, and security breaches. In addition, the system gives and accounting of the number of LMC employees discharged, suspended, and reprimanded for ethics violations. The information maintained by LMC's systems has aided both managers and the U.S. government in assessing the state of business ethics at the company.

LMC's renewed commitment to honesty, integrity, respect, trust, responsibility, and citizenship and its method for monitoring ethics compliance not only reduced the likelihood of being barred from the defense contracting business but also paved the way for the company to receive the 1998 American Business Ethics Award. Upon receiving the award, the company's chairman and CEO, Vance Coffman, said, "At Lockheed Martin, we have stressed that the first and most important unifying principle guiding us is ethical conduct, every day and everywhere we do business. Receiving the American Business Ethics Award is a strong signal that we are achieving our goal of putting our Corporation on a firm ethical foundation for the challenges of the 21st century."[17]

The Ethics Resource Center's conclusions on the actual practices of 2,000 U.S. corporations gives us keen insights into what organizations are doing today in actual practice to institutionalize ethics.[18] Organizations that see their ethics monitoring and enforcement methods as very effective share these characteristics:

- Written codes, policies, or guidelines
- Distribution of policies to all employees, not just management
- Reinforcement through communications, including videotapes, articles, posters, and public talks by company executives
- Additional training geared toward application of policies to everyday work situations
- Sources of information and advice, such as ombudspersons and hotlines
- Monitoring and enforcement through a Corporate Ethics Office and a Board of Directors Ethics Committee

Disciplining Violators of Ethical Norms

To truly institutionalize ethics in an organization, management must discipline violators of its accepted ethical standards. A major reason the general public and even employees in many organizations have questioned organizations' sincerity in desiring a more ethical environment has been organizations' unwillingness to discipline violators. Numerous top management officers have behaved unethically and yet been retained in their positions. For example, before Henry Boisvert, a testing supervisor with FMC Corporation, a government defense contractor, and Air Force Lieutenant Colonel James Burton prevailed in their fights to fix the Bradley fighting vehicle, Boisvert was fired and Burton was forced to take early retirement, while the officers who tried to stop the investigation were promoted.[19]

There have also been cases of top management overlooking or failing to penalize unethical behavior of direct reports at the lowest level. These evidences of inaction on management's or the board's part represent implicit approval of the individual's behavior. Fred Allen had argued that an organization should respond forcefully to the individual who is guilty of deliberately or flagrantly violating its code of ethics: "From the pinnacle of the corporate pyramid to its base, there can only be one course of action: dismissal. And should actual criminality be involved, there should be total cooperation with law enforcement authorities."[20]

The moral manager consistently rewards ethical conduct and disciplines unethical conduct at all levels in the organization, and these actions serve to uphold the standards and rules.[21] The effort on the part of management has to be complete in communicating to all, by way of disciplining offenders, that unethical behavior will not be tolerated in the organization. It is management's tacit approval of violations that seriously undermines efforts to institutionalize ethics in organizations.

CONCLUSION

Institutionalizing ethics in organizations means that it is made clear that preventing, reporting, and effectively and fairly correcting illegal or unethical actions, policies, and procedures are the responsibilities of organizations and their employees. Management cannot expect employees to be loyal to an organization that promotes or allows wrongdoing to its stakeholders. Whistle-blowing should be a last resort. A more active goal is to hire, train, and promote ethically and legally sensitive and responsive managers who communicate with and work for the welfare of all stakeholders.

Organizations committed to the institutionalization of an ethically responsible culture should also consider the impact of mentors or role models, reward systems, and career paths—all of which reinforce the culture and expectations and contribute to the institutionalization of ethics in the organization.

NOTES

1. T. V. Purcell and James Weber, *Institutionalizing Corporate Ethics: A Case History*, Special Study No. 71 (New York: The Presidents of the American Management Association, 1979).

2. L. W. Foy, "Business Ethics: A Reappraisal," Distinguished Lecture Series, Columbia Graduate School of Business (January 30, 1975), 2.

3. Linda Klebe Trevino, Laura Pincus Hartman and Michael Brown, "Moral Person and Moral Manager: How Executives Develop a Reputation for Ethical Leadership," *California Management Review* 42, no. 4 (2000), 134.

4. Harvey Gittler, "Listen to the Whistle-Blowers before It's Too Late," *The Wall Street Journal* (March 10, 1986), 16.

5. Lee L. Morgan, "Business Ethics Starts with the Individual," *Management Accounting* (March 1977), 14, 60.

6. Steven N. Brenner, *Influences on Corporate Ethics Programs* (San Diego, Calif.: International Association for Business and Society, March 16–18, 1990), 7.

7. Alan Weiss, "The Value System," *Personnel Administrator* 34, (July 1989), 40–41.

8. Ibid., 41.

9. O. C, Ferrell, J. C. Fraedrich and L. Ferrell, Business Ethics: Ethical Decision Making and Cases (4th ed.) Boston Mass.: Houghton Mifflin Company), 36.

10. Statement from Wendy's International. See: *http://www.investquest.com/ InvestQuest/w/wen/net/news/wenstmnt.htm* (November 23, 1998).

11. Susan Gaines, "Handing out Halos," *Business Ethics* (March/April, 1994), 20–24; See also Stephen J. Garone, *Business Ethics: Generating Trust in the 1990s and Beyond* (New York: The Conference Board, 1994).

12. *Ethics Officers Association: Overview and Benefits* (Waltham, Mass.: Bentley College Center for Business Ethics, 1996).

13. J. Wiscombe, "Don't Fear Whistle-Blowers." See: *http://workforce.com/ section/09feature/23/26/10/index.html*, 2002.

14. Sears Code of Business Conduct, 1997.

15. Gaines, "Handing out Halos," 22.

16. "Lockheed Martin's Corrective Actions after Being Fined for Violating U.S. Antibribery Laws," *The Wall Street Journal* (October 21, 1999), B1; Walker Information, *Assessing and Measuring Business Integrity* (Indianapolis, 2000).

17. *The Wall Street Journal*, "Lockheed Martin's Corrective Actions," B1.

18. Ethics Resource Center and Behavior Research Centre, *Ethics Policies and Programs in American Business* (Washington, 1990).

19. Robert P. Lawrence, "Go Ahead, Laugh at Army's Expense," *The San Diego Union-Tribune* (February 27, 1998), E12.

20. Fred T. Allen, "Corporate Morality: Is the Price Too High?" *The Wall Street Journal* (October 17, 1975), 16.

21. Trevino, Hartman, and Brown, "Moral Person and Moral Manager," 137.

11

Developing and Maintaining Ethical Employee-Employer Relationships

INTRODUCTION

Organizations are downsizing, restructuring, merging, and reinventing themselves. Mid-level management layers are diminishing. Functions are being eliminated and replaced by online automation and networked infrastructures. Knowledge workers with technological and people skills must manage processes and themselves in cyberspace with speed, efficiency, and accuracy. These and other changes continue to impact the relationships, rights, and obligations between employee stakeholders and organizations.

Chapter 4 discussed the major stakeholders' interests and responsibilities inside and outside of organizations. As for other stakeholders, it is in the organization's long-term interest to create and sustain employee-employer relationships or social contracts based on trust and respect. However, not all leaders and organizations demonstrate ethical competencies and due diligence with regard to their employee stakeholders.

Organizations have an implied social contract with employees. The contract is based on mutual trust, with the understanding that organizations have the interests of employees in mind. However, even social contracts can vary depending on economic and social changes in society.

A stakeholder approach to understanding organizations is grounded in the concept of a social contract. A social contract is a set of rules and assumptions about behavior patterns among the various elements of society. Like a legal contract, the social contract often involves a quid-pro-quo exchange.

The social contract between an organization and its employees is based on implicit as well as explicit agreements. For example, the success of many organizations is directly related to employee's confidence in and commitment to the organization. A loss of employee confidence and commitment can be detrimental to the organization. One way to retain and to reinforce employee confidence and commitment is by acting in an ethical manner, a manner that shows a concern for the organization's employees. Failure to do so can potentially lead to unethical employee actions.

A basic premise of this chapter is that the extent to which changing employee-employer relationships are understood and managed will determine the likelihood that unethical behavior will occur in the organization. Toward this end, this chapter discusses the implications of the changing social contract for organizational ethics—first discussing the origins of the changing social contract and the importance of building and maintaining ethical employee-employer relationships in organizations.

THE ORIGINS OF THE CHANGING SOCIAL CONTRACT

Companies in the United States from 1950 to 1980 enjoyed prosperity and world leadership. It was not unusual for many employees and their children to spend their entire working lives at one organization. Organizations invested considerable time and money in employee training and management development, and employees in turn embraced the corporate culture. Firing of long-term employees was an unheard-of practice, which protected a family-like atmosphere in many organizations. As a result, employees and management believed in a "cradle-to-grave" social contract: hard work and loyalty would be rewarded with job security and steady rewards (financial and promotional).

Traditional social contracts existed in organizations where there was stability, predictability, and growth. Organizations expected steady increases in revenue and the number of employees. Organizations saw their workforce as permanent, and tried to build loyalty among employees by making financial investments in training and by providing guaranteed long-term employment. Employees were committed to the organization and expected steady advancement up the corporate ladder. On the climb up the corporate ladder, the symbols of success were visible: vertical job growth (career paths were linear, job preparation generally meant one-time learning, and education and professional training were usually job-specific), steady salary increases, employee recognition plans, and perks like cars and country clubs for managers. Pensions, life insurance, and health-care plans that addressed long-term needs were funded by the organization.

The seeds of change are taking root, and with these changes new social contracts are developing between organizations and their members. No longer is the traditional social contract that once existed between the organization and the employee valid. Changes like those cited thus far have profoundly changed the ways in which organizations and their employees relate.

What is driving the collapse of the old social contract and emergence of the new? Three sweeping forces that began in the 1970s, grew in salience in the 1980s, and became dominant drivers in the 1990s are global competition, technology advances—especially in computers and telecommunications—and deregulation—especially of transportation and telecommunications. As a result of such forces, we have witnessed the destabilization of organizations and an old social contract. The new social contract places on employees more responsibility for their own success and prosperity in the employment relationship. Unlike the old social contract, the new social contract is not clear. For example, the old social contract between employees and corporations was predicated on a security-loyalty-paternalism pact. Job security, compensation, and advancement under the new social contract depend more on what the employee is contributing to the organization's mission.

The notion of adding value to the organization is critical to the new social contract. In exchange, companies are expected to provide learning opportunities, meaningful work, and honest communication, which is quite different from the attributes of lifetime employment, steady advancement, and loyalty offered under the traditional employee-corporation arrangement. It is easy to see how the old arrangement engendered an entitlement mentality on the part of employees. Table 11.1 presents some of the characteristics of the old and new social contracts.[1] Table 11.2 outlines the features of the new social contract between employers and employees.

Change, uncertainty, and continuous cuts in human resources in organizations will have an ongoing impact on the social contract. Clearly, there is a new social contract (or set of reciprocal understandings and expectations) regarding organizations' and employees' roles and responsibilities. Reorganizations, downsizings, mergers, and acquisitions will still threaten job security and career paths. An organization's work force will need to be flexible, with employees

TABLE 11.1 The Changing Social Contract between Employers and Employees

Old Social Contract	New Social Contract
Job security; long, stable career and employment relationships	Few tenure arrangements; jobs constantly at risk; employment as long as you add value to the organization
Life careers with one employer	Fewer life careers; employer changes common; careers more dynamic
Stable positions/job assignments	Temporary project assignments
Loyalty to employer; identification with employer	Loyalty to self and profession; diminished identification with employer
Paternalism; family-type relationships	Relationships far less warm and familial; no more parent/child relationships
Employee sense of entitlement	Personal responsibility for one's own career/job future
Stable, rising income	Pay that reflects contributions; pay for value added
Job-related skill training	Learning opportunities; employees in charge of their own education and updating

TABLE 11.2 One View of the New Social Contract between Employers and Employees

Outline for a New Social Contract

Employer Expectations of Employees	Employee Expectations of Employers
• Performance to the best of one's ability	• Fair pay and benefits proportionate to contribution to company success
• Commitment to the objectives of the firm	• Security tied to fortunes of the company and ability to perform
• Participation (suggestions)	• Respect, recognition, and participation
• Willingness to train to improve productivity	• Opportunities for growth
• Ethical and honest behavior	• Access to timely information and openness by candid leaders
	• Safe and healthy workplace

Joint Expectations

• Partnering replaces partnership.
• Employees are value-adding resources, not merely costs to be cut.
• Employee and employer must focus on customer needs and desires.

regularly recruited, hired, and retained for their particular skills for the short run as organizations focus less and less on long-term performance. Opportunities for advancement will remain limited by slower growth and leaner organizational structures with fewer levels of management. Dwindling career opportunities and greater emphasis on economy will force managers to reexamine their reliance on this definition as a motivator of performance. In addition, employees will continue to learn that good performance is no longer a guarantee of job security. Not only will the tangible symbols of success become less available, but the entire strata of career positions will continue to be obliterated in corporate downsizing. More and more employees recognize that they (1) can expect multiple careers, (2) have more responsibility for assessing and designing their own careers, (3) must seek new definitions of success, and (4) need to put more emphasis on lifelong learning to avoid obsolescence of their job skills.

For employees committed to life-long learning, working smarter rather than harder, and making their own opportunities, the new social contract is a positive situation. Organizational life will give them more opportunities to grow and be rewarded for creating value for internal and external customers of stakeholders. Promotions will be fewer and slower than under the old employment contract because organizations are flatter with fewer layers. But lateral moves from one project or function to another will provide lots of challenge for those who get results. Meanwhile, the new social contract is not good news for employees with an entitlement mentality. Despite the changes occurring in the world of work, these employees still believe the company owes them pay raises and promotions just for showing up for work. They also still tend to be inflexible and resistant to change.

The changing social contract also has implications for the organization. The new social contract has led to the increased recognition by organizations on how much they depend on employees who are willing to "go the extra mile" or have what has more commonly been referred to as organizational citizenship (OC). *Organizational citizenship* refers to behaviors that extend beyond the employee's normal job duties. They include avoiding unnecessary conflicts, helping others without selfish intent, gracefully tolerating occasional impositions, being involved in organizational activities, and performing tasks that extend beyond normal role requirements.[2] Good organizational citizens work cooperatively with coworkers and share resources. They forgive others for mistakes and help coworkers with their problems.

With more and more well-qualified workers competing for a shrinking number of jobs, the problems for organizations has moved from one of coaching employees with skill deficiencies to finding ways to motivate bright people with the carrot of promotion. In addition, old-style management techniques no longer apply and familiar incentives have evaporated, which makes the management of a brave new workforce considerably more challenging. The unilateral cancellation of the implied contract profoundly affects the surviving employees as well. Some of their most basic tenets—belief in fairness, equity, and justice—have been violated. Their sense of security has been destroyed, their identity and self-esteem are threatened, and organizations must be concerned about the implication that employees feel they can no longer trust management or the organization to look out for their welfare or to be truthful to them (that is, the contract is null and void). It is not surprising that company loyalty has quickly become extinct. Indeed, the employee-employer relationship has changed; thus, the need arises for organizations to better understand, clarify, and manage the social contract. One way to do this is first to recognize the increased importance of employee rights in the workplace.

EMPLOYEE RIGHTS IN THE WORKPLACE

Changes in the world of work and the workforce along with other changes and trends continue to create pressures for new ways of organizational thinking and for new relationships between organizations and employees who work for them—new relationships that often center on employee rights in a continually changing and dynamic world of work. A right can be understood as a "moral claim." A right is a claim because it corresponds with a duty on the part of the person against whom the right is held. For example, an employee claims that they have a right to be safe in their workplace. Employees hold this claim against their employer since the employer, has the duty to provide employees with this safety.

Understanding and effectively managing the rights of employees is important to a positive social contract between organizations and their employees. Employee rights may be afforded on the basis of economic, legal, or ethical sources of justification.

One right central to the employee rights movement is the right of employees to receive fair pay, which is relevant in at least three contexts. First, pay should be fair in an interpersonally comparative sense. Whether pay scales are based on seniority, achievement, or some other aspect(s), corporations have a duty to consider all employees equally. Hence, the cry "Equal pay for equal work" is a protest against alleged wage discrepancies (usually to the detriment of women and minorities) even when controls for seniority, achievement, and other relevant factors are considered. Second, pay should be fair in an intrapersonally comparative sense; as an individual's service to a corporation grows in length of time and (perhaps) in responsibility, he or she should receive comparatively more in the way of compensation.

Both these rights derive from equality, but the third context of fair pay, which is non-comparative and pertains to the notion of a minimum wage, derives from well-being. When we consider employees as persons who deserve respect, the justification for a minimum wage should be clear. As persons have goals and interests, a certain minimum standard of living is required. Whether this entails the existence of broader welfare rights held (against the government) by all persons, employed or not, is an open question; some claim that organizations (and others) are morally culpable for ignoring the plight of the homeless and jobless, but on the model of employees as persons, the homeless and jobless are not necessarily being treated by organizations as things because they are not being treated by organizations in any way at all.[3] Regardless, employees are persons with whom corporations have dealt, and have contracted to perform work. To hire a person for an appallingly meager wage is to use her or him as a means only, to treat her or him merely as an item on the balance sheet, acquiring services for as little as possible. Because many potential employees are in comparatively weak bargaining positions, the wage agreed upon, if unchecked, is likely to be very small in many situations (as was the case a century ago). An employee's right to a minimum wage is a recognition that the employee is a person, with goals and interests, and also that the maximization of shareholder wealth is insufficient justification for using a person as a mere tool for profit.

A second employee right is that of safety in the workplace. Employers have a duty to provide a safe work environment and to make improvements when necessary, since failing to do so risks the well-being of persons. There also exists the duty to inform workers of certain risks that cannot be avoided; not doing so amounts to a deliberate attempt to mislead in an effort to hold down labor costs.

A third employee right, more general in nature, is that of due process in the workplace. All employees, as persons who have goals, ought to be afforded a certain degree of participation in the decision-making processes of their companies. When firings or demotions are necessary, employees ought to be informed about the reasons (and indeed about the reasons behind any action by management that affects them), and perhaps even granted an appeal or hearing.

Finally, employees as persons have a right to privacy in the workplace (and also outside the workplace). This derives from the basic right to freedom, and at a minimum this entails the right to be left alone,[4] including the right to withhold from employers personal information that is not relevant to the job. Therefore, practices such as forcing employees to submit to polygraph tests (in order to ensure compliance with company rules) are morally questionable. The employee's inferior bargaining position with respect to available options makes her or him susceptible to exploitation; the polygraph test itself may be a form of exploitation (since the employee may have no viable alternative but to comply); and further, the information learned by the employer may in certain circumstances be used against the employee. Such policies therefore put employees at risk of losing viable options and thus of losing freedom. Whether a practice such as mandatory random drug testing violates this right is debatable, since companies (especially ones which entrust employees to protect public welfare, such as those in the transportation industry) do have a legitimate interest in securing drug-free employees. Even if a strong case can be made in favor of the permissibility of drug-testing requirements in certain fields, the inherent potential for employee harassment or other abuse by the employer means that acceptable guidelines must be instituted and strictly followed. Such testing, for example, must be truly random (to guard against discrimination), and must be conducted in such a way that the personal space of the persons being tested is not unnecessarily violated.

While such rights seem very general (and thus perhaps impractical), they can be used successfully by managers to enhance a positive social contract with employees when the underlying foundation of treating employees with respect as persons is firmly in place. Recognition of the basis of these rights will enable managers to discern what, exactly, is owed to employees and what is inordinate. Perhaps even more important, the foundation will provide a means for adjudication when rights conflict. In a proposed drug-testing policy, for example, one employee's right to a safe work environment may conflict with another's right to privacy. The appropriate course of action will be a function of which employee will be respected more as a person. It may also be the case that some compromise can be reached that respects both employees reasonably well. The important point is that employee rights with inadequate justification or with overly theoretical justification will not provide managers with a workable framework for moral reasoning in such instances.

This short list of employee rights is certainly incomplete, but these four suggestions are examples that seem straightforwardly to follow from the moral foundation of employees as persons. The last one, the right to privacy, is relevant to the example of a policy prohibiting dating between persons in the same office, the same department, or even the same company. The justification for such a policy is the correlation between the existence of such relationships and a decline in job performance. However, treating employees as persons requires not grouping them in statistical categories, at least not for the purpose of restricting their personal freedom. This policy therefore violates the employee's moral right to privacy; the choice of persons with whom to associate is, in short, none of the company's business. If there is a drop in job performance, then at that time the company may take certain actions (disciplinary or otherwise) to protect its interests; but the justification for any such action is poor job performance, not dating, and at no time may the employees be required to cease the relationship.

Human rights and social justice will continue to be increasingly revered in the workplace, as they are in the world at large. All organizations and their managers, accordingly, must be aware of and comfortable dealing with the following pressures.

Pressures for self-determination. People increasingly seek greater freedom to determine how to do their jobs and when to do them. Pressures for increased employee participation in the forms of meaningful and challenging jobs, self-managed teams, and alternative work schedules will continue to grow.

Pressures for employee rights. People expect their rights to be respected on the job as well as outside work. These include the rights of individual privacy, due process, free speech, free consent, freedom of conscience, and freedom from racial or sexual harassment.

Pressures for job security. People expect their security to be protected. This includes their physical well-being in terms of occupational safety and health matters, and their economic livelihood in terms of some form of guaranteed protection against downsizings and provisions for cost-of-living wage increases.

Pressures for equal employment opportunity. People expect and increasingly demand the right to employment without discrimination on the basis of age, gender, ethnic background, religion, or physical or mental ability. Among these demands will remain a concern for furthering the modest but dramatic gains made over the last two decades by women and minorities in the workplace. "Progress" will be applauded, but it will not be accepted as a substitute for true equality of opportunity.

Pressure for equity of earnings. People expect to be compensated for the "comparable worth" of their work contributions. What began as a concern for earnings differentials between women and men doing the same jobs continues to be extended to cross-occupational comparisons. Questions such as why a nurse or a K-12 teacher receives less pay than a carpenter and why a maintenance worker is paid more than a secretary are standard questions in today's world of work. They will continue to require answers other than the fact that certain occupations, such as nursing or teaching have traditionally been dominated by women, whereas others (such as carpentry) have been dominated by men.

Understanding and effectively responding to such related social pressures are important to the success of today's organizations. Equally important is the fact that organizations recognize that managing the rights of employees at work creates many ethical dilemmas in organizations. For example, privacy issues like computerized monitoring related to technology. Computerized monitoring constitutes an invasion of privacy in the minds of some individuals. The use of employee data from computerized information systems presents many ethical concerns. Safeguarding the employees' right of privacy while preserving access to the data for those who need it requires that the manager balance competing interests. Safeguarding the employees' right t privacy and at the same time preserving access to the data for those who need it requires that the manager balance competing interests.

Perhaps no issue generates as much need for managers to balance the interests of employees and the interests of the organization as the reality of AIDS in the workplace. New drugs have shown the promise of extended lives for people with human immunodeficiency virus (HIV), which means that HIV-infected individuals can remain in the workforce and stay productive. Managers may be caught in the middle between the rights of HIV-infected workers and the rights of coworkers who feel threatened.

Employers are not required to make concessions to coworkers, but employers do have obligations to educate, reassure, and provide emotional support to coworkers. Confidentiality may also be a difficult issue. Some employees with HIV or AIDS do not wish to waive confidentiality and do not want to reveal their condition to their coworkers because of fears of stigmatization or even reprisals. In any case, management should discuss with the affected employee the ramifications of trying to maintain confidentiality and should assure the employee that every effort will be made to prevent negative consequences for him or her in the workplace.

Laws exist that protect HIV-infected workers. For example, the Americans with Disabilities Act requires employers to treat HIV-infected workers as disabled individuals and to make reasonable accommodations for them. The ethical dilemmas involved with this situation, however, go far beyond the legal issues. How does a manager protect the dignity of the person with AIDS and preserve the morale and productivity of the work group when so much prejudice and ignorance surround this disease? Many organizations, such as Wells Fargo, believe the answer is education.[5] Wells Fargo has a written AIDS policy because of the special issues associated with the disease—such as confidentiality, employee socialization, coworker education, and counseling—that must be addressed. The Body Shop's employee education program consists of factual seminars combined with interactive theater workshops. The workshops depict a scenario in which an HIV-positive worker must make decisions, and the audience decides what the worker should do. This helps participants explore the emotional and social issues surrounding HIV.[6] Many fears arise because of a lack of knowledge about AIDS.

Failure to understand and respond to employee rights will have an impact on the employee and employer social contract, and employee loyalty and will increase the likelihood of unethical practices that will eventually result in harm to both the organization and its employees.

BUILDING AND MAINTAINING ETHICAL EMPLOYEE-EMPLOYER RELATIONSHIPS

Unfortunately some organizations are not always clear as to what their expectations of employees are. As a result, they do not talk about many areas nor pay attention to them. Mismatches between employee and employer expectations can occur by accident, out of neglect.

What is needed in today's organizations is for employees and organizations to carefully consider all areas of expectations in order to overcome the problem of clarity, which, if not addressed, can lead to dire circumstances for one or both parties. Too often this step does not occur because organizational managers and employees do not regularly consider it important. Creating and maintaining an ethically oriented culture can be enhanced if proactive attempts are made to increase the number of matches in the employer-employee contract and efforts are made to first ensure that the employee-employer contract is indeed ethical.

Being attentive to the need to regularly clarify what is an ever-changing employee-employer social contract is an important step in the management of and maintenance of ethical employee-employer contracts. This section discusses two employee-employer interactions (the employee-job relationship and the employee-organization relationship on organizational ethics) that if appropriately managed can help maintain an ethical employee-employer contract.

The Realistic Job Preview

Selection of employees is the first opportunity for an organization to reinforce the organization's ethical culture. Once new employees have been recruited and selected, they must adjust to the new job and organization. As evidenced by the high rate of turnover among new hires in the first few months, problems obviously arise at this point. One reason for the turnover may be that the job did not match newcomers' expectations or desires, resulting in a perceived violation of the employee-employer contract. The recruitment process may be partly responsible for this mismatch, as organizations and their recruiters tend to present jobs in very favorable terms in order to increase the number of employees hired. When these processes do not function well, unfortunate problems can arise, violating the employee-employer contract, as suggested in the experience of Nandi James:

When she began to major in marketing as a junior in college, Nandi James knew that someday she would work in that field. Once she completed her M.B.A., she was more positive than ever that marketing would be her life's work. Because of her excellent academic record, she received several outstanding job offers. She decided to accept an offer from one of the nation's largest consulting firms, believing that this job would allow her to gain experience in several areas of marketing and to engage in a variety of existing work. Her last day on campus, she told her favorite professor, "This has got to be one of the happiest days of my life, getting such a great career opportunity."

Recently, while visiting the college placement office, the professor was surprised to hear that Nandi had told the placement director that she was looking for another job. Since she had been with the consulting company less than a year, the professor was somewhat surprised. He decided to call Nandi and find out why she wanted to change jobs. This is what she told him: "I guess you can say my first experience with the real world was a 'reality shock.' Since joining this company, I have done nothing but gather data on phone surveys. All day long, I sit and talk on the phone, asking questions and checking off the answers. In graduate school, I was trained to be a manager, but here I am doing what any high school graduate can do. I talked to my boss, and he said that all employees have to pay their dues. Well, why didn't they tell me this while they were recruiting me? To say there was a conflict between the recruiting information and the real world would be a gross understatement. I'm an adult. Why didn't they provide me with realistic information and then let me decide if I still wanted the job? A little bit of accurate communication would have gone a long way." Nandi James's experience illustrates inconsistent decision making and shows how an organization can violate an employee-employer contract at the employee entry stage. Organizations can see to it that their Human Resources Management (HRM) department uses the realistic job preview (RJP), a down-to-earth presentation of both the favorable and unfavorable aspects of the job. Ideally, organizations must ensure that each stage of recruiting is honest and realistic. An RJP may take the form of a booklet or film about the job, realistic information delivered by an interviewer, or a work sample test that exposes the candidate to actual job conditions and activities.

Overall, RJPs can reduce turnover, lower recruits' expectations about the job, slightly reduce the job-offer acceptance rate, and slightly increase job satisfaction and commitment to the organization among new hires. Several reasons RJPs have these effects are as follows:

Self-selection. If the RJP helps the applicant realize that the job will not be personally satisfying, the applicant may choose not to take the job or select himself or herself out of the organization's selection process. Without this realistic information, the applicant might have accepted the offer and could have become an early turnover statistic (the result of a mismatch or the perception of a violation of the employee-employer contract).

Commitment to the decision. When the RJP is presented before the candidate accepts or rejects the job offer, the candidate feels that she or he has made an informed decision about the job. Having accepted a job known to include difficult moments or distasteful duties, a newcomer feels less justified in reversing the decision and quitting when an unpleasant event actually occurs.

Lowered expectations. The aim of an RJP is to lower, or make more realistic, the expectations that the newcomer holds about the job. One theory of job satisfaction states that dissatisfaction is a function of the discrepancy between what one expects and desires on a job and what one actually gets. Lowering expectations reduces the gap between expectations and reality; consequently, dissatisfaction decreases. Since dissatisfaction is one cause of turnover, this mechanism can explain both attitudinal and behavioral differences between RJP and no-RJP groups.

Coping. Unpleasant events are less stressful and more effectively dealt with if they are expected rather than if they are surprises. It is possible that the RJP operates by improving the ability of new hires to cope with negative aspects of the job. The RJP may stimulate newcomers to mentally rehearse their reactions to anticipated job problems and so increase their ability to deal with problems when they occur.

RJPs are most useful when organization present them early in the recruiting process (so that the self-selection and commitment processes can occur). RJPs are particularly effective for jobs in which there tends to be early high turnover and for entry-level jobs in which applicants are unlikely to have an accurate picture of the job or occupational field prior to applying. They make the most sense when there are numerous applicants for the available openings (if some decide to decline offers, the jobs can still be filled) and are most effective in reducing turnover when unemployment is low. In this situation, applicants will be most likely to turn down a job offer that does not suit them because they know that other jobs are readily available.

The RJP can be used by organizations to help clarify the social contract both at the early stages of the employee-employer relationship and during job reassignments (lateral moves, promotions, or demotions). However, like other means of clarifying the employee-employer contract, organizations must make sure that RJPs are tailored to the needs of the organization and that they include balanced presentations of positive and negative job information.

Setting Realistic Objectives or Goals

Just as important as RJPs to building and maintaining an ethical employee-employer social contract is the necessity that managers at all levels of the organization set realistic objectives or goals. A manager may quite innocently and inadvertently create a condition leading to unethical behavior on a direct report's part. Take the case of a marketing manager setting a sales goal of a 20 percent increase for the next year when a 10 percent increase is all that could be realistically expected, even with outstanding performance. In the absence of clearly established and communicated ethical norms, it is easy to see how a direct report might believe that he or she should go to any lengths to achieve the 10 percent goal. With a goal that is set too high, the salesperson faces a situation that is conducive to unethical behavior in order to please the marketing manager.

Managers at all levels of the organization must establish goals that are realistic—goals that can be achieved with current business practices. Under the pressure of unrealistic goals, otherwise responsible employees will often take the attitude that "anything goes" in order to comply with their manager's targets.

There are ethical implications to even the most routine managerial decisions, such as goal setting. Managers must be keenly sensitive to the possibility of innocently creating situations in which others may perceive a need or an incentive to do the wrong thing, as was the case at Salomon Brothers and Enron. Setting realistic objectives or goals increases the likelihood that employees won't go outside the lines and that doing the right thing will be institutionalized throughout the organization.

Business Ethics Training

Ethics training programs provides an excellent opportunity for organizations to communicate, build, and maintain ethical standards or expectations throughout the organization. This means educating managers and employees about what is ethical and what is not, which is important to the employee-employer social contract.

Ethics training efforts should provide opportunities to point out and discuss gray areas. Ethics courses and training can do the following:

- Provide employees with rationales, ideas, and vocabulary to help them participate effectively in ethical decision-making processes.
- Help employees identify the ethical dimensions of a business decision.
- Help employees understand the ambiguity inherent in ethical situations.
- Increase employees' awareness of their environment and organizational realities by abstracting and selecting ethical priorities.
- Increase employees' awareness of societal realities.
- Make employees aware that their actions define the company's ethical posture both internally and externally.
- Enhance conscientiousness and sensitivity to ethical issues and commitment to finding ethical solutions.
- Enhance moral reflectiveness and strengthen moral courage.
- Bring about a greater degree of fairness and honesty in the workplace.
- Eliminate the belief that unethical behavior is *ever* justifiable by stressing that
  - stretching the ethical boundaries results in unethical behavior.
  - whether discovered or not, an unethical act is just that.
  - an unethical act is never in the best interests of the company.
  - the organization is held responsible for the misconduct of its members.
- Respond more completely to the organization's social responsibilities.
- Improve the ethical climate of organizations by providing ethical concepts and tools for creating ethical codes and social audits.

Ethics training or courses should not advocate a set of rules from a single perspective nor offer only one best solution to specific ethical problems. Given the reality and circumstances of situations, more desirable and less desirable courses of action may exist. Decisions depend on facts, inferences, and rigorous, logical, ethical reasoning. Ethics courses or training should not promise superior or absolute ways of thinking and behaving in situations.

Ethical training can add value to the moral environment of an organization and to relationships in the workplace in the following ways:

- Finding a match between employee's and employer's values
- Managing the push-back point, where an employee's values are tested by peers, employees, and supervisors
- Handling an unethical directive from a boss
- Coping with a performance system that encourages cutting ethical corners

All of these are key to ethical employee-employer relationships.

Materials and formats typically used by organizations in their ethics training include the following: codes of ethics (as a training device), lectures, workshops/seminars, case studies, films/discussions, and articles/speeches. In 1997 Lockheed Martin introduced some humor into its ethics training by introducing the Dilbert-inspired board game, "The Ethics Challenge," for company-wide ethics training. To play the game, players (employees) move around the board by answering "Case File" questions such as, "You've been selected for a training course in Florida, and you want to go only for the vacation." Among the answers and their respective points are "Go, but skip the sessions" (0 points), "Ask their supervisor if it would be beneficial" (5 points), and the Dogbert answer, "Wear mouse ears to work and hum 'It's a Small World After All' all day." Sessions for the company's 185,000 employees were led by supervisors, not ethics officers. The chairman of the company kicked off the training by leading a training of those who reported to him directly.[7]

Business ethics training is an important mechanism for institutionalizing ethics in the organization and also further clarifying the employee-employer contract on organizational ethics.

CLARIFYING THE EMPLOYEE-EMPLOYER CONTRACT ON ORGANIZATIONAL ETHICS

There should be no doubt that ethical issues are a daily component of business. Ethical issues are more important today than ever and are involved in all facets of a business: decision making, arbitration, marketing and sales, financial reporting, personnel, appraisal, and leadership. Building and maintaining an ethical employee-employer contract can go to the heart of an organization's efforts to promote, institutionalize, and manage ethics within the organization. If appropriately reinforced and managed, the ethical requirements of the organization can serve as the foundation of the employee-employer contract, with the organization providing a culture that encourages and rewards the ethical behavior of employees. If employees' expectations are that an organization encourages ethical behavior but they find out through experience that the opposite is true, the employee-employer contract has been violated.

It is important for organizations to understand that clarity, discussion, and some give-and-take are often not enough to resolve some ethical mismatches. The major obstacles to the process are organizational norms that define some items as not legitimate areas for discussion. In addition, contract participants may be unwilling or unable to find a commonality of ethical expectations. Small but significant differences between the expectations of employees and the organizations may result in mismatches concerning ethical behavior.

There are also times when neither party in the contract fully knows all that must be included over the length of the contract. However, each party may act as though a stable frame of reference exists in which to define the relationship. The institutionalization and management of organizational ethics must be perceived and treated as an evolving set of mutual understandings as new ethical issues and concerns arise in organizations and in our society in general.

FINDING THE EMPLOYEE-ORGANIZATION MATCH IN ETHICAL EXPECTATIONS

The social contract specifies what the individual and the organization expect to give and receive from each other in the relationship; the process can go to the heart of building, institutionalizing, and managing ethics within an organization. If appropriately reinforced and managed, the ethical requirements of the organization can serve as the foundation of a social contract, with the organization providing a culture that encourages and rewards the ethical behavior of employees. Therefore, if an employee's expectations are that an organization encourages ethical behavior (or vice versa), only to find out through experience that the opposite is true, then the social contract has been violated.

A basic premise of this chapter is that social contracts made up primarily of matches in expectations of ethical behavior will (1) lead to greater institutionalization of ethics within the organization, (2) lead to ethical employee behavior, and (3) increase the length of time the individual and the organization are mutually committed to the institutionalization of ethics. The following four propositions further explain the relationships involved in the match between the ethical contributions and inducements in the social contract.

Understanding Ethical Expectations

Proposition 1. The more clearly an organization and its employees understand each other's ethical expectations, the higher the probability is of matching them. This can be accomplished to the degree to which (1) the individual and the organization have clearly thought out their own expectations toward giving and receiving; (2) open discussion of expectations is initiated by the organization, the individual, or both; and (3) the individual understands the organization's expectations and vice versa.

Barriers to Matching Ethical Expectations

Proposition 2. Clarity, discussion, and even some give-and-take are often not enough to resolve some ethical mismatches. The major obstacles to the process are organizational norms that define some items as not legitimate to talk about. In addition, contract participants often may be unwilling or unable to find a commonality of ethical expectations. Small but significant differences between the expectations of individuals and the organization may result in mismatches concerning ethical behavior.

Evolving Ethical Expectations

Proposition 3. The social contract typically is not static; rather, it is an evolving set of mutual expectations. Neither party to the contract fully knows everything it wants over the length of the contract. However, each party may act as if a stable frame of reference exists that defines the relationship. The building, institutionalization, and management of organizational ethics must also be perceived and treated as an evolving set of mutual expectations as new ethical issues and concerns arise in organizations and in society in general.

Interpreting the Ethical Contract

Proposition 4. Top executives and managers are agents of interdependence and must understand that ethical behavior does not develop automatically, but is communicated and reinforced from the top down. Interpreting the ethical contract is the function of the people in authority (particularly, top executives) acting on the organization's behalf. It is they who give life to the formal employment agreement, the meaning of the organizational structure, and very often the ethical behavior of an organization's employees, as was the case at Salomon Brothers and Enron. Early in their organizationalcareers,managersandemployeesdevelopenduringattitudes and expectations that are important to their future performance and success. Those attitudes and aspirations are directly related to their organization's expectations of them. Just as a mismatch of challenges and capabilities, of personal aspirations and company expectations, may sharply reduce an employee's long-term productivity, a similar mismatchonethicalexpectationscanresultinunethicalbehavior.

When organizations attend to the need for matching an organization's ethical expectations with those of its employees, the organization is in a better position to improve the institutionalization of ethics. When employees are expected by the organization to behave ethically and when employees have similar expectations of themselves, then ethics should be more institutionalized within the organization. Top management will have a far greater effect on developing the employees' ethics than will their peer group. The match of ethical expectations should also lead to a long-term organization and employee commitment to the persistence of ethical behavior. Boeing, Champion, International Chemical Bank, General Mills, Arthur Andersen, GTE, Hewlett-Packard, Johnson & Johnson, and Xerox are a few companies that have experienced the benefits of managing the employee-employer contract with their employees in their efforts to create and maintain an ethically oriented organization.

CREATING AND MAINTAINING ETHICAL WORKING CONDITIONS

Organizations are obliged to provide employees with a safe working environment and safe working conditions. The Occupational Safety and Health Administration (OSHA) and federal laws and regulations provide safety standards and enforce employer institution of the organization's own safety standards. The problems of organizations providing and of employees accepting safe working environments stem from (1) lack of knowledge and of available, reliable information about levels of health risks; (2) lack of appropriate compensation proportional to the level of occupational risk; and (3) employees accepting known risks when the employer does not offer safer alternatives. When the option is employment versus no employment, employees, especially in low-income, noncompetitive employment regions, often choose jobs with hazardous risks to their health or life.

Risk is, of course, an unavoidable part of many occupations. And so long as they (a) are fully compensated for assuming these risks and (b) freely and knowingly choose to accept the risk in exchange for the added compensation, then we may assume that their employer has acted ethically[8] and has not violated the employee-employer contract.

To maintain the likelihood of ethical employee-employer contracts, related to working conditions, the employer must take steps to ensure that employees are not being unfairly manipulated into accepting a risk unknowingly, unwillingly, or without due compensation. In particular employers should:

1. offer wages that reflect the risk premium prevalent in other similar but competitive labor markets.
2. insure their workers against unknown hazards; the employer should provide them with suitable health insurance programs.
3. singly or together with other organizations collect information on the health hazards that accompany a given job and make all such information available to workers. [9]

Reducing the potential for workplace hazards like the more obvious categories of mechanical injury, electrocution, and burns, and also extreme heat and cold, noisy machinery, rock dust, textile fiber dust, chemical fumes, mercury, lead, beryllium, arsenic, corrosives, skin irritants, and radiation is important to the maintenance of ethical employee-employer contracts. Not all organizations meet these obligations.

While organizations are not required by law to offer employees working conditions that provide meaningful tasks and job satisfaction, doing so can lead to increased performance, job satisfaction, and productivity and more positive and ethical employee-employer relationships. Employees work most productively when they can participate in the control of their tasks, when they are given responsibility for and autonomy over their assignments, and when they are treated with respect. Employees and organizations both gain when personal and organizational needs are met. Working environments that can provide conditions for this alignment contribute to creating and maintaining ethical employee-employer contracts.

DISMISSING OR FIRING EMPLOYEES: THE IMPORTANCE OF FAIR AND EQUITABLE TREATMENT

There are few actions that managers find harder to take than dismissing or firing an employee. Many managers confide that this task is especially hard when the reason is cost cutting. It's typically easier to justify firing someone who has not performed well—you can attribute the action to the employee: "If they had done a good job, I wouldn't have to let them go." But when an organization is downsizing or laying off large numbers of people, as we have seen in recent years, the task is tougher. It's often not the employee's fault. "I had eight years of excellent performance reviews," said a recently fired graphics arts specialist. "They showed them to me. What have I done wrong?"

Managers may argue that they have no alternatives. In many instances, as during downsizing, costs have to be trimmed if the organization is to be competitive. Those organizations that don't make the tough decisions will eventually fail in the marketplace against organizations that are "lean and mean." But do organizations have a moral obligation to repay their employees' long-term loyalty by providing job security?

Being fired can be devastating. Losing a job is not unlike suffering a divorce or the death of a close family member. It undermines people's self-esteem. It forces many to question their identity. It can cause mental illness, family breakups, and even suicides. Finding a new job can be a long and dehumanizing experience as evidenced, by the experiences of many employees during the last decade or so.

It's not as if there are no alternatives to firing people. For example, organizations have spread the cutbacks among all their employees. Instead of firing 20 percent of their staff, they have all employees cut their hours by 20 percent and take a commensurate pay cut. In the end, the extent to which organizations downsize in an ethical manner, the greater the likelihood employees will perceive that the organization is treating them equitably.

When employees are satisfied with their jobs, their status, compensation, benefits, job security, and their prospects for advancement are likely to be loyal to their organization. Employees who believe they are overworked and underpaid, are not given the recognition they deserve, or are dissatisfied with their working conditions are likely to become disgruntled and angry. They may, and often do, develop a desire to get even, and the result is all too often dishonesty, stealing, or some other unethical act.

Organizations can make a major difference here. They can provide training for supervisors and managers that focuses on the goal of fair and equitable treatment of employees. They can be the impetus for organization-wide programs to improve working conditions and thus to improve the employee-employer relationship.

An Ethical Discharge or Due Process System

Organizations can also make a difference in the employer-employee contract when they recognize and address those situations where organizational flaws generate conflicts, mismatches, or violations of the social contract. Three causes of such conflict are as follows. (1) Organizational incongruence creates a built-in opposition between task responsibilities. (2) Inadequate performance measures are used. For explamle, a purchasing department evaluated on the basis of negative measures of excess inventory may then fail to purchase adequately, which in turn may lead to conflict with the sales department. (3) Organizational complexity results in ambiguous communication, allowing employees to read what they want into communications. In such cases, utility for the organization and fairness to its employees dictates that the flaws be remedied. Dismissals based on conflicts originating in such flaws do not and should have a just cause foundation.

An employer can also exhibit fair and equitable treatment to its employees by stating in writing the reasons for discharge (e.g., under situations other than those resulting from economic reasons). No employee should have to experience the following scenario:

> Do you have any idea why you were fired?— "I think ultimately because they didn't like me. I think it's probably that simple. There are still people in the company who are quasi-alcoholics or who don't do any work. They're still there. And people who don't make waves. I had a lot of people working for me, and I was under a lot of pressure. I'm probably the kind of person who under those circumstances is not invisible. Probably what it came down to was simply that I was not liked. But I don't really know."[10]

There is no moral basis for the anxiety, self-doubt, and resentment often caused by such terminations. Dismissal may be justified in some cases, but the discharged employee cannot learn from the action if he or she does not understand its rationale. In addition, a written explanation of reasons for dismissal would encourage the manager to give the same reasons to his or her superiors, the discharged employee, and those responsible for the organization's due process procedure (the second element, after just cause) in an ethical discharge system.

Due Process

Due process is one of the most important underlying rights employees have in the workplace, because it affects most of their other rights. Due process refers to the right to have an impartial and fair hearing regarding employers' decisions, procedures, and rules that affect employees. As applied in the workplace, due process essentially refers to grievance procedures.

At a more general level, due process rights protect employees from arbitrary and illegitimate uses of power. These rights are based on the

Fifth and Fourteenth Amendments to the Constitution, which state that no person shall be deprived of "life, liberty, or property, without the due process of law."

The following procedural mechanisms are needed to ensure employees' right to due process in organizations:

- Right to a public hearing
- Right to have peer evaluations
- Right to obtain external arbitration
- Right to an open, mutually approved grievance procedure[11]

A succinct list of the characteristics of an ethical due process system is as follows:

1. It must be a procedure; it must follow rules. It must not be arbitrary.
2. It must be visible, well known enough so that potential violators of rights and victims of abuse know it.
3. It must be predictably effective. Employees must have confidence that previous decisions in favor of rights will be repeated.
4. It must be "institutionalized." That is, it must be a relatively permanent fixture in the organization, not a device that is here today, gone tomorrow.
5. It must be perceived as equitable. The standards used in judging a case must be respected and accepted by a majority of employees, bosses as well as subordinates.
6. It must be easy to use. Employees must be able to understand it without fear that procedural complexities will get the best of them.
7. It must apply to all employees.[12]

Although an ethical due process system can be implemented in a variety of ways and the best method will depend somewhat on the size and type of the organization, the following is a procedure that promises objectivity and fairness for a relatively large organization. The organization's Ethics and Social Responsibility Committee of the board of directors (constituted by an equal number of inside and outside directors) selects a termination-hearing panel of two company members and one member from the organization's legal counsel. Employees who have received a termination notice receive a written notice with an explanation for the termination five days before its effective date. Within this period the employee may elect to contest the dismissal by submitting a request for a termination hearing to the panel. The panel sets a hearing date ten to fourteen days after the effective termination date. The employee has the right to select a member of the organization's legal staff, a member of management, or an outside counsel to represent his or her case, and can make that selection any time after he or she has informed the panel of the request for a hearing. The manager who fired the employee is also entitled to representation. The member from the organization's outside legal counsel presides over the hearing. Both sides are entitled to call witnesses or additional resource people, who may be cross-examined. A stenographer is present to record the hearing. The hearing panel renders its decision within ten days. If the decision favors the employee, it is binding on management; if it favors management, it does not abrogate the employee's right to seek relief or legal remedy from state or federal courts. If the decision favors the employee, no record of the termination proceedings are retained in the employee's file.

In the end, it is important that the organization and employee realize that there are termination costs for both of them. In the case of just dismissals, where an employee has a good performance record, discharge may reduce efficiency. Many dismissals are harmful to morale and company image. Even just dismissals entail a waste of training and often a disruption of continuity. Organizations should take a close look at the impact of terminations, starting with a close look at their selection and performance appraisal systems. A major factor in separations may be under-hiring and over-hiring. A great deal of the agony of separation can be eliminated by working harder at the front end, the selection process, making sure not only that candidates can do the job, which is the easy part of the procedure, but also that they will do the job.

Three questions related to performance that if sufficiently answered, would prevent many terminations and resignations as the following: (1) Was the employee's job description regularly reviewed to determine if the employee was performing the duties prescribed? (2) Was the correlation between the employee's salary and his job description reviewed? (3) Were the employee's performance reviews carefully studied?

Even if an organization has an ethical discharge system, with just cause, due process, and mitigation mechanisms, the organization should be structured so that the dismissal issue seldom arises, other than as the result of economical necessity.

MAINTAINING ETHICAL EMPLOYEE-EMPLOYER CONTRACTS DURING MERGERS

While employees can reap benefits from mergers, mergers often mean dire consequences for the average employee, who may find that some form of job displacement ensues. Witness the impact of recent mergers in the financial or telecommunications industry or between two huge organizations such as British Petroleum and Amoco or Norwest and Wells Fargo banks, in which an excess of employees must be downsized. Mergers often leave the new, combined organizations with redundant departments, plants, and people.

How the organization manages the merger process can go a long way in maintaining an ethical employee-employer contract. The possibility of a successful ethical employee-employer contract during mergers is best accomplished when the organization keeps in mind one of the oldest theories of moral conduct based upon the assertion that a person's actions toward another should be considered in light of how that person would wish to be treated in the same situation. This perspective calls for key organizational leaders to examine the effects from the vantage point of those impacted. For example, in a merger situation, those initiating the consolidation should seriously consider the effects on employees from the vantage point of the employees. Would the top managers want to be treated in this way? If the answer is negative, then a reexamination of the process may be in order. According to this model, the dignity and importance of employees must be preserved in the process of consolidation in order to maintain an ethical employee-employer contract. If this is not possible, the process must be questioned; for the negative effect on employees impacts the organization.

Organizations should take measures to alleviate or to remove the negative consequences, if possible. Organizations committed to maintaining ethical employee-employer contracts they should adopt this framework of ethical analysis during the merger process, while also raising the following questions:

1. Are there ways to consolidate or merge that will not have negative consequences for employees?
2. Will each employee be treated with dignity and respect in the merger process?
3. If negative effects are unavoidable, are there mechanisms to alleviate or lessen the impact?
4. If there are negative consequences, can these be shared among various employee groups so that no individual group bears the full brunt of the consequences?
5. If any employees suffer loss, are there measures that can be taken to alleviate the loss?

CONCLUSION

When organizations pay attention to the development, clarification, and management of changing employee-organization relationships, they create progressive organizational cultures concerned with maintaining ethical employee-employer contracts. Top management personnel must play an active role in the development of such a culture and the ensuing employee-employer contracts. Because of continuing changes in the business environment, organizations, and employees, there must be corresponding changes in such areas as organizational recruiting, training and development, motivating, leading, communicating, and retaining strategies. Such changes require that managers at all levels of the organization be role models and champion ways of facilitating changes in organizations to maintain ethical employee-employer contracts. Such contracts are more likely when organizations develop comprehensive employment strategies and policies that recognize that today's contract is one of mutual benefit rather than one of job security and company loyalty.

Training programs also contribute to increasing the likelihood of an ethical employee-organization relationship or match. Training often involves statements from the CEO emphasizing ethical business practices, discussions of the corporate code of ethics, lectures, workshops or seminars, case studies, films/discussions, articles/speeches, and descriptions of procedures for dealing with or reporting unethical behavior.

As organizations become more competitive, as the contract between employees and employers continues to change, and as downsizing becomes a common practice, it is a necessity for employees and organizations to observe, study, interpret, and communicate with each other regarding their ethical expectations. As we move further into the twenty-first century, ethical employee-employer contracts are a valuable link in the individual and organizational performance process. Whether before (recruitment) or after (orientation or training) the employee enters the organization must work to decrease the likelihood that either party will experience living by anything other than an ethical employee-employer contract. To do so will likely prevent future Salomon Brothers and Enrons from taking such traumatic ethical falls.

NOTES

1. Kenneth Chilton and Murray Weidenbaum, *A New Social Contract for the American Workplace: Paternalism to Partnering* (St. Louis: Center for the Study of American Business, Washington University, 1994); Archie B. Carroll and Ann K. Buchholtz, *Business and Society: Ethics and Stakeholder Management*, 5th ed. (Mason, O.: South-Western, 2003).

2. P. M. Podsakoff, M. Ahearne, and S. B. MacKenzie, "Organizational Citizenship Behavior and the Quantity and Quality of Work Group Performance," *Journal of Applied Psychology* 83 (1997), 262–70.

3. J. Rowan, "The Moral Foundation of Employee Rights," *Journal of Business Ethics* 24, (2000), 355–61.

4. Patricia Werhane, *Persons, Rights, and Corporations* (Englewood Cliffs, N.J.: Prentice-Hall, 1985).

5. J. J. Koch, "Wells Fargo's and IBM's HIV Policies Help Protect Employees' Rights," *Personnel Journal* (October 9, 1990), 40–48.

6. A. Arkin, "Positive HIV and AIDS Policies at Work," *Personnel Management* (December 1994), 34–37.

7. "At Last: Humor in Ethics Training," *Business Ethics* (May/June 1997), 10.

8. R. F. Settle and B. A. Burton, "Occupational Safety and Health and the Public Interest," in *Public Interest Law*, ed. B. Weisbord, J. F. Handler, and N. K. Komesar (Berkeley: University of California Press, 1978).

9. Manuel G. Velasquez, *Business Ethics: Concepts and Cases*, 3rd ed. (Englewood Cliffs, N.J.: Prentice-Hall, 1992).

10. H. Maurer, *Not Working* (New York: Holt, Rinehart, and Winston, 1979), 20.

11. Werhane, *Persons, Rights, and Corporations*, 83.

12. D. W. Ewing, *Freedom Inside the Organization* (New York: E. P. Dutton, 1977).

Restoring Ethics Consciousness to the Workplace

INTRODUCTION

As evidenced by our discussion throughout this book and continuing news headlines, it is definitely a tough time to be in business. Navigating through the uncertain waters of the current economy, many organizations are buffeted by corporate scandals and tossed about by wild fluctuations in the stock market. As soon as the wave of mismanagement and deceit seems to subside, someone comes out with a revised earnings statement that $3 billion reported as profit was actually a loss, and we begin to sink again. It's an even tougher time to be at the helm. Tyco, WorldCom, Global Crossing, and Enron have run aground; and in each case, poor leadership has cost the company and the crew their livelihoods. CEOs pursued profits at the expense of everything else and doomed the organization.

In this unstable climate, it is not surprising that individuals have chosen an unethical path. Long-term investors are looking for a minimum 10 percent annual growth rate even as the market contracts, and more recent investors keep thinking that the enormous profits of the dot.com glory days are the norm. The profit motive is so strong it seems to overwhelm all other concerns. From the CEO to the accounting department, down to the district manager and department head, the focus shifts from what the business produces to the wealth it can create.

The problem appears to lie in a misunderstanding of the very essence of business. Business is all about creating unique products and services for customers. Businesses that succeed have managers and employees who are focused on being expert at their crafts and producing the most sophisticated products and services in the marketplace. It is not surprising that when businesses focus on their people and products, profits follow. Yet when the profit motive becomes the sole focal point, businesses get into trouble; the end result can be business failure.

As investor confidence tumbles and markets contract, the Bush administration has tried to solve the current crisis, demanding that CEOs sign off on their financial statements and adopt transparent accounting practices. The government is prosecuting white-collar crime and making lofty statements. They are preaching the gospel of full disclosure. While all these intentions are honorable, they will not be enough. Government regulation cannot stop a crime before it starts. Regulators can only provide guidelines and punish noncompliance. They cannot foster virtue or ethical consciousness. Unless individuals are acting out of a sense of moral responsibility, the current crisis will not pass. True ethical behavior must be internally driven. External agents can only force compliance, not encourage choice; ultimately, virtuous behavior is a choice.

This chapter highlights some of the important points discussed in this book while also suggesting that the way to avoid the fall of future giants is to return ethical consciousness to the workplace. This would begin by establishing a culture based on always doing the ethical right thing be it an individual employee, a team, or a whole organization. When leaders pay attention to developing and maintaining such a culture, they will be less likely to find their organizations confronted with a soiled reputation at best.

ESTABLISHING A CULTURE OF DOING THE ETHICAL RIGHT THING

To foster change and encourage individuals to act responsibly, good leadership and an ethically oriented culture are essential. Good leaders provide employees with a role model for their own behavior and keep the company grounded. But good leadership is not enough. Employees at all levels must be committed to ethical behavior. Businesses need managers who can embrace and strengthen the corporate culture of diligence and responsibility. There must be a cadre of people in any large-scale organization who have been trained not only in the language of business, but also in the language of ethics. This is where business schools can play a part.

While many MBA programs offer ethics curricula, few infuse an ethics focus into the core program. Most offer a stand-alone elective course, and recent research published in *The Journal for Education in Business* suggests that students retain relatively little of the content of these singleton courses. A more effective model is beginning to take hold, one that combines case studies of both applied and theoretical ethics, as well as an interdisciplinary focus throughout the MBA program, where ethics is taught as integral to all the courses a student takes. The pedagogy in these programs is moving toward teaching the lesson that good work, right action, and profitability are inextricably intertwined.

How can businesspeople be trained to choose ethical action? To choose well for themselves and for their companies? Business leaders hold the key to reform. Ethical action springs from virtue and ethical consciousness; virtue and ethical consciousness are learned from work done well; and good work is born in a supportive atmosphere. Therefore, the leader of any business must establish an organizational culture that encourages people to understand the core values of the company, to focus on creating a quality product and providing quality service, and to do their jobs better. Only in such an environment will individuals choose to act rightly and ethically, and only then will the business thrive.

This kind of visionary, disciplined leadership is rare anywhere, but it is particularly rare in the business world, where the raison d'être is often the external good of profit. Business is designed around a transactional model where leaders reward followers for work well done: you do your job, you get your paycheck; you do your job really well, you get your bonus. But this cannot be the only incentive for performing well and striving to improve. The motivation to provide the best products and services for customers, while adhering to the highest ethical standards, must be internally propelled.

Enron is a case in point. An outward model of social responsibility, Enron appeared to be environmentally responsible and community-minded, sponsoring numerous philanthropic projects in the Houston area. Beneath the veneer, however, Enron's culture was anything but responsible. Unethical leadership produced a culture of unethical behavior where cleverness trumped character. Former employees testified on Capitol Hill about a culture that rewarded unchecked ambition, where nothing but profits mattered, where higher profit demands forced employees to lie and encouraged accountants to cut corners. In this environment, added value was all that mattered, and employees were forced to stretch the rules further and further. Ultimately, employees responded to the climate established by their leaders, and that climate left no room for ethical behavior.

The culture of an organization need not, however, focus solely on transactional relationships. Instead, leaders can establish an environment where leaders and followers raise each other to higher levels of motivation and morality. In his seminal book, *Leadership*, James MacGregor Burns suggests that leadership induces followers "to act for certain goals that represent the values and the motivations—the wants and needs, the aspirations and expectations—of both leaders and followers."[1] He calls this kind of leadership "transforming" because it "raises the level of human conduct and ethical aspirations of both leader and led, and thus it has a transforming effect on both." With good leadership and inspired followers, companies can nurture ethical behavior and doing the right thing and move the organization forward.

How can we create such a culture, and once having created it, maintain it?

THE "PRACTICE" OF BUSINESS

In his book, *After Virtue*, Alisdair MacIntyre explains how creating and maintaining a virtuous culture might work.[2] MacIntyre posits a scheme for the individual to pursue an ethical lifestyle. Every person, he says, must engage in a "practice," a coherent and complex form of socially organized behavior. The purpose of any practice is to allow the individual to learn those virtues that are appropriate to, and definitive of, the particular practice. Every practice has an established set of rules that govern the behavior of members within that practice. Every practice also has standards of excellence that allow the individual to assess his own performance. Abiding by these rules provides the individual with a framework within which he can develop a healthy and productive life. Acknowledging and aspiring to the established standards of excellence allows the individual to strive continually for self-improvement while simultaneously advancing the practice. Institutions are necessary to keep the practice alive; they provide rules, maintain standards, and encourage growth.

MacIntyre's ideas, like others presented in this book, may be applied to the business world. Business, after all, can be defined as a "practice." There are certain rules that apply to every stakeholder: accurate accounting, honest treatment of investors and customers, and providing a quality product. There are role models—successful entrepreneurs, inventors, investors—and there are organizations that support the practice of business—corporate boards of directors, the NYSE, commodities markets. There are obvious internal goods that occur in unique ways in the business world: creativity, discipline, strategic thinking, teamwork, and service orientation. There are obvious external goods: money, power, fame.

As an example, Ukrop's grocery store in Richmond, Virginia, seems to have found a balance between principles (internal goods) and profitability (external goods). The company's mission is to serve its customers and community efficiently and effectively while treating customers, associates, and suppliers with the utmost respect. Part of the company's mission is also achieving profitable growth and long-term financial success while promoting an atmosphere of mutual trust, honesty, and integrity. This "practice" abides by the company's established set of rules of providing associates with a framework for developing healthy and productive lives.

New employees begin their four-session training with "Healthy Start," which includes an overview of Ukrop's retail and manufacturing operations and the company's commitment to the community. Who conducts the second session, which is about values? Bobby Ukrop, president of the company, along with the vice president of operations. That is right. The company's president trains all Ukrop's associates— baggers, cashiers, and stockers. Equally important, however, are the values themselves, which include superior customer service, teamwork, honesty, fairness, life long learning, competence, and the importance of quality. When a "practice" teaches and reinforces values, it encourages employees to strive for self-improvement and learn ethical behavior. When individual associates' values are in sync with company values, the practice is advanced.

This is directly related. MacIntyre's theory is that a life well lived is spent in search of internal goods, not external ones. Successful organizations know that by focusing on the core of their business and adhering to ethical standards, profit will follow. They also know that profits alone cannot sustain a company; once the bubble bursts, there is nothing substantial to sustain an organization. The substance comes from employees, not from the product. Disciplined, devoted workers will sustain a business through tough times.

CHANGING CORPORATE CULTURE

In their book *Corporate Cultures*, Terrence Deal and Allan Kennedy retell the story of S. C. Allyn, a retired chairman of the board of the National Cash Register Corporation. In August 1945, Allyn was among the first civilians to enter Germany at the end of World War II. As Allyn drove past the rubble of burned-out buildings and utter desolation, he came upon what was left of the NCR factory. Picking his way through the bricks, he came upon two NCR employees whom he had not seen for six years. Their clothes were torn and they were covered in grime, but they were busy clearing the debris. As he approached, they looked up and said, "We knew you would come!"[3] The company had survived the ravages of a world war.

Another prime example of strong ethical leadership is Howard Schultz, CEO and chief global strategist of Starbucks Coffee Company. In the current business climate, where increasing profits often takes precedence over ethical behavior, Schultz has managed to place ethical business practices at the top of his list, sometimes at the expense of profitability. Amazingly, Starbucks offers both full- and part-time employees equity in the form of annual stock options. In 1987, when the company was losing hundreds of thousands of dollars a year in its drive for expansion, he extended medical coverage for any "partner" working 20 hours or more. Paying 75 percent of the insurance premium costs Starbucks approximately $1,275 a year per worker, while hiring a new employee costs the company almost twice that amount. Schultz declared in a recent article, "If I look back at the last five years, it is the most important decision the company has made in relation to our growth."[4]

Since 1990, Starbucks' net sales have grown to $285 million, while net earnings have moved ahead to $13 million. Schultz credits the growth to the commitment of his employees and their dedication to providing a quality product and taking care of customers.

Schultz's strong ethical leadership has also been recognized in the business school community. In 2000, he was awarded Columbia Business School's Botwinick Prize in Business Ethics, which recognizes an outstanding business leader who adheres to the highest standards of ethical conduct.

Schultz said in a recent article, "a company can provide long-term value for shareholders without sacrificing its core belief in treating its employees with respect and dignity, both because we have a team of leaders who believe it is right and because it is the best way to do business."[5]

Business leaders must convey to their employees that they are involved in the "practice" of business, not just the job of making money. In order to create a corporate culture where individuals will choose right action and further the practice, business leaders need to focus corporate culture on internal goods. They must encourage their employees to adhere to the standard that Immanuel Kant sets out in *The Metaphysics of Morals*, "Always act in such a way that the maxim of your action can be willed as a universal law of humanity."[6] They need to convey to their employees that the work must come first. They need to avoid the siren song of external goods—a focus on profits alone—and focus on quality products and customer service. They must withstand pressure from corporate boards whose only concern is the profit margin. They need to acknowledge the heroes within their practice and provide tangible role models for employees to emulate.

It can also be put this way: "Corporate leadership must clearly identify an organization's mission and values in order to differentiate itself from the marketplace; if ethical behavior and a socially responsible attitude are intrinsic to these values, then strong leadership will be required to communicate this message to all employees, shareholders and board members, and hold them accountable."[7]

Leaders can provide the impetus for change. With vision and moral courage, they can redirect the ship and choose a new course.

A case in point is the new CEO of Procter and Gamble (P&G). Neither a flashy man nor an overwhelming personality, Alan G. Lafley is nevertheless an ethical leader. Lafley has turned P&G around by bringing it back to what it has always done well. What P&G did not need was a new Tide or a marketing gimmick to trick the consumer into buying a different product. What it needed was to sell more of the Tide it had always made and that consumers had always trusted. His plan seems to be working. By focusing on P&G's twelve biggest producers (all generate more than a billion dollars a year), he has righted the ship, and they seem to be on course for solid growth in the coming years.

What are Lafley's secrets? He knows his company's business and product line, having started in the trenches and worked his way through the company. He continues to work in the field, always seeking better ways to produce and market P&G's products. He listens to his employees—to all of them, individually—while informing them of the direction the company will take. He goes into the stores to see how retailers are displaying the products, and he works to gain their trust so that P&G's products get prime spots on the shelves. Basically, he works hard and he believes in what his company does.

In an interview with *Fortune*, Lafley said, "It is a basic strategy that worked for me in the Navy. . . . I learned there that even when you have a complex business there's a core, and the core is what generates most of the cash, most of the profits."[8]

While Lafley has promised the stockholders a 10 percent annual growth rate, it is less important to him than the company and what the company does well. He told *Fortune*, "What I'm trying to build into this organization is something that will last long after I am gone. This is a company that aspires to be around for 1,000 years."[9]

Indeed, stockholders may want rapid returns, but no company can survive long if it has not warranted the long-term attention of investors, and this cannot happen unless companies have earned the trust of employees and customers. In short, companies must first produce, and then they may profit. They must focus on the internal goods of their business and the products they produce rather than the external goods of the rewards they will reap. They must plant the seed and nurture the plant before they harvest the crop.

RETURNING ETHICS CONSCIOUSNESS TO THE WORKPLACE

Today's organizations must be committed to returning ethics consciousness to the workplace. As suggested throughout this book, organizational leaders can do this by changing the organization's culture, creating a climate for whistle-blowing, and providing a forum for dialogue and good moral conversation.

As highlighted in our discussion of Warren Buffett's tenure at the helm of Salomon Brothers in the early 1990s, ethical turnaround begin with ethical leadership. Returning ethics consciousness to the workplace ultimately means that organizational leaders reinforce an ethical culture. The five most important elements in changing and reinforcing an ethical culture are (1) what leaders pay attention to, (2) how leaders react to crises, (3) how leaders behave, (4) how leaders allocate rewards, and (5) how leaders hire and fire individuals.

Attention. Leaders in an organization communicate their priorities, values, and beliefs through the themes that consistently emerge from what they focus on. These themes are reflected in what they notice, comment on, measure, and control. If leaders are consistent in what they pay attention to, measure, and control, employees receive clear signals about what is important in the organization. If, however, leaders are inconsistent, employees spend a lot of time trying to decipher and find meaning in the inconsistent signals. Returning ethics consciousness to the workplace means that leaders focus attention on improving the ethical fiber of the organization by not disregarding the long-term implications of employee's actions in favor of the most recent bottom line profits.

Reaction to Crises. The way leaders deal with crises communicates a powerful message about culture. Returning ethics consciousness to the workplace means that leaders swiftly react to any ethical crisis facing the organization by complying with authorities and firing ethical wrongdoers. The organization's leaders must not lie or cover up ethical and legal transgressions and must avoid preserving ethical wrongdoers at any cost.

Role Modeling. Through role modeling, teaching, and coaching, leaders can reinforce values that support an ethical organizational culture.

Employees often emulate leaders' behavior and look to the leaders for cues to the appropriate behavior. Returning ethics consciousness to the workplace will occur when leaders convey the image of the moral manager. This means that leaders proactively set the example of honesty and integrity for the rest of the organization.

Allocation of Rewards. To ensure that values are accepted, leaders must reward behavior that is consistent with values and doing the right thing. Using rewards and discipline effectively may be the most powerful way for leaders to send signals about desirable and undesirable conduct. Returning ethics consciousness to the workplace means that those who accomplish their goals by behaving in ways consistent with stated values are rewarded and that a lack of commitment to ethical principles will ensure that employees will not be promoted.

Criteria for Selection and Dismissal. Powerful ways that leaders reinforce culture is through the selection of newcomers to the organization and the way it fires employees and the rationale behind the firing. Organizations must have clear policies on the criteria for selection and dismissal that employees understand. Reprimanding an employee who displays unethical behavior that is against the organization may be viewed as a failure to reinforce the values within the organization. Returning ethics consciousness to the workplace means that leaders must bring into the organization only employees who are committed to ethical principles and usher out all employees connected to ethical misconduct.

CREATE A CLIMATE FOR WHISTLE-BLOWING

Creating a culture where whistle-blowing is encouraged and whistle-blowers are safe is important to returning ethics consciousness to the workplace. This means that the organization:

1. Takes the time to manage whistle-blowing by communicating the conditions appropriate for the disclosure of wrongdoing.
2. Clearly delineates wrongful behavior and the appropriate ways to respond or disclose wrongdoing.
3. Recognizes that to silence a whistle-blower or to muzzle a watchdog is very likely to result in further compounding problems.
4. Creates a culture in which employees feel safe annd don't have to conceal and distort information.
5. Takes employees' complaints and whistle-blowers' information seriously.

6. Sets up channels and other mechanisms that not only allow but also promote healthy, open communication.
7. Conducts organizational audits or assessment to look at existing ethical standards (e.g., level of commitment from top management, the nature of training programs, communication tools such as help and hot lines, and the magnitude of organizational risks in matters ranging from internal harassment to product safety).
8. Integrates standards and ethical values into everything from hiring to firing—training, compensation, and so on.

Whistle-blowers should be perceived as heroes. Managers have a responsibility to listen and respond to their employees, especially regarding observations of and reporting of illegal and immoral acts. Mechanisms such as "ethics offices" are part of an organization's responsibility to provide due process for employees to report personal grievances, to obtain effective and just resolution of them, and to report the wrongdoings of others, including the employers.

PROVIDE A FORUM FOR DIALOGUE AND GOOD MORAL CONVERSATION

Providing a forum for dialogue is one of the most proactive gestures organizations can use to return ethics consciousness to the workplace. Dialogue encourages give-and-take and provides organization-sponsored opportunities for employees to discuss ethical expectations, individual and organizational actions, and ethically charged situations or gray areas. Dialogue leads to good moral conversation that in the long run promotes deeper commitment to the ethical employee-employer relationships or contracts and ethical practices in an organization.

Dialogue is good conversation and serves many purposes. It facilitates self-awareness and awareness of others. It is a source of learning. It is liberating, ensures that there is room for all voices, and lends itself to the creation of psychological safety, which opens the door for good moral conversations between different levels of employees in the organization.

Good conversation is a way for employees to develop "clear and compelling ethical views or positions" in and out of the workplace. Good conversation can have three main effects. First, it can legitimize ethical concern as an important dimension of life. Second, it is one way an employee can seek guidance and gain clarity about what to do in a particular situation. Finally, it is out of public discussion and agreement that feelings of ethical obligation ultimately arise. Thus, the essence of learning about and living within ethical boundaries in an organization is to be in dialogue with coworkers about the ethical rules of the road.

The primary purpose of engaging in moral conversation in organization's is to test, expand, enrich, and deepen employees' understanding of business ethics so that each employee can better apply principles, rules, virtues, structures, moral ideals, and background beliefs to problems encountered in business.

RECOGNIZE AN UNETHICAL ORGANIZATION

Organizational leaders who want to develop and maintain and employees who wish to be a part of an ethical organization have to be aware of the organization's ethical character (or culture). Employees can be as aware of the ethical character of a current or potential employer as they can of its economic health. For example, if an organization emphasizes short-term revenues over long-term results, it may be creating an unethical atmosphere. If an organization links its ethical behavior to a code of ethics but will not address the complexity of ethical dilemmas, then the code may merely be window dressing. Proactive organizations approach establishing a Code of Ethics as more than adopting a document. Some organizations establish board-level committees to monitor the ethical behavior of the organization. Ethics training programs in corporations also demonstrate a commitment to ethics in the workplace. However, such training initiatives should be proactive rather than reactive, as has been the case for many organizations to teach ethics in the post-Enron business world.[10]

An organization that encourages unethical behavior or discourages ethical behavior because of the financial implications will not be where you want to work. Ethical problems are not legal problems. An organization that fails to realize that distinction is at risk, as is one that only sees ethical problems as a public relations issue.

The treatment of employees can indicate the ethical nature of an organization. If employees are not treated as well as customers or if performance-appraisal standards are unfair or arbitrary, the company may be unethical. Additionally, an absence of procedures for handling ethical issues, the lack of a whistle-blowing mechanism, or even the lack of a basic communication avenue between employees and supervisors can indicate an organization that is ethically at risk. Finally, an organization that fails to recognize its obligations to the public as well as to its shareholders and expects you to leave your private ethics at home is an organization at risk for unethical behavior.[11]

INSTITUTIONALIZE ETHICAL BEHAVIOR

In the end, the only way organizations can avoid ethical falls is by constantly communicating their desire that employees at all levels behave ethically and responsibly. This means that organizational leaders use every opportunity to communicate what the organization stands for and against.

Establish the value. First and foremost in any organization's attempt to institutionalize ethical behavior is to establish ethical considerations as an organizational value. An organization's mission statement often details its goal of providing the highest quality product at the least cost. It recognizes the commitment to all stakeholders. In addition, it needs to add a commitment to an ethical standard.

Communicate the value. An organization must communicate its commitment to ethical values to employees and external stakeholders. Codes of conduct or ethics can be adopted. Distribution of such codes should not stop with upper and middle managers; all employees should be apprised of the corporate code of behavior. Communication cannot be limited to distribution, however, because actions speak louder than words.[12] Leaders and the organization are able to foster employee commitment to the organization goal of ethical behavior in the same way that they foster employees commitment to its other goals.

An employee has a commitment to an organization in direct relationship to that employee's involvement with the organization. A leader or manager can influence that commitment by making sure adherence to the ethical goal is rewarded with *visibility*; being explicit in its *expectations* regarding ethical or unethical behavior; making clear that ethical or unethical actions result in *irreversible* results, consistent punishment, or rewards; and finally, that employees take actions of their own *volition* to act ethically or unethically and are responsible for the outcomes.[13]

Select and train employees with ethical behavior in mind. Organizations can, include in their recruitment criteria the principles they look for in an employee as a moral actor. Several methods can be used to elicit this kind of information: honesty tests, background checks, and a signed commitment by the person to the Corporate Code of Ethics. Pizza Hut, Inc.'s top management looks for *integrity* when hiring and promoting employees in the organization. Integrity includes an internal allegiance to excellence, honesty, a sense of teamwork, and a balanced perspective on long-term goals and short-term profits.[14]

Early in the employment process, a *social contract* is formed between the employer and employee. Social contracts typically cover the inducement of the employer and the contribution of the employee. The degree to which both parties satisfy the expectations established by this contract affects the success of the relationship. It is important for organizations and employees to understand the expectations of the social contract as well. It is important for leaders and managers to understand that if the two do not or cannot agree on this aspect, then the relationship will suffer.

Because ethical behavior cannot be reduced to simple do's and don'ts, both parties have ever-changing expectations, and thus there must be opportunity and structure to address evolving.

Training employees to make an ethical analysis as part of their decision making is critical. Training can be formal, focused on the organization's goals and objectives and on techniques of decision making. Training can also be achieved through the normal socialization during orientation of a new employee. If the employer is operating ethically, then the role models whom the employees emulates will exhibit the proper ethical behavior. The system of rewards and punishment will confirm and reinforce ethical behavior.

While the points highlighted in this section will not guarantee that ethical missteps won't occur in an organization, they do increase the likelihood that the organization will avoid taking an ethical fall like the Salomon Brothers and Enrons of our time.

CONCLUSION: COMMITMENT TO ETHICAL ACTION

It may be a tough time to be in business, but an ethical orientation can help companies weather the storm. Organizations can withstand the lean years, but the only organizations that will do so are those whose organizational culture encourages right action and rewards ethical behavior. This breeds long-term trust from employees and customers and reassures investors. It is not enough to sign a paper that says your company is behaving ethically. It is not enough to give money to worthy causes and be "socially responsible," although it is a nice start. Organizations must reorient themselves to the practice of business. Another way to put this is: "If the next generation of managers is not trained to recognize that a competitive edge is no longer solely based on market share, then these companies—no matter how committed their leadership is to implementing an ethical approach to business—will fail to reach their desired state."[15]

Organizations must focus on doing the right things, the ethical things that helped them succeed from the first, and not be hypnotized by the bottom line. They must seek virtue for the good of the economy, their communities, the company, and the employees.

NOTES

1. James MacGregor Burns, *Leadership* (New York: Harper & Row, 1978), 380.

2. Alisdair Macintyre, *After Virtue: A Study in Moral Theory* (London: Duckworth, 1982).

3. Terrence E. Deal and Allan A. Kennedy, *Corporate Cultures: The Rites and Rituals of Corporate Life* (Reading, Mass.: Addison-Wesley, 1982).

4. M. Moss, "Uncompromising Principles and Commitment to Success." *William and Mary Business,* Fall/Winter (2002), 11.

5. Ibid.

6. Immanuel Kant, *The Metaphysics of Morals,* translated and edited by Mary Gregor (Cambridge, England: Cambridge University Press, 1996).

7. Ronald R. Sims, "Enron: How a Failure of Leadership, Culture and Unethical Behavior Brought a Giant to Its Knees," *William and Mary Business* (Fall/Winter 2002), 18–19.

8. Katrina Brooker, "The Un-CEO," *Fortune* (Sept. 16, 2002), 88–96.

9. Ibid.

10. Jonathan D. Salant, "After Enron, More Firms Teach Ethics," *Virginia Daily Press* (November 3, 2002), E1, E3.

11. Robert A. Cooke, "Danger Signs of Unethical Behavior: How to Determine If Your Firm Is at Ethical Risk," *Journal of Business Ethics* 10 (1991), 249–53.

12. Robert A. Giacalone and D. N. Ashworth, "From Lip Service to Community Service," *Business and Society Review* 66 (1988), 31–33.

13. Ronald R. Sims, "The Institutionalization of Organizational Ethics," *Journal of Business Ethics* 10 (1991), 493–506.

14. S. R. Reinemund, "Today's Ethics and Tomorrow's Work Place," *Business Forum* 17, no. 2 (1992), 6–9.

15. Sims, "Organizational Ethics," 19.

Index

ABOUT THE AUTHOR

RONALD R. SIMS is the Floyd Dewey Gottwald Senior Professor in the graduate school of business at the College of William and Mary, where he teaches organization behavior, leadership, business ethics, change of management and human resources management. He is the author or co-author of 20 books, among them *Teaching Business Ethics for Effective Learning* (Quorum Books, 2002).